The New History of England

General Editors
A. G. Dickens and Norman Gash

Aristocracy and People

Britain 1815–1865

Norman Gash

Harvard University Press
Cambridge, Massachusetts
1979

Library of Congress Cataloging in Publication Data

Gash, Norman
  Aristocracy and people.

  Bibliography: p.
  Includes index.
  1.   Great Britain—Politics and government—1800–1837.
2.   Great Britain—Politics and government—1837–1901.
3.   Great Britain—Nobility—History.   4.   Upper classes
—Great Britain—History.   5.   Great Britain—Economic
conditions—1760–1860.   I.   Title.
  DA535.G37   309.1′41′07   79–13638
  ISBN 0–674–04490–8

Preface

The plan of this volume is simple. Two introductory analytical sections (chapters 1 and 2) are followed by seven chronological chapters (chapters 3–9) covering the whole period from 1815 to 1865. These are rounded off by a separate section on foreign policy and war (chapter 10) and a final summary (chapter 11). In conformity with the general policy of the series, the affairs of Ireland are only touched on where they directly affect the history of the larger island. A similar and even more severe restriction applies to the British colonies and overseas empire. For the rest, though I cannot hope to have done justice to Scotland and Wales, I have tried not to forget them.

I take this opportunity of thanking the Court and Senate of St Andrews University for giving me leave of absence in the academic session 1975–6 during which, among other things, I began work on this book. This is also the proper place to express my gratitude to two friends, Professor P. Mathias of All Souls College, Oxford and Professor J. T. Ward of Strathclyde University, who read and criticized the first drafts of, respectively, chapter 1 and chapter 7. Two other friends and scholars, now dead, by their writings and conversations over many years taught me much about mid-Victorian society. It seemed fitting therefore to dedicate this book to their memory.

Norman Gash
St Salvator's College, St Andrews, December 1978

To the Memory
of
two Historians of
Victorian England

W. L. Burn and G. Kitson Clark

Contents

Introduction

The half century from 1815 to 1865 was the classic age when, on the return of peace, Britain met the full impact of those economic, technological, and demographic changes which have been given the evocative title of 'the industrial revolution'. For that reason it is not only an essential foundation for any historical study of modern Britain but has become the subject of much controversy. It is a tempting period for those who turn to history as a kind of storehouse of ideological illustrations. It is rich in evidence that can be extracted from its context to support doctrinaire arguments. Even the less committed find it difficult to discard conventional stereotypes of the 'evils of the industrial revolution' when they come to deal with the historical problems involved. In one sense we have never escaped from the 'Condition of England' question.

The early nineteenth-century reformers themselves helped to create this polemical atmosphere. In their concern for the poor, their zeal for removing social evils, they naturally gave publicity to what was bad, not what was good, in their own society. They were virtuous propagandists. The picture has been distorted still further by the effects on generations of readers of the Victorian social novelists. The literary tradition is almost invariably stronger than the historical. Often exaggerated in their descriptions, not infrequently anachronistic in their settings, they have done more to confuse than enlighten posterity on the real nature of Victorian society. Yet what in reality is demonstrated by the popularity of these novels in their own day is not public neglect, but public concern. The fashion for 'social protest' from about 1840 is a sign of social conscience; it reflected an interest, it did not create it. Take, for example, Disraeli's familiar concept of the Two Nations—the rich and the poor. It came in his novel *Sybil*, published in 1845 after a dozen years of public debate on the problems of the industrial poor, when Chartism was actually dying down, and the working classes beginning to see a permanent improvement in their standard of living. Disraeli, in other words, was following fashion, not leading it. Had the social novelists really been pioneer thinkers, directing their readers to new and

important truths, they would have been producing their books
between 1815 and 1825 when the special problems of the industrial
working classes were struggling for recognition. But in those years the
educated public were reading the romantic fiction of Sir Walter Scott
and Byron, or the middle-class novels of Jane Austen.

If the Two Nations concept had any validity, which is doubtful, it
was in the age of Peterloo rather than in the age of Chartism. By
1840 social concern had replaced social fear. But it would in any case
be a gross distortion to view early Victorian society in terms of rich
and poor. The contrast is too stark and too artificial. In fact no
such absolute gap existed. An immense and complex gradation of
classes and incomes stretched between the very rich and the very
poor. There were, moreover, other significant social differences
besides purely material circumstances. Two which had at least equal
importance for the early Victorians were the contrasts between the
new industrial world and the traditional rural society, and the gulf
of history and theology that separated anglicans and dissenters. But
these were not class divisions in the ordinary sense. They were
vertical lines of demarcation that ran downwards through rich and
poor alike.

The issues confronting British society in 1815 were in any case
larger and more complicated than simply that of industrialization.
Indeed Britain at that time was far from being primarily an industrial
society. What made the immediate post-Waterloo period so difficult
was not one but a combination of problems. Four distinct developments can be identified as imposing a strain on the social fabric, of
which industrialization was perhaps the least damaging. The other
three were, first, the great post-war slump in trade and manufacture;
second, the unprecedented expansion of population; and third, the
increasing urbanization of British society. Any one of these would
have caused difficulty for the government of the day. Together they
created an aggregate of social evils which took half a century to bring
under control.

Between the four there was no necessary historical connection.
The population was increasing rapidly in non-industrial Ireland and
rural England, as well as in the industrial districts, for reasons which
are still obscure. The growth of towns was reaching a critical point
in places untouched by the direct consequences of the industrial
revolution. When Chadwick looked for evidence of intolerable urban
conditions to publish in his classic 1842 report, he found them in
Bath, Brighton, Windsor and Edinburgh as well as in Manchester,
Wigan, Leeds and Glasgow. The Napoleonic Wars were the product
of the politics and diplomacy of the preceding period. It was a
struggle for the mastery of Europe, not for the markets of the world.

Yet it was almost inevitable that the dislocation and abnormal stimulus of war to the British economy should be followed by a period of acute depression. That all four problems presented themselves simultaneously was an accident of history which is still insufficiently recognized. Without the other three complications, the evolution of industrial Britain in the early nineteenth century would have been very different. The fact that they all came together was not only a misfortune for the generation whose fate it was to live in the thirty years after Waterloo; it has also distorted our retrospective view of the industrial revolution. Because industrialization came in a certain set of historical circumstances, those circumstances have come to be regarded as intrinsic features rather than as —what they really were—accidental accompaniments. Industrialization in itself did not cause the Napoleonic Wars nor the sensational increase in population nor the health problems of the British towns; but the history of the nineteenth century is often written as though industrialization was responsible for all those manifestations.

What can reasonably be argued is not only that post-war depression, over-population, and urban growth made the initial impact of industrialization on British society more painful than it need have been; but that without the wealth and skills produced by the industrial revolution British society would not have been able to master its post-war difficulties as well as it did. The state of Ireland in the first half of the century is a sufficient advertisement of what might have happened in the larger island had the same increase in population taken place without the cushioning effect of increased industrial productivity. As it was, there is a strong case for thinking that it was the staggering growth of population more than any other single factor which kept wages low and fostered unemployment in the generation after Waterloo. The times were difficult enough; without industrialization there might have been a social catastrophe. For all its harshness and crudities the industrial revolution was the saviour of British society in the conditions which prevailed between 1815 and 1865. It enabled the mass of the working classes to improve their standard of living, eat more and better food, have better houses and clothes, enjoy cheap travel, obtain more education, and organize themselves for further social and political advancement. The pace of improvement was uneven and its benefits not equally shared; but progress was significantly slowest for those classes furthest removed from the factory and the powered machine—the agricultural labourer, the handloom weaver, the Irish immigrant, and those engaged in unskilled small-scale employments where labour (especially female labour) was plentiful and wages conventionally low.

The long and still unfinished debate on the effects of the industrial revolution on standards of living has at least produced a measure of agreement among historians on some important issues. One is that living standards improved generally after 1842 and, arguably, had somewhat irregularly been improving since 1815. Another is that the task of plotting the precise rate of improvement for specific occupations and localities, made up in effect of individuals and families, is one of immense, and almost insoluble, complexity. A third is that the amount of social distress that existed before industrialization has been insufficiently taken into account as a basis of comparison. This is not because pre-industrial poverty, famine, and disease did not exist, but because there is so little readily accessible information to set against the wealth of detail elicited by the early Victorians about their own generation. There is less information because there was less interest and less concern.

Concern, however, either for the 'State of the Nation' as in Lord Liverpool's time or the 'Condition of England' in Peel's, was a mark of British society. It was a concern that manifested itself both in society at large and in government. It is a historical distortion to think solely in terms of individual reformers battling alone, as often portrayed, against a hostile or indifferent world. The ties that bound society together were in their multiplicity always stronger than the forces dividing it. In the emphasis on the heroic individual both the role of private philanthropy and the cumulative effect of governmental policy tend to be undervalued. Humdrum details of tariffs and taxes, for example, lack the personal interest of a career like that of Lord Shaftesbury. Yet it is probable that Peel's budgets of 1842, 1845 and 1846 did more for the working classes of Britain than all Shaftesbury's reforms put together. It is true that it was difficult for the early nineteenth-century state to respond quickly to social needs since it had never been designed for that purpose. But that is not to say that nothing was done. What is surprising is not that the system worked sluggishly at the start but that politicians and administrators showed so much flexibility. That mythical abstraction, *laissez-faire*, was neither the practice of governments nor the doctrine of many MPs. This in reality was an age of increasing experiment in state supervision, intervention and control. When it seemed politically expedient or morally desirable the legislature established precedents for interference in hitherto uncharted areas of social life. It was not, of course, a smooth, logical process. It proceeded by fits and starts; there were unsuccessful trials and not a few errors. But the governing classes on the whole proved remarkably resilient and adaptable. Their personal experience of public life—and of all the political élites of Europe the British aristocracy and gentry had the widest practical experience of governing—instilled into them a healthy realism and a generally tolerant attitude towards their aggrieved and often refractory fellow-countrymen.

Their patience and temper were often subjected to severe trials. The age of the Luddites and Chartists, of Peterloo, the Nottingham and Bristol riots, rural machine-breaking and incendiarism, was the most prolonged period of recurrent social disorder in modern British history. The strain on the governing class was made more nerve-racking by their vivid but misleading memories of the French Revolution of 1789. Violence on one side led to strong feelings on the other. Rich and poor, young and old, women and children, were exposed to frightening scenes and turbulent passions. This was the last period in British history in which great country houses were put in a state of defence against lawless attack, private individuals were called upon to defend their persons and property against riot and destruction, and unpopular cabinet ministers for a time went about armed in case of attempted assassination. Though the forces of law and order were stretched, however, the governing system never broke down and never looked as if it would break down.

The question is sometimes asked whether Britain came close to revolution in these years—in 1817, for instance, or 1831–2, or 1842. To decide how near something came to happening that in the event did not is a difficult and perhaps unrewarding task. But there are certain general considerations which deserve to be taken into account. In an organized state such as Britain was during this period there are probably three preconditions for revolution. First, the existence of an active revolutionary group ready to take over power; second, a loss of nerve on the part of the traditional governing classes; and third, the weakness or failure of the instruments for enforcing order. Unless at least two of these conditions are present, it is not easy for revolutions to take place. Of the first there is no real sign either among the radical reformers of 1816–22 or those of 1831–2 or the Chartist leaders of 1838–42. In each case they wanted reform, not revolution. Eccentric fanatics like the Spenceans or the Cato Street conspirators are irrelevant in this context. Of the second there is even less indication. Whatever faults the governing classes of Britain had in this period, cowardice was not one. It never occurred to either their friends or opponents that their nerve would give way. The criticism has usually been that they reacted too energetically to disorder. This may be so. If there was one lesson they had learnt from the French Revolution it was that weakness by authority at the start of civil disturbance was the surest means of making it more dangerous.

The third condition raises the question of the discipline in the

British army at this time. Up to 1829 the professional soldiers were
the main and often the only real protection against serious disorder
both in the metropolis and in the provinces. Even in London, as
late as the Chartist demonstration of April 1848, they acted as the
reserve force at the government's disposal. Had the army not
remained loyal and disciplined, their political rulers would have been
in grave difficulty. The army authorities were perfectly conscious of
this problem. In 1833, for example, the Grenadier Guards were
deliberately not recruiting men from the manufacturing towns in
order to lessen the risk of taking in political agitators. Yet there is
only one case on record of collective military insubordination for
what *might* have been political reasons. This was in London in June
1820 on the eve of the Queen's trial; when the capital was in a fever
of radical excitement. The offending battalion of the 3rd (Scots
Fusilier) Guards was promptly sent away to Portsmouth and
Plymouth and an official statement put out emphasizing that the
'symptoms of disorder' were 'unconnected with any political feeling
whatever'.[1]

Whether this was true or not, Wellington was clearly disturbed
by what had happened. What is noteworthy, however, is how isolated
the episode was and how rapidly it was dealt with. In general it is
clear that military discipline remained firm despite the difficult and
sometimes dangerous situations with the civilian population in which
the army was frequently involved. There are no grounds for thinking
that at any point the instruments in the hands of the government
for internal security purposes were other than reliable. That being
so, the chance of any subversive movement succeeding by sheer
force hardly existed. The famous letter sent by Francis Place to
Hobhouse in May 1832, warning ministers of the prospect, if
Wellington became prime minister, of 'a commotion in the nature of
a civil war', is no proof either that such a prospect was real or even
that Place thought so. His object was merely to stiffen the determination of the whig cabinet to stay in office. In effect, the whole purpose
of the national agitation in 1832 was to support one aristocratic
faction against another. But it is hard to believe that Place ever
seriously believed in the possibility of armed revolution. He told
Doherty, the cotton spinners' leader, in October 1831 that 'it was
absurd to expect such a combination among the working people as
would enable them to defeat the army and others who would not
quietly submit to be plundered'. Ten years later he was saying much
the same thing about the Chartists.

---

[1] They were officially ascribed to the dissatisfaction of the men with the new barrack
accommodation at the King's Mews, Charing Cross, and an unusually heavy roster of duties.

A similar realist, for all his radical sympathies, was General Charles Napier who commanded the disturbed northern district in 1839. 'Poor people.' he wrote of the Chartists in August of that year. 'They will suffer. They have set all England against them and their physical force—fools! We have the physical force, not they ... Poor men! How little they know of physical force!' There were one or two soldiers in the units in his command known to be Chartists or Chartist sympathizers. But they were too few to cause anxiety and the army authorities handled them with good sense. Later still, in April 1848, there was satisfaction among the upper classes that there had been no 'fraternization' between the London special constables and the Chartist demonstrators of the kind which had been the prelude to revolution on the continent. But by then whatever danger there might have been had passed away.

At no time, it seems reasonable to conclude, was revolution physically possible in Britain between 1815 and 1848. It is doubtful whether it was even envisaged by any substantial part of the population. When revolution occurred on the other side of the Channel in 1830 and 1848, the characteristic reaction of the complacent British public was to regard it as an attempt by benighted foreigners to catch up with British constitutional progress or as a horrid example of what happened in less fortunate countries. There was no parallel with the brittle authoritarian regimes abroad. British society was too interlocked, public opinion too influenced by moral and religious considerations, the governing classes too sensible and experienced, the government itself too resolute and efficient, for Britain to suffer the fate of the continental autocracies.

The views of educated foreigners on this point are illuminating since they had the priceless ability to make comparisons with society on the continent. Von Neumann, the Austrian *chargé d'affaires* for nearly twenty years, who thought at the time of the Queen's trial that, 'if ever this country was near a revolution, it is now,' was recording the following year that 'commonsense, of which there is so much in this country, has triumphed'. Princess Lieven, wife of the Russian ambassador, who had resided in London for an even longer period, made a more astringent remark at the time of the Tolpuddle trade union demonstration in London in 1834. There could be no real insurrectionary attempts in England, she wrote to her brother, 'because the masses here are cowardly and the classes are courageous'. A more acute observer than either, the Frenchman Alexis de Tocqueville, arrived at the same general conclusion after a rather more profound intellectual analysis of British politics and society. Coming to England in 1833 under the impression that the country was on the brink of a great revolution, he changed his mind after only a few weeks. 'If one understands by a revolution a violent and sudden change,' he concluded, 'then England does not seem ripe for such an event, and I see many reasons for thinking that it will never be so.'

The feature of British history in the first half of the nineteenth century is in fact the success of the aristocracy and gentry in retaining both the substance of their traditional political power and the social deference of other influential classes. Important concessions were made, the machinery of administration adjusted, a greater measure of political and social equality admitted, the power of public opinion recognized, and a larger responsibility of the rich towards the poor accepted. But the men who filled the House of Commons, the diplomatic corps, the civil service, the armed forces, the magistracy, the universities and the established church in 1865 differed little in social composition from their predecessors of 1815. To be in that position after the economic strains and social tensions of the thirty years that followed Waterloo was a remarkable tribute to their adaptability and good sense.

1 Country and People

I

The coming of the 'General Peace' in 1814 produced what the *Annual Register* described as 'a vast exportation of English tourists' to the continent from which they had been debarred for so long. It also brought over a group of foreign visitors curious to see the island society which had successfully resisted the might of the Napoleonic Empire. Their first impression was usually of the greenness of the grass and trees, and the universal presence of hedgerow and wood. Next they admired the neatness of the houses and farms, the trim fields and luxuriant crops, the fat cattle, the elegant country mansions of the gentry, and the landscaped parkland. 'England appears to have better trees, animals and men than any other country', observed one Swiss industrialist at the end of his first fortnight. Even when he penetrated across the border it was much the same story. Around Edinburgh 'the fields looked as if they had been manufactured on a rolling mill'; crops were planted so regularly that 'the farms had the appearance of a design printed on a piece of cotton cloth'.

The Lothians were the pride of Scottish agriculture. Elsewhere the enquiring traveller would have found much barren land, fewer trees, less enclosure. But in England the hedgerows, fields and coppices that constantly delighted the foreigner were an essential feature not only of the landscape but of the agricultural economy which had produced it. England was the most enclosed and the best cultivated country in Europe. By comparison with the open fields, heaths, marshes and ancient forests of the continent, the English landscape was as artificial as a garden. Little natural woodland remained and what there was had been thinned by the insatiable demands of the navy during the war. The largest royal forest was the New Forest; but its 67,000 acres possessed only 6,000 that were enclosed for growing timber in 1823. This was less than that of the Forest of Dean which was little more than a third of its nominal size.[1] Common and

---

[1] The royal forests covered just over 122,000 acres of which only 38,000 were enclosed for timber growing.

wasteland in England represented scarcely more than a fifth of the
total, compared with a third in Wales and over two thirds in
Scotland. The great enclosure movement was in its last phase. Except
in Wales and the northwest, there was no large-scale enclosing left to
do when George IV came to the throne in 1820. A few open fields
remained in England south of the Trent but they were already a
subject for comment. The task of English agriculture in the nineteenth century was not to enclose but to drain, sweeten and
fertilize the sour, waterlogged enclosures which had been inherited
along with the soft, wet English climate.

Though the British population had sometimes gone hungry, it had
contrived to feed itself throughout the twenty-two years of war. But
in 1814 and 1815 the continental visitor was less interested in the
efficiency of British farming than in the spectacular advance of
British manufacturing technology. In the lush green island there were
sights even more novel and exciting for the foreign—and even for the
native—observer than the outward evidence of high farming. 'All the
way along from Leeds to Sheffield it is coal and iron, and iron and
coal', recorded the countryman Cobbett in 1830 on one of his rare
incursions into northern England. Darkness fell before he reached
Sheffield and he was able to witness 'the iron furnaces in all the
horrible splendour of their everlasting blaze. Nothing can be conceived more grand or more terrific than the yellow waves of fire
that incessantly issue from the tops of these furnaces.' Escher, the
enquiring Swiss, gazed at Manchester like a Roman provincial
arriving at Heliopolis. In a quarter of an hour's walk he counted
over sixty spinning mills with their lofty chimneys stretching up into
the sky 'like great obelisks'. In the evening the vast four- and five-
storey buildings, illuminated by gaslight, looked even more mag-
nificent. 'It is impossible to imagine how grand is the sight of a big
cotton mill when a façade of 256 windows is lit as if the brightest
sunshine were streaming through the windows.'

Elsewhere there were even stranger sights. Near Sunderland in
1814 locomotive steamengines were at work, taking trains of from
thirty to forty waggons of coal at a time to the quayside for shipment.
Steamengines, 'like fearful ghostly figures', belching out black smoke,
hauled coal up from the pit, lowered the miners down, and pumped
water from the deep workings. Steamengines were used to lift heavy
weights, to operate lathes, to propel boats, to supply power for
rope-walks and breweries, and to heat factories. In the steamengine,
in fact, could be discerned a symbol of Britain's future industrial
dominance. What impressed observers on first encounter was the
combination of enormous power with ease of control. In 1816 another
continental visitor, also Swiss, saw at the collieries of the Birmingham

Coal Company machines raising coal from a depth of 600 feet, controlled by boys of fourteen. The process of substituting mechanical energy for the muscle, wind and water power on which mankind had relied since the dawn of history still had a long way to go; but potentially it was the most significant aspect of the industrial revolution which British society had brought into being behind the shelter of Nelson's navy.

Though the completion of the transport revolution represented by the passenger train had another fifteen years to wait, Britain already had, in addition to its agriculture and industry, the best transport system in the world. This was partly due to natural advantages. An elongated island with an enormous coastline relative to its landmass, with the sea never more than seventy miles from any town, with innumerable harbours, long inlets, and slow navigable rivers, was designed by nature for easy, and what was equally important, cheap communications. The coastal trade employed the larger part of the mercantile fleet and was responsible for the bulk of the cargoes landed at British ports. In 1824, the first year of official records, more than three quarters of the total tonnage arriving by sea came from other parts of the United Kingdom. The huge growth of London, for example, would have been impossible without cheap sea communications with the rest of the country, particularly with the coal fields of the northeast. In the previous half century the art of man had added to the facilities provided by nature. A great canal system, based on the iron and coal country of the industrial Midlands, linked all the main rivers and provided water transport between London, Bristol, Birmingham, Liverpool and Hull. For lighter loads and human passengers there were by 1818 in England and Wales 19,000 miles of paved streets and turnpikes, and 95,000 miles of public highway. By the end of George IV's reign there were 25,000 miles of turnpike in Great Britain, including 3,600 miles in Scotland, much of it reconstructed on the scientific principles of the ingenious Mr MacAdam. To travel from London to Edinburgh, which took ten days in the middle of the eighteenth century, now needed only forty-eight hours.

II

The population was growing at an unprecedented rate.[2] From nearly

[2] See appendix A for a tabular view of the increase in population, 1801–61.

eleven millions counted at the first and probably defective census of
1801, it had reached twelve and a half millions in 1811, and was to
continue to rise to nearly fourteen and a half millions (the highest
proportionate decennial increase ever recorded) in 1821, and over
twenty-one millions in 1851. Scotland, whose share of these totals was
1·8 millions in 1811 and just over two millions in 1821, was growing
less rapidly than Wales with its half million of population at the start
of the century; and Wales was growing fractionally less rapidly than
England. Nevertheless, the staggering fact remained that in the first
fifty years of the nineteenth century, in the lifetime of Peel,
Palmerston, Wellington and Macaulay, the population of Great
Britain almost doubled.

The reasons for this social phenomenon are still far from clear.
Given that both the English peerage and the Irish peasantry in the
last half of the eighteenth century were living longer and rearing more
children than in the past, it is not easy to isolate any particular
factor, such as nutrition, housing, industrialization, early marriage,
or better medical care, as the key to this demographic puzzle. It is
true that by the start of the nineteenth century bubonic plague,
leprosy, and scurvy had been eliminated, rickets, smallpox, and
typhus greatly reduced. Contemporaries had little doubt that the
death rate was falling and that people were living longer. Yet what is
equally worth noting is the continued heavy infantile mortality
without which the growth of population would have exerted an
almost intolerable pressure on the resources of the country. In the
five years (1838–42) following the compulsory registration of deaths
almost two-fifths of the total number in England and Wales were of
children under five years. On an average half the deaths were of
persons below the age of twenty, who were unlikely therefore to have
contributed in any statistically significant fashion to the breeding of
the next generation. The natural Malthusian check was still
operating to keep the population within manageable limits, even if
contemporaries were more concerned with the actual, as distinct from
the potential, rate of increase of population in what they were
beginning to regard as their own dangerously overcrowded island.

An expanding population and a high death rate had two consequences. In human terms alone Britain was a rapidly changing
society. Of the twenty-one millions alive in 1851, it was unlikely that
more than two and a half millions had been alive at the start of the
century; not more than half had been alive when the Reform Bill
was introduced in 1831. Half a generation disappeared in thirty
years, three quarters in fifty years. It was also a young society. In
the early nineteenth century half the population at any time was
under twenty. Since this age group was partially if not entirely

dependent on the half of the population aged between twenty and sixty, of whom in turn slightly less than half were male breadwinners, it was not surprising that the employment of women and children was an accepted feature of economic life—and a necessary feature. Without their aid it is difficult to see how any tolerable standard of living for the poor could have been maintained. This characteristic youthfulness of nineteenth-century British society may help to explain some other features: its emotionalism, its idealism, its naïvety, and, as far as crowds were concerned, its tendency to riot and disorder together with its timidity in the face of authority.

Migration both internal and abroad ensured that the population increase was not constant over the whole country. The influx of Irish into Lancashire, London and the west of Scotland probably helped to pull down living standards for the natives; but in crude numerical terms their numbers merely balanced the emigration from Great Britain. In the 1820s an average of 27,000 people a year were leaving the British Isles; in the following decade over 70,000 a year. Even before the great Irish famine in the late 1840s, there was a correlation between years of distress, such as 1826–9, 1830–32 and 1841–2, and peaks in the emigration chart. By 1841 nearly a million emigrants had been officially registered since 1821; by 1851 nearly 2·7 millions. To these should be added the two or three thousand convicts annually transported between 1825 and 1841 and probably many other emigrants that went unrecorded by customs officials. The majority of the emigrants were Irish and Scots and they went overwhelmingly to the North American continent, to Quebec and New York.

Internal migration, however, had even greater, certainly more visible, effects on the pattern of population. The 1841 census showed some 400,000 Irish-born inhabitants living in Great Britain, over two thirds in England, the rest mainly in Scotland. Despite their reputation for wandering, the group of Scots south of the border was comparatively small: some 110,000, mostly in England. The main movement of population inside Scotland was from the Highlands to the Lowlands. Scots that made the longer journey to England were usually men with a skilled trade or a little capital.

While currents of internal migration were beginning to mix the peoples of the British Isles, others were heaping the population into dense masses. In the decade ending in 1821 the fastest growing counties in England (some at twice the national average) were, in order of growth rate, Lancashire, Surrey, Sussex, Lincolnshire, Monmouth and the West Riding. In the following decade Monmouth displaced Lancashire, while Cheshire, Durham and Warwick moved up the list in front of Surrey and the West Riding. In the 1831–41

period Monmouth and Durham were ahead of Lancashire, followed
by Staffordshire, Surrey, Warwick and the West Riding: a significantly mixed group of districts representing heavy industry, the two
great textile areas, and one metropolitan county. In Wales during
these thirty years iron and steel made Glamorgan the one outstanding
area of expansion. In Scotland after 1821 Edinburgh and Lothians
were being outstripped by the Glasgow belt of Lanark and Dun-
bartonshire. At the other end of the scale the counties in England
with the slowest rate of growth were the North Riding, Hereford,
Westmorland and Cumberland; in Wales Merioneth and Radnor-
shire; in Scotland some of the central and southern rural counties.
Up to 1831, however, the population was still increasing everywhere,
even if the increase in some parts lagged well behind the national
average. Not until the 1841–51 decade did one English county,
Wiltshire, show an absolute decline and, in Wales, the hill-farming
counties of Radnor, Montgomery and Merioneth. In Scotland, on
the other hand, the social distortion produced by industrial concentration in the Clyde–Forth valley, and the slow depopulation of
rural areas elsewhere, was already visible before Victoria came to the
throne. The 1831–41 decade saw no less than eight counties with a
declining population—five in or bordering the Highlands (Argyll,
Kinross, Perthshire, Sutherland and Nairn) and three in the Lowlands (Dumfries, Peebles, and Haddington).

A feature of this growing unevenness of population was the rapid,
in some instances, extraordinarily rapid growth of towns. Histori-
cally, until the nineteenth century, the big towns were death-traps,
with mortality rates too high to ensure the maintenance of their
populations without continual reinforcement of healthy bodies from
the countryside. But from some conjectural date around 1800 the big
towns began to grow by natural increase as well as by immigration.
Even so, as late as the middle of the century, in London and the
seventy-one largest towns of England and Scotland nearly half the
inhabitants had been born elsewhere. In certain towns particularly
open to Irish immigration, like Glasgow, Liverpool and Manchester,
the proportion was more than half. Since the immigrants were
predominantly younger people, the birth rate in the growing towns
was abnormally high; this in turn accelerated the rate of expansion.
The seventy large towns (by which the statisticians meant those
with over 20,000 inhabitants in 1851) had accounted for 23 per cent
of the total population of Great Britain in 1801, 34 per cent
in 1851. They had increased by 189 per cent in the half century
compared with the 71 per cent growth rate of the countryside and small towns in the same period. What were statistically the
fastest growing towns did not, however, constitute a homogenous

group; and their diversity was a sign of the growing complexity of the society they served. They fell into six categories: mining, heavy industry, seaports, watering places, London and County towns. It was a mark of the opulence and mobility of Georgian and early Victorian society that in respect of rate of expansion, though not of course of absolute size of population, the fastest growing group were seaside holiday towns like Brighton, Margate, Weymouth and Torquay. These were followed closely by manufacturing towns, mining and hardware, and seaports, with London and the county towns at the foot of the list.

If London did not increase as far as other large towns or indeed the population as a whole, it was nevertheless the great leviathan of British cities. From over a million in 1811 it rose to 2·3 millions in 1851 and throughout the half century the population of London was more than half that of the rest of the seventy largest towns put together. All classes, a vast number of small industries, almost all trades and professions, were represented in London. It was the seat of government, the centre of finance, the greatest port. It had the largest concentration of peers and politicians, of solicitors and barristers, of physicians and surgeons, of costermongers, clerks and coal-porters, of merchants, shopkeepers, booksellers and newspaper editors—though, until the end of George IV's reign, no university. To feed, house, and police such a mass of population was by contemporary standards an enormous achievement. Yet though London had characteristic social features, it lacked political identity or economic unity. Too much was continually happening; too many interests, too many classes were involved in its everyday life for any one of them to predominate. The diversity of its economic life flattened the effects of slumps and booms. It was politically articulate, but rarely extreme, and never dangerous.

By comparison the next nine largest towns on the eve of the Reform Act had all strongly marked identities: Manchester, the cottonopolis of wealthy manufacturers, 'the chimney of the world', as Charles Napier described it in a moment of exasperation, full of 'rich rascals, poor rogues, drunken ragamuffins and prostitutes'; Liverpool, seat of great merchants and seagate to the Atlantic and America; Birmingham, the heart of the Black Country and home of small craftsmen; Bristol, the old West Country port with its strong colonial trade in sugar, rum, wine and tobacco; Leeds, the centre of the West Riding clothing trade; Plymouth and Portsmouth, the two great naval dockyard towns; Norwich, the declining capital of the once wealthy East Anglian textile industry; and Newcastle, the expanding capital of the northeastern coal and iron fields.

The other notable feature of urban development was that, except

in Edinburgh and one or two other Scottish towns where there was
a tradition of flatted tenements, the towns grew outwards. Most of the
working classes, in town as in country, lived in their own houses
even if they had to let out one or two rooms to lodgers. The middle
classes were beginning to move out from the centre, creating the
characteristic suburban zones. What smoke and soot did in some
towns, high rents did in others. Long before the traveller reached the
outskirts of London he became aware of the metropolitan influence.
On the nine miles between London and the Surrey market town of
Croydon, where the hounds still met, there were in 1822 rows of
houses lining the road for nearly half the way: as ugly a bit of country,
thought Cobbett, as any in England. Round the metropolis and large
industrial towns like Birmingham and Sheffield the visible signs of
rapid expansion were sometimes depressing: blighted countryside,
'Land to be Sold' notices, fresh gravel-pits, new brick-kilns, and a
'band of black vegetable gardens, reeking with town manure'.[3] Near
Cheltenham, on the other hand, a steadily expanding inland spa,
Cobbett found 'rows of white tenements, with green balconies' from
which he inferred the hateful presence of 'an assembly of tax-eaters'.

Where there was acute pressure on cheap accommodation in the
centre, as in the wynds of Glasgow or the cellars of Liverpool and
Leeds, conditions were dreadful. Even in the rows of workers' houses
on the outskirts there were examples of jerry-building. During the
Napoleonic Wars, when costs of materials, land and labour rose
sharply, the temptations before the small builder must have been
great. Yet the new working-class accommodation was probably no
worse, and often much better than the rural cottages many of them
had left. Even jerry-building had its part in the scheme of things.
Most of it was to last for the rest of the century. The problems arose
more from the increasing density of housing and isolation from the
antiseptic qualities of the countryside. What was remarkable was that
the building industry was not only keeping abreast of the rising tide
of population but, if anything, slightly ahead of it. Even in the
industrial areas the housing situation did not deteriorate and in some
had probably improved by the accession of George IV.[4] Scarcity of
accommodation was more likely in the rural areas where building
costs were higher and farmers sometimes pulled down the meaner
kind of rural hovel to save poor law assessments, in this way herding
the labourers into villages several miles from their work.

³ This description comes from an article in the *Journal of the Royal Agricultural Society* XVII
(1866), p. 491 n. but the same sights could be seen on the outskirts of large towns throughout
the period.
⁴ See C. W. Chalklin, *The Provincial Towns of Georgian England*, chapter 12.

III

While population trends indicated the pattern of the future, the structure and habits of Britain were largely those of a pre-industrial society. The majority of people lived either in the countryside or in small, semi-rural towns. They were to continue to do so until the second half of the century. The land—socially, economically, politically, and by almost every criterion except foreign trade—was still the largest single interest. Even though rents had risen, sometimes to double their pre-war level, ownership of land for purely agricultural purposes was not a particularly profitable investment. But many of the large estates had themselves been caught up in the industrial expansion. The English landed aristocracy had always shown a businesslike awareness that land could be made to serve a variety of uses. The marquess of Westminster with his estates in Mayfair and Belgravia, the duke of Bedford with his Bloomsbury site, the earls of Durham and Londonderry with their coal fields in Durham and Northumberland, were merely outstanding figures in a large group of landowners who through urban development, harbour-building, canals and turnpikes, and the exploitation of minerals such as coal, iron, copper, lead and tin, reaped a handsome profit from the non-agricultural purposes to which land could be put.

For the majority of less fortunate landed proprietors, whose estates brought in nothing but agricultural rents, the value of landownership was not to be measured in purely economic terms. Land was important because it carried with it membership of a particular social class. Had it not been for the social significance of being a landed proprietor, land would have been less expensive and more profitable. The great survey of 1872 disclosed that four fifths of the land in the United Kingdom was owned by less than 7,000 individuals. A quarter of England was occupied by large estates of over 10,000 acres. In Wales and Scotland the greater part of the soil belonged to the gentry and aristocracy. It is unlikely that the position in 1815 was markedly different. The upper crust of this landed class was formed by the 300 or so families who possessed a title, an income from between £3,000 and anything up to and over £50,000 a year, a country seat and probably another house in London. This hereditary peerage had expanded rapidly under Pitt and his immediate successors. It was a useful form of political patronage since it entailed no charge on the public purse—a consideration to which both ministers and public were growing sensitive. When Wellington was created a duke, a grateful House of Commons voted money for an estate to support him in that dignity; but this was exceptional. Normally a peerage required preceding proof of material affluence. Lord Eldon, who declared in 1825 that the emoluments from his office of lord chancellor were little more than £9,000 a year (they were generally believed to be twice that), accepted promotion from baron to earl in 1821 only with reluctance since 'my fortune is not more than equal to my present rank'. Partly as a result, even after Pitt and Liverpool, the peerage was a relatively select order. By the time of the first Reform Act the peers numbered about 350. Thereafter the rate of peerage-making slackened and by the time of the second Reform Act in 1867 the total was little more than 400.

Outside the peerage was the great mass of landed gentry. In England there were about 3,000 of them in 1872; in the United Kingdom as a whole perhaps as many as 4,000. Between them and the peers was a social rather than an economic division. The richer commoners were wealthier than the poorer peers. Probably as many as half the men enjoying an income of £10,000 or more from land were not peers. Colonel Beaumont[5] of Northumberland, with an income of up to £100,000 from lead mines in Yorkshire, as well as landed estates elsewhere, could probably have bought out half the House of Lords. But the majority of the gentry were men of more modest means, with rent-rolls from £3,000 down to a mere £1,000 a year. Below them in the social hierarchy was a less definable, shifting class of inferior county society—gentlemen farmers, lawyers, doctors, bankers, retired tradesmen, ex-army and navy officers—who filled the gap between the gentry and their tenants, and are immortalized for posterity in the pages of Surtees's novels.

The true landed class of gentry and aristocracy, together little more perhaps in 1815 than some 4,000 families, constituted the traditional governing élite. Since 1688 they had dominated the political life of the kingdom. They controlled the electoral system, filled the benches in both houses of parliament, supplied the bulk of the clergy of the Church of England, the officer corps of the army and navy and the upper ranks of the diplomatic service. They commanded the militia; with the clergy they monopolized the magistracy; and through grand juries and quarter sessions they governed the countryside. Oxford and Cambridge had become finishing schools for their sons; contemporary painting and architecture reflected their aspirations and pursuits. They were conventionally regarded as, and to some extent actually were, a closely knit caste, and perhaps tended to be more so as the century wore on. The obvious distinction of hereditary title, including beside the

---

[5] Colonel Thomas Richard Beaumont (1758–1829), MP for Northumberland 1795–1818.

peerage proper the baronetcy, was underpinned by an elaborate legal system of entail, settlement and primogeniture, designed to preserve and transmit the integrity of the estates from which they derived their status. Not land, but (as Gladstone once observed) land in the possession of families was the essence of the 'landed interest'; and he, like many others, regarded it as the main source of Britain's social strength. By the time Sanford and Townsend produced their two-volume work on *The Great Governing Families of England* in 1865, they recognized that what, in ordinary terms, was referred to as 'the aristocracy' was no more than the larger owners of land. It was this, rather than title or ancient lineage, which constituted the 'real and permanent aristocratic power in English politics'.

Yet from another point of view this appearance of a closed caste was deceptive. Within the 'aristocracy', in Townsend's loose definition, were enormous variations of wealth, outlook, and social origin. The 'landed interest' of which the aristocracy were the natural spokesmen was not a horizontal but a vertical division of society, embracing tenants and freeholders, clergy and lawyers, auctioneers, landagents, millers, corn merchants, brewers, blacksmiths, butchers, bakers, innkeepers and an endless list of crafts and trades which served the needs of those who owned, farmed, or worked on the land. To society as a whole the aristocracy was linked not only by ties of influence and clientage but by blood and marriage. The absence of a legal caste of 'nobility' in British society meant that their younger sons and daughters were continually being absorbed into the non-aristocratic classes without title or without estates. At the same time the 'aristocracy' was being constantly reinforced by talented or fortunate families from below. Ambitious politicians, political lawyers, successful generals and admirals could carve out a fortune and a peerage for themselves in a single lifetime. If the political system up to the age of Liverpool was something of a lottery, the financial and social rewards for the fortunate few were often high.

Other families had to be content with the more conventional climb up the social ladder, represented by a baronetcy in the first generation, followed by further public service and promotion to a peerage in the second or third. In default of a title, actual ownership of land was in itself a social asset. The 'landed gentry' in fact were in a state of continuous flux. It was always possible to 'set up as a gentleman'; and the traditional ambition of successful bankers, merchants, and manufacturers to acquire gentility ensured a steady infusion of plebeian blood into the ranks of the landowning classes. At the start of the nineteenth century there were innumerable examples of this form of social metamorphosis: Darby from the iron trade, Boulton from engineering, the Peels, Marshalls, Arkwrights,

Fieldens and Strutts from textiles, the Whitbreads from brewing, the
Smiths and Barings from finance. Round Glasgow the wealthier
merchants had been investing in estate purchases for a generation
before Waterloo.

The middle classes from whom these new-style gentry came were
a heterogeneous collection: industrialists and merchants, professional
men, farmers and shopkeepers, families of independent means,
differing widely in wealth, education and political outlook. The
industrial manufacturers themselves were of no identifiable type. A
few came from the ranks of the small gentry, some from simple
yeoman families; others were skilled workmen who made their way
upwards by thrift, diligence and technical knowledge. There were
conservative anglicans among them but also a perhaps disproportionate number of Quakers, Unitarians and dissenters with a
strong moral sense, liberal political views and independent outlook.
Many were sturdy individualists who took a pride in their order and
had no desire to turn themselves into bastard gentlemen with a
country house and a miniature estate. In Scotland where living
standards were simpler, there were fears in 1825 that this class would
fall below the proposed special juryman qualification of a £30 house
or £100 in land. Cockburn spoke of 'a very great number of rich and
respectable manufacturers, who live in houses not rented at £30, and
who, having no land, have no valuation'. Such families lived in solid
but unostentatious comfort, their houses were commodious, and they
ate well. In London Escher found a typical middle-class lunch
(salmon, roast beef, potatoes and green peas, sweets, fruits and salad
washed down with port and madeira) too much for his Swiss stomach.
In Manchester he discovered that 'everybody who is well off ... has
a greenhouse in which he grows considerable quantities of grapes,
peaches etc.'. Among the manufacturers in Glasgow, though he
remarked on the barefooted maids waiting at table and an inordinate
amount of churchgoing and grace-saying on Sundays, he found the
meals as good as in England and the houses more comfortable and
spacious than in London.

Families such as these were part of the group described by the
1831 census as 'capitalists, bankers, professional and other educated
men' whose total of 214,000 in that year was larger than that of either
farmers employing labour or 'persons of independent means'. The
census of 1841 enabled this rudimentary analysis to be carried a little
further. In England the three great and easily identifiable professions
—church, law and medicine—totalled 50,000 with the law taking
rather less, the other two rather more than a third each. In Scotland
the total was just under 10,000 with doctors and lawyers both slightly
outnumbering the clergy. Only in religious and backward Wales did

the 1,600 clergy more than equal lawyers and doctors put together. A more amorphous group, double the size of the three traditional professions, was that comprehensively listed as bankers, merchants, brokers, agents, clerks, shopkeepers and the representatives of literature, science and the fine arts. Of these there were over 120,000 in England (a quarter of them in Middlesex); 3,000 in Wales; and 18,000 in Scotland (a fifth in Edinburgh). To these should be added about 17,000 civil servants and 25,000 parochial, town, church and police officers, though doubtless some of them fell short of the strict criteria for educated persons. It is arguable whether they should be included in even a loose definition of the 'middle classes'.

If they are included, it is possible to arrive at a figure of well under quarter of a million for the entrepreneurial, wage- and salary-earning middle class (out of a total of just over four and a half million adult males) at the time of the 1841 census. Even at this level, British society was still strongly pyramidal in structure, with a relatively small middle class above the broad mass of working-class population. Indeed this figure of quarter of a million is itself probably an overstatement. Allowing for the general population increase between 1811 and 1841 the equivalent figure for 1815 would be approximately 175,000. A rough check can be applied to this figure by the statistics available for the last year of Pitt's wartime income tax. The number of persons charged for income tax under schedule D (income from trade, industry and professional profits)[6] numbered just over 160,000 in the year ending 1816. The somewhat cynical commissioners of the inland revenue estimated in 1869 that some 40 per cent of those making returns under schedule D failed to give a true statement of their income. Since taxpayers in 1815 were unlikely to have been more scrupulous than in 1869, it is reasonable to assume that a figure of 160,000 is an understatement of those actually in receipt of an income of £50. By how much an understatement it is impossible to know and difficult to guess. But any addition would bring the total still closer to the other figure of 175,000 projected backwards from the 1841 census. The tentative conclusion must be that in 1815 the middle classes in Britain, excluding persons of independent means and farmers, were represented by between 165,000 and 175,000 individuals, unmarried or heads of families.

If £1,000 per annum is accepted as the lower limit of income for the gentry and aristocracy, £50 per annum is as good a line of demarcation as any for the middle classes. What was the lower limit

---

[6] The other forms of income distinguished were from ownership (schedule A) or occupation (schedule B) of land; from public stocks and shares (schedule C); and from official salaries and pensions (schedule E). See the *Report of the Commissioners of Inland Revenue for the Years 1856–69*, Cd. 1870 I, pp. 130–31, II, p. 189.

for the wartime income tax, a comfortable wage for a journeyman carpenter in the London of the young Charles Dickens[7] and the attractive pay of Peel's new metropolitan police, was enough to maintain with economy lower middle-class appearances. From £100 to £200 a year represented comfort; and it was on this kind of income that the bulk of the middle classes supported themselves. Of the schedule D taxpayers at the time of Waterloo a majority (58 per cent) returned incomes of under £100 a year. The great mass (88 per cent) of them had, or declared that they had, incomes of under £300 a year. At the top of the scale some salaries and incomes were undoubtedly high. Only after £5,000 did the revenue commissioners think it unnecessary to specify any further categories. But these higher reaches of the tax system were occupied by a relatively small number of persons. Less than 5,000 returned incomes of over £1,000, the point at which the middle classes in terms of wealth could be said to overlap the lower ranks of the landed gentry.[8]

Apart from commerce and industry the three established professions of the church, the law and medicine all offered careers in which a combination of patronage, talent and luck might lead to social distinction as well as material opulence. The professions in fact formed a kind of bridge between the aristocracy and the middle classes in more ways than one. Denman in 1825 (seven years before he became lord chief justice and nine before he became Lord Denman of Dovedale) argued that £4,000 per annum was a sufficient salary for a high court judge. 'It was impossible, by any increase of salary, that they could ever be raised to an equality with the great. At present they might be said to be at the head of people of middling fortune, which was better than being at the foot of the higher order.' But what the professions offered was prestige as well as money. The church was of course an estate in itself whose episcopal heads sat in the House of Lords as spiritual peers. But the leaders of the legal and medical professions, if not on an equality with the great, were at least a respectable adjunct to the aristocratic world in which they found their more lucrative clients. Barristers could aspire to a judgeship or, if their bent was political, the alternative route of a parliamentary seat and in due course one of the handful of politico-legal posts, headed by the Lord Chancellorship, which every government had at its disposal. Court physicians, like court painters, could hope for a knighthood; and a fashionable doctor in London could earn as much

---

[7] See *Sketches by Boz* (1836) 'Characters' chapter 4, for the description of Mr Samuel Wilkins, journeyman carpenter. 'His earnings were all-sufficient for his wants, varying from eighteen shillings to one pound five, weekly; his manner undeniable—his Sabbath waistcoats dazzling.'

[8] Many schedule D taxpayers must also have been in receipt of income from government stock (schedule C) but the fundholders were more likely to be found among the wealthier classes, including the landed gentry, than those with incomes of under £100.

as a cabinet minister. All three professions were gentlemanly in the accepted social sense. Their membership implied a university career and a classical education. They constituted powerful, self-governing and self-recruiting groups closely identified with the outlook and interests of the governing classes: the clergy through the two old universities and the hierarchy of the establishment; the doctors through the Royal Colleges of Physicians and Surgeons; and the barristers through the Inns of Court.

It was a sign of the growing size and complexity of the English middle classes, however, that by 1815 the old predominance of the three learned professions was being challenged at many points. Already by 1811 there were more non-anglican places of worship in the towns of England and Wales than anglican. The Methodist movement and the parallel nonconformist revival of the late eighteenth century had produced a mass of unestablished clergy, many educated in the dissenting academics and training colleges or even in the case of Methodist clergy in the old universities themselves, some at least of whom were the equals of their anglican brethren in classical and theological learning. The evangelical revival at its height led to a sometimes disastrous emphasis on fervent oratory and there were justifiable criticisms of the intellectual quality of some of the preachers who made their appearance. But by the 1830s all the nonconformist churches were making steady efforts to improve the professional training of their younger clergy. Other considerations apart, the rising social aspirations of their congregations made such a development necessary. 'All our people in trade now give a boarding school education to their children', wrote a Methodist superintendent on the Bath circuit in 1828, 'and an unlettered pastor with a provincial dialect sounds but ungracious on their ear'.

An analogous process was at work in the two secular professions. The Apothecaries Act of 1815, enabling the society of apothecaries to regulate training and admittance to the profession, was at once a victory for the country doctors over the obstructive monopoly of the Royal College of Physicians and an assertion of a new professional status for ordinary practitioners. When in the year of the first Reform Act the body which later became the British Medical Association was founded (at Worcester) as the Provincial Medical and Surgical Association, it was essentially a general practitioners' union. Similarly the body later known as the Law Society, established in 1825 as the Society of Attorneys and Solicitors,[9] was given a royal charter in

---

[9] The difference was that attorneys were technically officers of the common law courts and solicitors of the Court of Chancery. The same man could qualify as both. The distinction disappeared in 1874 when the attorneys took the name of solicitors, popularly held to be the more respectable classification.

1831 to enable it to provide a proper legal education for the more numerous but less fashionable section of the legal profession. Within half a dozen years the first serious qualifying legal examinations were being held for attorneys. The barristers remained exempt from such ungentlemanly inflictions until 1872.

By these characteristic methods of education, association and examination the middle classes were in effect securing a career for the talents of their children outside the old monopolistic professions, a career which no longer needed the stamp of an Oxford or Cambridge degree or nominal membership of the anglican church. It was, however, a process not only of rivalry but of imitation. In creating for themselves these new professions they were in effect assimilating themselves to the aristocratic pattern set by the barristers, physicians and established clergy.

The expansion of the number of professional associations was a sign of the growing size and ambition of the more prosperous middle classes. The same features a little lower down in the social scale produced the insecurity and competitiveness mentioned by many writers when they surveyed British society. As W. J. Fox put it with excessive bluntness in 1835, 'in the middle classes we note an almost universal unfixedness of position. Every man is rising or falling or hoping that he shall rise, or fearing that he shall sink.' The aristocracy as a class were too assured, economically and socially, to fear loss of status. The mass of the poor had no rational hope of moving upward in the social scale. But, so Fox thought, throughout the rest of the middle classes (he was expressly excluding the professions and the farming community) there was a ceaseless struggle, a sense of dependence on a precarious income, and therefore 'a continual anxiety to increase the amount of that income or to prevent its sinking to a smaller amount'. This competitive spirit encouraged enterprise and energy. It also, Fox alleged, had some disagreeable features: materialism, selfishness and snobbery, a disposition to look above for leadership, jealousy and sectarianism at their own level, and an excessive emphasis on outward morality.[10]

The language of a Unitarian minister, reproving from his own pulpit the faults of his own age and class, need not be taken literally. But too many observers made similar comments for Fox's strictures to be dismissed entirely. For the lower middle classes at any rate – the master craftsman, the small shopkeeper, the clerk in the city office— hard work and respectability were the outward marks of the painfully narrow margin of economic superiority which kept them above the

[10] W. J. Fox, *Morality and the Classes of Society* (1835), III *The Mercantile and Middle Classes.* The book was based on a series of lectures delivered at his Finsbury chapel.

mass of the labouring poor. Similarly the competition of a cut-throat business world, the reckless spirit of speculation sometimes exhibited, the constant fear of bankruptcy, help to explain if not to justify the harshness sometimes displayed towards employees by the small employer working on limited capital. It has been remarked how in Dickens, that supreme portrayer of the Victorian lower middle classes, there is an obsessive interest in the work people do for a living, in the material comforts of life, and in the power of money to make the difference between indebtedness and independence, success and failure, happiness and misery.[11]

The middle classes as a whole showed perhaps wider variations of wealth, education, economic security, and political outlook than the classes above or below them. What can be loosely described as a middle-class culture was beginning to be a dominant influence in morality, art and literature long before Victoria came to the throne. But it was not the work of a class that was either united in its aspirations or conscious of its power. This lack of social and political homogeneity, important in itself, resulted from the even more important circumstance that the middle classes did not constitute a fixed or even easily definable social caste. They were emphatically the middle *classes*, a plural concept as opposed to the singular noun *bourgeoisie* of European countries. Their 'universal unfixedness of position', in Fox's phrase, was no more than the fluidity of British society more actively at work than at any other level. The middle classes embraced the social detritus of the aristocracy, the upward migrants from the working classes, and much of the solid talent, wealth, and intellect of the country. Their diversity, looseness and disunity were simply signs of a high degree of social activity and mobility. Compared with most continental states, if not with the American Republic on the other side of the Atlantic, Britain was already becoming an open society.

IV

What were beginning to be known as the working classes also exhibited a variety of occupations, rewards, and conditions of life. The typical worker, however, if such an abstraction can be made from the impersonal figures of the census returns, was employed neither in a factory nor in the processes of industrial manufacture. The broad

[11] See Humphrey House, *The Dickens World*, chapter 3.

analysis of occupations provided by the 1831 census showed that the
number of adult males in the manufacturing industry was only half
that of the agricultural labourers and only two thirds that of the mass
of labourers who were neither industrial nor agricultural. Even in the
industrial sector, the great cotton mills of Lancashire and Glasgow
and the deep coal mines of the northeast that attracted the attention
of the foreign visitor, were untypical. Apart from textiles, iron, and
coal among the large industries, brewing, glass-making and shipyards
among the small, the British manufacturing industry was an
agglomeration of small, separate enterprises. The metal trades of
Birmingham and Sheffield, for example, were dominated by small
firms, with employers often working alongside their men. Simple
articles in constant demand, like locks, hinges and brackets, were
manufactured by individual mechanics in their own homes and sold
to the wholesale merchants. The outworkers who collected iron rods
from the nail-masters and returned the finished article, the button-
makers, the needle- and pin-makers, worked on the same system.
Sometimes a family carried on both forms of manufacture. The father
of George Holyoake, the radical agitator, was a senior and respected
workman in the Eagle Foundry at Birmingham in the period after
Waterloo. His wife ran a little workshop at home making horn buttons
and as a small boy Holyoake learnt to wind copper wire on a lathe,
stamp it into shanks, and cut the shanks with shears 'which often
strained my little hands'.

Even among textiles, cotton was the only branch in which up to the
middle of the century the large factory was the principal unit. Cotton
manufacture caught the eye of industrialists, reformers and politicians because its three great characteristics—regional concentration, use of steam power, and large factories— were a novelty in
the British economy. It was however an impressive novelty. By 1815
the larger mills in Manchester and the west of Scotland were
employing three hundred or more workers, the very large concerns
over a thousand. Many smaller and therefore less conspicuous firms
existed but they were to be gradually squeezed out of existence in
the next generation. Even so, there still remained a large army of
outworkers carrying on spinning and weaving. In 1831 the total
number employed in the cotton industry has been estimated as
approximately 400,000. Of these only half worked in mills and
perhaps more than half were women and children. In the rest of the
textile industry—woollens, worsteds, clothing, silks and lace—the
organization was in the form of a long chain extending from the
retailer, the wholesale merchant or warehouseman, and the middleman or putter-out, to the domestic or outworker with his (usually)
rented loom or frame. The handloom weaver, whether as in Man-

chester, Paisley and Liverpool forming a species of urban proletariat, or as in parts of Yorkshire and Lancashire living in a rural cottage with a garden and sometimes poultry or a pig, was the largest class of outworker. But the domestic worker, obtaining his raw materials from a middleman and working at home, was the characteristic labour force of many other analogous industries—the hosiery workers of Leicestershire and Nottinghamshire, for example, or the knitters and lace-makers of the southern counties.

One consequence of the universal domestic system was the involvement of the whole family in the work on which they depended for their livelihood. The wife, when free from cooking, cleaning, mending and childbearing, the children as soon as they were old enough, at six or seven, to carry out the simpler repetitive processes, all joined in the main economic activity of the household. There was nothing to astonish either the native or foreign observer in this. It was the immemorial custom for women and children of the poorer classes to assist in the father's occupation or to supplement his earnings by some other form of gainful employment. The hours they worked, though irregular, were often long, and for the children the discipline of the parents often severe. Whether being in a family was enough to offset bad working conditions, tiredness and occasional harsh treatment is irrelevant. It was an accepted and traditional practice which none questioned as long as it was confined to the home. Often indeed the practice of regarding the whole family as a working unit was carried over into the early cotton mills and coal mines; and employers were sometimes obliged to take younger children than they really wanted to allow the family to stay together. The precocious training of children in particular kinds of work to supplement the output of the father tended of course to prolong the existence of certain traditional forms of employment, notably handloom weaving, long after they had ceased to provide an adequate economic reward. 'Surprising as it may appear,' wrote a sympathetic observer of the Bethnal Green and Spitalfields weavers in 1841, 'the Weaver, while deploring the depressed condition of his trade, as soon as his children are capable of exercising their upper and lower extremities, puts them as a matter of course in the loom, and so perpetuates a famished and discontented race.' The immobility inherent in the domestic system does much to explain why the hopeless struggle of the handloom weavers against the machine was maintained so long.

Even that larger part of the non-agricultural population which was not engaged in industrial manufacture worked for the most part in small units. The building trade, which including the unskilled labourers probably employed more men than any other industry outside agriculture, was essentially a small firm activity with bricklayers, carpenters, plasterers and slaters often working alongside the master builder. The same was broadly true of most of the thousand-odd trades and occupations by which the British people earned their daily bread. The tailors in their workroom, the clerks in offices and counterhands in shops, the porters in the market and at the quayside, the ostlers in the stables, the compositors in the printing rooms, all carried on their work in small groups under the direct supervision if not under the constant eye of their employer. This was particularly true of one of the largest but most ignored of all occupations—the domestic servant. Even allowing for some confusion in the census returns between household servants and living-in labourers on farms, there were well over half a million female domestic servants in Great Britain in 1831, and over a million male and female servants in 1841, more than all the men, women and children employed in all the textile manufactures at the same date. Voteless and unorganized, they nevertheless lived (however cramped for space) under their employers' roof, often ate much the same sort of food, and some-times, when out of livery, wore their cast-off clothing. In their own ambiguous way they formed yet another link between the rich and the poor.

V

The largest industry of all was, as it had always been, agriculture. A great part of the population spent their time in producing food for the rest. The country had to depend almost entirely on itself for its staple article of diet, bread; and as in medieval days, or indeed under the Tudors and Stuarts, the class most vulnerable to the unpredict-able and uncontrollable vagaries of the British climate were the poor. A bad harvest meant shortage of corn, high prices, suffering, social discontent and sometimes rioting. Until the repeal of the corn laws in 1846, the result of the British harvest was the most important single factor in regulating the cost of living for the lower classes.[12] The vicissitudes of the weather produced great variation in the cost of wheat not only from year to year but from month to month. The average price was 78s. 6d. a quarter in 1816, only 44s. 7d. in 1822. These annual averages in turn concealed considerable fluctuations. In 1828 the weekly average price was 51s. 6d. at the end of January, 75s. 3d. at the beginning of December; and this was in no way exceptional. In the following year it was 75s. 3d. early in February falling to 56s. 3d. in the second week of December. It is not surprising

[12] See appendix B for the yearly average price of wheat, 1811–64.

that the state of the harvest was something that entered into the calculations of politicians or that for thirty years the corn laws were a topic of national debate.

The organization of agriculture in the good farming land of England had already assumed its characteristic triple pattern of land-owner, tenant farmer and landless labourer. But a prevailing pattern did not imply complete uniformity. Enclosure and consolidation of estates in the eighteenth century had tended inevitably to reduce the number of small proprietors and subsistence peasants. For an agricultural estate to pay its way an adequate rent-roll was necessary; and rents depended on efficient tenant farmers. Nevertheless, the small farmer and freeholder were an unconscionable long time dying. In some areas, like Kent with its specialized orchards, hop-growing and market gardening, they were probably on the increase. According to the 1831 census as many as a third of the total number of occupying agricultural families were of the continental peasant type, farming their own land with no hired labour. On the other hand many of these were concentrated in the Highlands of Scotland, Wales and the west of England. But even in Cornwall, for example, a traditional area of small farms, there were only 3,600 who farmed without labourers as against 4,600 who farmed with. In England as a whole 60 per cent of the farmers employed labour as compared with 50 per cent in Wales and 33 per cent in Scotland.

In all there were in 1831 over 355,000 farmers of one kind or another, with or without hired labour, of whom approximately two thirds were in England. Of the remainder a third were in Wales, two thirds in Scotland. They formed a formidable social and economic interest, even if the differing needs of arable and grazing, cold clay and light loam, corn, meat, fruit and vegetables, ensured that the farmers did not always speak as a body or with only one voice. As a social class the British farmers and freeholders after 1832, since most of them were enfranchised by the celebrated Reform Act of that year, must have constituted something like a third of the national parliamentary electorate. The disproportionate weighting of the boroughs in the representative structure and the traditional respect for landlord wishes at country elections robbed that electoral strength of much of its effectiveness. Nevertheless, the farming interest was a powerful one. Few sections of the population outside the small ruling class were so well placed, economically, socially and electorally, to bring their influence to bear on the legislature.

Consolidation of farms, high prices and high profits during the war had enriched the farming community financially and elevated it socially. By continental standards Britain, particularly England, was a country of large farms. A hundred acres, which in Germany or

France would rank as a large, in England would be the upper limit of a small farm. Over a large part of southern and Midland England most farms were above that limit. Many, especially those with down-land sheep-runs or moorland pasture or on recently enclosed land, were considerably larger. That statistical concept, the average farm, is of little value as a guide since hardly anywhere was there one predominant type of farm, and nearly everywhere a wide mixture. But in the middle of the century, and probably earlier, less than a quarter of the farming land in England and Wales was held in farms of under a hundred acres. In Scotland, where most of the land was owned by the gentry and aristocracy, the large farms of several hundred acres run by the professional tenant farmer dominated the great arable districts of the Lothians and the southeast Lowlands in the post-Waterloo era. While small farms still flourished in the southwest and northeast, in the very different economy of the Highlands the process of clearing away the tacksmen and cottars had already started.

Contemporaries both before and after Waterloo had unkind remarks to make about farmers who rode to hounds, whose wives kept smart gigs, and whose daughters learned the piano and went to seminaries for young ladies instead of working in the dairy and poultry yard. Not all farmers aspired to such marks of gentility, but presumably enough did to give a basis for a widespread conviction. 'They are got very hard-hearted', said an old Sussex labourer to a parliamentary committee in 1837. 'When I was young a farmer and his wife used to ride both upon a horse with a pillion ... and another thing, the farmer used to keep a good many servants in the house ... but now they have got gigs and fine hunting horses.' Widening class divisions were no doubt one influence tending to exclude the labourer from his employer's house, the high cost of provisions another. It was also more economical to give piecework or hire by the day or week instead of for the whole year. Increasingly young single labourers had to live in the overcrowded parental cottage or in common lodging houses in sometimes distant villages. The substitution of the casual cash nexus for the older, more permanent relationship contributed to the growing sourness of rural life.

Popular tradition has, however, exaggerated both the speed of the decline in the living-in farm servant and the social loss which it represented. As late as the middle of the century there was still an average of nearly one indoor male servant to every farm, even though this figure would include the stable boy of the foxhunting and gig-driving farmer and the unmarried farm worker of higher status, the shepherd, carter or fogger. In the small dale farms of Cleveland described by Atkinson the practice of having workers of both sexes living at the farm was still common in the middle of the century. The overcrowding, moreover, was as bad as in the ordinary labourers' cottages. Surviving accounts do not suggest that living as one of a group of labourers on a farm was a particularly refining experience. One old man survived to the end of the century to record his recollections of conditions when working as a boy in the 1830s on a large arable farm in Somerset, where there were a considerable number of living-in workers both male and female. They existed on stale, often mildewed, bread, rancid bacon, potatoes and turnips which they prepared themselves and cooked on a wood fire; and, he added concisely, 'as for morality there was just as much as with the dogs and cats.'[13]

Working for the farmers, or for those at least who hired labour, was an army of over 800,000 (887,000 according to the 1831 census) —an average of just over five to each employer in England, just under three in Scotland and Wales. These were men over twenty; but boys, women and girls were also part of the agricultural labour force, if only at specialized tasks or at busy periods in spring and autumn. In terms of families, a more realistic basis, there were about five labouring households to each employing household, rather more in England, rather less in Scotland and Wales. Their numbers were still growing, though less so than the population of the towns and industrial counties. Only after 1851 was there an absolute decline. But migration to the towns, to a smaller extent overseas, was taking off much of the natural increase in the first part of the century. It is surprising that it did not take more. Wartime expansion and inflation had left British agriculture in 1815 over-manned and over-capitalized. The next twenty years, marked for the most part by good harvests, were a period of general stagnancy for British farmers. In the long run the only remedy was an increase in consumption, either individual or through sheer aggregate growth of population. The short-term remedies were less pleasant: lowered wages, under-employment, masked by heavy subsidization from the poor rate.

Low as his economic status was, the condition of the agricultural labourer still differed widely from one part of the country to another. One marked contrast was between the north of England, where a smaller rural population and competition from the industrial districts kept wages up, and the south and east, the historic centres of English population, where they remained low and after Waterloo seemed to be getting lower. James Caird's map published in his *English Agriculture in 1850* showed the line of division as starting at Chester and curving through Shropshire, Worcester, Warwickshire, Leicester-

---

[13] Mrs Cobden Unwin, *The Hungry Forties* (1904), p. 176.

shire to the Wash. North of the line wages were predominantly high, south of it predominantly low. There was another equally important line of division between arable and pasture. This vertical line ran down between Cumberland and Northumberland, through York-shire to the western boundaries of Lincoln, Huntingdon, Bedfordshire and Hertfordshire, crossed the Thames at Faringdon, and through Wiltshire to meet the Channel at Lyme Regis. West of the line were the predominantly grazing counties, east of it the predomin-antly corn counties. It was in the corn-growing counties east of the line, the districts of high farming where the plough was master, that the labourers were left with fewest resources. Cobbett never failed to remark on this paradox. 'Another proof of the truth of my old observation: *rich land* and *poor labourers*,' he noted when riding across Romney Marsh in 1823; and later the same year on the Isle of Thanet, 'invariably have I observed that the richer the soil, and the more destitute of woods; that is to say, the more purely a corn country, the more miserable the labourers.'

It was the southeastern quarter formed by the intersection of these two lines, that part of England where the Speenhamland system of supplementary allowances from the poor rate was most entrenched and where the great agricultural riots of 1816 and 1830 took place, that most nearly resembled a vast rural slum—nearly but not altogether. Even apart from regional variations, the influence of an individual landowner, less often that of an individual farmer, could make an essential difference to the comfort of the rural labourer. On large estates wealthy proprietors could and often did provide decent cottages with gardens and at the same time prevent the more demoralized and shiftless poor from finding a settlement. The dis-tinction between an 'open' and a 'closed' parish was often significant in terms of prosperity and cleanliness. But the 'closed' parish could only exist by pushing certain social problems on the backs of its 'open' neighbours. In one of his rural rides in 1826 Cobbett found the best and worst place for labourers both within the one county of Hamp-shire, the first deriving solely from the high wages paid by one proprietor. Yet this did not prevent the general state of the poor in Hampshire and Wiltshire from being among the most depressing he encountered on all his travels through the English countryside. Local cottage industries by which women and girls could earn extra money, like button-making in Dorset, glove-making in the West Country, straw-plaiting in some of the Midland counties, could for the individual family make the difference between comfort and in-digence. Even so, these were on the whole declining industries; the pay was bad, so too the conditions of work. Poaching for the London game market was another profitable sideline, though the gentry (no doubt prejudiced) alleged that the proceeds usually went on drink.

Though the problem was uneven, it is clear that over a large part of southern and eastern England the agricultural population was among the worst paid, fed and housed of all the classes of the community. Agricultural wages barely sufficed to keep a man and his family at subsistence level. Even the quality of his food was inferior. In the northern counties and Scottish Lowlands the rural poor lived mainly on oatmeal (often cooked as porridge), milk, butter, potatoes, pork and bacon—a well balanced diet to which some observers attributed the greater strength and endurance of the northern labourer. In the south the staple article of consumption was bread, usually (though not always and rarely the best) wheaten bread. Surviving accounts frequently mention flour made from tailings, bran, or damaged grain sold cheap by the farmers, which produced a grey lumpy loaf, hard without and sticky within. Butcher's meat, even milk and butter, were usually beyond their means; cheese and lard were the main additions, together with potatoes or some other vegetable. On rare occasions there might be a small piece of bacon, butcher's offal, or salt fish as a special treat. Tea was made from burnt crusts or used tea-leaves begged from a wealthier household. The innumerable diet sheets compiled by social investigators probably represent the basic minimum rather than the average actual consumption. It is hard otherwise to see how families survived. People do not as a rule allow themselves literally to starve in a food-producing environment. Poaching hares, rabbits and pheasants, stealing potatoes, turnips, swedes, peas and beans from the fields, oats from the stable, and poultry from the farmyard, was a normal feature of country life, though naturally such matters were not mentioned in the accounts given by cottagers to enquiring gentlemen from the Poor Law Commission.

Even with these supplementations, however, many country labourers lived in permanent penury, with barely enough nutritious food to sustain their strength for hard manual work, and unable to save money for old age. Payment of rent and purchase of clothes came from additional piecework at harvest or women's work in the fields. Any adverse occurrence—illness, accident, unemployment, a large number of small children—meant recourse to parish relief. Where the Speenhamland system was in operation (and it was by no means universal even in the south and east) it offered some safeguard against fluctuating bread prices and some assistance with a large family. But after 1815 many poor law authorities tended to reduce the scale of assistance in the face of increasing pressure on parochial relief funds. Moreover, the rate-in-aid, while providing an insurance against absolute destitution, had the effect of keeping down wages,

putting thrifty and hardworking men on the same level as the idle
and improvident, and discouraging movement away from overcrowded parishes.

The poverty of a large part of the rural working class was reflected
in the state of their housing. Since the labourer could not afford to
pay a remunerative rent, there was no direct economic incentive to
provide him with adequate accommodation. Over the country as a
whole there was a wide variety of labourers' cottages: stone, brick,
wattle and daub, mud and board, with roofs of tile, slate, or thatch.
Contemporary descriptions are apt to single out the worst because
a reforming conscience was already at work. But even Cobbett
is to be found praising cottages he passed in Sussex, Suffolk and
Worcestershire. Except on good estates, however, the best rarely had
more than two rooms and many only one for the entire family, in
which to live, eat, procreate and sleep. Floors were usually bare earth;
water came from streams, ditches or surface wells; the provision of
privies was not yet regarded as a necessity. Though many had
gardens, not all did. The worst were those put up on commons or
wasteland, often owned by the cottager himself. Cobbett saw some
near Cricklade in Wiltshire that were 'little better than pig-beds ...
wretched hovels ... stuck upon little bits of ground on the roadside'.

Even the higher wages of the north did not mean better living
conditions. Paradoxically cottages were generally better in the south
and east, the old agricultural centres of England that had benefited
from a century or more of improving landlords, than in the more
rapidly developed farmlands of Scotland, Wales and the north of
England. In Leicestershire Cobbett found 'miserable sheds ... hovels
made of mud and straw; bits of glass, or of old off-cast windows,
without frame or hinge frequently, but merely stuck in the mud wall'.
Where, as was customary on the Borders and in the Scottish Lowlands, labourers were housed on the farm in return for supplying
additional 'bondage' work, the barrack-like accommodation provided was often worse than that of the horses. Alexander Somerville
described the 'row of shabby looking tiled sheds' in the Lammermoor
district of Berwickshire where he was born in 1811: one room for
each family, clay floors, no ceiling, no cupboards or fittings of any
kind. The labourers had iron bars which they used to make a fire-
place and took away with them when they left. Among the few
possessions of the Somerville family was a pane of glass which they
carried round from farm to farm, fixing it in the wall of each hovel
they occupied to form a window.

Conditions like these were no novelty. The rural poor lived, as
far as housing, food and clothing were concerned, much as they had
lived since Tudor times. Except in the imagination of romantic tories

like Cobbett or sensitive poets like Gray, there was no past golden age which the country labourer had once enjoyed. There had been no catastrophic decline in his social position. The Napoleonic Wars, while providing him with abundant work, had not raised his wages sufficiently to keep pace with inflation; enclosure and high farming had not improved, sometimes had worsened, his lot. But these were marginal circumstances. What was new was the awakening humanitarianism, already observable in the late eighteenth century, which was beginning to consider seriously the plight of the poor. What was increasingly clear was that the growth in national prosperity affecting most other classes had left the largest single class of worker untouched. While others were escaping, the country labourer was still caught in the age-old trap of poverty from which timidity, ignorance and the paralysing effect of the poor laws made it difficult for him to escape. Primitive housing, lack of sanitation, gross intermingling of the sexes, probably did not trouble him much: the poor had always lived under those conditions. It was the reforming gentry, the Benthamite administrator, the clergy with their professional concern for morality and decency, who were disturbed by such things. The Reverend John Atkinson, arriving in his lonely Yorkshire parish in 1847, though shocked by 'the shameful immorality of the usages and manners' prevailing there, accepted that it was simply a continuation from 'older and strangely less refined days'. The labourer himself was more practical. A few shillings on his wages, meat once a week, more regular employment, was all he asked of society—asked but did not get.

VI

At the bottom of the social scale were the vagrants, the outcasts, and the criminals. They were a heterogeneous collection: the thieves, fences, pimps, prostitutes and homeless gangs of children in the metropolis and other large cities; the pedlars, tramps, beggars and gypsies of the countryside; the crowds of touts, roughs and hangers-on who congregated round the racecourses, fairgrounds, prize-rings and cockpits. Of violent organized crime there was relatively little; the highwaymen and footpads of the previous century had largely died out. Evidence heard by the House of Commons committee on the police of the metropolis in 1816 emphasized London's bad reputation for open prostitution (worse than that of any other European capital) and the enormous growth in juvenile delinquency as a result of the hordes of parentless children who infested parts of the city. But there was general agreement that highway robbery and crimes of violence had diminished. The main problem was theft in all its ramifications: from pickpocketing and petty stealing from open doors and windows to the brazen depredations of river pirates and dockyard thieves who levied daily toll on the vast quantity of valuable cargoes that passed in and out of the port of London.

This was crime in its metropolitan form. Twenty-three years later another committee, examining the need for a county police, described other aspects of the problem. It was a daunting list: the gangs who travelled round between race meetings and fairs, making their living from petty crime, pickpocketing, assaulting and robbing individuals, occasional burglary; the vagrants and sham beggars who intimidated women in isolated houses and cottages; the tramps and gypsies who stole washing from the line, poultry from the yard and sometimes horses from the fields; the specialists who pilfered from goods waggons and passenger coaches along the highroads; the wreckers and smugglers among the fishing population all round the coast. Most villages had a cheap lodging house for trampers and 'travellers', the haunt of thieves and prostitutes; and the poor perhaps suffered proportionately more than the rich from this lawless under-world because of their inability to protect themselves. An enormous amount of petty crime was carried on, the 1839 committee gravely concluded, for the sake of the superior profits to be expected from such a mode of life compared with the ordinary rewards of honest industry. The observation, though doubtless true, is not a novel one.

Britain, in fact, when set against the larger states of western Europe, was a singularly disorderly and undisciplined country. People were free to behave as they thought fit, subject to the uncertain and tardy consequences of the law should they be identified, caught and proved in a court to have broken it. The ferocious penalties prescribed by the legislature even for minor crimes were a reflection of the weakness of the machinery for detecting and prosecuting the criminal. In England the historic institution of parochial constables was ineffective in both town and country. Even in London the reforming Middlesex Justices' Act of 1792 had left magistrates with constabulary forces too small and decentralized to be able to police the teeming streets of the metropolis. In Scotland there was a slightly stronger tradition of effective policing in the large cities and in some counties, the latter probably originating in the measures taken during the disturbed Jacobite years of the first half of the eighteenth century. But even in Scotland there was much room for improvement. In England an efficient police was regarded even by the educated public as an un-British and tyrannical institution,

'odious and repulsive' to use the language of a parliamentary committee which considered the matter in 1818. For once honourable
members were speaking the language of the people. If it was a choice
between liberty and order, there was no question which the public
preferred. While admitting the problem, they chose optimistically to
put their trust in the gradual progress of civilization and such
characteristic Georgian institutions as private societies for the amendment of morals or the prosecution of felons.

The problem, however, did not seem a desperate one; it was
certainly not new. The governing classes were used to the unruly
habits of their fellow-countrymen and on the whole took a tolerant
view of their excesses. De Tocqueville thought that the licence given
to the lower classes in England actually strengthened the aristocracy
by emphasizing to the respectable middle classes the dangers of pure
democracy. It is unlikely that this sophisticated reflection was consciously present in the minds of the ruling class. More probably they
recognized even in the more disorderly manifestations of the true-
born Englishman an instinct for individual liberty and a quality of
brute courage which they themselves both admired and in large
measure possessed. Cobbett spoke for nearly all his countrymen
except the 'Saints' and professionally religious when he stoutly
defended popular sports involving risk of life and limb. 'They tend to
make the people bold,' he wrote, 'they produce a communication of
notions of hardihood; they serve to remind men of the importance
of bodily strength; they, each in its sphere, occasion a transient
relaxation from labout; they tend, in short, to keep alive, even among
the lowest of the people, some idea of independence.'

Love of sport was common to the top and bottom of society; and
sport in Regency England was both brutal and disorderly. Like the
Spaniards with their bullfights, the English were notorious in Europe
for their bullock-baiting, boxing matches, quarter-staff and cudgel-
playing, their addiction to hard physical exercise, and their passion
for watching bloody fights whether between men or animals. A
battle with fists was a favourite method of settling a quarrel and it
was not unknown for some of them to end in the death of one of the
combatants. In the more professional encounters in the prize-ring,
the bare-knuckle technique of the pugilists and the practice of ending
each round at the first fall led to protracted and sanguinary battles
in which the repeated cutting and bruising of the flesh and sheer
physical exhaustion were more likely to decide the issue than a knock-
out. At the end of the fight at Newmarket in 1807, in which Gully
beat Gregson after thirty-six rounds, not only were both men
'hideously disfigured and scarcely able to get off the knees of their
bottle-holders' but the seconds themselves were drenched with blood

from their principals. Nevertheless the age of Gully, Dutch Sam, Cribb and Molyneux was the golden age of the patronage of the ring by the aristocracy. When Cribb, the all-England champion trained by Captain Barclay, fought Molyneux in 1811 at an open-air site in Rutlandshire, they were watched by a crowd of several thousand, of whom it was estimated that a quarter were nobility and gentry from the surrounding countryside. At the end of the fight Molyneux was carried out the ring speechless and senseless while the triumphant Cribb was 'received by his honourable friends and patrons like a Nelson returning from a naval victory'. A French newspaper which published a description of the fight and the names of the 'noble amateurs' who attended, added sarcastically that 'certainly the English nobility stand alone in their taste for this singular and degrading spectacle'.[14]

While the aristocracy were taking up the popular sport of pugilism, the people had been invading the aristocratic pastime of horseracing. By the end of the Napoleonic Wars the Derby, Oaks, One Thousand and Two Thousand Guineas, St Leger and Ascot Gold Cup were already national institutions. With the coming of peace the amount of prize money and the number of races steadily increased. By the accession of Victoria it was estimated that there were nearly 150 places in Great Britain where race meetings were held, sometimes two or three times a year. The emergence of the professional bookmakers in the early years of the nineteenth century was a sign of the growing public-interest in horseracing and betting. They were then called 'bettors-round' to distinguish them from sportsmen who wagered among themselves on a single horse. Sometimes, more offensively, they were referred to as 'legs' which was merely an abbreviation for 'blacklegs'. As it was not unknown for them to make a horse 'safe', as it was styled, by corrupting trainers or jockeys, or interfering with the horse itself, the latter title was not unjustified. Dan Dawson, who achieved a species of immortality in 1812 by being hanged for poisoning racehorses at Newmarket, was firmly believed by all racing men to have been working for the notorious bookmaker brothers, Jem and Joseph Bland. But until Lord George Bentinck and his almost equally autocratic successor Admiral Rous came to preside over the Jockey Club in the middle decades of the century, aristocratic owners themselves habitually indulged in practices for which they would have been warned off the turf a generation later. The main sporting object of Englishmen of all kinds was to win and make money; they were not too particular how they did it.

[14] *Annual Register 1807*, p. 499; *ibid. 1811*, pp. 110–11. Tom Cribb went on to a career which included sparring before the Emperor of Russia and the King of Prussia in 1814 and guarding the entrance to Westminster Hall at the coronation of George IV.

There was a similar mingling of classes in other sports. Cricket was a village game in the southern counties of England before it became fashionable at universities and public schools. 'If', observed Miss Mitford, a great lover of the game, when describing a match between neighbouring parishes in 1819, 'there be any gentlemen amongst them, it is well—if not, it is so much the better.' It seems to have been the gentry on the other hand who popularized cricket in Yorkshire. Cock-fighting was a favourite North Country amusement for miners but there were many country squires who attended cocking mains, bred birds and sometimes staged fights in their own drawing-rooms. Farmers rode to hounds even with the aristocratic Quorn and Pytchley and lesser folk followed on foot or (more vexatiously for the foxhunter) drew coverts with their own dogs on Sundays. Among the members of Grantley Berkeley's stag-hunt in the Vale of Harrow in the 1820s were a coal merchant and that well known London pastrycook Mr Gunter. The scholars of Westminster School would turn out to watch bull- and bear-baiting spectacles in the metropolis. Men like Squire Osbaldeston would race, row or box against anyone, gentleman or commoner.

It was an age in which the sporting aristocrat regarded the noble art of self-defence as important a part of his education as French or dancing. Many of them were more than ready to demonstrate their skill, usually with success, on any of their social inferiors who were insolent or aggressive. The Prince Regent himself in his younger days had taken lessons from Jackson, the conqueror of Mendoza, and along with his personal reminiscences of the battle of Salamanca was wont to relate how he had once thrashed a Brighton butcher on the Sussex Downs. Undergraduates at Oxford and Cambridge took lessons from professional pugilists and fought in the streets with the townees. On one famous occasion that future sporting ornament of the church the Reverend John Russell (who gave his name to the breed of terriers) won a sparring match with two others from Exeter College against three representatives from that very superior college Christ Church.

Fighting in fact seemed one of the Englishman's main amusements. When the Methodist-educated Lovett came up to London from distant Cornwall in 1821 he noticed with astonishment the number of black eyes and damaged faces among the labourers going to work on Monday morning, the result of their weekend sprees. A species of amateur pugilism was one of the common Sunday entertainments in the working-class quarters of London with nobody interfering except the wives, who would occasionally fight each other. In the Black Country a newly appointed clergyman about the time of Waterloo discovered that one of the habits of his parishioners was to stage fights in public houses between women, naked to the waist and their hair cut short, with their husbands acting as the seconds. The first fight witnessed by young Holyoake (born in Birmingham in 1817) was between two women who having quarrelled adjourned to a piece of open ground, 'stripped so that bosoms and arms were bare' and began sparring. 'In their neighbourhood fighting would be common,' he added indulgently. 'Their husbands might be boxers.'

The countryside could be as rough as the towns. A Congregational minister in East Anglia described the amusements of village people about 1840 as 'sottish and brutal'. Dog-fighting, cock-fighting and badger-baiting were popular. Regular pugilistic encounters between young men, sometimes two or three in a row, were frequently staged in the churchyard among the graves. Sometimes a gang of youths in one village would pit themselves against those of the next and feuds would break out that made it unsafe for an isolated man to cross the parish boundary into enemy territory. It was the same further north. When Atkinson went to his neglected, primitive, semi-pagan parish on the moors of Cleveland in 1847 he met several survivors of this class of village rowdy, 'men whose pastime it had been, if not whose object and desire, to provoke a row or a scuffle, and to fight it out then and there.... Rows, scuffles, scrimmages had been the rule then.... Hardly contested boxing-bouts, with a cruel amount of "punishment", were of continual occurrence.'[15] Ten years later, at the Scouring of the White Horse revels in Berkshire in 1857 affectionately described by that muscular Christian Tom Hughes, the old rough country sports were still in evidence even though refined opinion was beginning to turn against them. They included back-sword (that is, cudgel fighting) contests in which contestants hit at arms, shoulders and chest while seeking the decisive, blood-letting crack on the skull which settled the match; and elbow-and-collar wrestling in which hacking the shins was part of the game, though on this occasion the committee disallowed the wearing of iron-tipped boots. These were formal spectacles watched by women and children, in which the men were often fighting in teams for their parish or county. But, said the local parson reminiscently, 'there used to be some very brutal play in out of the way places, where the revels were got up by publicans'. What the genuine article was like in an earlier age appears from Bamford's description of a typical Lancashire public house fight near Bury in 1817. 'It was all fair play,' he observed mildly, 'though certainly of a rough sort.' The men stripped to the waist, went outside to an open piece of turf and then grappled in an encounter which resembled all-in wrestling varied by throttling

---

[15] J. C. Atkinson, *Forty Years in a Moorland Parish* (1923), p. 27.

and savage kicking at legs and knees, 'until the white bones were seen grinning through the gashes in their legs and their stockings were soaked in blood'. This particular fight only ended when one of the men seemed dead.

With so little concern for themselves, men felt even less for animals. In the 1820s Richard Martin of Galway MP, 'Humanity Dick', made several attempts to bring in bills to prohibit bull- and bear-baiting and other cruel sports. But the home secretary Peel (who was not an inhumane man) resolutely opposed any legislation to restrict the amusements of the poor while leaving the pleasures of the rich untouched. Cruelty, he argued realistically, was inherent in most sports and any abuses would gradually be swept away by the growing intelligence and refinement of the nation. A favourite sport of the Spitalfields weavers in London was bullock-hunting. Gangs of men and boys would intercept an animal from one of the herds being taken to Smithfield Market, drive it into a side street and torment it with sticks and dogs until the maddened beast would turn on its attackers and a kind of bullfight ensued. Peel's Metropolitan Police put an end to that, rather than the increasing refinement of the Spitalfields weavers. In 1835, after the Reform Bill, a Cruelty to Animals Act forbade bull- and bear-baiting and another in 1849 cock-fighting. But the practices still went on in certain parts of the country. Bull-baiting remained a common pastime in the Black Country, a parliamentary committee was told in 1838, and the colliers were much attached to it. Despite the 1835 act riots broke out when attempts were made to put down the sport; until in 1837 Lord Dartmouth, on the occasion of the annual three days of bull-baiting in Birmingham, staged a successful counter-attraction by throwing open his park for amusements of a milder nature—sack-races, hurdle-races and similar contests. To promote their popularity among the people and doubtless to add to their social prestige, he attended with his family on all three days.[16]

The Britain which produced the infantrymen of Albuera and Badajoz was not a gentle society; and the process of taming it was a slow one. The election-gang battles of bargees and butchers, the nocturnal affrays between poachers and gamekeepers, the brutal methods employed by trade unionists to coerce employers and black-legs, arose naturally from the habits of the age. Hardship, acceptance of pain and a measure of callousness were as much features of life in hospitals and public schools as in the army and navy, or among the lower classes. The harshness of some millowners, the savage treatment of working women and children by butty-masters and

[16] *PP 1837–8* vii, p. 96 (*Report of Select Committee on the Education of the Poorer Classes*).

factory overseers, were not peculiar products of the industrial system;
they simply reflected the general modes of behaviour in society at
that time. Among the aristocracy themselves sheer physical courage,
the ability to face danger unflinchingly and endure pain stoically—
pluck or 'bottom' as it was called in contemporary slang—was one of
the most prized manly qualities. For some of them the sporting tastes
of the period overrode all other interests. George Osbaldeston, the
'squire of England' who died in 1866 at the age of eighty, wrote his
autobiography without mentioning the Reform Act, the repeal of the
corn laws, or the Crimean War; and the *Waterloo* he records was the
name of a horse. Many of his social inferiors were perhaps equally
indifferent. At the time of the Reform Bill a political lecturer, going
to speak at a village near Manchester, was gratified at the sight of
streams of men moving in the same direction. Expressing to some of
them his pleasure at their interest in politics, he received the surprised
reply, 'nay, mon, it's nobbut a dog-feight'. McCabe, who tells the
story, added condescendingly that this was a clear mark of the
'helplessness and degradation of the bulk of the workers' at that
time.[17] But that was a late-Victorian verdict.

[17] *Life and letters of George Holyoake*, edited by J. McCabe (1908) 1, p. 16 n.

2 Government and Religion

I

In 1815, and for long after, management of British society was largely in the hands of local authorities, both public and private. The responsibilities of the state were primarily in the field of external relations—the defence of the realm and the regulation of trade. Internally it was little more than a tax-raising, justice-enforcing, order-preserving agency. The only other important service it performed for the public was the transport of mail. Even in the fundamental matter of law and order it was only an authority of last resort. When the local forces of control were inadequate, the state could bring in the ultimate sanction of the army. Central justice was administered by a mere twelve high court judges who between them ran the three central courts at Westminster—Kings's Bench, Common Pleas and Exchequer—and travelled round the provinces at regular intervals to ensure that all prisoners, whatever their offence, were tried, punished or released and the gaols cleared, at least twice a year.

In relation to the numbers and wealth of British society the scope of central government was remarkably small, the size of its executive departments and the revenues at its disposal correspondingly limited. This, for the general public, was a matter for congratulation rather than otherwise. The engrained attitudes inherited from the eighteenth century were simple, and on past experience not unjustified. Governments, it was thought, would always use their power of appointment as a form of political patronage and government administration in consequence would always be expensive and inefficient. These accredited defects were magnified in radical eyes by the conviction that the whole structure was riddled with class bias. Wartime inflation, the steep rise in personal taxation, and the alarming expansion of the national debt strengthened still further these inherent prejudices against enlarging the amount and increasing the cost of state administration. The cry for 'cheap and

efficient government' raised alike by the pre-1820 radicals, the
reformers of 1831-2 and the Chartists of the 1830s and 1840s, was a
demand not for more government but for less. Cheapness in effect
was a mark of efficiency; the best government was that which
administered least. Early nineteenth-century British society was overwhelmingly individualistic. The controversies which engaged most
public attention were those which involved a redistribution of power,
not an extension of governmental activity in itself.

It was this combination of prejudice and parsimony which formed
the real limits to state action rather than any official subscription to
laissez-faire as a policy. While there was no acceptance of a collectivist
philosophy, there was equally no doctrinaire adherence to a rule of
non-intervention in the social and economic life of the community.
The country gentry who formed the bulk of the House of Commons
were accustomed to governing in their own localities; they had no
prejudice against regulation and control in the abstract. When
questions of legislative intervention arose, the considerations which
weighed with them were the practical ones. Was there an evident
utility in what was proposed? Would it cost money? Was there a
moral or humanitarian issue involved? Would it disturb local or class
susceptibilities, vested interests, the rights of property? Would it
enlarge ministerial patronage? But even before 1830 a legislature that
could pass the 1817 Poor Employment Act authorizing loans for
providing public works, the elder Peel's factory act of 1819 protecting
children in cotton mills, the 1828 act regulating emigrant traffic
across the Atlantic, or on a humbler scale the statute of 1827
minutely specifying conditions of hiring for the London watermen
who carried passengers on the Thames,[1] was clearly wedded to no
particular theory. Theory was something the House of Commons
avoided. It preferred to act in known cases, for particular purposes,
when the pressures and arguments in favour of action on balance
outweighed those against. If the results were meagre, illogical and
untidy, at least its freedom of action was never at risk.

Even the fashionable theoretical views on the nature and object of
state intervention, though possessing greater coherence, did not offer
an unqualified solution. It was true that much of the argument of the
classical economists was directed towards dismantling the top-heavy
structure of legislative control built up in preceding centuries; and
an important part of the reforms of the 1820s and 1830s consisted in
the repeal of obsolete or unwanted legislation. The free-trade
doctrine in itself was inevitably, within its own sphere, a *laissez-faire*

---

[1] Act for the better regulation of watermen and lightermen of the River Thames (7 & 8
Geo. IV c. 75). For further examples of interventionist legislation at this period see W. S.
Holdsworth, *History of English Law* XIII, pp. 323 ff.

doctrine. The view which Lord Liverpool once expressed when deprecating state interference in industrial life, that 'government or Parliament never meddle with these matters at all but they do harm, more or less', was one that permeated the thinking of much of the nineteenth century. Defenders of particular interests against the inquisitiveness of parliament could always find helpful quotations from the writings of economists to reinforce their case. Yet the classical authorities from Adam Smith to J. R. McCulloch presented a more diverse and qualified intellectual attitude than was usually evident in those who invoked their authority. *Laissez-faire*, whether interpreted as the removal of restrictive legislation or as the market freedom to buy and sell goods or services, was only a means to an end. It was a species of mechanism whereby liberty, progress and prosperity could be achieved within society.

The classical economists as a whole were always prepared to assign a significant role to the state. Its primary functions were certainly to carry out the elementary duties of guaranteeing order, administering justice and guarding the realm. But it was also its business to protect those who were incapable of protecting themselves; and to do those things from which all would benefit but which no individual motive or interest would ensure being done. Under these headings much could subsequently be justified that was never originally envisaged; and as social problems multiplied, the economists like the rest of the public had to adjust, sometimes equivocate, and not infrequently disagree. What in the last analysis prevented political economy from being a lifeless and restrictive philosophy was that it was regarded by its exponents as an instrument of social reform. It was significant, for example, that the majority of the classical economists favoured state support for education. They were concerned to improve humanity; at heart they were pragmatic reformers. Even if their means were sometimes ill-chosen, their end was that 'Progress of the Nation' which the statistician G. R. Porter chose as the title of the book he published in 1836. Moral and social improvement, or in the phrase popularized by Bentham, 'the greatest happiness of the greatest number', was the characteristic aim of the classical economists rather than *laissez-faire* as an end in itself.

The precise role of the state in promoting this happiness was open to discussion; but, in the writings of Bentham himself, there was no doubt of the importance attached to state action as a lever for reform. Indeed, it was only when he began to despair of the adoption of his schemes by an aristocratic legislature that he turned political radical. For him, as for many other radicals, political reform became a necessary condition of administrative improvement. But this was historical accident rather than logical necessity. Bentham's political

radicalism and philosophic individualism certainly lent themselves to
a *laissez-faire* interpretation. The greatest good of the greatest
number, it could be argued, was best secured by 'maximizing liberty'.
Fundamentally, however, Bentham was an administrative reformer;
and both he and his disciples constantly looked to the state as the
prime agency for carrying their plans into effect.

To attempt an assessment of Bentham's influence on nineteenth-
century legislation and administration is a fruitless and perhaps a
pointless task. Bentham and the utilitarians were themselves products
of their society. Had Bentham never lived, most of the reforms
popularly ascribed to his influence would probably have come about.
The evident obsolescence of so much of British law and so many
British institutions; the new problems and larger demands of a rapidly
evolving society; the shifts in political power; the rational tradition
of the eighteenth century—all these would have ensured a broadly
similar response. Bentham provided a formidable cutting-edge to the
intellectual arguments. In the school of utilitarians who acknowledged in some degree his authority were men of considerable
influence in various fields of public life: Hume, Grote, Brougham
and Place among the politicians, Black and Fonblanque among the
journalists, Ricardo, Mill, McCulloch among the economists, Chadwick and Southwood Smith among the administrators, even Whately
and Blomfield on the episcopal bench. The foundation of the
Westminster Review in 1824 as the organ of philosophic radicalism was
a characteristic intellectual middle-class tribute to his influence.
When the administratively inexperienced whig government came to
power in 1830, some of these leading utilitarians became their
advisers, consultants and officials.

Yet though Bentham and the utilitarians helped to colour the
thought of their age, few pure examples of Benthamite reforms ever
found their way to the statute book. Legal reform, for example, as
initiated by Peel in the 1820s and continued by Brougham and the
whigs in the 1830s, was carried out on an empirical and not a
doctrinaire basis. The strict Benthamite principles which Chadwick
tried to write into the new poor law of 1834 were modified in
subsequent redrafting and further modified in actual practice.
Bentham provided a copious flow of ideas; but he and his disciples
were unable to secure the adoption of an administrative code, or
even the fragments of a code. At bottom his inexorable rationalism,
demanding equally rationalist reaction in others for success, con-
flicted with both human nature and political expediency. It was not
an accident that Edwin Chadwick, the most rigid of Bentham's
followers, became the best hated bureaucrat in Britain.

In practice the expansion of governmental activity in the early nineteenth century was inadequate, unplanned, piecemeal and spasmodic. It was a response to practical problems, to flagrant evils, to moral and humanitarian feelings. It owed much to pressure groups, to individual reformers, and in some cases to the innate tendency of bureaucracy to find fresh tasks for itself. But while there were some bold pioneer achievements, there were many compromises and some humiliating retreats. State interference was not something that was welcomed in principle either by the bulk of the electorate, the ratepayers and taxpayers, or by the politicians themselves. There is little justification for connecting the interventionist legislation of the 1832–50 period with the rise of organized political parties equipped with firm majorities able to put their policies into effect. Impressive as this period is in the growth of government activity, the increase in parliamentary committees of enquiry and royal commissions which were the index of that growth starts in 1820 rather than in 1832; and the significant post-1830 social legislation owed little to party programmes or party majorities. The 1833 factory act and the 1834 poor law, like the Ten Hours Act of 1847 and the Public Health Act of 1848, were passed in sessions when the whigs were far from possessing a firm party majority in the Commons. The whig educational scheme of 1839 was defeated, as were the educational proposals in the ministerial factory bill of 1843 under a conservative administration. Ashley's Mines Act of 1842 was essentially a private member's bill and the royal commission which preceded it had been granted two years earlier by the previous government. At most it can be argued that the Reform Act of 1832 and the subsequent party governments brought about a greater sensitivity to public opinion and a greater readiness to intervene where defects and abuses were clearly proved.

Such issues, however, were scarcely issues of 'politics' in the sense generally understood by politicians and the public. Take, for example, the advice tendered by Prince Albert to Samuel Wilberforce when he was appointed to the diocese of Oxford in 1845. A bishop, the prince suggested helpfully,

> ought to abstain *completely* from mixing himself up with the politics of the day, and beyond giving a general support to the Queen's Government, and occasionally voting for it, should take no part in the discussion of State affairs (for instance, Corn Laws, Game Laws, Trade or Financial Questions, etc.); but he should come forward whenever the interests of humanity are at stake, and give boldly and manfully his advice to the House and Country (I mean questions like Negro Emancipation, education of the people, improvement of the health of towns, measures for the recreation of the poor, against cruelty to animals, for regulating factory labour, etc.).[2]

---

[2] Quoted in S. C. Carpenter, *Church and People*, p. 260.

As long as this distinction between 'state affairs' and 'the interests of humanity' remained in the minds of politicians, it was unlikely that any party or government would regard the intervention of the state to secure a specific social reform as more than a kind of side issue which circumstances might throw up from time to time.

Even if the contemporary outlook had favoured intervention, the administrative apparatus in the hands of the ministers after Waterloo was hardly conducive to an extension of state activity or the furtherance of strong executive action. One basic weakness of the constitution was the looseness of the control exercised by the executive over the legislature. It was a defect, however, more obvious to ministers than to the public. Radical criticism of the House of Commons, by concentrating on the defects and abuses of the electoral system, tended to imply that the House was therefore under the domination of the ministers. It was true, of course, that the representative system was completely antiquated and at least partially corrupt. Leeds and Manchester had no separate MPs; the fields and earthworks of Old Sarum had two. Over half the English boroughs had electorates of less than 300. Many boroughs were venal; most of their elections disorderly. English counties were so expensive to contest that their representation was usually settled by compromise or tacit acceptance of the dominant influences. The north and north-west of England were under-represented compared with the south and southeast. The boroughs, with 465 seats as against the 188 for the counties, were grossly overweighted. The return for some constituencies could be bought as a simple financial transaction; many depended on the decision of individuals. About 275 borough MPs, it was estimated, owed their seats to direct nomination.

Any mechanical analysis of the electoral system, in fact, by bringing into prominence certain features, could present a powerful case for reform. When to bribery and nomination were added the more intangible factors of influence and connection, the case seemed overwhelming. T. H. B. Oldfield the contemporary historian of parliamentary representation, claimed in 1819 that over 70 per cent of the House of Commons were 'sent to Parliament by private nomination, and through the influence of Peers and opulent Commoners'.[3] Vague and extravagant as this assertion was, the fact that it could form part of contemporary debate was a sign of the times. In the corrupt 'borough system' the radical reformers saw the main explanation for what they also believed to be a corrupt governmental system.

This widespread belief contained two fallacies. It ignored the

[3] *Key to the House of Commons* (1820), p. 37.

degree of independence inside and the power of public opinion outside the House of Commons; and it failed to observe that control of elections by individuals did not necessarily mean that they or the MPs whom they returned were subservient to government. In fact, for a third of a century before Waterloo, the physical means of influencing the legislature possessed by the executive had been steadily declining. Starting with Burke's act of 1782 over a thousand sinecures had been abolished before the end of the century. By 1815 only about 350 sinecure posts existed, many of which were due to expire on the death of their holders. The 1817 enquiry which resulted in the abolition or regulation of some 300 offices was virtually the end of the 'economical reform' campaign started by the Rockingham whigs a generation earlier. A select Commons committee reported in 1822 that of less than seventy 'ministerial dependents' in the House (excluding a few life or honorary appointments), fifty were holding 'efficient' offices. Another committee appointed by the whigs when they came to power found in 1834 that of an alleged one hundred government sinecures only fifty could be regarded as such.

Over the same period diminishing sources of unappropriated revenue and stricter parliamentary accounting had also destroyed the government's ability to purchase seats in the electoral market. Indeed, the only major source of patronage left to them was the honours system. But this was of limited effectiveness. It did not directly affect the electorate; there were constraints on its application in any given case; and the personal integrity of the ministers, not to speak of the prestige of the peerage, was closely involved. Though Liverpool carried on the Pittite system of fairly lavish grants, later prime ministers like Peel and Russell were noticeably less generous. Not surprisingly, for those in a position to distinguish between factual reality and radical fiction, there were complaints from the professional politicians that executive influence had been so reduced as to be no longer dependable. As early as 1809 Thomas Grenville declared that 'the influence of what they call corruption is, for practical purposes, too small rather than too great'. Ten years later, when discussing with Castlereagh the 'unstable state' of the ministry, Arbuthnot (treasury secretary since 1809) pointed out that 'it is to be remembered that with all our sweeping reductions of patronage, I have not the tie I once had upon the independent members'. Subsequent prime ministers—Grey, Melbourne, Peel and Russell—clearly lacked the means of influencing the legislature possessed in the eighteenth century by Walpole, North and Pitt. But it was during the Liverpool ministry from 1812 to 1827 that this lack was first painfully felt. The Reform Act of 1832 was only the final stroke.

A further handicap to government was to be found in the con-

ventions and procedures of the House of Commons. So far from being
designed to facilitate public business, the lower house still bore the
characteristics of a body whose historic function was to criticize
government and obtain redress for grievances rather than assist
ministers of the crown to govern the country. Motions by individual
MPs still took precedence over public business. Miscellaneous
debates could be started on the introduction of petitions or as a matter
of urgency by private members. Repeated motions for adjournment,
even when repeatedly defeated, could so consume parliamentary
time as to achieve their object in the abandonment of debate.
Though ministers were responsible for organizing the work of the
Commons, they were obliged in practice to give a major share of
parliamentary time to the House as a whole. The total time available
was in any case not excessive. Following the old agricultural rhythm,
parliamentary sessions usually ran from late January or February to
July; and business did not begin until about four o'clock in the
afternoon. Of the six months' parliamentary session government
could not confidently count on the equivalent of more than half. It
was not an allotment that left much for other than strictly routine
and necessary business. Controversial legislation extraneous to the
essential work of government was easily obstructed and called for
great pertinacity by ministers to push it through to the statute book.
That the system worked at all was an achievement. That it did so
was mainly because the rows of country gentry on the backbenches
were content as a rule to leave debating to the acknowledged orators
on either side. Bad and boring speakers were summarily and sometimes brutally extinguished. But when after 1832 public interest and
constituency pressures increased the number of members anxious to
demonstrate their assiduity in *Hansard*, even this safeguard disappeared.

     It was a system that was bound to show strain under the growing
amount of work that fell on the House after 1815. Nevertheless, only
after several decades of increasing pressure on parliamentary time,
particularly from the vast increase in petitioning, did the Commons
amend some of its procedures in the 1840s to allow more time for
government and less to the private member. For a whole generation
after the Reform Act parliament was clearly reluctant to give up
any of the time-honoured practices that had enabled it to limit the
powers of the executive in earlier ages; not until after the second
Reform Act of 1867 did it begin to recognize that if government
now was in reality an organ of the legislature, it must have the right
to control the business of the legislature. Until then ministers
continued to be dependent on the goodwill of the Commons for the
despatch of business; and in time of crisis or party conflict they could

find their work intolerably obstructed. Without the growth of party organization after 1834 the position of the executive would have been impossible; and as Melbourne, Peel and Russell all discovered, even party in its early period was not the most reliable of instruments.

II

There was another set of limitations: those inherent in the actual machinery of the executive itself. The central departments of the state suffered from two handicaps: their small size and the indifferent quality of their personnel. There were in fact only three really large departments, all significantly revenue-collecting agencies. These were Customs, Excise, and Stamps and Taxes, which between them employed nearly 20,000 officials stationed all over the country. The only other sizable civil department was the Post Office which employed less than 1,500. Comparable in size though not in function were the services' supply departments (Ordnance, Admiralty and Naval) which together had an establishment of about 4,000. By comparison the central policy departments which formed the main instruments of government were minute. In the early 1820s, after the post-war economies had taken place, the Home Office had a staff of seventeen, including the secretary of state but excluding porters and cleaners. The Colonial Office, responsible for more than thirty colonies scattered round the globe, was even smaller, with an effective staff of fourteen. Even the Foreign Office, with its daily mass of diplomatic and consular correspondence, had a staff of less than three dozen. Not surprisingly there were constant complaints from the permanent officials of overwork; to which were not infrequently added alarming accounts of crowded and unhealthy accommodation. When to the sharp post-war cuts in establishment were added in 1821 proposals to reduce salaries, the clerks in the Colonial Office were reported to be sulky and mutinous. They were probably not the only department whose morale suffered.

Inadequate staffing was one defect; another was sheer mediocrity. A career in the civil service (though the term was only just appearing) offered little more than security and respectability. The work was dull, the main occupation of the permanent staff being routine copying of letters. The system was defended as a means of ensuring a thorough grounding in departmental practice and policy; but the absence of any formal distinction between the administrative and clerical duties must have added to its unattractiveness as a career.

A profession which offered little more than years of monotonous quill-pushing for all except a few could hardly expect to recruit the ablest young men. In practice the civil service had to make do with the unambitious, the lazy and the incompetent. A considerable responsibility was therefore thrown on the political head. His office was largely what he made it; he was not only the mainspring of policy but the deviser of detail. The permanent officials were there to do his bidding rather than tender him advice.

The system was not, however, wholly inefficient and in the early decades of the century was slowly improving. Abolition of fees and sinecures made necessary a stricter method of departmental accounting and a regular scheme of pensions and salaries. The growing distinction between political appointments and permanent officials provided greater security of tenure and made the service more attractive as a career. The informal, gentlemanly atmosphere in many departments and their virtual autonomy under their political chief allowed opportunities for piecemeal reform by regulation rather than legislation. The last twenty years of the Georgian period in fact saw a steady and on the whole successful effort to make the civil service economical, unpolitical and incorruptible. These were assets not to be despised. The not unimportant matter of efficiency depended, however, largely on the quality of intake; and it was here that the main difficulties arose.

Until the development of competitive examinations after the middle of the century, entrance into the civil service was normally through personal recommendation, and the intensification of party rivalries after 1834 possibly accentuated the political aspect of civil service patronage. Though this method of recruitment offered some assurance of social homogeneity (not to mention nepotism), it was hardly a guarantee of intellectual standards. But if the system was calculated to produce mediocrity, there were some saving features. Since the end of the eighteenth century there had been a growing practice in various departments of probationary periods which enabled unsatisfactory candidates to be weeded out after a year or two. By 1832 most departments had age limits for new entrants and some a form (though little more than a form) of qualifying examination. Moreover, what was almost as important as the quality of the young recruit was the system of promoting established officials. Power of promotion usually lay with the departmental head who had some personal interest in selecting the ablest men. From 1837 the policy was increasingly followed of deciding internal promotions in the revenue departments by merit rather than by seniority.

The system, as it existed up to and beyond the middle of the century, was an uneasy compromise between the aspirations of an increasingly professional civil service and the reluctance of ministers and chief whips to give up the considerable if low grade patronage still in their possession. Some civil servants were undoubtedly idle, some incompetent, many no more than routine hacks. But the standing weight of mediocrity was at least offset by the right of a head of a department to bring in able men from outside for senior and responsible posts. Many of them were barristers by training, like George Harrison, assistant secretary at the Treasury, 1805–26, Henry Hobhouse, under-secretary at the Home Office under Sidmouth and Peel, Sir James Stephen, under-secretary at the Colonial Office, 1836–47, and William Gregory, Irish under-secretary, 1812–31. Such men obviously found their work sufficiently interesting and re-munerative to become permanent officials. Part of the attraction was that they were helping to advise their political chiefs and shape policy. In an irregular way an administrative as distinct from a clerical grade was beginning to emerge.

This slow improvement in departmental efficiency was assisted by the growing weight and complexity of departmental business. The post-war campaign for retrenchment, for example, revealed the practical inability of the House of Commons to control governmental expenditure once the vote had been granted. This led to an increasing emphasis on the duty of the Treasury to undertake this role with the result that a larger share of effective treasury business was handled by the senior clerks. Though the primacy of the Treasury in the civil service hierarchy did not finally come until after 1866, the consolidation of financial administration between 1815 and 1835 already put it in a position of considerable influence. At the Foreign Office the enhanced role of Britain in world affairs after 1815 and a succession of able foreign secretaries meant a large increase in diplomatic activity and an expansion of staff. By 1841 its effective strength had risen to forty-five, an establishment which was to serve its purposes for the rest of the century. The hybrid department of War and Colonies found that the virtual cessation of its military responsibilities after Waterloo was more than counterbalanced by the new problems thrown up by the enlarged British colonial empire. Lord Bathurst, secretary from 1812 to 1827, was virtually the founder of the modern Colonial Office. Sheer pressure of work, together with Bathurst's flexible style of administration, made it the first depart-ment of state in which the political heads devolved much actual decision-making to the permanent officials. Its staff enlarged steadily until by the 1820s it numbered twenty-seven besides supernumerary clerks. The Board of Trade, originally a consultative committee of the Privy Council, after 1815 became involved in the tariff reforms of the Liverpool government. Under a succession of able presidents and vice-presidents·like Wallace, Huskisson and Poulett Thomson, and some outstanding permanent officials like Deacon Hume, G. R. Porter and J. MacGregor, it became a centre of free-trade influence within the government. By the early 1840s its effective staff had risen from twenty in 1830 to thirty and thereafter expanded even faster.

Significantly these three departments were all of them (two exclusively and one partly) concerned with external British interests. For the more domestic offices of state it was a period of slower growth. The Home Office was a case in point. In 1812 *The Times* had stigmatized it as 'the sink of all the imbecility attached to every Ministry for the last thirty years'. Not until Peel launched his eight-year programme of legal and criminal reform in 1822 did it acquire something of the prestige of the other secretaries' departments. As late as 1841 when he gave the Colonial Office to the ex-whig leader Stanley and the Home Office to his follower Sir James Graham, it still ranked third in the hierarchy. Such enhanced importance as it possessed was not reflected in any significant expansion in size. From a low point in 1822 of only seventeen effective officials it grew to twenty-one under Melbourne in the early 1830s and twenty-two under Graham in·the early 1840s. Even this modest enlargement was probably less a matter of deliberate policy than a return to normal staffing after the unreasonable reductions of the 1817–21 era.

III

What was true of the Home Office broadly applied to the state as a whole, not only in the Georgian era but well into Victoria's reign. Though improvements were slowly taking place in the quality and conditions of service of its personnel, the central departments of government were neither intellectually prepared nor physically equipped to take over a major directive function in British society. There was no public demand for them to assume such a role; no general conviction that they were competent for it; no readiness on the part of the taxpayer to finance it. The regulation of society, such as it was, remained primarily the care of local authorities, reinforced by a miscellany of *ad hoc* voluntary and statutory bodies.

At the apex of the local hierarchy was the lord lieutenant of the county, usually one of the wealthier landowning peers. He was the king's representative in the county, the county spokesman to the central government. Though he was frequently absent and his routine duties were slight, his prestige was considerable and in times of emergency his leadership (or lack of it) important. Home secretaries had no hesitation in ordering lords lieutenant back to their localities when trouble threatened and were accustomed to using them as a general channel of communication with the county JPs. An active lord lieutenant corresponded regularly with the Home Office, occupied the chair at magistrates' meetings, explained government policy, and took the initiative in quelling disorder and prosecuting rioters. He called out the militia, cooperated with the regular forces stationed in his district, and on occasion organized a rudimentary intelligence service. The vice-lieutenant and deputy-lieutenants, mainly substantial landowners, acted as a kind of consultative and executive committee, known collectively as the lieutenancy, which could be called together in time of crisis. The other principal royal officer in the county was the sheriff who, though saddled with many historic electoral and judicial duties, was customarily of lower social status. It was an elective, annual and unpopular office and its importance had much declined.

Next in order of local significance were the magistrates, the men who individually and collectively were primarily responsible for the preservation of peace in their districts. Appointed by royal commission, normally on the recommendation of the lord lieutenant, and subject generally to a property qualification, the JP had power to suppress riots and affrays, apprehend and commit felons and inferior offenders, issue warrants for arrest, and summon constables, yeomanry, militia or military to his aid. Sitting with another magistrate in petty sessions he could exercise summary jurisdiction over minor offenders; with a full bench at quarter sessions he helped to try more serious offences, remitting the major crimes to the assizes. In addition to these primary duties, a mass of administrative tasks were handled by the magistracy in special session or in the grand jury of the county to an extent which made them the effective county government. The maids of all work under the Tudors and Stuarts had become masters of the districts in which their property lay, partly by the steady accumulation during the eighteenth century of various statutory duties, partly by a silent expansion of their authority based on local precedent and practice. They saw to the up-keep of roads and bridges, settled the county and approved the parish rates, appointed or endorsed the appointment of surveyors of roads, overseers of the poor and constables of the hundreds and parishes. They supervised workhouses and prisons, decided poor-law policy, and in specific cases could themselves order relief.

To be a magistrate was to possess a desirable social status. To be an active and conscientious magistrate was another matter. It required much time and energy, and on occasions it involved con-

siderable unpleasantness and sometimes personal danger. With no
organized body of police, rarely even a single efficient constable to
support him, a JP was expected in time of disturbance to make an
individual effort to quell trouble before summoning assistance; and
assistance when summoned might not always be forthcoming. The
constables of the hundreds and parishes were too few and ineffective
to cope with disorder of any size. The swearing-in of special
constables, drawn from the more respectable inhabitants, could only
be justified in an emergency. The theoretical power of summoning all
householders to keep watch and ward was unpopular and rarely
exercised. The problem was most acute in the industrial areas where
the mobs were larger, the social controls more lax, and the
magistrates fewer. In the north of England there was a general
shortage of magistrates and not all those appointed possessed the
requisite qualities of courage and activity. There was a certain
reluctance, both political and social, to appoint JPs from the
industrial middle classes; and the county magistrates called in to deal
with urban troubles were often out of their element.

The nature of the untrained, unpaid, voluntary magistracy made
it inevitable that over the country as a whole the burden of work
fell on a minority of active and conscientious men. Many of them were
clergy of the Church of England, whose education and sense of duty
made them particularly suitable for the magistracy; in some parishes
they were the only ones. Between 1815 and 1830 clerical magistrates
formed about a quarter of the bench in England and Wales. In
terms of attendance and activity the proportion was even higher.
Whether these magisterial functions strengthened their spiritual
influence or redounded to the credit of the church as an institution
was more doubtful. In rural parishes, where the traditional disciplinary role of the church in the sphere of morals had not yet
completely died out, little harm perhaps was done. In other areas the
clergyman-magistrate was decidedly unpopular. The radicals certainly denounced with relish the incongruity of the two roles. It was
the subject of one of Cruickshank's most savage political caricatures
in 1819 and it gave point to the argument that the church was
simply an institution designed to support the state.

Standing aloof from the county administration were the corporate
towns with their own historic rights of self-government and hierarchy
of officials, some of them *ex-officio* magistrates—mayors, aldermen,
bailiffs and common council—varying with the terms of their different charters. Some had a democratic element, most were close,
self-perpetuating oligarchies of urban gentry, wealthy merchants and
manufacturers. Nepotism, patronage, peculation, favouritism, were
common; contemporaries took such things for granted and were not

unduly shocked. But the corporations had their own individualities. They were not all completely corrupt, or completely inefficient. At their best they provided a reasonably good, even an economical administration of some aspects of municipal affairs. At their worst they were no more than permanent managers of certain properties and revenues. Few of them, however, regarded themselves as responsible in any direct sense to the population which they served. A jaundiced observer might be pardoned for wondering whether the corporations existed for the benefit of the towns or the towns for the benefit of the corporations. They were the constitutional representatives of their community; they formed a legal entity, a corporate body with certain privileges, property, powers and obligations. But they were not the political representatives, still less the delegates of the inhabitants. Tory corporations were criticized by local whigs and dissenters excluded from place and power; the occasional whig-dissenting corporation faced the opposition of excluded tories and anglicans.

But though errors and abuses were exposed to acrimonious public comment, there was no great pressure on existing corporations to enlarge the services which they offered to the ratepayers. When in the social or economic life of the towns new needs arose, these were more often supplied by specific agencies, set up usually by private act of parliament, independently of the town corporation: street commissioners, paving, lighting and scavenging authorities, water boards, harbour trustees, police commissioners, watch committees, fairs and market supervisors, and that recent Georgian innovation, gas companies. Sometimes a number of these functions were collectively exercised by a statutory body of improvement commissioners. These might be either nominated or elected, and in either case were capable of rivalling the authority of the corporation itself. By 1830 there were over two hundred of them. In the counties there was the same system, if the word is appropriate, of miscellaneous statutory bodies— bridge toll companies, turnpike trustees, poor-law unions—replacing or overlapping the traditional structure of local government. For most of the eighteenth century parliament had been active, not in setting up central administrative bodies, but in using its legal sovereignty to delegate administrative authority to innumerable local organizations. In this peculiar English way the country had been enabled to supply its wants by voluntary local effort, with a minimum of expense to the general taxpayer and without any central accumulation of power. But the result was the chaos of conflicting, competing jurisdictions which confronted the administrative reformers of the early nineteenth century.

A particular problem was posed by the once-rural townships

and parishes which industry had transformed into dense urban agglomerations. They included such places as Birmingham, Bolton, Halifax, Huddersfield, Manchester and Stockport which were already familiar names in the manufacturing world. Such overgrown communities could not fit into the rural paternalism of squire and parson and yet lacked the traditional governing institutions of the corporate boroughs. A conspicuous example of the administrative anachronisms created by the industrial revolution was Manchester. In the sixty years from 1770 to 1830 the population of the township increased from about 24,000 to 142,000. Around it the growing townships of Cheetham, Hulme, Chorlton Row and Ardwick formed a ring of satellite populations which could pour into the centre of Manchester in time of unrest. Even by early nineteenth-century standards the government of Manchester was a curiosity. The unit for quarter sessions was the hundred of Salford; the ecclesiastical unit the parish of Manchester. The township itself was governed by the medieval manorial court-leet which annually appointed a borough reeve and two constables from among the merchants and manufacturers of the town. To assist these amateur officials there was a permanent, salaried deputy-constable (from 1803 to 1823 the notorious Nadin, described with some exaggeration as the real ruler of Manchester), and a few unpopular beadles. Administration of justice was in the hands of county JPs; poor relief and payment of constables' accounts was the business of the overseer of the poor and the churchwardens. To stiffen this antiquated array of jurisdictions there was also the statutory Manchester Police Commission set up in 1792. This was the eighteenth century, not the modern sense of the word 'police' (from policy, meaning internal government). It was responsible for street-cleaning, repairs and improvements, lighting, night watch and fire precautions. The problem of enforcing order in this raw industrial community was clearly insoluble under such a system and Manchester in the early nineteenth century was proverbial for its riotous habits.

At the base of the pyramid of local administration was the parish, still a vital and vigorous unit of self-government. Though based on the old ecclesiastical territorial division, its government and responsibilities were as much civil as religious. The ruling body was the parish meeting, known from its traditional meeting-place as the vestry. This could either be open to all householders or freemen— the common or open vestry—or confined to a representative body of wealthier inhabitants—the closed vestry. The vestry was sometimes a demagogic assembly, sometimes a self-perpetuating oligarchy of ratepayers. In the rural parishes the parson and leading farmers ruled unchallenged and composed their differences in private. In the towns the vestrymen were not infrequently a corrupt, politically minded and quarrelsome body. Nevertheless the vestry remained an indispensable piece of machinery for fixing rates, electing churchwardens, appointing parochial officers, deciding on the amount of expenditure for the relief of the poor, upkeep of church fabric and maintenance of roads, and for criticizing actions taken by town councils or magistrates. It supplied a democratic element in local government which could with a certain optimism be regarded as the historical embodiment of English political liberty. Since there was neither uniformity of practice nor certainty in law on such matters as frequency of meetings, qualifications for membership, and right of voting, material for disputes were always present in the larger town parishes. A common source of acrimony were the incessant disputes between anglican incumbents and dissenting churchwardens over the church rate. But poor law administration and cost of relief were also controversial issues.

IV

Tithe and church rate, parochial government, clerical magistrates, bishops in the House of Lords, anglican monopoly of the two English universities of Oxford and Cambridge were all outward signs of that union of church and state which to many conservative people was the fundamental feature of the constitution preserved by the 1688 Revolution and the Hanoverian succession. Like most of the other historic institutions of English society after 1815 the church offered a broad target for the critics. Indeed, because its ecclesiastical character had sheltered it from the late eighteenth-century political reform movements, it was even more in need of repair and renovation than its secular counterpart. Its organizational defects were notorious: among them nepotism, absenteeism, sinecures, pluralism, gross inequality of stipends, maldistribution of its human and financial resources, lack of professional training for its ordinands, decay of episcopal discipline, absence of any central representative assembly, and the preoccupation of the episcopate with their parliamentary and political functions. Along with this institutional obsolescence went obvious spiritual deficiencies. Materially, with the growth of land values, the position of the inferior clergy, drawing their revenue from glebe and tithe, had improved considerably since the days of Addison and Defoe. But the greater social respectability of the anglican clergy and their closer assimilation with the ruling classes had led to a certain tepidness of religious zeal and neglect of the vital offices of the church which was observable at all levels.

The price of establishment had been in effect a considerable loss of autonomy. Of its approximately 10,000 benefices the patronage of about 50 per cent belonged to lay patrons, 10 per cent to the crown and municipal corporations, and only 40 per cent to the church itself, including the Oxford and Cambridge colleges. Even without the anti-clerical stimulus of the French Revolution, it was inevitable that in radical eyes the church seemed part of the established framework of society, sharing the social and political attitudes of the ruling classes. In one sense this was neither unhistoric nor discreditable. The role of the Christian church in European society had traditionally been to enjoin personal morality, social duty and civil harmony. But in an age of social fluidity and political unrest an undue emphasis on these to the exclusion of other Christian virtues placed the church in a vulnerable position. It was dangerously easy in these circumstances for an anti-establishment attitude to become part of the liberal and progressive creed; equally easy for anglicans to interpret dissent and opposition to the establishment as a political danger to the state.

Generalizations about the state of the church in the early nineteenth century tend to relate to the system rather than to the individuals. Yet to the laity what counted most was the character of the clergy they encountered in daily life. The effectiveness of the church was measured by the quality of the incumbent. Among the ten thousand parochial clergy were to be found zealous parsons, worldly parsons, poetic parsons, scholarly parsons, scientific parsons, hunting parsons, drunken parsons, immoral parsons and absentee parsons. The power of the patron, the contemporary view of the church as a genteel career, the negligence of bishops in their pastoral capacity, the disuse of clerical courts, the almost unassailable right of the incumbent to the 'freehold' of his office, made the clergy of the Church of England intensely individualistic—too much so for the good of the church as a corporate institution. But though the church undoubtedly harboured eccentrics and ne'er-do-wells, the majority of clergy fell into neither category. 'The working clergy of the Church of England are, perhaps, taking them as a body, as good men as any in the world', observed Cobbett in 1831 with more generosity than most of his fellow-radicals would have shown. Even so it was significant that public opinion distinguished between 'working clergy' and the rest.

A good parson, however, had to be present in his parish to be able to do good; and one great defect of the church in the post-Waterloo period was the absenteeism which was the inevitable accompaniment of pluralism. The low stipends of many livings, even of some bishoprics, explained if it did not justify the practice of holding several offices simultaneously. Before the Ecclesiastical Commission began its labours in 1835, the yearly incomes from church benefices varied enormously from under £50 to over £2,000: but the average was approximately £285. Pluralism brought the average income of beneficed clergy up to about £418. But the result was that in 40 per cent of the parishes in the post-war period the legal incumbent was non-resident. This did not mean that these parishes were without a resident cleric of any kind. Most pluralists installed a curate at a lower salary, the average being £80 per annum; but not all did. In the early 1830s there were about a thousand parishes without even a resident curate.

An even more profound weakness was the failure of the church to adjust to the demographic changes that had taken place in English society. It was a double failure. In the first place the parochial organization was even older than the parliamentary representation and like it had remained largely unchanged for centuries. In both systems the historical geography of medieval society had ensured that the centre of gravity was in south and southeast England. Here, in the old centres of population, the parishes were clustered more densely. North of a line from the Humber to the Mersey there were fewer of them in proportion to geographical area and they were therefore larger in size. The other problem was created by the rapid growth of towns. In the north the boundaries of a single parish might now contain a great new industrial town. Even in London the parochial system had been overwhelmed by the teeming population of its streets and alleys. St Pancras in 1815 had 50,000 inhabitants and a church that could seat 200. By the time Victoria came to the throne conditions were even worse. In 1840 the parish of St George's, Hanover Square, had 73,000 inhabitants.

But even this was not so bad as the state of some of the northern towns. Leeds had a population in 1831 of over 123,000 comprising old Leeds and a number of other townships within the parochial boundaries. Though there were some thirteen other churches and chapels to serve this sprawling community, most of them were perpetual curacies without cure of souls. The bulk of the formal parochial duties fell on the mother church where the vicar was assisted only by a curate and a clerk in holy orders. In the early 1840s the hard-pressed staff of the parish church celebrated each year some 1,000 weddings, 1,300 funerals and 1,800 christenings. When Hook became vicar of Leeds in 1837 he found his predecessor's two assistants, who spent most of their time on these duties, were not surprisingly doing their best to discourage other forms of church service during the week. Yet the legal and moral obligations of the established church were inescapable. Before the act of 1836 made provision for state registration of births, deaths and marriages, the Church of England had a virtual monopoly of the ceremonies connected with them. Even after that date social custom brought people to the parish church for those purposes who were never seen there at any other time. As late as ten years after the 1836 legislation, Church of England marriages were eight times as many as those carried out either in registry offices or by other religious denominations, though in terms of actual membership it is probable that the establishment could claim no more than half of the church and chapel-going population.

In the period after Waterloo it was clear that the pastoral responsibilities of the church exceeded its administrative capacity. Because it was the national church it still had a national function. Yet because it was an established church it was crippled by its lack of autonomy. Though the parochial system covered the whole country, changed circumstances had in many areas made that system totally inadequate. Yet it was difficult to change this system. The creation of a new parish, the building of a new parish church, could only be done through act of parliament. It was this constraint that made the church so vulnerable to competition from other denominations.

The dead hand of state control, the superiority of private enterprise, were never better illustrated than in the multiplication of Methodist and dissenting chapels in populous districts where the choked and swollen historic anglican parishes had long ceased to be effective pastoral units. When a new dissenting chapel involved merely the hiring of a hall and a magistrate's licence and a new anglican parish a parliamentary statute, the scales were heavily weighted against the establishment. It was not a problem peculiar to anglicanism. In Scotland the established Presbyterian church was also suffering from over-rigidity in the face of its competitors. In the century prior to 1834, recorded Cockburn, 600 dissenting chapels had been built compared with only sixty-three for the established Kirk. Not until the General Assembly in 1833 raised the forty chapels endowed by the government in the Highlands to the status of parish churches and a church extension movement resulted in the addition of some 214 churches and parishes to the existing system did the Church of Scotland by the middle of the century begin to overcome its deficiencies. Until then St Cuthbert's parish in Edinburgh, for example, and the Barony in Glasgow were as bad as Leeds or the worst of the London parishes.

V

The ossification of Church of England organization in 1815 was
peculiarly dangerous in view of the startling growth in the previous
generation of Methodism and the 'old Dissent' denominations. To a
great extent the church had itself contributed to the expansion of
the Protestant sects by its failure to make its traditional 'cure of souls'
a reality in all parts of the country. The new statistical information
gained from diocesan returns, from the censuses of 1801 and 1811,
and from parliamentary enquiries like that instituted by Sidmouth
in 1809, revealed to anglicans not only their own deficiencies but the
progress made by the other churches. A return from the bishops in
1811 of the number of places of worship in parishes of over 1,000
inhabitants in England and Wales showed that dissenting chapels
and churches already outnumbered those of the establishment by
seven to five.[4] Though many of these buildings were small, defective
returns and the omission of private houses used for prayer meetings
probably made the real dissenting total even greater. Though exact
figures of religious membership, as distinct from the number of
religious buildings, were unobtainable, it was not difficult for church-
ment to arrive at two disquieting conclusions. The first was that
though anglicans still had a majority in the country as a whole, in
some towns they were equalled if not outnumbered by dissenters. The
second, even more ominous, was that dissent was growing faster than
the establishment. Twice as many licences had been taken out for
dissenting places of worship between 1795 and 1808 as in the previous
twenty years. Lord Harrowby was not alone in entertaining the
fears he expressed during a debate in the upper house in 1810 that
the country was drifting towards 'that most alarming of all situations,
in which the religion of the Established Church would not be the
religion of the majority of the people'. For the first time since the
seventeenth century the church was in danger of losing its hold on the
nation.

The shift in the religious balance had been brought about by
the evangelical revival of the previous half century. In the first decade
of George II's reign Protestant dissenters from the established church
numbered perhaps no more than 3 per cent of the population and
were still declining; by the death of George III in 1820 they formed
perhaps 30 per cent. In the middle of the nineteenth century their
church and chapel capacity and actual congregations virtually

[4] Anglican 2547, non-anglican 3457 (*Annual Register 1811*, p. 268).

equalled those of the establishment. At the heart of this great transformation was the Methodist movement. By 1820 its enrolled class membership was not far short of 200,000; its adherents probably five times as many. In numbers it was as strong as all the other Protestant sects put together. The main Wesleyan connection possessed, moreover, what the other dissenting denominations lacked —a strong centralized administration. For this it was indebted to the organizing tradition bequeathed by its founder. Superimposed on its three hundred English circuits with their superintendents and itinerant preachers was the 'Legal Hundred' of senior ministers who had inherited Wesley's authority. Meeting in annual conference they constituted the legislative, executive and disciplinary core of the Methodist movement. Even this, however, was insufficient for its steadily expanding membership. District meetings (nineteen in England), composed of all the preachers within the area, and the standing committee of privileges set up in 1803, helped to stiffen Methodist organization after Wesley's death. But it was only with the emergence of Jabez Bunting, the new 'pope' of the Wesleyan Methodists, who became assistant secretary, then secretary, and in 1820 for the first time president of the Conference, that the movement consolidated its strength. To Bunting, more than any one man, Wesleyanism owed its financial stability, theological unity and social discipline in the generation after Waterloo.

This continuation of what were essentially Wesley's own principles was not achieved without the internal conflicts which are the characteristic marks of historic Protestantism. The secession of the Kilhamites or New Connection in 1797, the Independent Methodists in 1806, the Primitive Methodists in 1812 and the Protestant Methodists in 1827, were in essence the protests of lay democracy against the ecclesiastical ghost of John Wesley sitting enthroned in the Methodist Conference. Despite these schisms, the Wesleyan Methodists remained the most formidable of all the domestic rivals to the established church up to 1841, the point at which they reached their highest membership relative to the size of the population. It was true that strictly speaking Methodism was not a branch of historic nonconformity. It had started as a movement within the Church of England and as late as 1839 its centenary handbook described the Wesleyan Methodists as 'occupying a distinct and peculiar position between strict Churchmanship and systematic Dissent'. The continued use by Methodists of such phrases as 'the United Societies', 'the Methodist Connexion' or 'the People called Methodists' was evidence of the bond which still united them to the anglican church. Yet Wesley himself, by ordaining ministers, had set the movement on the path of separation. After his death the 1795

Plan of Pacification, permitting the administration of the sacrament by preachers licensed by the Conference, continued along the same road. The title of 'Reverend' authorized in 1818 and the annual ordination services started in 1836 merely completed the transformation of the Wesleyan ministry from a body of irregular anglican preachers into a separate clerical order.

Long before Victoria came to the throne the Wesleyan Methodists constituted the best organized and for certain purposes the most efficient religious body in England. Bunting in his prime was at the head of the most powerful vehicle for protest, petition and publicity in British society. That before 1841 it was rarely used for this purpose, and never against the Church of England, was a testimony to the traditional Methodist reluctance to intervene in secular politics, to Bunting's political conservatism, and to its historic sympathy with the establishment. Nevertheless, looking at its growing strength and disciplined leadership, anglicans might well feel that here, in the latest schism from the Church of England rather than in the old seventeenth-century nonconformist churches, was their real rival for the allegiance of the English churchgoing population.

Yet the evangelical revival had also done much for historic dissent. In particular the Independents, or Congregationalists as they were beginning to be known, and the Baptists had been invigorated by the new wave of religious fervour. In some cases they had inherited unattached congregations left by Whitefield's 'Calvinistic Methodist' movement. But even without this adventitious source of recruitment, they underwent a notable phase of expansion which was reflected in Sunday schools, new training colleges for their preachers, an interest in social philanthropy and the launching of home missionary campaigns, especially among the Congregationalists. The other members of 'old Dissent' covered by the Toleration Act of 1689, though not untouched by contemporary evangelical activity, showed less elasticity. The Quakers were too inbred and pietistic to take part in a wave of popular religious expansion; and the Presbyterians, who at the start of the eighteenth century had constituted the most numerous and influential branch of English Dissent, were steadily declining into a narrow though rational and tolerant sect of Unitarians. The old framework of national dissenting organization dating from Walpole's time continued, however, despite the altered balance of strength. The Protestant Dissenting Deputies of the Three Denominations (Presbyterians, Independents and Baptists) met regularly in London to provide an experienced, cautious, metropolitan leadership on legal and parliamentary matters. The general body of deputies (laymen elected by congregations in and around London) numbered about 150 and met as a rule once a year. The effective work was carried on by the Committee of Deputies of about twenty-one members, most of them prosperous, influential members of the mercantile and professional classes. In addition there was the general body of ministers of the Three Denominations who met annually in their more democratic but less effective representative assembly.

This impressive traditional structure apart, English Dissent remained both divided and decentralized. There were divergences of outlook between the provincial congregations and the metropolitan Deputies. There was a growing doctrinal rift between the Unitarian Presbyterians and the two orthodox Calvinist denominations which created bitter disputes over public policy and chapel ownership long before the actual Unitarian secession of 1836. The largest sects, the Congregationalists and the Baptists, were informal societies rather than unified churches. Their 'unions' in the early years of the nineteenth century were no more than voluntary organizations for particular purposes such as home and foreign missionary work. It was not until after 1832 that effective Congregational and Baptist Unions took shape. Until then dissent was still an amorphous even though pervasive influence in national life.

While it was beyond doubt that the Congregationalists were by far the most numerous of the Three Denominations, perhaps more than twice the size of the other two put together, in social terms Congregationalists, Baptists and Methodists had common characteristics. Their membership included a range of classes and occupations, from merchants and manufacturers down to unskilled labourers and farm workers; but the bulk of their adherents, probably over half, were made up of skilled artisans—weavers, spinners, tailors, carpenters, shoemakers, masons and the like. The significant difference between the Methodists and the other denominations was not social but geographical. 'Old Dissent' had, so to speak, flourished in the interstices of the establishment, forming congregations from those antipathetic politically or socially to the Church of England, or simply neglected by it. Its strength was in the south and west, in London and the small towns, in the larger villages, the places in fact where the establishment was also most firmly entrenched. This close local rivalry fostered that intensity of church–chapel antagonism that was such a feature of Victorian society. On the other hand, given the greater social prestige of anglicanism, it also helped perhaps to restrict the growth of old dissent compared with Methodism. Wesley's movement by contrast won its greatest successes in the areas neglected by both anglicanism and dissent. He had not only sought to convert the poor and outcast; he had gone to those parts of the country where the parochial system was weakest and the Church of England most evidently failing in its duties. His typical mission fields had been among the colliers of the northeast and southwest, the textile workers of Yorkshire and Lancashire, the fishing population of the east and west coasts, and the Celtic fringe of Wales and Cornwall. Early Methodism did not so much compete with the existing churches, whether anglican or nonconformist; it flowed into the gaps they had left.

VI

The years from 1815 to 1832 marked the period of greatest anglican weakness, relative to the other Protestant churches, since the Commonwealth. Critical as the position of the establishment was, however, it was not hopeless. Already there were signs of activity, reform and regeneration. Like the rest of English Protestantism, the Church of England had felt the inspiration of the evangelical revival. The evangelical party within the establishment had been closely associated with such interdenominational organizations as the Religious Tract Society. The preponderantly anglican Church Missionary Society of 1799 and British and Foreign Bible Society of 1804 owed almost everything to their zeal and enlightenment. The great anti-slavery campaign, which secured the abolition of the trade in 1807 and of the institution itself in 1833, has tended to obscure both in Wilberforce's personal career and among evangelical anglicans generally their parallel interest in education and social philanthropy. In missionary efforts abroad and the Sunday school movement at home evangelical anglicans individually, if not the anglican church collectively, took a prominent part.

The Clapham Sect of Wilberforce, James Stephen, Henry Thornton, Zachary Macaulay and Hannah More represented only a minority, often an unpopular minority, within the establishment; but they had an influence in politics out of all proportion to their numbers. There was also a more specifically clerical evangelical party at Cambridge led by Charles Simeon and Isaac Milner, the pluralist dean of Carlisle and president of Queens' College. The practice initiated by Simeon after Waterloo of purchasing advowsons from a central fund enabled a steady trickle of young evangelical clergy, often Cambridge-trained, to be directed towards selected areas. At Birmingham, by the start of Victoria's reign, they dominated the Anglican party in the town and largely as a consequence of their friendly relations with dissenters, church rates there were abolished by local agreement in 1832. At Sheffield the Methodist super-

intendent reported in 1829 that though his society was making
converts among the poor, the rich were flocking to the new anglican
churches. 'Two new ones have been opened and a third is nearly
finished. All supplied by what are called evangelical clergymen,
chiefly young, active, and zealous men, who strive to equal us in every
good work.'[5]

Reforming zeal was not, however, a prerogative of the evangelicals
within the church. Indeed, it could be argued that since they were
chiefly concerned to save souls and preach the gospel, the actual
reform of the Church of England owed more to the high church party.
Even before Waterloo the orthodox supporters of the establishment,
critical of indiscriminate evangelical enthusiasm, were beginning
their countermeasures. The Quaker Joseph Lancaster's unsectarian
educational society of 1808 (renamed the British and Foreign Schools
Society in 1814) was answered in 1811 by the significantly named
National Society for the Promotion of the Education of the Poor in
the Principles of the Church of England. Simultaneously leading
members of the Anglican laity were turning their attention to the
lack of church accommodation in London and elsewhere. Before the
war ended the government was pressed to take action and early in
1816 Lord Liverpool received a memorial from some 120 influential
laymen, stressing the 'danger to which the constitution of this country
both in church and state is exposed from the want of places of public
worship, particularly for persons of the middle and lower classes' and
arguing that it was one of the chief duties of parliament 'to provide
places of worship for the members of the established religion'.

Post-war financial stringency prevented immediate action by the
politicians but pressure on the cabinet did not relax. The moving
spirit behind the campaign was the group of high churchmen known
by contra-distinction as the 'Clapton Sect', or 'Hackney Phalanx',
grouped round the two Watsons, the Reverend H. H. Norris, and
Archdeacon Daubeny. Joshua Watson, their most energetic representative, was a wealthy winemerchant who had retired in 1812 to
devote himself to the high church effort. His brother was rector of
Hackney and he was connected by marriage with other anglican
clergy. The group included bishops and judges among its sympathizers, and through Charles Lloyd, later bishop of Oxford, and
Christopher Wordsworth, later master of Trinity College Cambridge, had allies in both universities. The Hackney Phalanx had
been responsible for the creation of the National Society in 1811 and
in 1818 they scored their greatest triumph by securing a Church
Building Commission with a parliamentary grant of one million

[5] *Early Correspondence of J. Bunting 1820–29*, edited by W. R. Ward, p. 208 (Camden
Society, 4th series XI).

pounds. In 1824 the unexpected repayment of an Austrian loan enabled another half million to be added to the fund. By the time of the 1832 Reform Act not only had most of this money already been expended but at least an equivalent amount had been raised by private and parochial subscription for the same purpose. Even this related only to the work of the Church Building Commission; it took no account of churches and chapels erected independently. In all it has been calculated that £6 millions were spent between 1818 and 1833 on church building.

Despite timid toryism among its clergy, torpor and entrenched abuses in the structure of its organization, the Church of England at many scattered points was already showing signs of a reforming spirit. There was even occasional cooperation between the rival parties of evangelicals and high churchmen. Legislation in 1796 and 1803 had done a little, though only a little, to meet the problems of curates's stipends and non-residence. In 1813 a bill introduced by Lord Harrowby laid down minimum stipends for curates varying with the size of the parish. In 1817 a general act consolidated the earlier measures. Though they disagreed on details, both anglican parties contributed to the passing of this legislation which was designed not only to assist the underpaid curates but to encourage residence by official incumbents and stricter attention to parochial duties.

The effects of these measures were scarcely revolutionary; but at least the winds of change were beginning to blow, however gently. The first evangelical bishop to be appointed was Henry Ryder in 1815, who enjoyed an uncovenanted advantage in being the brother of a cabinet minister. But something of a quiet episcopal transformation was taking place between 1815 and 1830 with such bishops as Law of Chester who in 1817 founded and endowed a training college at St Bees for ordinands unable to go to Oxford or Cambridge; Bishop Burgess of St Davids who in 1822 started a similar college at Lampeter; Charles Sumner who revolutionized the sprawling diocese of Winchester to which he was appointed in 1827; his brother J. B. Sumner who did comparable work at Chester between 1828 and 1848; Kaye who became bishop of Bristol in 1820 and of Lincoln in 1827; the energetic Blomfield who was appointed to the diocese of Chester in 1824 and London in 1828; and the cautious but reforming Howley who after fifteen years at London became archbishop of Canterbury in 1828. Even before the Reform Bill became law the church was beginning the long, difficult task of putting its house in order. In church as in state, though this went largely unperceived by radical critics, the age of reform had already started.

3 The Peterloo Years

I

The government whose strategy was crowned by Waterloo was substantially that formed by Perceval in 1809. Of the five administrations which followed Pitt's resignation in 1801, Perceval's had proved the most efficient and durable. Yet when, after Perceval's assassination in 1812, Lord Liverpool was confirmed as his successor, it appeared to be a consequence less of his own merits than of the reluctance of more talented politicians to take office. It was the exigencies of the war and Wellington's victories in the Peninsula that enabled the new premier to consolidate his position. By 1815 the rival claims to the Pittite political inheritance which had seemed so strong three years earlier had virtually disappeared. Canning had accepted the Lisbon embassy in 1814, a halfway house to his re-entry into the ministry in 1816. Grenville's alliance with the whigs, which had withered in the last few years of the war, failed to revive with the coming of peace. The end of the long war, however, meant that the government entered on a new and unpredictable phase. The patriotic feeling and military prestige that had sustained it did not long survive the great European contest. Ministers had to learn the art, disused for nearly quarter of a century, of governing a civil population which could now afford exclusive attention on its domestic problems. As the brief period of illusory peace in 1814 had already demonstrated, the cabinet would in future have to adjust itself to a more assertive House of Commons, parliament to a more assertive public.

The position of the ministry was made more difficult by the generic weakness of British executive government in the early nineteenth century. The constitutional development of the previous thirty years had produced a stage of parliamentary government in which power and responsibility rested to a remarkable extent with a small, semi-permanent group of professional politicians and administrators. The cabinet bridged the gap between the decline of the power of the crown in the eighteenth century and the rise of organized party in the nineteenth. But this unique period of quasi-independence was only possible at the cost of considerable limitation on its actual exercise of power. Since 1810 the monarch had ceased to play a significant role in politics; and George IV, both as regent and king, was too indolent, capricious and unpopular to be capable of strengthening the ministers whom he continued in office. At the same time the cumulative effect of the administrative and 'economical' reforms pursued by all governments since 1782 had materially weakened the ability of the executive to influence individual members of the House of Commons. More significant still, public opinion was no longer prepared to tolerate the time-honoured methods of political 'management' that had served Walpole and Newcastle. It was a sign of the sensitivity of both ministers and the public to the charge of ruling through patronage that a majority of less than sixty (the approximate number of MPs officially connected with the government in the Commons) was rarely regarded as morally, however politically, satisfactory.

In the absence of an organized party system ministers had to work their measures through parliament, relying on their prestige as servants of the crown, their better sources of information, their debating talent and inferentially on the superior merits of their proposals. Parliament in the last resort was the arbiter of policy. The legislature with its collective experience, presumed wisdom, and undoubted power was the filter through which public opinion ('that great compound of folly, weakness, prejudice, wrong feeling, right feeling, obstinacy and newspaper paragraphs,' as the cynical young Peel once described it) had to pass before it could achieve the respectability that entitled it to a hearing by the ministers of the crown. For direct manipulation of public opinion government was neither technically nor psychologically equipped. Most newspapers and periodicals were in the hands of the opposition or neutrals; and one of the lessons that had to be assimilated by Liverpool's cabinet in the next five years was that with an active and articulate public, political virtue could not rely on intrinsic but unproclaimed merits to win its just reward. By 1815 the national press had almost entirely emancipated itself from government influence. Secret service money could not compete with the profits from large circulation and heavy advertising. The damage which the reputation of being a 'government paper' inflicted on both those sources of revenue was more than any Treasury subsidy was worth. The only journals that sought ministerial assistance were those whose support was not worth having.

In the House of Commons there were two dominant features: the presence of a large body of independent MPs interposed between 'government' and 'opposition', and the lack of adequate sanctions to enforce voting discipline or even attendance at debates. The old Foxite opposition which had appropriated the title 'whig' only numbered about 150–60 and even at full strength could never seriously threaten the government without considerable reinforcement from the independent MPs. It was the corresponding object of ministers, with only a marginally more numerous body of 'thick and thin' supporters on whom they could confidently rely, to attract as large a number of independents as possible in order to isolate the whigs. Majorities in divisions rose and fell with the popularity of the proposals and the lateness of the session; and though the party men on either side of the House rarely voted against their leaders, abstention was a widely practised and equally damaging form of silent disapproval. Though government spokesmen had the advantage of authority, the whigs were aided by the antique rules of the House which gave individual MPs wide latitude for obstruction and delay. The whigs moreover, closely knit by social ties and lavish hospitality, tended to remain in London during the summer when independent members favourable to the government were slipping away.

The system would have been unworkable had it not been for a residual sense of responsibility among the country gentlemen; a general, though not invariable, disposition to support the ministers of the crown; and a reluctance in and out of parliament to see the whigs return to power. Whig opposition to the war effort and whig association with radicalism were sufficiently fresh in the public memory to make many moderate men still regard them as a factious and irresponsible set of politicians. The House of Commons as a body was ready to criticize, limit and on occasion overturn ministerial policy; it was not anxious to overturn the cabinet itself. This was part of Liverpool's strength; the rest lay in the prestige and talent of the ministers themselves. Liverpool himself, in his mid-forties nearing the summit of his powers, was one of the most experienced prime ministers in British history. Entering parliament at the age of twenty he had served in all three secretaryships of state before his colleagues put him forward as their leader in 1812. Though he remained a curiously sensitive man, the diffidence of his early years had been mastered and in the cabinet he showed qualities of firmness, tact and judgement which made him indispensable.

The technical weakness of his administration in 1815 was that out of a cabinet of thirteen, nine were in the House of Lords, among them Sidmouth, Eldon, Bathurst and Melville, as well as the prime minister himself. Of the House of Commons ministers Vansittart was a poor speaker, Bragge Bathurst and Pole worse than useless. Virtually the entire frontbench responsibility rested on Castlereagh, who as foreign secretary had more excuse than any for being absent. Though not a fluent debater he was formidable when attacked; and the House of Commons respected and trusted him as they never, for example, trusted Canning. Nevertheless, it was a heavy burden for one man to carry. There were promising young men in junior office; Palmerston the secretary at war, for example, and Peel the Irish secretary. But they were not in the cabinet and their largely departmental activities could not compensate for the thinness of front-line support for Castlereagh as Leader of the House.

The deficiencies of the government in the lower house were thrown into sharp relief by two events at the outset of its post-war career: the passing of the corn law of 1815 and the rejection of the income tax in 1816. The future of the British corn trade had been discussed in parliament as early as 1813 by Parnell and Irish landowners. It became an urgent matter in the eyes of British landlords and farmers when the great harvest of 1813 sent prices tumbling and peace in 1814 brought foreign grain imports and the promise of more to come. The all-party Commons committee which examined the problem in 1814 concluded that a fair remunerative price for wheat was 80s. a quarter, the approximate wartime average. In the hope of securing an agreed reasonable solution the cabinet decided to take responsibility for a new corn bill in the 1815 session. Liverpool and Huskisson would have liked to have included in it the principle of a sliding scale; but in private meetings with leading agriculturalists they reluctantly gave way to the pressure for absolute prohibition when the price fell below 80s. with free entry above that figure. Parliament would obviously insist on strong protective legislation of some sort; and it was hoped that the ministerial concession would reconcile the country gentry to the unpopular financial measures which the government knew would be necessary when the war was over. In any case the cabinet could not be indifferent to the fate of the country's largest single economic interest. Rents, prices and costs had risen sharply since the 1790s; and it was not unreasonable for the legislature to ease the transition from the inflated conditions of war to the more testing climate of peace of which the 1814 slump was a sharp foretaste. Even the few doctrinaire free traders who advocated abolition of all restrictions admitted that the immediate effect on the agricultural industry would be painful. Protection on the other hand could conscientiously be defended as likely to provide the country with a more stable supply of food than would result from partial dependence on intermittent and costly imports from abroad.

The fact remained that the bill was designed to safeguard

agriculture in its wartime state and to keep the level of profits, prices and rents near, if not at, their wartime level. To the population at large it seemed that they were being called on to maintain the landed interest in the state of opulence to which providence in the shape of a twenty-years war had accustomed it. There was a mass of petitioning against the bill from manufacturers, towns, and industrial labourers, and outbreaks of riot in towns as far apart as Edinburgh, Norwich and Canterbury. The London mob, in the hearty eighteenth-century tradition, for several days demonstrated outside parliament and smashed the windows of available ministerial houses. Though this whiff of violence hardened rather than weakened the resolution of the House of Commons, the popular instinct was not altogether at fault. Previous corn laws, by a judicious mixture of import checks and export bounties, had tried to maintain a stable market in corn, through good years and bad, at a level satisfactory to consumer and producer alike. The 1815 act introduced a new principle of prohibition designed to favour the producer. It was the first clear clash of interest between the landed interest and the rest of the country, and the corn laws remained a permanent radical grievance for the next thirty years.

For the government the consequences were almost entirely disastrous. By making it a ministerial measure, they saddled themselves with the odium of class legislation without reaping the advantage of political support from the classes intended as its beneficiaries. The illusion that a prohibitory tariff would safeguard the farmer vanished almost as soon as the bill was on the statute book. Two good harvest in 1814 and 1815 brought prices down to nearly half the level of 1812, with a trail of bankruptcies and rent reductions. During the thirteen years in which the 1815 act was in operation the annual average wheat price went above 80s. a quarter in only two years and in one year sank as low as 44s. 7d. The experience confirmed the belief of theorists that parliament was powerless against the iron laws of economics; but this was of little comfort to a government which had given the impression of promising a security which in practice was never, and could never be, realized. Even the hope that the measure would reconcile the gentry and farmers to a continuation of high taxation proved delusory. When the proposal to renew the income tax came before the Commons as part of the 1816 budget, they rejected it by a majority of 37.

Over the income tax the ministers had an even better case than on corn. No reasonable person could doubt that heavy government expenditure would have to continue for some years after Waterloo, and that even when it settled to a peacetime level, it would be substantially higher than in the years before 1793. The immediate needs of the army of occupation in France had to be met; allied subsidies already contracted had to be paid; the defence needs of the empire had been enlarged by the addition of another seventeen colonies; the national debt had risen to unprecedented heights; there was a 'dead-weight' of war pensions and half-pay; and the value of the pound had fallen. The campaign against the income tax (or property tax as it was still misleadingly called) was inspired not by its amount, however, but by its character. It was almost universally regarded as an inquisitorial, un-English mode of taxation, justified only by the overriding needs of a state at war. It was widely, though wrongly, believed that when it had been introduced, there had been a promise that it would last only for the duration of the war, and that the Liverpool ministry had repeated that pledge when, on the news of Napoleon's escape from Elba, they rescinded their proposal to terminate the tax in 1814. The British people were war-weary and tax-weary; and of all taxes, this was the most vulnerable. Every class of taxpayer, farmer and manufacturer, town and country, disliked it; and the whig parliamentary opposition, scenting a popular issue for the first time in many years, applied themselves to the task of organizing a national campaign of agitation.

With no prominent newspaper prepared to state the government case, the cabinet was unconscionably tardy in reacting to the clamour. Nevertheless, they made a number of important alleviations in the scope of the tax, reduced the standard rate by half, and hoped that the normal influences of government and the plain necessities of the situation would see them through. Up to the last they expected a majority of forty. What destroyed their expectations was the adverse vote of some eighty usual government supporters and the absence—or deliberate abstention—of about an equivalent number. In the first important trial of executive strength in the post-war period they had been ignominiously defeated; and they had been defeated because the House of Commons had been more sensitive to public opinion, however selfish and short-sighted, than the ministers. It was a defeat that had protracted consequences. For the moment, as Castlereagh bluntly told the Prince Regent, it left the government with £12 millions clear revenue with which to meet an expenditure of £30 millions. As a result the government was forced back on a ruinous policy of borrowing from which it did not begin to extricate itself for another three years. In the long run it helped to worsen relations, not between industry and agriculture as in the case of the corn laws, but between rich and poor. By divesting themselves of a direct tax which fell most heavily on the rich, the legislature obliged the executive to rely on indirect taxation which proportionately fell most heavily on the poor.

There was another more insidious consequence. The defeat on the income tax whetted the public appetite for more economies and revealed to the opposition the vulnerable flank of the ministry under peace conditions. Given the universal popular demand for 'cheap government', the cabinet could no longer rely on the goodwill of the independent MPs unless it was seen to be making determined efforts to eliminate every unnecessary form of expenditure. For the next two years much of the time of ministers was spent departmentally in cutting government estimates to the bone and publicly in defending them against parliamentary attacks. The peacetime establishments for the army and navy, which they had hoped to settle in 1816, were once again reduced; the Civil List was pared down; the civil departments repeatedly pruned; a 10 per cent cut made in official salaries. By 1818 the process of enforced retrenchment had reached a stage when the basic structure of the state was endangered.

II

What gave continuous force to the campaign for economy was the prolonged distress in the country. To a large section of the public the connection between the two was self-evident. Since the days of Wilkes and American independence, governmental inefficiency had been ascribed to corruption and corruption to financial profligacy. After Waterloo this simple political equation was extended further. Disorder in the country was due to economic distress; distress to heavy taxation; and heavy taxation to the inefficiency and extravagance of the government. There was a modicum of truth in the argument that governmental policy had contributed to national distress, though not the kind of truth that the critics were prepared to recognize. The sharp reduction in government expenditure (the reverse side of tax reduction) added to post-war deflation; the discharge of a third of a million men from the fighting forces (over 300,000 in 1816 followed by another 32,000 in 1817) flooded the already congested labour market. Once the artificial conditions of war had disappeared, however, the basic causes of economic distress were the instability of the textile industry in terms of overseas trade, and the instability of the agricultural industry in terms of harvest yield. Neither of them was very amenable to legislation at Westminster. The collapse of the South American market in 1810, and the trade war with the United States which effectively began in 1811, had already produced the first and largest wave of Luddite disorders

in the Midlands, Yorkshire and Lancashire. The return of peace on
both sides of the Atlantic in 1814–15 gave a transitory stimulus to
the overloaded textile industry but by 1816 a general trade depression
set in once more. At the same time, with bad weather and an
anticipated poor harvest, the cost of bread began to move steadily
towards the famine prices of 1817 and 1818.

The distress was widespread. Classes as varied as domestic weavers
in Lancashire, iron-workers in South Wales and sailors on the
Liverpool–Dublin run suffered wage reductions or actual unemployment. With distress came the traditional protests—riot and destruction. The most serious industrial disorder was among the hosiers
and lace-makers in Leicestershire and Nottinghamshire, a notoriously
depressed and overcrowded manufacturing area with a previous
history of Luddite outbreaks. It took the form of scattered machine-
breaking incidents of which the most serious was a determined
assault on a large lace factory at Loughborough which destroyed
over two dozen machines worth many thousand pounds. The
disturbances finally died down in 1817 after seven rioters had been
executed. The attacks seem to have been largely the work of a
comparatively small gang of young men operating as almost professional machine-breakers, assisted financially if not actually paid by
the rank and file of the workers. The local manufacturers, gentry
and magistrates, taught by their previous experience, were on this
occasion unusually active in protecting mills and detecting the ringleaders.

The most severe rioting in 1816, however, was not industrial but
rural. Starting in April and going on intermittently until the end of
May, in Cambridgeshire, Essex, Suffolk, Norfolk and Huntingdon,
there were attacks on the houses and shops of millers, butchers
and bakers, demands for money and beer, rick-burning and
destruction of threshing and other agricultural machines. Women
were prominent in the raids on food shops; and there was some
evidence that among the men were poachers and recently discharged
soldiers. At Littleport and Ely, towards the end of May, the rioting
was of a more violent nature. Money was extorted from the principal
farmers and shopkeepers; houses were sacked and everything
valuable taken; and the mob took possession of firearms. About
eighty arrests were made and at a special assize at Ely twenty-four
rioters received sentences of death, of which nineteen were subsequently commuted for imprisonment or transportation—a judicial
reprisal which even local opinion thought excessive. It is clear that the
East Anglian riots were primarily food riots, directed against those
traditionally unpopular figures, the millers, butchers and bakers, and
were accompanied by demands for employment and higher wages.

Elsewhere in the country there was a trail of similar but less dangerous incidents—from Bideford in Devon, where there were riots in May to prevent a cargo of potatoes leaving the harbour, to Dundee in Forfar where in December a mob several thousand strong plundered over a hundred provision shops and sacked the house of a wealthy corn dealer.

The general distress produced demonstrations of various kinds. The unemployed miners of the Midlands dragged waggons of coal round the countryside partly to raise money, partly to advertise their plight. Though devoid of politics and perfectly peaceful, their action was disliked by the authorities as a breach of the vagrancy laws. There was, however, considerable public sympathy. Two parties advancing on London were met at St Albans and Maidenhead Thicket by metropolitan magistrates who arranged for the purchase of the coal and provided the men with money to return home. Parties of colliers elsewhere met with similar understanding by both magistrates and public. Of a different nature was the Spa Field riot at London in December. The occasion was a series of meetings organized by the Spencean Society and addressed by the great radical orator, Hunt. The main purpose was to organize petitions from the distressed labouring classes to the Prince Regent but at the second meeting Watson and his fellow Spenceans, having harangued the crowd on their own account, led a small party off into the City to plunder gunsmiths shops. Watson, Thistlewood and two others were subsequently prosecuted for high treason but acquitted. The gravity of the charge lent an exaggerated significance to the amateur terrorism of the Spenceans. An indictment for robbery with violence would have been enough, with the advantage of probably securing a verdict. To attempt to convince a London jury that Watson and his group seriously intended to levy war against the crown was a self-defeating exercise only explicable in the excited atmosphere prevailing at the time.

Disorders, demonstrations and fears went on throughout the following year. It began inauspiciously with what was believed to be two shots fired at the Prince Regent on his way to open parliament, and continued with further industrial strikes and disorders. In March 1817 a planned mass procession from Manchester to London to petition the crown for parliamentary reform was met by a somewhat excessive concentration of civil and military force. Only a small party, evading arrests and obstructions at Manchester and Stockport, got as far as Macclesfield; none arrived at their proclaimed destination. The 'march of the Blanketeers', similar in pattern to the colliers' more successful march with their coal waggons, has been over-dramatized because of its political character. It was in fact a

singularly clumsy and useless gesture organized by some of the wilder
Lancashire radicals. Bamford asked one of the marchers afterwards
what they would have done had they reached the capital. 'Done?'
he replied. 'Why iv wee'd nobbo' gett'n to Lunnon, we shud ha'
tan th' nation an' sattl't o'th dett.' This was Cobbettite doctrine
in its crudest vernacular form. That the prisoners taken were finally
released without trial was a sufficient proof of the harmlessness of
the whole business.

Two other incidents in that disturbed summer were scarcely more
dangerous though the intention was different and the consequences
in one case tragic. On the night of 8 June two separate bands of
men, a few hundred strong, one from Pentridge and other Derbyshire
villages, the other from parishes round Huddersfield, gathered for
action under the persuasion that a general rising of working people
was to take place next day. During the night both parties broke into
private dwelling houses to get money and arms, and in the course of
one attack a servant was killed. Their visible isolation the following
morning, when cavalry and yeomanry were sent to investigate, was
enough to disperse them. Jeremiah Brandreth, the Pentridge leader
who had committed the murder, together with two others were
arraigned for high treason before a special commission at Derby and
subsequently executed. The Huddersfield men, with fewer arrests
and no convictions, even on the minor charges of burglary which
were all that were preferred against them, escaped scot-free. The
antiquated and brutal machinery of the law, even when brought to
bear on popular disorder, was both irregular and inefficient.

III

What faced the government in 1816 and 1817 was prolonged and
widespread economic distress and social discontent, which produced
innumerable incidents of differing degrees of illegality and violence,
from simple industrial disputes to the opportunistic tactics of a few
theoretical revolutionaries. Riot and disorder were the immemorial
reaction of the common people to distress and grievance. The highly
localized outbreaks of Luddism, like the rural machine-breaking of
1816, arose from wider, more permanent features of British society:
inadequate relief in time of unemployment, bad industrial relations,
lack of accepted methods of wage negotiations, vulnerability of
employers to forcible action, absence of an effective police, and the
general weakness of the forces of law and order. Violence was

common because it was an instinctive answer and because there was
nothing to stop it in its early stages.

But Luddism was not the only product of these chaotic industrial
conditions. Trade unions were pursuing similar objects by different
methods, even though their technical illegality made their actions
equally conspiratorial and suspect. Political agitators were trying to
harness the force of popular discontent to the cause of parliamentary
reform. Between Luddism, unionism and radicalism there was no
clear line of demarcation. At different times the same sort of men
could be found engaging in all three. It was not surprising that
among the discontented and distressed there was confusion of purpose
and method, among the authorities fear and misunderstanding. Over
both lay the shadow of what had happened in Europe during the
previous twenty-five years.

Warned by the French Revolution, instructed by Burke, middle-
aged Englishmen of education and property—or a large part of them
—associated political democracy with confiscation of wealth, attacks
on the church, anarchy and military despotism. Their knowledge of
classical literature informed them that this had also been the
experience of the ancient world. The word 'Jacobin' was still part
of current political vocabulary. It was used to describe the rejection
of legal authority not based on democratic representation; but it
was a word drenched with the emotions of the recent historical past.
What was particularly frightening to many was that sympathy with
the principles of the French Revolution, which in 1793 had been the
mark of an intellectual minority, seemed after Waterloo to have
spread to the mass of the people. In 1791 the Birmingham crowd
had sacked the houses of dissenters and radicals; there were no
'Church and King mobs' after 1815. 'We must not,' Robert Southey,
the poet and political philosopher, adjured the prime minister in
March 1817, 'be blind to the signs of these perilous times. The spirit
of Jacobinism which influenced men in my sphere of life four and
twenty years ago (myself and men like me, among others) has
disappeared from that class and sunk into the rabble.'

The political radicals themselves traced their intellectual descent
from late eighteenth-century writers like Paine, Cartwright and
Burgh. In a more muted form they were carrying on the great
debate on the rights of man and the legitimacy of government
which had been opened by Burke and Paine in 1790. There were
even more extreme ideas being advocated, less important though
more obnoxious, such as the semi-socialist views on land nationaliza-
tion of that serious and speculative bookseller Thomas Spence whose
influence was perpetuated after his death in 1814 by various
Spencean Societies. More respectable were the Hampden Clubs,

formed under the inspiration of the veteran pre-war reformer, Major Cartwright, to provide a popular basis for a new parliamentary reform campaign. His missionary tours in the north and Midlands in 1812 and 1813 had resulted in the formation among workmen and artisans of Hampden Clubs and Union Societies, estimated by 1817 to number as many as a hundred and fifty. They paid a small subscription, took in radical periodicals like Cobbett's *Political Register*, and were in touch with the central Hampden Club in London.

Social discontent and radical agitation were not, however, synonymous. The East Anglian riots had no political content. Luddism was an economic and not a political protest, only differing from earlier industrial troubles by its concentrated violence in certain areas. If the tradition preserved (and perhaps somewhat dramatized) by Frank Peel in his *Risings of the Luddites* is accurate, John Baines, the old republican who in 1813 was sentenced to transportation for alleged connection with Luddite disorders, had been the leading spirit in a small group of men known as 'Tom Painers' who used to meet at a public house near Halifax. But there is no clear evidence that Baines was actually involved in the Luddite attacks; and one example alone is hardly conclusive. The evidence for the internal history of Luddism is fragmentary; but lack of information is scarcely a justification for erecting wider theories of its political motivation. The more intelligent artisans in the better-paid trades, where union organization was already established, had a slightly more sophisticated level of political interest. Among these skilled and far from illiterate workmen there was a thin but continuous tradition of radical ideas dating from the 1790s: the doctrine of the sovereignty of the people, the theory of the aristocracy as a usurping class and the conviction that the Revolutionary and Napoleonic Wars were undertaken primarily to suppress liberalism at home and maintain despotism abroad.

The working classes, like the middle classes, were made up of many layers intersected by both occupational and regional differences. Nevertheless, compared with the years before 1790, they had many more men in their ranks who were socially and politically articulate. One contributory cause at least was the spread of Methodism in the industrial districts in the fifty years preceding Waterloo. Though the claim is sometimes put forward that Methodism was the great prophylactic of the British people against revolution, the work of Methodist Sunday schools in spreading literacy among the industrial poor was a tangible element in the growth of popular political consciousness. Hone and Bamford the radicals, Lovett and Cooper the Chartists, all came from Methodist

families where the parents attached importance to education for their
children and were ready to make sacrifices for that purpose. The
adoption by the radical and Chartist movements of the system of
classes, leaders and delegates was an indication of working-class
familiarity with the Methodist organization; and many of the early
nineteenth-century popular reform movements in their earnestness
and moral fervour resembled a secular religion rather than ordinary
political associations.

It was true that the official leadership of the Wesleyan Methodist
movement was both other-worldly and politically conservative. At
the time of the Pentridge incident in 1817 the Methodist Conference
passed a resolution against disaffection; and it remained loyal to the
government over the Queen's trial in 1820 when popular feeling
was on Caroline's side. This outward political conformity, however,
concealed a conflict of ideas and classes within the Methodist movement itself. There were divisions of opinion between the poorer
chapel congregations in the centres of industrial towns and the
middle-class members of new chapels in the prosperous suburbs,
between circuit superintendents representing the official attitude and
the resident class leaders and local preachers. The increasing reliance
of the Methodist establishment on their wealthy laity, while yielding
both financial and political rewards, aroused anger and discontent
among the more proletarian rank and file.

'Our system', wrote Jabez Bunting, the great leader of the
Methodist connection in 1821, 'is not democracy. The interests of the
people it substantially provides for, but not by a plan of universal
suffrage, than which nothing could be more fatal to real liberty,
whether in church or state.' Nevertheless, Bunting had to use all his
considerable influence to keep the radical wing of Methodism in
check and preserve the facade of unity. W. H. Stephenson, a
discontented local preacher who taught in a Sunday school at Burton
colliery in the Newcastle circuit, declared in 1819 that three quarters
of the Methodists there were radical reformers. If that was an
exaggeration, it is clear at least that the decision to support the
address published by the Wesleyan Central Committee of Privileges
a few months after Peterloo, recommending the expulsion of members
who persisted in identifying themselves with factious and disloyal
political activities, led to the loss of some of the rank and file, and
strong criticism from others. The offshoots of the movement, the
Kilhamites (New Connection) and the Primitive Methodists, who
insisted on greater lay democracy in their organization, had fewer
qualms and in some areas openly took the lead in political agitation.
As for trade unionism, its early history abounds with mention
of intelligent and articulate Methodists, especially Primitive

Methodists, who occupied official positions from check-weighers and committee chairmen to county and national delegates. Two local Methodist preachers organized the miners at Kersal in Lancashire in 1818 and Tommy Hepburn, a Primitive Methodist, was the miners' leader in Northumberland and Durham at the time of the Reform Act.

The trade unions themselves were another element in the complicated social and political pattern after Waterloo. The power of JPs to fix wages, long obsolete, had been abolished in both England and Scotland in 1813. Combinations in restraint of trade, including collective action to regulate hours and wages, remained illegal until 1824. This did not prevent their existence, though it added to the suspicion with which the authorities regarded them. It was estimated in 1817 by one Home Office correspondent that there were more than twenty different trades or manufactures in which regular workers' associations existed which organized strikes for higher wages and corresponded with similar societies elsewhere. These for the most part were the aristocracy of the working classes, members of a skilled trade and when employed earning good money: seamen, shipwrights, miners, metal workers, cloth-finishers, calico printers, flax-dressers, journeymen tailors, shoemakers, bricklayers, masons and hatters.

Against these powerful associations the law was virtually inoperative. The notoriety of Pitt's combination acts of 1799–1800 has obscured both the intentions and effects of those not very important pieces of legislation. They made nothing illegal that was not illegal before; and the existing law prescribed harsher penalties than were provided by Pitt's acts. The prime object of the 1800 law was to secure a more effectual legal procedure, by authorizing summary jurisdiction by JPs in place of the dilatory and uncertain method of indictment at quarter sessions. In Scotland, where there were no combination laws, the penalties for illegal trade associations could be harsher than in England. In 1813, under the ordinary Scottish law of conspiracy, sentences of up to eighteen months imprisonment were passed on a group of Glasgow trade unionists. Pitt's act reduced the maximum penalty in England to three months imprisonment as compared with seven years transportation under previous law. The real criticism of what in some respects was a comparatively mild measure, was that whereas the older, more severe laws had been primarily designed to prevent workers from usurping the magistrate's right to fix wages, the conbination laws of 1799–1800 were passed when that alternative safeguard had in practice disappeared. The 1800 act, however, proved almost totally ineffective. The penalties were too slight to be a deterrent while recourse to the law was always unpopular. Employers were often afraid to prosecute, magistrates often reluctant to act. The government refused to undertake official prosecutions. The attitude of the Home Office was one of non-intervention except when a breach of the peace was involved. Parliament was unwilling to increase penalties and often showed sympathy with the men. The occasional warning or punitive actions by employers that came to the courts were mainly under common law.

Efforts to suppress unions through the law, like attempts to break strikes by force, tended to lead to further disorder, sometimes on a spectacular scale. In 1820 an attempt was made by magistrates at Swansea to commit thirteen copper-smelters for illegal combination. Their fellow-workmen prevented them from being taken to gaol and when three of them were subsequently arrested and lodged in Swansea prison, a crowd of over a hundred men armed with bludgeons marched into the town, broke open the prison and fetched them out. At Coalbrookdale the following year colliers, on strike against reduced wages, went round closing the ironworks. When a body of yeomanry cavalry were sent to intercept them, the miners, about 3,000 strong, took up a defensive position on some slag tips. In the skirmish which followed one rioter was killed, another died later of injuries and six were committed for trial at the next assize. Social conflict of this nature was clearly not indefinitely sustainable. By the mid-1820s it was obvious to many magistrates and employers that they were fighting a losing battle against the unions. Some believed that wages were better left to the ordinary laws of supply and demand; a few were frankly pessimistic. A manufacturer (who was also a JP) in Glasgow complained in 1823 that 'by combined resistance and private intimidation, the servants are rendering themselves absolute masters of the will and the property of their employers' not only in fixing the level of wages but in regulating terms of work and types of men employed.

The methods used by the trade unions to enforce discipline and punish blacklegs were various, and sometimes not pretty. The Glasgow cotton spinners had an ugly habit of throwing vitriol at the faces of their victims. In the northeast, among the coastal seamen of Sunderland and Tyneside, there was a practice of tarring and feathering, sometimes exposure in a homemade pillory, even for minor offences like absence without explanation from union meetings. Elsewhere reports of gunpowder explosions, pistol shots from unseen assailants, attacks on individuals and damage to private houses, all contributed to the impression of violence which frequently surrounded trade union activities. The outbreak of Luddism in Nottinghamshire in 1814 was preceded and probably provoked by the failure of the framework-knitters' Nottingham Union, founded in 1812, to obtain an increase in the rates they were paid; and there was a strong suspicion in 1816 that the Luddite gangs were directed by some form of union committee. Though direct connection between the unions and the machine-breakers was difficult to prove, it was not easy for authorities to discriminate. The inevitable secrecy of their discussions, the oaths that were exacted of loyalty and silence, the well guarded meetings in public houses, the camouflage of Friendly Societies, the despatch of delegates to different parts of the country, even the occasional processions with banners and music through the streets, helped to make magistrates and politicians regard trade unions with uneasiness and suspicion.

There was, however, a more direct sense in which Southey's remark that Jacobinism had descended to the masses was justified. In many ways the industrial unrest of 1816–17 marked the end of Midlands Luddism and the conversion of a substantial body of working-class opinion to parliamentary reform. Machine-breaking did little to improve conditions. Whether intended merely to intimidate specific employers into abandoning objectionable practices or giving higher prices for finished piecework, which was the main object of the hosiers and lacemakers in the Midlands, or to limit competition with the skilled hand-workers which was the motive of the croppers or cloth-finishers in the West Riding, the effect of Luddite disorders was transitory. Machine-breaking was primarily a weapon of coercion, a kind of ungentle industrial bargaining. In itself it could do little to solve the problems of the hand-workers whose prosperity was bound up with the industry to which they belonged and who could do little even if they wished to prevent the steady growth of machine technology.

The man who more than any other helped to turn the thoughts of the discontented working classes to parliamentary reform was William Cobbett. In his *Letter to the Luddites* he argued the folly of opposing machinery and in the winter of 1816 he began publishing reprints of articles from his *Political Register* in the form of unstamped twopenny pamphlets designed for a wider public. Simultaneously he announced his support for manhood suffrage rather than the enfranchisement of all direct taxpayers which he had been advocating only shortly before. The most powerful single influence in popular journalism was now on the side of Cartwright and the democratic radicals as opposed to the more dilettante and aristocratic Sir Francis Burdett.

Cobbett was a tory radical rather than a doctrinaire democrat; and his conversion to the extreme radical views of Hunt and Cartwright came comparatively late. To the end his real targets were

corruption, sinecures, taxation and the national debt. He took up
parliamentary reform only because he became convinced that the
House of Commons in its existing form would never accept the
drastic financial programme he advocated. Parliamentary reform
for him was merely a means to an end; but once he adopted it,
he was able to offer his working-class followers an attractive and
immediate political alternative to Luddism. 'He directed his readers',
wrote Bamford in a classic passage, 'to the true cause of their
sufferings—misgovernment; and to its proper corrective—parliamentary reform'.

There was of course a profound fallacy in Cobbett's teaching.
Misgovernment was not the cause of social distress after 1815; nor
was the country being particularly ill and certainly not extravagantly
governed at any time between 1815 and 1830. The first Reform Act
when it came was therefore a disappointment to the working classes;
and it is hard to believe that manhood suffrage in 1832 would have
brought them any greater benefit. What was important, however,
was that they were led to believe that parliamentary reform would
benefit them. At a time when opposition politicians and the respectable middle classes were singularly cool in their approach to this
fifty-year-old issue, it was taken up with enthusiasm by the discontented industrial proletariat. Not until a dozen years after
Cobbett's death in 1835 did this faith, which he had done more
than any other single man to instil, begin to lose its hold on the
working classes.

Parliamentary reform, moreover, as argued by Cobbett, was not
an abstract issue but directly related to contemporary politics. To
demand a reconstruction of the legislature was to condemn the
parliamentary oligarchy; to assert misgovernment was to condemn
the persons and policies of the ministers. To impute to both responsibility for the state of the country was to suggest a degree of
political culpability almost amounting to moral crime. Much of the
savagery of post-Waterloo politics derived from a genuine conviction
of the personal blame attaching to government for all that was
happening in the country. For those growing to manhood in these
post-war years it was one of the formative influences of their life.
Thomas Cooper, the future Chartist leader, as a schoolboy in Gainsborough between 1816 and 1820 made friends with the men in a
brush-making shop close to his home, all 'determined politicians' and
followers of Cobbett, Wooler and Hunt. They lent him radical
literature and talked to him of those 'villainous rascals' Castlereagh,
Sidmouth and Eldon, 'until I hated the Liverpool Ministry, and its
master, bitterly, and believed that the sufferings of the poor were
chiefly attributable to them'.

The popular radical press of Cobbett and Wooler, the provincial tours of radical orators, the network of Hampden and other political clubs, provided working-class radicals with a measure of national unity. Cartwright, Hunt, Cobbett and Burdett in the metropolis constituted a kind of collective national leadership. But what was of more importance than the details of this rudimentary radical organization was that social discontent was being harnessed to a specific political objective. The aristocracy of radical leadership was never a very cordial or united group. Burdett was indolent and snobbish, Hunt vain and domineering, Cartwright old and complacent, Cobbett rough and dogmatic. They fought jealously to safeguard their own personal prestige; and their differences over policy were as much temperamental as tactical. Demagogues rarely make good bedfellows. Yet in their different ways they were men of personality and talent; they believed in their cause; and they offered at least the appearance of powerful leadership by men of national reputation and higher social standing then the masses to whom they appealed.

IV

Confronted with a situation of such confusion and complexity, it was understandable that ministers found it difficult to distinguish accurately between causes and effects, Luddism and bread riots, distress and sedition, social protest and political subversion. Disorder presented itself not as a single identifiable problem but as a succession of regional symptoms, indicating a kind of social 'distemper' (to use a word which came naturally to their minds) of whose real nature and origin they could not be sure.

For distress among the poor in time of trade depression there was a considerable amount of public sympathy and a general readiness to subscribe to relief funds. In addition there was often sharp criticism of manufacturers, especially from clergy, magistrates, and army officers who were the classes professionally involved in the consequences of disorder. At Manchester in 1819 public opinion was clearly on the side of the weavers, the most distressed of all the various trades which went on strike in that disturbed summer. In Coventry the following year, when the ribbon-makers stopped work in protest against a reduction in the prices paid for their work, the magistrates asked the master manufacturers to consider increasing the amount—for which they received the public thanks of the men.

Sometimes the better employers themselves protested against the action of their competitors in lowering wages. In Leicester during the troubles of 1817 the poor law authorities, no doubt with a prudent eye on the rates, put themselves on the side of the framework-knitters against the masters. Most of the parishes concerned agreed not to sanction the supplementation of low wages out of the poor rate and to relieve workmen who gave up their frames in protest against low prices. There was, one JP reported, 'a sort of warfare between the parish officers and the hosiers'. Though the magistrates tried to preserve the impartiality of their position, their sympathies too were clearly with the men. 'Such is their .predilection for the stockingers (and the men are all aware of this)', wrote one aggrieved master hosier to the Home Secretary, 'that it is next to impossible to maintain any kind of subordination.' At one stage in the long dispute the employers were so resentful that they contemplated indicting the lord lieutenant, mayor, aldermen and clergy who subscribed to the relief fund for the stockingers on a charge of criminal conspiracy to keep up wages.

The rioters and strikers themselves often appealed to other social classes to assist them; their dislike was directed against individuals, not (initially at least) against the well-to-do or the authorities. Only when more peaceful methods of securing redress failed did their mood tend to harden. In this there was something more than a tactical move to obtain sympathy. There was a long tradition among workmen of looking to the law for protection. Elizabethan legislation had enshrined in statutory form the right of the magistrate to fix a fair rate of wages, of the able-bodied to be given work, and of the infirm to be given aid. The appeals and petitions from workmen in different trades to the king, the House of Commons and magistrates in quarter session that had been common in the eighteenth century continued in the nineteenth. A feature of the Luddite troubles was the recurrent appeal to authority. One Luddite publication put it into rhyme.

> Let the wise and the great lend their aid and advice,
> Nor e'er their assistance withdraw,
> Till full fashioned work at the old fashioned price
> Is established by custom and law.

Similar appeals were common in other industrial disputes. At Sunderland in 1817 there was a request by seamen on strike to the rector of Wearmouth and another magistrate to mediate between them and the shipowners. At Oldham in 1818 the weavers put out a printed address to the gentlemen and landowners of the district giving a statement (a remarkably reasonable one) of their grievances. In 1819 at Nottingham the framework-knitters on strike made an appeal in pathetic terms to 'the Nobility, Gentry and Clergy of the

County' and in particular to the duke of Newcastle as lord lieutenant. 'You have been so good as to look upon me as a friend,' wrote the duke when responding to the appeal. He went to Nottingham and advised the hosiers to grant the men the full price for their work that they were asking.

As long as workmen carried on their industrial disputes peaceably, the manufacturers tended to be an isolated group. It was when disorder and destruction of property began that the authorities had to intervene against the men and public sympathy cooled. A similar effect was produced by the introduction of political objectives and organization. It was a distinction also noticeable in the attitude of the government towards industrial unrest. As far as purely industrial disputes were concerned, the Home Office uniformly urged the removal of points of conflict rather than resistance and repression. During the disturbances on Tyneside in 1815 Sidmouth was critical both of the shipowners for refusing to meet their men and of the magistrates for not attempting mediation. Though he agreed that the forcible blockade of the port must cease, he deprecated subsequent action against any but the most prominent offenders. Military commanders were instructed that disputes between masters and men were private matters and they should only intervene if there was an actual breach of the peace. Requests for stiffening the law against trade combinations received a discouraging reply. The law officers advised, for example, against any attempt to prosecute the men concerned in the attempt to form a general union of trades at Manchester in 1819. During the Manchester strike of 1818 the Home Office observed that the weavers appeared to have just ground for their complaints and if so, the masters should raise their wages. Government had reason to complain, wrote Hobhouse, the under-secretary to a JP at Prestwich, of manufacturers who provoked combinations 'by relying on the support of the law instead of considering the justice of the demands made on them'.

On the other hand the Home Office was in certain circumstances ready to advise manufacturers to make use of the law when it appeared that there was a general conspiracy of unions to intimidate them, and magistrates to watch and if necessary prosecute political agitators who seemed to be fomenting industrial trouble. Like many magistrates and gentry the Home Office officials were convinced not only of the widespread activity of what Hobhouse once called 'disaffected demagogues' but of the existence among them of a general wish to start a national revolution. Though the evidence available to the government was fragmentary, there was enough to give colour to this theory and not enough to disprove it. The ignorance and delusion on both sides was compounded by some of the sources on which the authorities relied for their information. The case of Oliver the spy in 1817 brought odium on Lord Sidmouth as Home Secretary because it was taken up by the press and the parliamentary opposition. But spies had been used by Sidmouth's predecessors and continued to be employed after him by Peel. In fact general use was made of spies and informers not only by the Home Office but by local JPs, borough officials and district military commanders; and a good deal of public money was disbursed in this way. An intelligence and security service, often with regular soldiers or militiamen operating in plain clothes, was a standard feature of military organization in the disturbed districts. The metropolitan magistrates used spies to find out what was going on in the Spencean Societies and Hampden Clubs of London. In Scotland similar agents were employed by the Lord Advocate's office. The Home Office itself was constantly approached by people who wanted to give, or rather sell, information in times of disorder. With no national police force, no trained detectives other than a handful of Bow Street runners, the authorities would have been even more ignorant and helpless had they not made use of such means to get warning of trouble beforehand and evidence for conviction afterwards. They would have been negligent in their duties had they not done so.

But the use of amateur agents is a hazardous practice. The tendency of spies and agents was to emphasize the political element in economic disputes, to exaggerate the size and ramifications of the organizations they uncovered, and, worst of all, to stimulate the illegal activities which it was their business to report to their employers. To make themselves acceptable to local radicals men like Oliver would claim to be delegates from a central organization in London; and this in turn helped to foster among the more credulous and violent provincials the idea of a nationwide conspiracy. It is difficult otherwise to account for the two simultaneous incidents near Nottingham and Huddersfield in June 1817. Brandreth, the leader of the Pentridge 'rising', certainly attributed his tragic end to Oliver. The authorities were not blind to the difficulty of finding suitable agents and the unreliability of many of those employed; but even with these allowances, the weight and consistency of the information which accumulated were enough to convince minds already predisposed to belief. Not all spies were *agents provocateurs*; not all of them were useless. But at best they were defective and at worst deceptive instruments.

Information from such sources, even though the most dubious reports were discarded, was among the evidence placed before the secret committees appointed by both houses of parliament at the start of the 1817 session to consider the state of the country. The disorders of 1816, culminating in a series of political reform meetings in England and Scotland during the autumn, and the Spa Fields riot in December, had decided the government to seek additional powers. The cabinet was by then honestly convinced that the 'disaffected demagogues' were deliberately trying to stir up revolution. When Hunt at the first Spa Fields meeting appeared with the insignia of the French Revolution—a pike, a cap of liberty and a tricolour flag— and a 'Committee of Public Safety' was formed in London to organize radical petitions to parliament, it was not difficult to accept that there were grounds for an enquiry. The only difference between ministers was that Sidmouth wanted to arm himself immediately with emergency powers, Liverpool wished to make a convincing case before asking parliament to legislate.

In the third week of February the two committees made their reports. They omitted on security grounds the detailed evidence on which they had arrived at their conclusions but the tenor of both documents was the same. Under the guise of societies and clubs, some ostensibly seeking parliamentary reform, others of a different character, there was an organized revolutionary movement in existence, even though the activities of these secret clubs and societies were largely confined to the lower classes and to the industrial areas of Lancashire and the Midlands in England and the Glasgow area in Scotland. By the end of March the government was given the legislation it asked for: compulsory licensing of rooms used for political meetings, a prohibition on federations of societies and meetings of over fifty persons without magistrates' permission, dissolution of the Spencean societies, suspension of *habeas corpus* for persons arrested on charges of treason, and the death penalty for inciting members of the armed forces to mutiny. Independent opinion in parliament was strongly behind the ministers; the whigs, divided on the issue, could only muster a token opposition. If the government's information was substantially true, and the opposition was in no position to disprove it, action was clearly demanded. All men of forty or more could remember how the weakness of authority in the early days of the French Revolution had led on to anarchy. Those, who like Lord Grenville had even older memories, could recollect how, for lack of judicious firmness at the outset, the Gordon riots of 1780 had handed the capital over to a drunken and marauding mob. Though the Commons were still harrying the government over retrenchment, they were happy to give them what powers seemed necessary to preserve law and order. 'We separated,' wrote Castlereagh with satisfaction at the end of the session, 'the question of economy from that of seditious reform.' He added: 'and we became masters of both'; but that was premature rejoicing.

In the event the effects of the 1817 measures (including a further suspension of *habeas corpus* from June to January 1818) were both slight and temporary. In all forty-four persons were arrested by the government on suspicion of treason. Of these thirty-seven were detained, of whom one was soon released, another discharged on compassionate grounds and a third died in prison. Of the remaining thirty-four, committed on sworn evidence to detention, all by January 1818 had been released; most of them by early December. It was not exactly a reign of terror. The parliamentary committees at least were satisfied that the powers entrusted to the executive government had been exercised with as much leniency as circumstances allowed. A more subjective account of what happened was later provided by Bamford, the Lancashire radical. Arrested at the end of March, he was taken to London, examined by the Privy Council and finally released at the end of April with an avuncular warning from Lord Sidmouth. After being given a present of some clothes and taken to see the sights of the town by one of the king's messengers who had escorted him from Lancashire, he was put on a coach for home—and a prompt renewal of his radical activities at Middleton.

It was true that the Hampden and other clubs were for a time discontinued; and Cobbett (still under sureties for keeping the peace after his release from prison in 1812) fled to America to avoid possible costly legal action against his 'Twopenny Trash'. But once established overseas he resumed publication of the *Register* and in the interval the gap was filled by two other radical publications started at the beginning of 1817—Wooler's *Black Dwarf* and the *Reformist Register* published by Hone and Francis Place. It was characteristic of executive weakness that the government was totally unable to control the press. Sidmouth's circular of March 1817, reminding magistrates that persons selling seditious literature could be arrested and held to bail, evoked little response in the provinces. The government's own venture into the quicksands of press prosecutions was singularly unlucky. Douglas, a preacher charged with using seditious language in a sermon, was acquitted in the High Court of Justiciary at Edinburgh in May. Hone, whose profane and witty parodies of the Creed, Litany, and Catechism were regarded by the pious as peculiarly offensive, was found not guilty of blasphemous libel by sympathetic London jurymen in December to the cheers of the waiting multitude. The only effect was to give Hone's works gratuitous publicity and create an eager public for the full account of the trials which he promptly published with lavish quotations from the offending material. A public subscription was raised which enabled him to set up in a larger bookshop and continue, in alliance with the caricaturist George Cruickshank, those illustrated rhyming satires on the ministry which were one of the most effective pieces of radical propaganda during the next two or three years. The government could not compete with this kind of popular journalism; nor did it want (or would have been given) the extraordinary censorship powers which alone could have repressed it.

Further reports from the secret committees in February 1818, devoted mainly to the Nottingham and Huddersfield incidents of the previous June, kept alive the notion that a general rising had been contemplated even if not actually organized. While paying tribute to the loyalty of the great mass of the population, the committees emphasized the danger of the prevalent doctrine that economic distress was caused by the defects in the constitution and warned magistrates not to relax their vigilance. The warning was soon justified. In the summer there were signs that political clubs and associations were starting up once more in the industrial areas, and the movement became unmistakable with the appearance of Political Protestant Societies and Union Clubs the following year. There was even (to the scandal of the old-fashioned) a Female Reform Society at Blackburn which urged the wives and daughters of the working classes to instil into their children 'a deeply rooted hatred of our tyrannical rulers'. That the efforts of Cartwright, Cobbett and Hunt during the past few years were beginning to bear fruit was shown by the events of 1819. In that year a serious attempt was made by the radical reformers, as they were now known, to overcome the resistance of the governing classes by means of mass demonstrations. The campaign was launched in January at a parliamentary reform meeting at Manchester where banners bearing the mottoes 'Rights of Man', 'Universal Suffrage' and 'No Corn Laws' were prominently displayed. Hunt, the principal speaker, told his audience that mere petitioning of parliament was useless and advised them to come forward as Englishmen to claim their rights. In June there was a series of mass meetings in the industrial districts of Lancashire, Yorkshire, the Midlands and the west of Scotland. Though peaceably conducted, the burden of the speeches at all these meetings was the same. The sufferings of the people were due to the inadequacies and extravagance of government and the remedy lay in annual parliaments and universal suffrage.

What was particularly objectionable in the eyes of the constitutionalists was the spread of the idea implicit in the Spencean 'Union of non-represented people' movement of 1818, that the doctrine of popular sovereignty and the rights of man justified the formal election of representatives in those large towns which were not parliamentary boroughs. From this it was only a step to the assertion that a national convention or assembly had the authority to override a parliament which had ceased to be a true representation of the people.[1] The radicals themselves perhaps did not fully appreciate the sensitivity of the governing class to this implicit challenge to the legislature. Since the final victory over Stuart despotism in 1688, parliament had been regarded by all conventional constitutional writers as the palladium of British liberties. To suggest that another elected body might replace its authority was even more subversive than a campaign for its reform. It was this implicitly revolutionary movement, rather than the simple demands for universal suffrage and annual parliaments, that was the forerunner to Peterloo.

In June and July mass meetings were held at Stockport, Oldham, Leeds, Birmingham, London and Manchester. At Birmingham in July a crowd, variously estimated as between 15,000 and 30,000, elected by show of hands the eccentric aristocratic radical Sir Charles Wolseley (a lesser Burdett who had been at the Stockport meeting and sent an encouraging message to the Birmingham one) as their 'legislatorial attorney and representative of Birmingham'. A meeting at Leeds resolved to follow this example as soon as a suitable person could be found. Wooler, who was present at the Birmingham meeting, welcomed these developments because he believed that they would bring to a head the conflict between the aristocracy and the people. Other radicals, less doctrinaire and certainly less explicit, probably saw in them no more than a flamboyant advertisement for the claims of the unrepresented towns. The Home Office seemed more of Wooler's opinion and reacted sharply. Wolseley was arrested and held to bail for his seditious language at Stockport; and at the end of the month a royal proclamation was issued against seditious and treasonable meetings, particularly those claiming 'in gross violation of the law' to elect representatives to sit in the Commons. Fortified by the legal advice of the Home Office, the local magistrates issued a warning against a third meeting, for the same purpose as at Birmingham, which was planned for 9 August in Manchester. The Manchester Radical Union then decided to postpone the meeting until 16 August when they would proceed not to elect a representative but merely (in a careful phrase) consider the propriety of adopting legal and effective measures to obtain a reform of parliament. It was to be addressed by Hunt, the oratorical idol of the radical movement.

On 16 August occurred the confusion, errors and bloodshed at St Peter's Field. The magistrates decided to arrest Hunt on the hustings before he could speak. The size of the crowd, probably about 60,000, made the use of the military for this purpose necessary. By accident the local yeomanry arrived before the regular force of

[1] T. M. Persinnen, 'Association, convention and anti-parliament in British radical politics 1771–1848', *EHR* LXXXVIII.

hussars. The yeomanry almost instantly got into difficulties from the denseness of the crowd, obstructions on the ground and their own indiscipline. They were believed to be under attack and the hussars were sent in to extricate them. When it was all over about a dozen people were dead or dying, some hundreds badly injured. The country was shocked at the news; and within a week 'Peterloo', the satiric title coined with reference to the government's other great military victory at Waterloo, had passed into the political vocabulary of the British nation. Simultaneously Lord Sidmouth expressed the thanks of the Prince Regent to the Manchester magistrates and yeomanry for their 'prompt, decisive and efficient measures for the preservation of the public tranquillity'.

Peterloo was a blunder; it was hardly a massacre. Possibly half the deaths, probably even more of the non-fatal injuries, were among those who were trampled underfoot by horses and the crowd in the panic that ensued. The public indignation was a mark both of the strong liberal feeling in the country and of the general restraint normally exercised by the authorities in dealing with large political assemblies. It was because Peterloo was uncharacteristic that it achieved notoriety. The magistrates had made two mistakes: in endeavouring to arrest Hunt at the meeting, and in sending in the amateur, unpopular and politically minded Manchester and Salford Yeomanry, a raw volunteer unit formed after the Blanketeers' March incident two years earlier. The Manchester JPs were men of only ordinary ability; they shared the alarms and credulity of their class. Their nerves had been stretched by the protracted disputes among the cotton spinners and the series of political meetings in 1819. The radicals with growing confidence had been using increasingly inflammatory language. Wolseley at Stockport had talked of storming the English Bastille; Hunt at the Smithfield meeting in London had spoken in defence of a resolution not to obey laws not passed by a freely elected democratic assembly.

There had been actions as well as words. A police officer escorting the Reverend Joseph Harrison, a Methodist preacher and leading Stockport radical arrested on the hustings at Smithfield (an unhappy precedent for Peterloo), was pistolled by a young weaver on arrival back at Stockport and was fortunate to survive. Another cause of alarm to the magistracy was the growing habit among the political unions of marching and drilling. Processions with music and flags were a feature of working-class demonstrations in the industrial areas. Perhaps it was a tradition inherited from town trade guilds or rustic feasts and revels. At all events it added colour and pageantry to lives that had little enough of such things. Practically it could be justified, or at least rationalized, as a method of getting large bodies of people into a limited space with order and despatch. But the presence among the radical clubs of regular army veterans and ex-militiamen made the drilling take a pronounced military form, even to the extent of carrying sticks and clapping the hands as if to simulate a volley of musketry. The day before Peterloo, in the small hours of the morning, a constable with a few companions came across a body of several hundred men drilling on White Moss, some five miles from Manchester. He was attacked, beaten with sticks, and made to swear that he would never be a king's man.

Given the atmosphere of panic and revolution in Manchester at the time, the conduct of the magistrates on 16 August was under-standable. It was foolish but not vindictive. Had they weighed more attentively the advice of the Home Office, hardened by long official experience, the disaster would not have occurred. The officials at Whitehall, in particular Sidmouth and his under-secretary Hob-house, were always careful to stress that meetings and speeches should not be deemed illegal until they had proved themselves to be so, that the dispersal of crowds and the arrest of individuals was a matter of expediency, timing and judgement. But the Home Office, distant twenty-four hours and nearly two hundred miles from the scene of the trouble, was obliged to leave a reasonable latitude of decision to the men on the spot. It was this which made it impossible subsequently to disown their actions. For the maintenance of law and order in the provinces the magistracy—unpaid, voluntary and amateur—was the government's first line of defence; behind them there was nothing but the army. To have penalized the Manchester JPs for an error of judgement committed in trying circumstances would have shaken the morale of the magistracy all over the king-dom. 'When I say that the proceedings of the magistrates at Manchester on the 16th. ult. were justifiable,' the prime minister wrote to Canning, 'you will understand me as not by any means deciding that the course which they pursued on that occasion was in all its parts prudent ... but ... there remained no alternative but to support them.' As it was, the government was already finding considerable difficulty in getting magistrates to act.

In itself Peterloo neither overawed the radicals nor drove the government into panic measures. There were immediate meetings of protest at Leeds, Birmingham and other industrial towns, even a second minor Peterloo during September at Paisley in Scotland. There, despite a warning from magistrates, the reformers persisted in holding a mass outdoor meeting. An attempt by the authorities to break up a procession through the town afterwards was resisted; and a general riot ensued in which over a period of several days houses were gutted and people robbed. In the end cavalry had to be brought from Glasgow to restore order; but though there were many wounded, there was no loss of life. What disturbed the government was not Peterloo or Paisley but the attempt of the whig opposition to make political capital out of the widespread public indignation. Sidmouth, it was true, pressed immediately for stronger legislative sanctions; but he had been of that opinion even before 16 August. Lord Liverpool was more restrained. He did not want an early meeting of parliament which would only advertise the government's alarm; and he thought that it would be unwise to ask for fresh powers until the mood of the country gentlemen was ascertained.

During September, however, with some hesitation and initial disunion, the whigs took up Peterloo as a political issue. Whig politicians addressed urban protest meetings; and preparations were made for organizing a series of county meetings. Nine in fact took place in October and November; five more were attempted but without success; two were planned but abandoned when parliament was summoned. It was not exactly a national campaign; but it came near to one and it effectively put the whigs at the head of the country-wide movement of protest. The crucial event was the meeting in Yorkshire where the requisition had been supported by the lord lieutenant, Earl Fitzwilliam, one of the wealthiest and most influential of the whig peers. His example stiffened the wavering resolution of whigs elsewhere and decided the government to appeal to parliament. Within a few days the lines of party battle hardened still further. The Prince Regent, in a reply to an address from liverymen of the City of London, had already condemned the demand for an enquiry into the Manchester affair. Fitzwilliam's public support for the resolution of the Yorkshire meeting, which both called for an enquiry and attacked the ministry, was clearly an improper action for a lord lieutenant, the local representative of the crown. His prompt dismissal closed the ranks of the opposition and advertised to the ministerial supporters that the government was in earnest.

The summoning of parliament in November and the Six Acts were therefore as much a product of parliamentary party warfare as of the actual state of the country. Outside the central industrial areas of England and the west of Scotland, in fact, there had been little disturbance. By November even the industrial areas had quietened down; the harvest was good; and trade was reviving. Only in Scotland, where reports were flying round in the late autumn of an intended rising by the radical weavers of Glasgow and the respectable citizens of Edinburgh mustered in an Armed Association, did the alarms continue until the end of the year. But for the government the only effective answer to whig propaganda in the country was a full

debate in the Commons; and to justify the premature recall of
parliament the ministers had to be ready with emergency legislation
proposals. In the event, besides the gloomy encouragement of Lord
Grenville who told the prime minister in November that 'the object
of effecting a revolution in this country by inflaming the worst
passions of the lowest orders of society has been unremittedly pursued
for many years past', soundings among government supporters
showed a feeling in favour of strong action. When the Commons met,
a whig demand for an enquiry into Peterloo was easily defeated
and the subsequent debates on the six bills brought forward by the
government placed the opposition in an uncomfortable position. The
Grenvillites and the independent members evinced a gratifying desire
to stand by the ministers at a time when law, order and property
were threatened; and aided by the readiness of the government to
accept amendments from the floors of both Houses, all the emergency
legislation went through by the end of the year.

The sinister reputation of the Six Acts, as they became known in
radical and popular vocabulary, is hardly borne out by an
examination of their contents. The two that involved most interference with personal liberty—those giving power to magistrates to
search for arms in specified towns and counties and prohibiting
unauthorized mass meetings for political purposes—were only
temporary and were not renewed when they expired. Three others—
to prevent delays in legal processes, stop evasion of the newspaper
stamp duty, and provide for the destruction of publications found
by the courts to be blasphemous or seditious libels—were merely
attempts to amend defects in existing law. The facilities open to the
accused to delay both trial and sentence, in cases involving blas-
phemy or treasonable conspiracy, had long been a source of embarrassment. By traversing (that is, denying) the indictment, a step
which automatically secured postponement to a subsequent session,
and then moving in arrest of judgement at the postponed trial,
defendants released on bail could enjoy up to twelve months'
immunity during which they were free to repeat the original offence
as often as they liked. The sixth act, forbidding unauthorized military
organizations and training, was a prohibition which most modern
governments regard as essential.

The real criticism of the Six Acts is not that they put a powerful
instrument of coercion in the hands of the executive, but that for
the most part they were misdirected and ineffective. The violent
scenes at the time of the Queen's trial a year later and the flood
of libellous radical publications which accompanied it, were clear
proof of the inefficiency of any laws which government could devise,
and parliament would accept, for the purpose of repressing popular

agitation. At the same time the relative moderation of the 1819 legislation, and the scrupulousness with which ministers and law officers handled the traditional British rights of free speech and free assembly, reflected their desire to work within the framework of the constitution and avoid any imputation of arbitrary action. Lord Liverpool was always conscious of the need to distinguish between deliberate political agitation and genuine social grievance. His legislation, both in 1817 and 1819, was simply designed to isolate and muzzle the agitators. If he over-reacted, it was because of lack of reliable information on the exact extent of seditious activities and a prudent desire to run no risks. His policy was primarily a preventive one. Firmness at the outset would make unnecessary more stringent action later on. To enforce law and order, to reassure the timid and peaceable, was in his judgement the best way of avoiding any slide towards arbitrary rule. His argument in the House of Lords in November 1819 that what the government proposed was 'in furtherance of the principles of the constitution, and for the purpose of protecting the people of this country against a series of evils which, if not checked, must subvert their laws and liberties' was not only an expression of honest opinion but based on more substance than subsequent critics have been ready to credit. At bottom his object was to preserve the rule of law.

The problem before cabinet and parliament in these years can easily be underestimated. All the evidence that came to them from magistrates, army officers and their own spies, indicated the existence of networks of local political reform societies, the circulation of inflammatory and sometimes subversive literature, the constant movement of delegates between the provinces and London, some purchase and manufacture of arms, and surreptitious drilling. The severe hardships and discontents in the industrial areas easily led to widespread rioting; government powers to repress disorder were limited; the small peace establishment army was already stretched to the limit. Both cabinet and parliament could be excused for thinking there was a real danger, that additional powers were necessary, and that they should be used firmly. As late as the spring of 1820 the clash between yeomanry and a party of armed Glasgow weavers at Bonnymuir near Falkirk, and the appearance in the Huddersfield and Barnsley districts of bands of radical workmen carrying pikes and pistols, kept alive the fears of a general rising. The whig opposition were right in asserting that there was no organized national conspiracy; but their views were as much based on belief and conjecture as those of the government, perhaps more so. They made much in 1817 of the provocative activities of Oliver (first uncovered by the *Leeds Mercury*) but the use of spies did not create, it merely exaggerated the danger. It was inevitable that some action would be taken by the ministers. They were often urged to do more; they could hardly have done less.

Towards the poor in general the attitude of the ministry was paternalistic rather than repressive. It was true that the teaching of the classical economists pointed to the uselessness if not actual harmfulness of state interference in economic matters; and the poverty of means at the government's disposal seriously limited executive initiative. Nevertheless, as practical politicians the cabinet did not allow the doctrinaire philosophy of *laissez-faire* to dictate their actions. Lord Liverpool, for example, warmly supported the first Sir Robert Peel's campaign to regulate the employment of children in textile mills which secured the act of 1819. The previous year the Church Building Act allocated a million pounds for new churches in urban and industrial areas—the first time since the reign of Anne that the state had taken any responsibility for the spiritual and educational needs of the population. There was a trickle of other remedial legislation. In 1816 discharged soldiers were allowed to set up in trade in any part of the kingdom. In the disturbed and distressed year 1817 a truck act was extended to cover workmen in collieries and the iron and steel industries; a second act was passed to encourage savings banks; and a third (even more remarkable for the principle it embodied) empowered the crown to advance loans for public works and fisheries in the United Kingdom with the object of providing employment for the poor. In 1819 an act was passed to encourage Friendly Societies, those early manifestations of self-help on the part of the rural and industrial working classes, by giving them specific safeguards and privileges. Little of this well intended but limited legislation was very effective in practice; but at least it demonstrated that the government was not without a social conscience and in certain circumstances was prepared to ignore prevailing economic theory.

The judicial consequences of Peterloo were relatively slight. The following March Hunt, Bamford, and two others were found guilty of unlawful assembly. After the usual delays Hunt was sentenced to thirty months' imprisonment, the others to one year. Hunt served his time in Ilchester gaol, a bad prison where his treatment seems to have been unusually harsh. Bamford and the others, sent to Lincoln prison, were sympathetically handled by the local magistrates and lived comfortably until the time came for their release. Bamford was allowed to have his wife with him, and to receive letters, newspapers, pamphlets, and money from well-wishers and fellow-reformers in the country. Sir Francis Burdett, who after Peterloo had written a characteristically provocative letter to his

Westminster constituents, speaking of a 'reign of terror and blood' and comparing the Prince Regent with James II, was found guilty of seditious libel, fined £2,000 (a heavy fine but he was an extremely wealthy man) and sentenced to three months' imprisonment. Wolseley and Harrison, for their part in the Stockport meeting, were sentenced to eighteen months. How little this served to damp down the radical reform movement was seen by the resurgence of the radical press, the return of Cobbett in November 1819, and Burdett's triumphant victory at the top of poll for Westminster in the 1820 election. Even Thistlewood's vicious but crack-brained Cato Street conspiracy to assassinate the cabinet in February 1820, of which the government had prior warning through their agents, did little to rally uncommitted opinion. For by the spring of 1820 the 'Queen's affair' was about to usher in the worst political crisis that Liverpool's harassed government ever had to face.

4 The Government and the State of the Nation

I

It was a mark of the admirable British mixture of liberty and security, wrote a political pamphleteer approvingly in 1821, that 'while no Administration in England can withstand the sentiments of the people, the Government is always able to despise the clamour of the mob'.[1] But while in 1819 the clamour of the mob had been disregarded, it was painfully clear that Lord Liverpool and his colleagues had not been able to enlist the sentiments of the people. The same anonymous but sympathetic writer observed discouragingly that 'the Ministers who had gained a considerable degree of credit for their conduct of the war, had lost it almost entirely by the occurrences of the peace'. While few sensible men believed that the government was responsible for the ills of society, many illogically but understandably felt that there was something lacking in their efforts. The ministers had been in power for many years; all the post-war distress and disorder, if not caused by their actions, had happened under their administration. Yet they had done little that was constructive; they had shown no clear line of policy even within the accepted sphere of governmental responsibility. They had lived by shifts and contrivances; when not actually in retreat, they had been on the defence.

For a cabinet whose influence depended in large part on its prestige, this decline in public confidence was both ominous and demoralizing. A feature of the first post-war general election in 1818, noted the Grenvillite W. W. Wynn, was 'the unwillingness of most of the new members to be considered as belonging to Government'. Ward, a Canningite, remarked on the additional strength and confidence of the opposition. 'The government don't seem much beloved. It has quite spent the popularity of the war.' Huskisson

---

[1] *A Political View of The Times; or A Dispassionate Enquiry into the Manners and Conduct of the Ministry and Opposition*, anon. (London 1821), p. 139.

reported to the prime minster from Sussex that radical propaganda was affecting even the farming community. 'They despise the Whigs; but they are no longer what they were ten years ago in their attachment to the old Tory interests and principles which are prevalent in the Nobility and Gentry. . . . Be assured that the feeling is strong in the country, that we have not done enough.' Peel, the ablest of the administration's young men, settling down in England after six arduous years as Irish secretary, was struck by the gap which seemed to have opened up between opinion in the country and the policy of the cabinet. 'Do not you think,' he asked his friend Croker in March 1820, 'that there is a feeling, becoming daily more general and more confirmed . . . in favour of some undefined change in the mode of governing the country?'

The ministers themselves were not unaware of their growing isolation. The problem was how to break out of the administrative straitjacket in which public prejudice and parliamentary parsimony had encased them since 1816. To repress Jacobinism, though necessary, was no remedy; the cure would only come with the return of prosperity and employment. If government could not actually manufacture those conditions, it must at least be seen to be fostering them. Any measures proposed would have to be acceptable to parliament; but ministerial policy to be successful would have to appeal to a wider body of public opinion. To argue that the limitations on government action had been placed there by the legislature, though largely true, was an insufficient excuse. The duty of ministers was to administer the affairs of the country efficiently or to make way for those who could.

The immediate problem was financial. The radicals complained of the weight of taxation; and to the unsophisticated the contrast between the £50 or £55 millions raised annually in revenue after Waterloo and the £16 or £17 millions that had sufficed before the war was a striking one. But there was little that the cabinet could do about it. The limited machinery of the state was already being run as cheaply as possible. Nearly 80 per cent of the revenue was swallowed up by interest on the national debt, another 8 per cent by war pensions and retired service pay, another 3 per cent by interest on loans which the reluctance of the Commons to grant adequate taxes made necessary. It was not surprising that Cobbett complained about the 'tax eaters'. The government virtually controlled only about 9 per cent of their normal revenue. Of the total governmental expenditure of £69 millions for the year ending January 1818, for example, no less than £51 millions were absorbed by the national debt, short-term exchequer bills, and the 'deadweight' of approximately £5 millions for service half-pay and pensions. Of the remaining £18 millions available for what might be called 'normal' government purposes, the greater part (£12 and a half millions) went on the army, navy and ordnance, leaving a mere £5 and a half millions for civil administration and miscellaneous services. With a net revenue from all sources of £56 millions, Vansittart had to meet a deficit of £13 millions, which he did by issuing exchequer bills. The only point on which the government could fairly be criticized was the stubborn retention of the sinking fund. To borrow, at a higher rate of interest than was carried by the loan it was designed to pay off, was an economic absurdity which merely meant that the burden of floating indebtedness had to be funded at regular intervals and added to the permanent national debt which it was its function to reduce. The only justification was that the sinking fund, consecrated by the authority of Pitt, had a psychological value in maintaining public confidence.

It was a preposterous situation that could scarcely be permitted by any self-respecting body of ministers to continue much longer. After three years of continual concession to what Castlereagh in an ill-advised moment called the 'ignorant impatience of taxation', the government made up its mind to stand and fight, if necessary to stake its existence on the acceptance by parliament of the cabinet's policy. It was this crucial decision, and not the irrelevant episode of Peterloo, that made the year 1819 the turning-point in the post-war history of the Liverpool administration. Inevitably, in the circumstances, the determination of the government to embark on a more constructive policy was directed first to the field of finance.

At the start of the 1819 session, six months before the wild scenes at Manchester, two select committees were appointed in the House of Commons, one on currency and the other on public finance. The first, chaired by Peel but including all the important ministers in the Commons, recommended in May a return to cash payments by successive stages ending in 1823. Most financial experts, including in theory even the Bank of England, favoured an end to the wartime paper currency system. The strongest argument against the return to a metallic-based currency was that wartime debts incurred when money was cheap would now be repayable when money was dear; but this was unavoidable. As a result of post-war deflation the pound had already risen from its low point of 30 per cent devaluation in 1813 to only 4 per cent devaluation in 1819. To the government, as well as to whig liberal economists like Ricardo, the return to a fixed gold standard seemed essential for any policy of sound finance. In the event the transition was accomplished with less difficulty and more speed than had been anticipated. In 1821, two years before the statutory period expired, the Bank of England began to cash notes up to £5 in the new gold coinage of sovereigns and half-sovereigns authorized in 1816.

The second phase of the new ministerial policy was more controversial. But by early summer the cabinet's mood had been stiffened by the slack attendance of government members in the new House of Commons, falling majorities and several not unimportant opposition victories on other issues.

> I am quite satisfied [the prime minister wrote sharply to Lord Eldon on 10 May] ... that if we cannot carry out what has been proposed, it is far, far better for the country that we should cease to be the Government. After the defeats we have already experienced during this Session, our remaining in office is a *positive* evil. It confounds all idea of government in the minds of men. It disgraces us *personally*, and renders us less capable every day of being of any real service to the country. ... A strong and decisive effort can alone redeem our character and credit, and is as necessary for the country as it is for ourselves.

In the event the strong line proved the safest. As usual when a whig opposition campaign seemed on the brink of a decisive victory, the country gentlemen began to desert them. The resolutions of the public finance committee were carried in June by a majority of nearly 200 and the session that had started so ill for the ministers ended on a note of triumph.

Vansittart's long-delayed budget of 1819, incorporating the principles laid down by the financial committee, if not quite the 'new system of finance' that it was described as in a government pamphlet, was at least a watershed in the financial history of the government after Waterloo. In broad outline it imposed £3 millions of new taxes and took £12 millions out of the sacred sinking fund as a substantial contribution towards balancing the budget. Even this was not enough; and the remainder was made up in the usual way by loans and exchequer bills. But it was the first step towards solvency, the first real enunciation of the principle which Huskisson had been labouring behind the scenes to instil—that the only true sinking fund was a surplus of revenue over expenditure, and that only by achieving this could public confidence be restored and the credit of the government established. The subsidiary arrangements for maintaining the sinking fund at £5 millions and gradually reducing the national debt by conversion of stock from a higher to a lower rate of interest were only devices to assist this primary policy.

Success, however, depended on making more productive the main source of revenue, customs and excise. Short of reviving the income tax (and only Herries was heroic enough in 1819 to argue for this), the government had inevitably to rely on indirect taxes; and the yield from these fluctuated with the economic activity of the country. A recovery in trade and manufacture was therefore the next objective. For Lord Liverpool, a liberal economist brought up like Pitt and Grenville in the school of Adam Smith, the only way to stimulate the sluggish post-war economy was to lower the high tariff wall which surrounded British industry, and loosen the mass of commercial regulations which restricted the flow of British trade. By 1820 the time seemed ripe for the first move.

With the complaints of manufacturing distress being joined by the lamentations of the agriculturalists, and a dawning realization that the campaign for retrenchment and economy had virtually exhausted its usefulness, there was a growing readiness among politicians to consider fundamental issues of economic policy. The extent of free-trade feeling in the mercantile classes themselves has been exaggerated. The famous free-trade petition of the London merchants early in the 1820 session owed less to genuine conviction in the City than to the private campaign of the economist Tooke. It met with little response until it received the encouragement of the prime minister and was taken up by the influential banker Henry Thornton. But the favourable response that the petition met in the House of Commons provided a useful background for the government's own initiative.

Liverpool's great free-trade speech of 26 May 1820 was the first time that a British prime minister firmly and unequivocally stated the advantages of an unrestricted freedom of trade. Some contended, he observed, that Britain had risen to greatness because of her protective system. 'Others, of whom I am one, believe that we have risen *in spite* of that system.' He reassured his audience that he had no thought of abandoning agricultural protection; and absolute freedom of trade was out of the question. But he emphasized the interdependence of agriculture, industry and commerce—'what is for the benefit of the one, must be beneficial to the rest'—and indicated various ways in which a start could be made in relaxing the commercial system. The two committees, one from each House, set up to examine the question of foreign trade, laid down the strategy of the new approach. The report of the Commons committee, introduced in July by Wallace, the vice-president of the Board of Trade, was particularly outspoken. The skill, enterprise and capital of British merchants and manufacturers, it argued, required only fair and open competition for success. The greatest boon that could be bestowed on them was as much freedom from interference as possible. All restrictions not justified by political expediency or other special considerations should be abolished, the navigation laws should be modified, and the system of bonded warehouses extended.

In little more than twelve months, therefore, the government had captured the initiative in both financial and commercial policy. It was under Vansittart and Wallace that the blueprints were drawn for the great reforms of the 1820s which brought Robinson and Huskisson so much—and perhaps such excessive—acclaim. The gap between the years of planning in 1819–20 and the years of fruition in 1823–6 was caused not by the impact of new ministers or by any change of policy but by one fortuitous and unpredictable event: the Queen's affair of 1820–21. At the very dawn of recovery, the administration was reduced to its lowest point of unpopularity and political weakness, and even threatened for a time with an end to its existence.

II

The death in 1817 of Princess Charlotte, the Regent's only child and George III's only legitimate grandchild, had several momentous consequences. It led to a flurry of marriages among the elderly royal dukes—Cambridge, Clarence and Kent—in 1818. It also removed the Prince Regent's last scruple at severing the ties between himself and his estranged wife Caroline who had lived abroad since 1815. The report of the so-called Milan Commission of 1818 confirmed European gossip and left no doubt in the minds of the Regent and his ministers that Caroline had been guilty of adultery. The problem of the relationship between George and his vulgar, silly, ill-used wife was not new. It had existed ever since the 'Delicate Investigation' of 1806; but even when, after Waterloo, evidence of grounds for divorce began to accumulate, the ministers were disinclined to advise any action. George's only remedy was through the law; and the law offered only two solutions, both politically dangerous. To sue in the ecclesiastical courts for a separation *a mensa et thoro* (absolute divorce was not recognized by the church) would enable the Princess's counsel to bring forward in extenuation evidence of the Regent's own marital delinquencies. It might even uncover the scandal of George's illegal marriage with Mrs Fitzherbert in 1785. The only practical alternative was to promote a private bill for release from the ties of marriage (*a vinculo matrimonii*) at the cost of an unsavoury political wrangle in parliament. With the Regent more intent than ever on divorce, the only gleam of hope in a highly unpleasant outlook was the knowledge, conveyed to the government in 1819 by Caroline's legal adviser Henry Brougham, that she might be prepared for a settlement.

The death of George III in January 1820, bringing with it the strong possibility that the Princess would return to England to demand her legal rights as queen consort, brought matters to a head. George IV's immediate demand for the omission from the Liturgy of the customary prayers for the queen was reluctantly conceded by the cabinet in the hope of winning his assent to some amicable arrangement that avoided a legal divorce. Though refusal would have precipitated a crisis between King and ministers, the decision proved a tactical error. In seeking to placate the King, the cabinet merely outraged the Queen. The omission from the Liturgy stung Caroline into a vindication of her rights; and when legal proceedings against her were instituted, it seemed to have prejudged her case before any evidence was heard. Though with great difficulty the ministers persuaded the King to accept a separation settlement to be ratified by act of parliament, Caroline impartially brushed aside the liberal offers of the government, the warning of legal sanctions, and the embarrassed advice of Brougham. In June she arrived in London to the cheers of welcoming crowds and took up residence at the house of the radical Alderman Wood. The contest was now both public and political.

When the final negotiations between the cabinet and the Queen's advisers predictably broke down, and an eleventh-hour appeal to Caroline by an unhappy House of Commons was rejected, the government had no option but to proceed with their threat of formal proceedings. In July a bill of pains and penalties was introduced in the House of Lords where counsel and witnesses could be heard at the bar. From August to October the whole kingdom was fed on the unsavoury evidence of a royal divorce. Though Liverpool conducted the proceedings with fairness and dignity, the government's case was doomed from the start. To the ordinary people George's profligacy and extravagances were notorious. They had heard little previously about Caroline's life on the continent and cheerfully disbelieved all foreign witnesses. The upper classes, though sceptical of Caroline's innocence, thought her offence the lesser of the two. Even those not unsympathetic to the King felt that the attempt to prove her guilt could only do harm to the monarchy. Free of such scruples the radical writers and cartoonists plunged joyfully into the steamy controversy, depicting the King as an ageing voluptuary surrounded by fawning, brutal ministers ready to gratify his every wish, and Caroline as the model of injured, female purity. It was in these years, beginning with the publication of *The Queen's Matrimonial Ladder*, that the devastating combination of Hone's burlesque verse and Cruickshank's satiric illustrations reached its pinnacle of popular success.

The feverish excitement gripped the whole country. In Scotland, unaffected by the Liturgy prohibition, and with a dour Presbyterian prejudice against an earthly head of the church, not only secessionist but many established clergy prayed fervently for the Queen by name. At a public meeting at Edinburgh at the end of the year some 17,000 signatures were obtained for a petition calling on the King to dismiss his ministers. It was the first anti-governmental public meeting in the Scottish capital in the post-war period. Everywhere the public wrath was directed as much against the cabinet as against the crown; and ministers suffered most because they had most to lose. Even the whig peers took a hand in the party game. Though the government, in deference to the scruples of the bishops, were prepared to drop the divorce clause, a majority which included whigs led by Lord Grey insisted on retaining it in order to ensure the ultimate rejection of the bill. It passed, but only by a majority of nine; and since on this showing it would never get through the Commons, the bill was abandoned.

It was the most spectacular defeat for the government since 1816. Next session, encouraged by innumerable public meetings during the recess and a mass of petitions in favour of the Queen, the opposition moved in for the kill. Since the question of the Queen's allowance still had to be settled, in addition to such acrimonious issues as the Liturgy and the coronation, a further struggle in the Commons was unavoidable. Once more, however, the whigs had underestimated the government's ability to survive. By yielding to public opinion, despite their technical victory in the House of Lords, by making it clear that no further disclosures or penal measures were contemplated, by leaving the financial question of the Queen's allowance to the Commons, the ministers made it easy for the independent MPs to resume their natural political allegiance. They had not been edified by the spectacle of Caroline holding court at Brandenburgh House as queen of radical England; they were even more distrustful of the apparent whig proclivity for exploiting the passions and prejudices of the multitude. The government was saved from both censure and defeat by majorities of over a hundred; and Caroline's opportune death in 1821 soon after the close of session put an end to the parliamentary inquest on 'the Queen's affair'. Even in the country, after one last flurry of popular feeling in August when her funeral cortège was forcibly diverted through the City on its way to Harwich, interest soon died down.

The wounds inflicted on the ministry, however, went deeper than parliament or the public realized. George IV, angered by the failure of his cabinet and morbidly sensitive to his own unpopularity, had seriously contemplated during the winter recess a change of ministers. An entirely new administration might bring the Queen's business to a rapid and satisfactory end, restore public confidence in the govern-

ment, and even perhaps transfer the odium of the whole affair from
the King to his dismissed servants. Tentative soundings in November,
however, with both whigs and Grenvillites, proved discouraging.
Until the Commons definitely declared themselves against the
ministry, no other body of men had much prospect of commanding
a majority. Even if the whigs eventually came to power, their policy
not only with regard to the Queen but on such larger matters as
Catholic Emancipation was likely to be in flat contradiction to the
wishes of the crown. Nevertheless, knowledge of these overtures did
nothing to calm Liverpool's nerves, already stretched by the Queen's
trial; and the rift soon widened with the conflict over Canning's
future.

Canning had once been on friendly terms with Caroline. Some,
including the King, believed that they had been more than friendly.
In 1820 Canning thought that the institution of legal proceedings
after the removal of her name from the Prayer Book had piled
injustice on error. He absented himself from England during the trial,
resigned office in December and was beginning to weigh the prospects
of his wrecked career at home against the possibility of a lucrative
appointment in India. His withdrawal left Castlereagh once more
the only real debater on the government front bench. Peel, the
only other able government politician out of office, declined an offer
of the vacancy Canning had left at the India Board since like him he
felt unable to defend the government's handling of the divorce issue.
Though in the end the ministers survived the 1821 session without
notable disaster, it was clear that strength would have to be recruited
somewhere. Liverpool's instinct was to reinstate Canning, take in Peel,
and find minor office for some of the less inefficient Grenvillites who
had been signalling for some time their readiness to join the government. He encountered opposition from the King, who did not wish
to see Canning in office ever again, from many of his own colleagues
who were beginning to think it would be better to let Canning depart
in peace, and from Castlereagh who showed an almost pathological
jealousy of anything that might weaken his authority in the
Commons. A half-hearted offer of the India Board to Peel in May
met with another refusal. This was followed in June by a peremptory
message from the King to the effect that he saw no reason, and
therefore did not intend, to change the existing structure of his
ministry. Relations between the King and his harassed prime
minister reached a point at which Liverpool, profoundly depressed by
the death of his wife the same month, was prepared to believe that
a plot was on foot to destroy the government. If Canning were to be
proscribed, he wrote agitatedly to his friend Arbuthnot, the King
would have to look for another prime minister.

Only gradually, through the mediation of other members of the cabinet, did the strained atmosphere relax. But by the end of the year it proved possible to arrive at an acceptable compromise. Canning was to go to India as governor-general; Sidmouth at last consented to retire from the Home Office to make way for Peel; C. W. Wynn, a Grenvillite, went to the India Board; and the alliance was further cemented by a dukedom for Lord Grenville's ambitious nephew, the marquess of Buckingham. It had been a personal as well as a constitutional crisis: and both sides made concessions. Liverpool had maintained the right of a prime minister to select his own cabinet, at the cost of yielding in practice to the general feeling of his colleagues against Canning. The King showed himself helpful and conciliatory in the official arrangements, especially on India which had always been Canning's alternative ambition. What was most important was that the ministry had strengthened itself for a further period of office after two years of acute weakness. Though they had lost Canning's debating skill in the Commons, they had gained Peel. In absorbing the Grenvillites, they denied to the King the only rival political group to which he could turn other than the whigs. 'I regard this,' wrote Castlereagh to the prime minister in December, in a triumph of sense over syntax, 'as constituting the preponderating motive for forming this connection, which having once incorporated with your management, I think your Government will be equal to any emergency.'

In the end the reconstruction went further than anyone could have anticipated at the start of 1822. In August Castlereagh's suicide, of which his obsessive attitude in 1821 was perhaps a forewarning, transformed Canning's position. After a brief battle of wills with the King he succeeded as foreign secretary and leader of the House of Commons—the 'whole inheritance' for which he had unsuccessfully bid in 1812. In turn Canning's influence strengthened Liverpool's feeling after the unsatisfactory 1821 session that a further reinforcement of the ministry in the House of Commons would not come amiss. Vansittart therefore was induced to go into honourable retirement as Lord Bexley. Robinson, with the double recommendation of having been both Castlereagh's and Canning's favourite for the post, became chancellor of the exchequer. Huskisson, more identified as a follower of Canning, became president of the Board of Trade with the promise of an early seat in the cabinet. At the start of the 1823 session, with a front bench that had been almost totally reshaped since 1821, the government possessed a more formidable team in the Commons than at any time since 1812.

To achieve this had been the primary motive in all the ministerial changes of these years. The mythical transformation of the ministry

from 'reactionary tory' before 1822 to 'liberal tory' afterwards was
the invention of subsequent historians. Liverpool's object was not to
alter course but to reorganize his crew for a voyage that had already
started. All the new appointments, with the negligible exception of
the Grenvillite Wynn, went to men who had served the administration during the dark years of 1816–19. Robinson had been con-
tinuously in office since 1809 and president of the Board of Trade
since 1818. Huskisson, though in the comparatively minor office of
Woods and Forests, had been an influential member of Liverpool's
little 'economic cabinet' long before 1820. The detachment from
continental commitments which became the hallmark of Canning's
foreign policy had already been foreshadowed in Castlereagh's state
paper of 1820. The first of Peel's criminal reforms had been prepared
under Sidmouth. Had Vansittart remained as chancellor of the
exchequer or Wallace, the able vice-president of the Board of Trade,
succeeded Robinson in place of Huskisson, it is unlikely that the
financial and fiscal reforms of the 1820s would have been any
different. Vansittart's reputation has suffered unfairly partly from the
financial straits to which the government was reduced after 1816 and
partly from his awkward phraseology and peculiar accents in debate.
Robinson, though not demonstrably a better financier, was by
contrast a pleasant and popular figure in the Commons. Huskisson,
on the other hand, was never liked by the country gentlemen because
of his shyness and furtive manner.

What was new was the alteration in the personal balance of power
within the government. Canning's inheritance of Castlereagh's
central position, under a prime minister who had always been his
best and sometimes his only friend in the cabinet, worked a profound
change in the private relationships among ministers. 'Ours is not, nor
never has been a *controversial* Cabinet,' wrote Wellington with
emphatic negatives in 1821. After 1822 that was no longer true.
Canning's flamboyant foreign policy, skilfully publicized in terms
flattering to British insular prejudices and contrasting strongly with
Castlereagh's aristocratic, continental affinities, was a powerful
ingredient in the government's growing reputation for liberalism. But
it was a different picture inside the administration. His constant
meddling, his passion for political manipulation, and what was
thought by jealous colleagues to be the excessive partiality shown
to him by Liverpool, all conspired to confirm the reputation for
intrigue and ambition which he had made for himself in early life.
Increasingly the cabinet began to form into the Canningite and anti-
Canningite groupings which came into the open so dramatically in
1827. In an administration more active, more powerful, more
popular without, more divided within, than it had been before,

Liverpool's conciliatory leadership was more than ever indispensable.

III

By the beginning of 1822 the cabinet's basic social and economic thinking was fully developed. They denied that the distress in the country was due to heavy taxation. Since 1815 taxes had been reduced by £17 millions; economies in administration had been carried to the limit. The rising wealth and population of the country were well able to support a larger government revenue than in 1792. What the complaining agriculturalists really needed was an expanding market; what had damaged them was not heavy taxation but the fall in government expenditure and public consumption after the war. A market could not be supplied to order. All that ministers could do was to press forward with their task of maintaining public credit, restoring financial confidence, encouraging trade and industry. If the government was successful in producing a clear surplus of £5 millions, this would place in their hands, as Castlereagh told the Commons in one of his periodic economic lectures, 'a most powerful instrument, if wisely and properly used, for rapidly promoting the regeneration of the public prosperity'. Agriculture, manufacture and commerce depended on each other for economic health. The government was not prepared to bring forward any further monopolistic legislation on behalf of the landed interest. Cheap food was a boon to the mass of the people and led to increased consumption. If marginal land could not yield a profit, it must submit to the laws of supply and demand. There was no intention of departing from the basic principle of providing protection for agriculture; but there was a strong case for lowering the level of entry for foreign corn and introducing a sliding scale to regulate the impact of imports on the home market.

Looking ahead the cabinet could feel reasonably confident. It was when they cast their eyes on the House of Commons that doubts assailed them. The eleventh-hour extrication from the Queen's divorce entanglement did not mean that the parliamentary basis of power was any more assured. The general election of 1820 made necessary by the new reign had lost them some supporters, slightly strengthened the opposition, and worst of all had injected into the new House the mood of general discontent which characterized the country at large. To add to all their ministerial troubles a series of

good harvest from 1819 to 1822 brought agricultural prices tumbling
until by the winter of 1822 wheat was down to under 39s., the lowest
for thirty years. In the 1821 and 1822 sessions the government was
under almost constant attack from a variety of quarters: agriculturalists demanding more protection and less taxation, retrenchment
fanatics pressing for further economies in the public services, cheap
money exponents who criticized the 1819 currency legislation, whig
and radical advocates of parliamentary reform. The most alarming
symptom was that a substantial number of independent country
gentry seemed disposed to countenance many if not all of these
nostrums. In the 1821 session a combination of disgruntled agriculturalists and opposition whigs forced the government to repeal
the tax on farm horses (a loss of nearly £½ million) and the pressure
intensified the following year. The House of Commons, as Ward had
wryly noted in 1819, seemed determined that the government would
always stumble even if it never fell. In May 1822 the ministers were
driven to the ultimate sanction of announcing that they would treat
any further defeat as a question of confidence. This brought the
House to its senses and preserved the ministry for the rest of the
session; but it had been a demoralizing experience.

The root of the trouble was that the cabinet had not yet imposed
its will on the Commons or produced a series of connected measures
that would be acceptable to parliament and the public. It was still
failing to give the country the firm leadership it wanted. Though the
ministers had not come unprepared in the 1822 session, they had
been forced into various shifts and expedients, and had made many
concessions. This, as the prime minister observed to Huskisson at the
end of the session, was 'neither creditable for the Government, nor
safe for the Country'. It was not surprising that Liverpool was
determined, after Castlereagh's death that summer, that the King's
susceptibilities must be overruled and Canning brought back into the
ministry.

From 1823, however, the spadework of the previous years began
to yield its harvest. Vansittart's ingenious budget of 1822 in which he
contrived to manufacture a surplus even while dispensing with £3·3
millions of taxes, started his successor off with a handsome legacy of
nearly £5 millions excess revenue. With trade recovering Robinson
was able to budget for an even greater surplus of £7 millions which,
after allowing for the £5 millions earmarked for debt redemption,
gave him £2 millions which he used to reduce taxation. This was a
political rather than an economic gesture. The following year (1824)
the government embarked on a more ambitious programme. Looking
ahead to 1827 they estimated that they would have over the whole
five-year period since 1823 a clear surplus of £4 millions even after

deducting the standard sinking fund contributions. In 1824 and again in 1825 duties were lowered on a whole range of consumer goods and raw materials for industry, including iron, coal, wool, silk, hemp, coffee, wine and rum. The most gratifying feature was that despite the lowering of duties, rising consumption and a greater volume of trade kept the revenue buoyant and even enabled further direct taxes to be taken off. Even when the financial crisis of 1825 and the subsequent recession of 1826 brought the first phase of economic recovery to a halt, Robinson was still able to reckon on a small revenue surplus for 1827.

It had been a remarkable period of prosperity which the country was not to experience again until Peel applied the same formula in the 1840s. The free-trade policy could scarcely have had a better vindication. In four years (1822–5) taxation had been reduced by nearly £12 millions. Simultaneously the healthy state of the stock market had made it possible to reduce the interest on a large block of the national debt from 5 per cent to 4 per cent and in 1824 from 4 per cent to 3½ per cent representing a total saving of £1½ million annually on debt interest. The national debt both funded and unfunded had decreased and its charges fallen by another million. With a legislature and public that had become almost morbidly sensitive to public expenditure these achievements considerably enhanced the government's authority. The ministers were not slow to point the political moral. The government and the legislature, observed Robinson cheerfully in the last session of the parliament elected in 1820, 'may boldly face our constituents in whatever part of the country, and at whatever time we may be called upon to appeal to them'. The previous year Lord Lansdowne, the leader of the opposition in the House of Lords, had handsomely congratulated the government on the flourishing and tranquil state of the kingdom. In his reply the prime minister dwelt complacently on the 'unprecedented, unparalleled prosperity of every part of the country', reaffirmed the general principle of free trade as the foundation of economic success and called for an even bolder advance along the path which ministerial initiative had opened up.

An important contribution both to the buoyancy of the revenue and the rising level of national economic activity had been made by the Board of Trade. In 1820 British foreign trade was smothered in a mass of legislation, nearly 2,000 statutes in all, some of which dated from the fourteenth century. They imposed not only tariffs on imports but duties on the export of goods and machinery, and restrictions on the emigration of skilled workmen. While some of this legislative accumulation of the centuries was either anomalous, obsolete, or ineffective, the navigation acts dating from the seventeenth century were still in operation. Their primary object was to preserve British maritime strength, both in ships and seamen, by a severely restrictive system which reserved all coastal, colonial and non-European trade for British shipping. The loss of the American colonies had made some modification of the code necessary but the general protective principle still remained intact.

The first attack on this system was made in 1821 when Wallace introduced a bill founded on the reports of the foreign trade committee to lower the duties on timber imported from northern Europe. Since 1815 the British colonies in north America, despite the long Atlantic haul, had secured a virtual monopoly of the timber trade. The significance of Wallace's bill was that it was specifically designed to open up trade with northern Europe for the benefit of British manufacturers; and that it was put on the statute book against the protests of the powerful colonial and shipping interests. It had not taken ministers long to discover that while there might be an intellectual acceptance of the principles of free trade, most trades and industries were apt to discover special reasons why it should not apply to themselves. Encouraged by this success, however, Wallace gave notice of the general scheme of reform which the government had in mind: the simplification and rationalization of the great body of commercial legislation; a relaxation of the navigation acts; and encouragement to foreign shipping to use British ports by a reduction in harbour dues and provision of duty-free warehouses. The five acts passed the following session (1822) under Wallace's guidance constituted the first great instalment of this programme. The purpose behind the legislation was clear. It was to loosen monopolies, remove restrictions, extend freedom of international commerce, promote British trade even at the apparent expense of British shipping and in general to make Britain the commercial emporium of the world. There was still a long way to go to complete freedom of trade; but the first steps had been taken. The guiding principle that the government had asserted was that national needs must take precedence over sectional interests.

Wallace, resigning in 1823 in protest at Huskisson's promotion over his head to the presidency of the Board of Trade, has (like Vansittart) received less than proper recognition. It was left to Huskisson, in charge of the remaining part of the government's commercial programme, to win the credit that should equitably be shared by several men, including Liverpool himself. Under his direction, however, the remaining years of the administration saw warehousing legislation to allow foreign goods to use British ports as a free entrepôt; the great series of reciprocity acts by which most foreign states in Europe and America negotiated agreements for mutual abolition or adjustment of discriminatory duties; the collaboration with Robinson over the budgetary tariff reductions; and the consolidation and simplification of the customs regulations mainly carried out by Deacon Hume, the controller of customs.

Huskisson's more personal contribution was twofold. First was his growing emphasis (foreshadowing the arguments of Cobden and Bright fifteen years later) on free trade as a moral force promoting international cooperation and harmony. As foreigners sometimes unkindly observed, the British liked to have ethical arguments for lining their pockets. Next was his contention that the old mercantile system which had led to the loss of the American colonies must be replaced by a more liberal and preferential policy towards colonial trade and manufactures. Colonies must be assured of freedom and prosperity under the shelter of the imperial flag and the imperial connection preserved through the bonds of self-interest. A species of utilitarian imperialism was not perhaps the highest of ideals; but it was at least a corrective to the pessimism which the loss of America had engendered. Against the doubtings of those who believed in the inevitable separation of the rest of the colonies, Huskisson showed his optimism and imagination by arguing that at best a solid and mutually profitable imperial union might be created, while at worst separation when it came would not be the result of pettiness and selfishness by the mother country. 'England cannot afford to be little,' he said finely. 'She must be what she is or nothing.'

Huskisson, like Lord Liverpool and others of his colleagues, was a practical economist in the tradition of Adam Smith, not a *laissez-faire* dogmatist. Indeed his imperial preference policy cut across the strict free-trade theory. He regarded free trade as a signpost pointing the way, not as a set of rigid rails from which it was dangerous to diverge. In 1824 he supported Hume's doctrinaire committee which reported in favour of abolishing all legal restrictions on the export of machinery, the emigration of artisans and trade combinations. On the other hand he introduced the Passenger Transport Act of 1828 which imposed the first effective regulations on the malodorous north Atlantic emigration traffic. The repeal of the Combination Acts in 1824 was largely based on the view of the Benthamite radicals that coercion had produced association and the repeal of the acts by the legislature would see the end of combinations among the men. The wave of strikes and fresh union demands that followed in the next twelve months in the west of Scotland, Lancashire, the Midlands and the northeast made the ministers reconsider the problem. The new law passed in 1825, largely at the instigation of Peel and the Home Office, while not attempting to make illegal either trade unions or collective bargaining, laid down a maximum penalty of three months' imprisonment for the use of threats or molestation specifically to promote strikes, enforce union membership or impose restrictions on employers. Simultaneously Ellenborough's act of 1803, making murderous attacks by cutting, wounding and stabbing a capital offence, was extended to Scotland with the addition of a special clause on vitriol-throwing. This legislation was intended not to suppress or harass the trade unions but to prevent them from abusing their power. The violent methods employed against non-unionists or imported 'blackleg' labour in the 1824–5 disputes—two murders and many persons injured in Ireland, a Glasgow weaver pistolled in the back, a Lancashire miner almost beaten to death, attacks on seamen at Sunderland—demonstrated that the task of reconciling trade union power and individual liberty was not going to be easy.

Peel's larger programme of reform at the Home Office was characteristic of the new course which the government felt able to adopt after 1821. While responding to public opinion, the department had a policy of its own and was not afraid to propose controversial measures or resist popular demands. The long campaign for criminal law reform carried on by the Romilly, Mackintosh, Buxton group of whig humanitarians had as its primary object the simplification of the complicated mass of statute law and its replacement by a more merciful code: the emotional issue of capital punishment was central to the whole campaign. While accepting the principle of reform and agreeing with most of the recommendations of Mackintosh's 1819 committee, Peel was not anxious for the relaxation to be pursued in isolation from an improvement in the means of crime prevention and detection. As a result of the classic series of reforming statutes which he put through between 1822 and 1827, consolidating and amending the great body of English criminal law, many capital offences were swept away. But most of these had almost ceased in practice to be punished by execution and Peel was disinclined to go as far as the whig reformers and indeed much of the educated public would have liked. His tenure of the Home Office did in fact see a considerable drop in the number of executions: an annual average in England and Wales of 61 for 1822–6 as compared with 108 for 1817–21. But he preferred to combine a relative strict code with a flexible use of judicial reprieve until the effects of his legal reforms were clear.

Two considerations prompted this cautious attitude. One was the absence of any satisfactory system of secondary punishment in the existing prisons; the other was the steady increase in criminal committals and convictions, far exceeding the rate of growth of population, in the period since Waterloo. Of equal importance in his view was the question, neglected by the whig reformers, of law enforcement and crime prevention. At the start of his secretaryship he took up the matter of public order in London, where the rowdy scenes at the time of the Queen's trial and subsequent funeral, and the enforced employment of the military, had proved of great embarrassment to the government. There had already been in fact a formal recommendation from Wellington, following the 'mutiny' in the guards in 1820, to entrust the policing of the metropolis to some other force than the regular army. The parliamentary committee secured by Peel in 1822, however, returned a flat negative on the central issue of establishing a strong, centralized police force in the capital to replace the small staffs attached, mainly for detective purposes, to the separate metropolitan magistrates' courts. It was clear that the engrained prejudice of both politicians and the general public that the existence of an effective police would mean a curtailment of traditional British liberties was too deep-seated to be overcome at the first attempt. In 1795 the former Glasgow magistrate Colquhoun in his book *The Police of the Metropolis* had put forward the novel thesis that the prime function of a good police system was crime-prevention. Though accepted by the experts, including many Benthamites, this was not a concept easily understood by the mass of the British people. After his initial rebuff the home secretary allowed four years to pass before making preparations for a second attempt. If over capital punishment the Home Office lagged behind public opinion, over police reform it was clearly ahead.

IV

In their years of success and popularity between 1822 and 1827 the unsolved problem for ministers was provided by the agriculturalists. It was a political rather than an economic problem. Economically the cabinet felt that the agricultural industry must learn to adjust to peacetime conditions. They were not blind to the standing paradox that when farmers complained of low prices, the country was benefiting from cheap food. Politically however, they had to do, or appear to be doing, something. The agricultural interest had a powerful, indeed in the eyes of many of the public a disproportionate, influence in the legislature and its spokesmen were the independent country gentlemen whose support the government could not afford to lose.

The high prices for wheat which contributed to industrial unrest between 1816 and 1818 had kept the agricultural interest tolerably content. But when in 1817 and 1818 prices rose above the statutory level of 80s. a quarter, and wheat was allowed into the country from abroad, the farmers took fright. The year 1818, which was marked by the largest import of foreign corn so far experienced, saw the first attempt by farmers to organize a national movement for higher protection. This was the Central Agricultural Association, founded by the wealthy West Country solicitor and sheepfarmer George Webb Hall, to encourage local county protection societies and bring pressure to bear on the government for a higher and virtually prohibitive duty on all foreign corn. By the end of 1819 twenty counties, mainly in the southern half of England, were sending delegates to the central association meetings and a membership of some fifty local associations was claimed. A semi-political movement run by wealthy tenant farmers was not altogether to the liking of the landowning gentry; and Webb Hall's economic theories, when exposed to the cross-questioning of experts on the 1821 parliamentary committee, seemed remarkably naïve. Nevertheless, he had done enough to attract the attention of some agricultural MPs and parliament could not permanently ignore real dissatisfaction among farmers.

The next few years saw control of the agriculturalist movement pass into the hands of its natural social leaders in the House of Commons. In 1819 came the first of a series of four consecutive good harvests which kept corn prices abnormally depressed until the spring of 1823. By 1821 the accumulation of grain and the continued low state of the market had produced something of an agricultural panic. To mounting complaints in the Commons of agricultural distress the government offered the time-honoured palliative of a select committee. Well seeded with free-trade economists like Ricardo and Huskisson, the committee did little to satisfy the protectionists. Its report, drafted by Huskisson, was mainly designed to explain how the existing difficulties had arisen and why it was impossible for the legislature to remedy them. But it did suggest that a duty on imported grain, counterbalanced by a lowering of the level at which imports were permitted, might help ease the sudden transition from total prohibition to free importation under existing law when the 80s. point was reached. The continuing flood of petitions complaining of distress led to a renewal of the committee in 1822. Its report repeated the 1821 suggestion and on this basis the government passed the 1822 corn act imposing a graduated scale of duties on foreign corn between the 70s. and 85s. price levels. Since, however, the clause of the 1815 act, forbidding the entry of corn until the domestic price reached 80s., was not repealed, and that price was never in fact reached during the lifetime of the 1822 act, it remained a dead letter.

As a piece of legislation the 1822 corn law is only explicable as a holding operation on the part of the government while they were considering a more permanent measure. At the moment their political weakness in the Commons discouraged any immediate initiative. For the ministers the disquieting aspect of the agricultural agitation was its tendency to stir up a whole range of other issues. While the fact of agricultural distress was undeniable, not all agriculturalists were convinced that higher protection was either feasible or helpful. One of the reasons for the decline of Webb Hall's Agricultural Association was the rivalry it encountered from the champions of other remedies: the retrenchment school who saw in government extravagance the root of all evil; the country gentry who hoped for a reduction in taxation to offset reduced rents and at times even seemed to favour a compulsory reduction of the interest on the national debt; farmers who thought that tithes and poor rate constituted a more pressing grievance for the agricultural producer; men like Cobbett and some of the radical whigs who argued that the country's affairs would never be put right until parliament had been reformed; and financial theorists like Attwood of Birmingham who by 1820 was propagating in the *Farmers Journal* his view that the currency act of 1819 and the ending of cheap money was the real source of the nation's difficulties.

Worst of all from the ministerial point of view was the growing restiveness of the independent MPs and the attempt by some of them to take control of policy. In 1821 and 1822 there was something like an agricultural revolt in the Commons led by men such as Lethbridge of Somerset, Knatchbull of Kent and Gooch of Suffolk, familiarly known as the 'Boodle cabinet' from the club of that name much frequented by tory squires. 'The country gentlemen,' wrote Wellington sharply in March 1822, 'treat the Government exceedingly ill. . . . What I complain of is their acting in concert, and as a party independent of, and without consultation with, the Government, which they profess to support, but really oppose.' Liverpool was determined, however, not to give way on any major point of policy. Retrenchment and economy was one thing: to abandon the 1819 currency act—Peel's act as it was becoming known, not altogether to Peel's advantage—or pass a more stringent corn law was another. 'It is the duty of Government and of Parliament to hold the balance between all the great interests of the country, *as even as possible*,' he said firmly in a debate on agricultural distress in the House of Lords in February 1822. 'The agricultural is not the *only* interest in Great Britain. It is not even the *most numerous*.' The agriculturalists were

not to hear such plain speaking from a prime minister again until
Peel repealed the corn laws in 1846.

If the government needed any encouragement in their task of
holding the balance between the great interests of the country, it
came with the success of its free-trade commercial policy and the
growing criticism from industrialists and merchants, in proportion as
their own legislative protection diminished, at the continued high
protection for agriculture. The rise in wheat prices from 1823
onward, the financial crisis of 1825, and the manufacturing depression of 1826, brought fresh popular demands for the abolition or
reduction of duties on foreign corn. Faced with a return of industrial
unemployment and social discontent the government in the 1826
session secured statutory permission to release bonded corn at a low
rate of duty for a limited period and if necessary to admit further
supplies of foreign corn during the recess by order in council. The
half million quarters of wheat released from bond helped to stabilize
prices at less than 60s. a quarter and the entry subsequently
authorized by the cabinet on its own responsibility for oats, rye, peas
and beans (the crops that suffered most from the drought of 1826)
further alleviated the food situation. Meanwhile the ministers made
it clear that they intended in the new parliament to bring forward
a definitive revision of the 1815 corn act.

By this date most sensible landowners had realized that the day of
high prices and high rents had gone for ever. In 1825 the government
had sent William Jacob to investigate the potential size of corn
exports to Britain from northern Europe. His report, published in
April 1826, showed that there was little likelihood of large-scale
importation of grain from the continent and that a duty of 10s. or
12s. a quarter would be enough to protect the British grower when
the domestic price was between 60s. and 64s. Jacob's report offered
one kind of argument. The industrial rioting in Lancashire in the
same month, where nearly a thousand power looms were destroyed
by hungry, unemployed cotton workers, provided another. There
was no Peterloo in 1826, no re-enactment of any of the expired
repressive legislation. The attitude of the Home Office was conditioned by the knowledge that the disorder was due entirely to
economic causes. Public controversy centred on such practical
matters as corn laws, free trade, financial credit and banking reform.
There was little radical agitation. The country gentry were not called
on to rally in defence of a threatened political system. They were
cast for the more invidious role of beneficiaries of an economic
monopoly. More clearly than ever before the 1826 session marked the
point at which the landed interest went permanently over to the
defensive against the claims of the rest of the community. Their only

hope was to get agreement at parliamentary level on some adjusted level of protection which would be acceptable to the country and tolerable for the agriculturalists. 'The charm of the power of the Landed Interest,' pronounced the whig Creevey in May 1826, 'is gone.'

The strength displayed by the ministry in overcoming agricultural opposition in 1826 derived from many sources: the initiative and leadership they had shown since 1822, the success of their commercial and financial policies, the liberal outlook that seemed to pervade all the great departments of state and the sympathy that had been established between government thinking and informed public opinion. They were in the position of a national executive ruling in the national interest through, rather than on behalf of, a landowning parliament. To achieve this position had been one of Liverpool's main aims ever since 1819. An anonymous but well known to be government-inspired and probably government-written pamphlet, *The State of the Nation*,[2] published just before the 1822 session to explain ministerial policy, emphasized this point on its first page. His Majesty's ministers, it affirmed, recognized that their reputation and influence depended on the way in which they discharged their duties and that 'the goodwill of the people towards government has in all ages proved the readiest means of an effective administration'. The ministry therefore anxiously desired 'to stand well in public opinion' not only for their own sake, but because a general persuasion that the government was actively pursuing the welfare of the country would promote social harmony and render unnecessary the kind of legislation 'required in more turbulent times to repress public disorders'. At bottom Liverpool's policy was a social policy designed to close the gap between the state and society and to allay discontent by spreading prosperity. It was also a conservative policy, designed to blunt radical attacks on the constitution by demonstrating that the aristocratic system was capable of producing an administration that looked to national needs and worked for national ends.

Nevertheless, a policy of conservatism, however liberal and enlightened, was still fundamentally a policy of preserving the essential features of the constitution inherited from the eighteenth century. It was here that the ministers could sometimes feel that, despite all their

---

[2] It was published by Hatchard & Son, Piccadilly, the firm usually employed to print the more important speeches of Liverpool and Castlereagh, and ran into at least seven editions. Von Neumann, the Austrian diplomat, stated specifically that it was issued by the government shortly before the start of the session, because of lack of support from the country gentlemen, and that it had a useful effect. *Diary of Philipp von Neumann*, edited by E. B. Chancellor (1928) I, p. 91. For the efforts of the ministry after 1820 to secure better publicity for their efforts see *Historical Manuscripts Commission Bathurst*, p. 489, Arbuthnot to Bathurst, 29 November 1820.

success and popularity, the currents of public opinion were flowing against them. Among the educated classes in both England and Scotland the idea of parliamentary reform was beginning to make headway, not as a matter of immediate necessity but as an ultimately desirable eventuality. Writing in 1820 to Copleston, provost of Oriel College, Oxford, and future bishop of Llandaff, the Canningite Ward confessed that 'when I see the progress that reform seems to be making not only among the vulgar, but among persons, like yourself, of understanding and education, clear of interested motives and party fanaticism, my spirits fail me'.

Lack of success in bringing the government down over the Queen's affair had stimulated the whigs to try this alternative method of exploiting popular feeling. Russell's reform motion in 1822 attracted 164 votes, the largest ever mustered on such an issue since Pitt's youthful effort in 1785. In 1823 Lord Archibald Hamilton's motion to reform the narrow representative system of the Scottish counties was defeated by only thirty-five votes, an encouraging result greeted by loud cheers from the opposition benches. A tangible factor in the gradual conversion of the whigs to reform as a party measure was the publicity given to an analysis[3] of divisions in the 1822 session. This showed that the strength of the government derived preponderantly from the Irish and Scottish constituencies and from the close boroughs in England, while most anti-ministerialist votes had come from members representing English counties and the more popular urban constituencies. Even more disquieting was the attitude of the country gentry who in 1821, over the disfranchisement of the corrupt borough of Grampound, had overruled the ministers and voted to transfer the seats to Leeds. Though the House of Lords rejected this and on Liverpool's motion gave the seats to the West Riding, this tactical success brought little comfort to the prime minister. If the normally conservative country gentlemen believed that agitation in the country could be soothed by piecemeal concession, he concluded, the whole principle of reform would soon be accepted. The House of Lords could not act indefinitely as the watchdog of the old constitution.

While ready to punish individual cases of corruption, Liverpool was opposed to any systematic reconstruction of the electoral system. If examples were to be made, he preferred to transfer forfeited seats to the larger counties. The county representatives, he told his cabinet, 'if not generally the ablest members in the House, are certainly those who have the greatest stake in the country, and may be trusted for the most part in periods of difficulty and danger';

---

[3] *An Alphabetical List of Members of the Commons House of Parliament* (1822). A digest of the contents is given in the *Annual Register 1823*, pp. 15–16.

whereas the grant of representation for the new industrial areas would merely result in the return of men 'least likely to be steadily attached to the good order of society'. Fortunately for the cabinet the years 1821–2 were abnormal and by the mid-1820s interest in electoral reform both in parliament and the country seemed to have evaporated. Canning's classic and eloquent defences of the old order, based largely on Edmund Burkes's arguments, were acceptable to the governing classes and a large section of public opinion because the system, despite its defects and anomalies, was producing sensible, enlightened and efficient government. With Cobbett's thesis so clearly disproved, there seemed little point in endeavouring on abstract grounds to alter the parliamentary basis of what Lord Bathurst, with little exaggeration, had called in 1825 'the most popular administration which this country has for some time had'. Prosperity for the time being killed reform.

Even party politics was at a discount. With no radical wind to fill their sails, the whig opposition fell once more into the doldrums. The ministers had outbid them for the support of moderate liberal opinion in the country and a section of their own party, the free-trade economists, readily cooperated with the government to defeat the protectionists and agriculturalists. The real core of opposition to ministerial policy was to be found not among the whigs, but among the country gentlemen who conventionally ranked as government supporters. Agriculturalists and protectionists by interest and in- stinct, uneasy at the progress of liberal ideas, jealous of the growing importance of commerce and industry, frustrated at their inability to get legislative concessions to the landed interest, they found themselves in an increasingly shapeless political world in which their proper role was not obvious either to themselves or to others.

While the danger of parliamentary reform seemed temporarily shelved, the other great constitutional issue of Catholic Emancipation was a permanent irritant. With a mass of tory squires forming a solid 'Protestant' party on the one side and the whigs an almost equally solid 'Catholic' party on the other, the government was suspended uneasily between them, without unity and without policy. The Pittite tradition, on all other matters a unifying influence, on this had bequeathed nothing but weakness and division. Pitt had both proposed and subsequently repudiated a final settlement which would put Roman Catholics in a position of complete political equality with Protestants. Pittite politicians could use their master's name to justify totally opposed attitudes. The impossibility of securing unity had led in 1812 to an agreement that the cabinet would remain neutral on the issue, that it would not be raised as a matter of government policy, and that if it were raised independently

in parliament, members of the administration would be free to speak
and vote as they pleased. It was a confession of weakness that brought
strains and difficulties, not least to the Irish executive. But without
it Liverpool's administration could not have been formed, and would
not have lasted. Nevertheless, nothing could prevent the issue from
being brought up almost annually in parliament in one form or
another; and as the long, unresolved argument dragged on from one
session to the next, all the leading politicians began to be labelled
'Protestant' or 'Catholic' according to the stand they took and the
lengthening record of commitment created by past votes and
speeches.

Up to 1822 the balance of power in the cabinet was held by the
'Protestants' who included senior ministers like Sidmouth, Eldon and
Bathurst as well as the prime minister himself. Castlereagh, the
leading 'Catholic' minister, though faithful to the principle which
had made him resign with Pitt in 1801, loyally accepted the cabinet
agreement not to make it an internal issue; and Canning, when he
returned to the cabinet in 1816, thought it wise to live down his
chequered past rather than cause fresh controversies. After 1823 the
situation changed. Canning was now leader of the Commons and the
prime minister's right-hand man; the Grenvillites had brought in a
fresh accession of 'Catholic' sympathies; and the not unconnected
choice of Earl Wellesley as lord lieutenant of Ireland in 1822 was
significantly the first 'Catholic' appointment to the head of the Irish
executive since the whig Talents administration of 1806. More
important still, after 1823 the renewal of Catholic agitation in Ireland
under O'Connell and the Catholic Association brought about a more
dangerous situation in the other island and a greater urgency to
Catholic debates in parliament.

Already in 1821, in the aftermath of the Queen's trial, the House
of Commons had given a small but decisive majority for Plunket's
bill to relieve Catholic disabilities, even though it was subsequently
thrown out by the Lords. In 1822 Canning's bill (introduced after
his appointment to India) for admitting Catholic peers to the
parliament also passed the Commons before meeting its inevitable
fate in the upper house. In 1825 came Burdett's comprehensive effort
which flanked the central Catholic relief bill with two subordinate
measures (the 'wings' as they were known) designed to allay
Protestant fears: a bill to provide for the payment of Irish Catholic
clergy and another to abolish the 40s. freehold franchise in the Irish
counties. The triumphant progress of Burdett's main bill through
the Commons (it passed its third reading in May by twenty-one
votes) produced a cabinet crisis. Faced with the opposition of all his
senior colleagues in the Commons (Canning, Robinson, Huskisson

and Wynn) and encountering a succession of defeats on all aspects of
the bill, Peel offered his resignation. Since the great debate of 1817,
which earned him his seat for Oxford University, Peel had been the
leading 'Protestant' spokesman in the Commons. In the situation
created by Burdett's success he concluded that his position as minister
was an embarrassment both to himself and to the government.

Simultaneously Liverpool raised the question of his own retirement. Though he had little doubt of his ability to persuade the
Lords to reject Burdett's measure, as they had rejected similar bills
in previous years, this could only be in the nature of a final gesture.
It was impossible for the upper house to go on for ever staving off
the deliberate wishes of the Commons. Moreover, Peel's departure
would be such an actual and symbolic loss to the 'Protestant' party
in the government that the prime minister felt he could not honour-
ably continue at its head. In the end Wellington and Bathurst, the
influential elder statesmen of the cabinet, persuaded Peel and Liverpool to refrain from a step which would clearly lead to the collapse
of the entire government. In that event, as Peel could see for
himself, the only possible outcome would be a ministry under
Canning pledged to emancipation.

But all was not yet over. When Burdett's bill met its expected
defeat in the Lords (aided by a sensational speech by the duke of
York, the presumptive heir to the throne) the crisis entered on its
second stage. Canning now asked for a special cabinet meeting to
consider the Catholic question and told Liverpool that the government could not remain neutral on the issue any longer. Once more
the prime minister was caught in a dilemma. Though Bathurst and
no doubt others would have been prepared to let Canning resign,
Liverpool was as loath to lose him as he was Peel. In the end counsels
of moderation once more prevailed. In a series of cabinet meetings
at the end of May Canning, finding himself opposed even by
'Catholic' colleagues like Robinson and Melville, gave way to the
general feeling. For their part Liverpool and Peel agreed that the size
of the Protestant majority in the Lords provided them with enough
justification for staying in office. It was obvious to everyone that
Canning's proposal, though not without a certain political logic,
would break up the government. This in the last resort none of them
were prepared to contemplate. Agreeing still to disagree on the
most controversial issue in domestic politics, the Liverpool administration safely surmounted its most difficult crisis since 1820. But the
strains left on its members were slow to disappear.

As most ministers realized, the crisis had only been postponed.
Many must have feared that when it did come, the inevitable result
would be that, in Liverpool's pessimistic phrase, 'the Protestant's

cause must go to the wall'. All that the cabinet had bought was time.
When the ministers discussed their immediate future, they agreed not
to hold a general election until the summer of 1826, the last practicable date, to keep the question of a new corn bill in suspense
during the last session of the old parliament, and to discourage any
renewal of the Catholic issue. When it came, the general election of
June 1826 offered the usual desultory series of local contests rather
than any grand clash of parties and principles, though it was
estimated that the 'Protestants' had slightly increased their numbers.
The electorate was always more anti-Catholic than the Commons.
But this made little difference to a cabinet that had always found
its main source of strength within itself. That unity was now visibly
crumbling. Liverpool, morbidly anticipating that his administration
would finally founder on the emancipation issue the following session,
was already a tired man, nearing the end of his physical resources.
In December 1826, for the third time since the divorce crisis of 1820,
he was seriously ill from hypertension and low pulse-rate. The
problem of his successor was now something more than a remote
contingency. Wellington, indifferent on the Catholic question, disliked Canning's foreign policy and was not the only one to distrust
his systematic attempts to curry favour with the king. Peel, the
ablest minister in the Commons after Canning, was drifting into a
closer relationship with Wellington. The uneasy equilibrium in the
cabinet hung on the fragile health of the prematurely aged man
(only fifty-six but apart from one period of thirteen months con-
tinuously in office since 1793) who in January 1827 was ordered by his
doctors off to Bath for a month's convalescence.

5 The Constitutional Revolution

I

In February 1827 Lord Liverpool suffered a severe stroke. After six weeks of confusion and delay his wife sent in his formal resignation. In December 1828 the most underrated prime minister of the century died almost unnoticed. Liverpool's government, in structure and appearance the last of the long eighteenth-century administrations, in outlook and achievement was the first of the nineteenth-century conservative ministries. Its members looked back to Pitt in the 1790s; its policy anticipated that of Peel in the 1840s. The essence of the Liverpool system was opposition to constitutional changes combined with innovation in administrative and social policy. The two aspects were not separate; together they formed an integrated response to the problems of government after Waterloo. But because it was the response of a cabinet rather than of a party, it lacked a foundation of permanent strength; and the personal continuity between the cabinets of 1822–7 and 1841–6 has been curiously overlooked.

The extent to which the Liverpool administration depended on Lord Liverpool was shown by the disintegration of cabinet unity and policy direction during the next three years. With the end of the fifteen-year-old political empire, a kind of balkanization of politics ensued. The 'succession' ministries of Canning, Goderich and Wellington represented the fragmentation of the old governmental connection rather than any new alignment. Those ministries were sufficiently imbued with the Liverpool tradition to attempt, sometimes successfully, a continuation of the reforming policies of the 1819–26 era. But their growing weakness, caused initially more by personal difficulties than any deliberate withdrawal of parliamentary support, forced them to internal compromise and external concession on issues where Liverpool had been able to maintain a firm stand. Compromise and concession broke up their support in the House of Commons still further. In the end, after quarter of a century of opposition, the whigs under Lord Grey seemed the only group

capable of forming an administration, not so much from their own
intrinsic strength as from the utter disunity of their former opponents.

The King's choice of Canning to succeed Liverpool as prime
minister produced the first schism. It seemed a reasonable choice.
Canning was the ablest of the senior members of the cabinet; he
already led the Commons; his claims were indisputable. But his
appointment in April was followed by the resignations of half the
old cabinet. Some, like Peel's, had been anticipated, but not all.
Most were from 'Protestants' but some 'Protestants' stayed in office
while Melville a 'Catholic' went out. At bottom it was not merely
Protestant feeling or opposition to Canning's foreign policy that
broke up the administration but a deep, unconquerable distrust of
the man himself. Deserted by half his colleagues, Canning had to
fill the vacancies by taking in whigs. Not all the leading whigs were
prepared to join him, particularly in the absence of any pledge on
Catholic Emancipation. Lord Grey in fact regarded the coalition
as a betrayal of whig principles, though his definition of principle
was perhaps coloured by his dislike of Canning. For the bulk of the
party under Lord Lansdowne the prospect of office and delight at
ending the long tory domination were enough. How the fragile
alliance would have fared, what Canning would have done about
emancipation and parliamentary reform, was never to be known.
Four months later he was dead.

Robinson, who had assumed the title of Goderich when he took
over the leadership of the House of Lords for Canning in April 1827,
now took over the cabinet. Harassed by a neurotic wife, surrounded
by lukewarm and intriguing colleagues, he was temperamentally
unfitted to assert any mastery over his divided administration. As the
only prime minister who never met parliament, he has been treated
somewhat contemptuously by posterity. But the malicious epithets
of 'Goody Goderich' and the 'Blubberer' suggest a more foolish man
than he actually was. It was Huskisson's nerve that collapsed, not
his; and it was the King, fearful of a further lurch towards the whigs,
who was responsible for easing his amiable, unassertive prime
minister out of office in January 1828.

In selecting the duke of Wellington as his successor, the King was
looking for a strong man to rally traditional support from peers and
commoners behind the executive after the weakness and divisions
of the previous twelve months. His field of choice was painfully
limited. Most of the senior members of Liverpool's administration
were either too old or too discredited by recent events. The only
real alternative was Peel, who at the age of forty was not too young
for the premiership in a society that preferred to judge men by
performance rather than age. But he was suffered under two dis-

advantages. He was the acknowledged champion of the 'Protestant' party and his appointment would give a distinct anti-Catholic flavour to his government. What counted even more against him in the eyes of George IV and many orthodox tories was his liberalism on all other matters. The choice of Wellington was natural enough, as that of Canning had been; but the disadvantages were even clearer. Not all were happy to see, for the first time since Cromwell, a professional soldier at the head of civil government, particularly in an age when the army was the only effective peace-keeping force. The unanimous view of the cabinet that he would have to resign from his post of commander-in-chief was a mark of their sensitivity on the subject.

Wellington of course was not merely a soldier. His victory over Napoleon and his own strong character had given him enormous prestige among the aristocracy. He had been a member of Liverpool's cabinet between 1818 and 1827 and had considerable diplomatic experience. He was a good administrator and he had political courage. Once convinced of the necessity of a measure, he would see it through unflinchingly. He was as averse to compromise as he was careless of consistency. In politics, however, by a complete reversal of his military abilities, he was an excellent subordinate but a disastrous leader. His great weakness was his indifference to public opinion and his remoteness from ordinary parliamentary life. Accustomed to the discipline of the army, insulated by the deference of his own social circle, he was ill at ease in the more ambiguous and equalitarian relationships of politics. In a matter-of-fact way he was aware of his defects; but as 'the retained servant of the Sovereign' (his own characteristic phrase) he felt it his duty to respond to any call from the crown for his services. Moreover he thought there was a need for all those who belonged to the *parti conservateur*, in the continental vocabulary which came naturally to him, to stand together for the preservation of the fundamental institutions of the state against radicals and levellers, among whom he was apt to class Canning and Huskisson.

Peel, politically the ablest of the seceders of 1827, was Wellington's inevitable second-in-command, a professional chief of staff to his amateur political general. Under his influence the new administration was deliberately designed to be a reunification of 'Lord Liverpool's old party' in its latest form. The omission of men like Eldon, Westmoreland and Vansittart, and the retention of the Canningites (Huskisson, Palmerston, Grant, Dudley and Lamb) was the first disappointment for those ultra-tories who mistakenly saw in the duke the champion of reaction. The reunification, however, did not last long. Though the Canningites were never isolated on policy, they isolated themselves personally. The prickliness of Grant and Huskisson made cabinet life difficult; the insistence of the Canningites on acting as a group made it impossible. The East Retford bill on which they retired in May 1828 was a relatively minor issue; but Huskisson's offer of resignation was the third to emanate from the Canningites in four months. Huskisson's temperamental defects (obvious before but worse since Canning's fatherly influence had been removed), together with the duke's ill-concealed impatience, brought about the final break. But the fundamental cause lay in the disruption of Liverpool's cabinet a year earlier.

The departure of the Canningites and their replacement by men of inferior ability, the only reinforcements available from the small stock of government reserves, did not materially affect policy. For Peel the return to the Home Office enabled him to complete the programme of legal reform left unfinished in 1827. The only slight setback came over his forgery bill in 1830 when Mackintosh secured a small majority for reducing still further the types of forgery for which the death penalty was still retained. Though the cabinet agreed to accept the amendment, the House of Lords restored the original clause. But in fact no one was hanged for forgery after 1830. Of more lasting consequence was the Home Secretary's success in obtaining a police committee which reported favourably in 1828. The following year, profiting by the distraction of public interest over Catholic Emancipation, he succeeded with a remarkable absence of debate in putting through his metropolitan police bill. Aided by an admirable choice of the first two commissioners, Rowan and Mayne, and based on the preventive principles of Colquhoun, the new force, whose members went on their beats in September 1829 with their blue uniforms, top hats and truncheons, was the first efficient body of civil police that England had ever possessed. Peel did not remain in office long enough to carry out his plans for the country as a whole, but his Metropolitan Police provided the model and recruiting-ground for similar forces set up in borough and county during the middle decades of the century. Though the whigs were lukewarm and the radicals (though not the Benthamites) hostile, with the public at large the 'Peelers' or 'Bobbys', as they were called after their founder, soon became an accepted and popular London institution. It was the first great administrative step towards a more ordered society.

The remaining items left over from the Liverpool era did not fare so well. The corn bill which Liverpool had prepared before his collapse provided a sliding scale of duties to operate around the pivot price of 60s., ceasing entirely at 70s. a quarter. Introduced by Canning in March 1827 it passed through the Commons with comfortable majorities despite bitter attacks from the agriculturalists. In the House of Lords, largely because of a misunderstanding between Huskisson and Wellington, it was slightly amended to prevent bonded corn coming on the market until the price reached 66s. Taking the view that the amendment destroyed the principle of the bill (though that was not the universal opinion), Canning as prime minister postponed the issue until the following session. He suspected a political intrigue against his new government and both in public and private expressed considerable irritation. Next session Huskisson, now a member of Wellington's cabinet, took the matter up once more. After some friction it was finally agreed, largely through Peel's mediation, to accept a compromise between Canning's bill, which most of the cabinet favoured, and the duke's agricultural partialities. The new bill was similar to the old except that between 60s. and 70s. a quarter the scale of duty was increased and foreign wheat was not admitted free until the domestic price reached 73s. In this form it passed and the acts of 1815 and 1822 were repealed. Though perhaps most of the duke's cabinet, and certainly Huskisson, were not happy over the details, at least the principle of absolute prohibition up to 80s. had been abandoned and a sliding scale operating from 72s. downwards put in its place.

Less than free traders wanted, more than agriculturalists approved, it was a not unreasonable compromise. In a sense it was Lord Liverpool's last legacy to his country. It represented the formal retreat from the high prohibitive tariff of 1815 and a response to the mounting public and press attacks on corn law monopolists and iniquitous landlords. The majorities for Canning's bill in 1827 and Huskisson's bill in 1828 were a sign of the general readiness of the gentry to learn the lesson Lord Liverpool had tried to teach. Some indeed by 1828 had even become converts to free trade. In this they were influenced by more than merely economic considerations. At the time of the debates in the Lords over the 1827 bill Canning had said bitterly in private conversation that 'they ought to see that we are on the brink of a great struggle between property and population. Such a struggle is only to be averted by the mildest and most liberal legislation'. The bulk of the House of Commons by that date were of much the same opinion. What remained to be seen was whether any protective legislation would prove satisfactory to the public on a matter that affected the food of the poor and depended on the vagaries of the British climate.

On finance and tariff reform these years saw the Liverpool policy come to a halt and two opportunities missed of securing the one measure which would have given it renewed momentum. The general trade depression which lasted almost without a break from

1827 to 1831 had its inevitable effect on the revenue. Though there were budget surpluses in every year up to 1830, they were insufficient to justify any further tariff reductions. Liverpool had long ago foreseen that the only remedy for this situation lay in an increase in direct taxation. He told Canning privately in 1824 that the limits of tax reduction had been reached and that the true policy (if they could do it) was to add to direct taxation and reduce indirect. As it was, direct taxation in Britain was under £4 millions per annum, less in proportion to total revenue than in any other European state. Increasingly the opinion was gaining ground among the experts that the only way out of the persistent financial stalemate was to restore the income tax. Herries as chancellor of the exchequer was preparing for this when the Goderich ministry collapsed. In the following Wellington administration several cabinet ministers including Peel, Herries and Goulburn, the new chancellor, were agreed that time had come for a fundamental recasting of the revenue system. Only the resistance of the duke and the majority of their colleagues prevented Goulburn from incorporating a proposal for a modified income tax in his 1830 budget. The second opportunity of putting the finances of the country on a permanently sound footing was thus let slip.

In public Peel spoke in strong terms of the need to alleviate the burden on the poorer classes by reducing indirect taxation. In cabinet he stressed the importance of reaching such plutocrats as the financier Rothschild, Baring (another wealthy banker) and his own father (a textile millionaire) as well as absentee Irish landowners. Goulburn's budget speech of 1830 contained a striking enunciation of the government's desire to follow the principle of affording the greatest possible relief to the urban and working classes. The abolition of the beer and leather duties he put forward as an earnest of his intentions was, however, only a faint substitute for an income tax. Behind the scenes Peel and Herries continued to warn their aristocratic colleagues that such a tax would have to be introduced the following session. But in less than twelve months they were out of office. It was another twelve years before Peel, supported by other survivors of the Liverpool ministry—Goulburn, Herries and Robinson—could return to that fundamental problem.

II

Parliamentary weakness and Wellingtonian conservatism ensured that the 1827–30 administrations were memorable less for innovation than for concession. It was a curious paradox, in view of Wellington's lack of dogmatic religion, that the formation of his ministry at once brought down on him demands from both Protestants and Catholics. It was not however a coincidence; the timing of both demands was dictated by the vulnerability of his parliamentary position.

The first attack came over the Test and Corporation Acts, those largely symbolic testimonies to the old anglican supremacy in the state. Though after Waterloo the Protestant Deputies seemed to have relapsed into a policy of political conservatism, the storm over Brougham's educational bill in 1820 indicated the strength of dissenting feeling in the country when it appeared that their interests were being sacrificed to the established church. The ministers of the Three Denominations and the militant Protestant Society set up a united committee to exert pressure on parliament and the bill was hastily dropped after the first reading. This easy success encouraged those more aggressive dissenters who felt that their traditional representatives in London were unnecessarily diffident.

Much of this dissenting confidence arose from a consciousness of their growing numbers and importance in post-war society, aided by what the Protestant Deputies described in 1823 as the 'rapid progress of knowledge and just views of civil government' and the 'increasing liberality of the times'. The gathering movement for complete religious equality in the 1820s derived less from an abstract passion for a principle than from the social aspirations of a rising class. The characteristic nonconformist virtues of frugality, prudence and integrity assisted its members to success in worldly life. The consolidation of the dissenting churches fostered a sense of social respectability. Both developments strengthened the desire for the legal rehabilitation represented by a repeal of the Test and Corporation Acts. Social mobility and social status were incomplete without the disappearance from civil life of all religious distinctions.

Both sides were agreed that the Test and Corporation Acts were mainly symbolic—that dissenters could and did occupy important offices and become members of corporations. Since in the decade preceding the repeal of those acts three dissenters had held the office of lord mayor of London, to argue otherwise would have been absurd. What the great body of dissenters wanted was to break down the social prejudice that lay behind the legislative symbol. An official statement issued in 1827 by the Protestant Deputies argued that while in practice dissenters could hope to fill many public positions of influence and distinction, not as many did as might, partly because of social and official prejudice, partly because of the reluctance of conscientious dissenters to 'purchase eminent success by a sacrifice of principle'. Eminent success in worldly affairs was, however, evidently regarded by them as a legitimate ambition which ought to be open to all. At bottom it was social equality rather than religious toleration that was behind the campaign to abolish the Test and Corporation Acts.

Although the absence of practical hardship robbed the question of any political urgency, repeal of the acts might have come earlier than it did. What complicated the issue was the Catholic question. Up to 1827 there was every reason to believe that repeal of the Test and Corporation Acts would only come as part of a general religious settlement in which the main feature would be Catholic Emancipation. Liberal politicians like Russell and Palmerston thought in fact that the granting of religious equality to Protestant dissenters might postpone idefinitely the emancipation of the Roman Catholics which was their primary concern. The Protestant Deputies under their veteran chairman William Smith, the Unitarian MP for Norwich, were accustomed to working through the parliamentary politicians and tended to accept their views on tactics, all the more since in this case these agreed with their own convictions on the indivisibility of the principle of religious toleration. The more democratic dissenting bodies in the country not only favoured a more independent line, but disliked having their cause linked with that of Catholic Emancipation. Among the mass of ordinary dissenting congregations, as among the rank and file of the Methodists, anti-Catholic feeling was still a powerful emotion. This internal disagreement over both tactics and principle was the main reason for the absence of dissenting initiative in the early 1820s. Not until the defeat of Burdett's motion in 1827 did the opportunity seem to present itself for a separate Protestant campaign for the repeal of the Test and Corporation Acts. A United Committee was set up to head the agitation and draft petitions were circulated to dissenting congregations all over the country. The accession of Canning as prime minister, however, and the junction with his government of a large section of the whigs, brought the campaign to an abrupt halt. Canning was pledged not to consider the repeal of the Test and Corporation Acts in advance of emancipation and his new whig allies were not prepared to jeopardize the future of the coalition on what to them was a side issue.

Next session the situation was reversed. With Wellington in office, and the whigs reunited in opposition, the parliamentary alignments once more favoured the dissenters. The still suspicious Protestant Society, which had run a separate campaign in 1827, was mollified by a declaration from the United Committee that it would not form any alliance with the Catholics. The way was now clear for a great if somewhat misleading demonstration of Protestant dissenting solidarity. Backed by the disciplined response of the dissenting congregations, conveyed in a mass of petitions to the House of Commons, Lord John Russell in February carried a motion to repeal the acts. Though formal opposition had come from the government, there was no disposition on the part of the cabinet to make it a contentious issue. The government had no automatic majority to enforce policy; the dissenting interest was strong in many constituencies; and in the House of Commons there was a clear preponderance of feeling in favour of repeal. Peel as home secretary virtually took charge of the ensuing bill and to mollify anglican susceptibilities he devised, in consultation with the bishops, a substitute for the old sacramental test in the form of a declaration binding the taker not to injure the established church. The declaration was to be compulsory for those chosen for corporation offices and at the discretion of the crown for civil posts. In the House of Lords the majority of bishops voted for the bill, though at the suggestion of the bishop of Llandaff an addition was made to the declaration of the phrase 'upon the true faith of a Christian'—a formula which had the technical effect of excluding atheists, Jews and (arguably) Unitarians.

Though Peel did not think this an improvement, to avoid controversy the amendment was accepted and by May all the formalities were concluded. After years of dissenting discussion and preparation, the easy passage of the bill was almost an anticlimax. Once the Commons had accepted Russell's motion, no resistance was offered by church leaders, not even by that citadel of orthodox Anglicanism, Oxford University. Though it was, as the *Annual Register* observed in its review of the year, 'the first successful blow that had been aimed at the supremacy of the Established Church since the Revolution', the absence of any real will to resist was a significant commentary on the altered nature of English society.

III

In its broadest terms Catholic Emancipation the following year raised the same issues as the repeal of the Test and Corporation Acts. The arguments on its behalf scarcely needed recapitulation. Justice, liberalism, expediency all spoke in favour of admitting Catholics to full political equality. There was an intellectual case against it, but it was largely historical. To abandon the specifically Protestant character of the state was to abandon something that had

been established by the Reformation in the sixteenth century and
preserved in the seventeenth at the cost of expelling the lawful
dynasty. In 1689, as old Lord Eldon once reminded the House of
Lords, it had been decided 'that this country should have a Protestant
King, a Protestant Parliament and a Protestant Government'. Under
the constitution thus formed Britain had achieved domestic peace,
imperial greatness and material prosperity. It had stood the test of
time as no other European monarchy had done. In such circumstances it did not seem illogical to distinguish between religious
toleration and political power. To admit Catholics to the latter was
to change the principle on which the constitution was founded.
Men from middle-class backgrounds like Eldon, Sidmouth, Peel,
even Liverpool himself, who with their families had risen to wealth
and fame under that constitution, often supported it as fervently as
the old aristocracy. Some of them were convinced, moreover, that
religion could not be divorced from the state without damage to
both. The purpose of the establishment, as Eldon pointed out, was
not to make the church political but to make the state religious.

Political issues, though sometimes influenced by intellectual
considerations, are rarely decided by them. Had it been only a
question of the English Roman Catholics, there would have been
no difficulty. A tiny minority of the nation, socially isolated,
politically passive, the English Catholics formed a kind of hermit
community that offered no conceivable political danger. Both Peel
and Liverpool supported bills introduced in 1823 and 1824 to
enfranchise English Catholics; and both were in favour of admitting
them to office on the same terms as dissenters, under the protection
of annual indemnity acts. But the issue never presented itself in those
safe and limited English terms. Catholic Emancipation involved
Ireland and the whole controversy was an illustration of the unique
ability of Ireland to translate English problems into a completely
different idiom. In one sense there was a close analogy between the
two countries. The emancipation movement in Ireland was essentially a demand of the rising Catholic middle classes—small gentry,
lawyers, merchants, journalists, shopkeepers—for social equality.
To that extent the dissenting intellectuals were right to couple
Catholic Emancipation with the repeal of the Test and Corporation
Acts. But in both countries the primary emancipation issue was
distorted by two other considerations—Roman Catholic autonomy
and Irish political separatism. Catholic Irish nationalism was the
uniquely blended phenomenon which transformed the simple question of religious disabilities into a matter affecting the unity and
security of the British Isles.

At the political and parliamentary level the obvious division was between those who regarded emancipation as a necessary completion of Pitt's Act of Union and those who believed that emancipation, by giving political power to the native Catholics, would lead inevitably to Irish independence. In practice this was further complicated by the friction and misunderstanding that had grown up between the professional, ministerial politicians who had to accept the cabinet rule of neutrality, and the independent, 'amateur' MPs who having no official responsibilities could afford the luxury of conscientious partisanship. The suspicions which existed between whigs and Canningites, for example, had their counterpart in the jealousies of ultra-tory peers and MPs at the liberalism of the cabinet in 1825 and in the rumours which swept London that Lord Liverpool was about to give way over Burdett's bill.

Though politicians were divided, however, the overwhelming preponderance of feeling in the country was anti-Catholic. The 1825 crisis had revealed both the depth of Protestant fervour and the plain fact that the 'Catholic' majority in the House of Commons did not represent the true wishes of the people. For the clergy of the establishment, who took a prominent part in petitioning parliament, the church of Rome was the historic enemy. Protestant dissenters could charitably be regarded as seceded members of the Church of England; but Catholicism was the ancient rival with whom there could be no compromise if anglican legitimacy was to be upheld. On this issue at least there were few sectarian or social divisions in English society. Peers, landowners, manufacturers, dissenting congregations, all joined in denouncing emancipation. Among Methodists, following the example of Wesley himself and deeply influenced by the experiences of their congregations in Ireland, anti-Catholicism was at least as strong as in the anglican church. The strength of Methodist opposition was concealed only by the personal influence of their remarkable leader, Jabez Bunting, one of the few prominent Wesleyans in favour of emancipation, and the traditional reluctance of the Committee of Privileges to intervene in political matters except when Methodist interests were directly involved. Bunting, however, had to resist considerable pressure. 'Many of our preachers and people', he wrote in February 1829, 'are goading each other to petition against it *as Methodists*.' Lower down the scale, in a society where a worn volume of Foxe's *Book of Martyrs* was often a treasured possession in the cottages of the poor along with the Bible and *Pilgrim's Progress*, the historic anti-Roman prejudice was still passionately alive. 'The difficulty is neither with the King nor with the Cabinet,' observed the *Edinburgh Review* in 1827, 'neither with the Commons nor with the Lords. It is with the people of England.' No general election had ever yielded a majority for emancipation;

and whenever it was made an electoral issue, Protestantism had been strengthened. The people of England would never have passed Catholic Emancipation in 1829; and it was as well for that cause that the country was still ruled by an oligarchy.

In the summer of 1828 the House of Commons, which had already agreed to repeal the Test and Corporation Acts, put on record its opinion that there should be a final and conciliatory adjustment of the laws affecting Roman Catholics. The motion, introduced by Burdett, passed by six votes; and though a parallel resolution was defeated in the Lords, the sands were clearly running out for the Protestant party. To both Wellington and Peel it seemed that Catholic Emancipation was now only a matter of time and opportunity. In the event O'Connell precipitated the decision by demonstrating that continued delay would endanger the Union. The general election of 1826 had already revealed the political influence of the Irish parish priests and the new Catholic Association. The accession to power of the Wellington administration freed O'Connell from the restraints he had carefully observed as long as there was a chance of obtaining emancipation peacefully at the hands of the Canningites. The peasant meetings held all over Ireland early in 1828 and O'Connell's return for Co. Clare at a by-election in July, although as a Catholic he could not take his seat in parliament, confronted the government with a direct challenge.

Ministers were now in a fundamental dilemma. Without sharper coercive powers than they already possessed, the Catholic Association could not be suppressed. Yet a House of Commons that had voted for Burdett's bill would certainly refuse to pass a coercion bill unless accompanied by emancipation. To dissolve parliament and go to the electorate on a cry of 'No Popery' would probably yield a Protestant majority; but such a step would be politically unwise and practically difficult. Wellington's cabinet, like all since 1809, had been based on a principle of neutrality towards emancipation and contained both 'Protestants' and 'Catholics'. A new policy of explicit resistance would necessitate the formation of an exclusively 'Protestant' cabinet. Even if one could be formed, a general election would involve Ireland; and what had been done once in Co. Clare could be repeated in a score of Irish counties. The Irish representative system would become a farce; the electoral influence of the landed gentry would suffer irreparable damage; and the new cabinet would be faced with an immediate crisis. Behind the political dilemma was the larger threat of civil disorder. Although O'Connell was basically a constitutional agitator, he was too much of a demagogue not to make use of the menace of actual rebellion. As the tension mounted, the Irish secretary at the end of September warned his government to make their military arrangements as though Ireland were 'on the eve of rebellion or civil war'. Two months earlier Wellington had summed up the position in a brutally explicit letter to the King. With rebellion pending in Ireland, he observed grimly, the government was faced at home with a parliament it dared not dissolve, with a majority in it which favoured emancipation.

By July 1828 the duke in fact had made up his mind that Catholic Emancipation must be conceded. His main problem was with the King who was reluctant even to allow the matter to be considered by the cabinet, though the prime minister gained little support from the bishops when they were eventually brought into the discussions. It was partly these difficulties behind the scenes, partly Wellington's argument that his aid was indispensable in the House of Commons, that finally persuaded Peel to stay in office and take charge of the bill. The cost to the home secretary's reputation was enormous, not only in the loss of his seat for Oxford University where he quixotically exposed himself to a by-election, but in the immediate reproaches and lasting doubts which followed his change of front. Nevertheless his continued presence in the cabinet was decisive. All the points he had been arguing for with Wellington in the autumn were substantially incorporated in the bill. The duke, despite his public reputation as a diehard tory, had never belonged to the ultra-Protestant group. In 1825 he had startled his colleagues by producing a plan for an agreement with the Papacy, endowment of the Catholic clergy in Ireland, and government supervision of their higher appointments. He made similar proposals to Peel in 1828; but now that the crisis had arrived, the home secretary came out firmly for a simple, permanent solution containing as few seeds of future trouble as possible.

As passed, the act was framed on Peelite, not Wellingtonian lines. Catholics were admitted to all but a handful of offices of state, the exceptions being those representing or directly connected with the crown. The 'securities' that had been discussed so much during the previous fifteen years were discarded. There was to be no concordat with the Pope; no crown veto on episcopal appointments; no payment of priests. The only tangible safeguard was political: a bill to raise the Irish county franchise to £10 in place of the old 40s. freehold. The clauses dealing with ecclesiastical titles and monastic orders were of secondary importance and in the event proved useless. In effect Catholics were to be admitted to full membership of the state in its political and administrative aspect; but there was to be no place for the Roman Catholic church as an institution. Without a degree of control already rejected by the Roman hierarchy in Ireland such a place could not be found for it; and even if feasible, it is difficult to dissent from Peel's view that such a relationship, imposed by a Protestant, secular state, would have led to constant friction.

Introduced at the beginning of March 1829, the emancipation bill was law by the middle of April. The rapidity of its passage was proof of the parliamentary feeling in its favour. Now that for the first time the government had taken the initiative, even the House of Lords was prepared to acquiesce. The opposition in parliament, however, was only a pale reflection of the impassioned feeling without. For the Protestant party in the country defeat was bad enough. To be betrayed by Wellington and Peel, whom they had once regarded as Protestant champions, reduced them to anger, mortification and despair. Equally disturbing was the consciousness that parliament had failed either to maintain the anglican character of the state or to represent the real opinion of the nation. It had acted neither as conservative oligarchy nor as democratic assembly. The simple partisan explanation was that parliament had behaved as it did because it was unduly and perhaps corruptly influenced by the executive. It was not surprising that some ultra-Protestant tories came to the conclusion that there was more to be said for a reform of parliament than they had so far been prepared to admit, a reform which would eliminate the unconstitutional control of government and individual borough owners, and restore the landed interest to its proper place in the legislature. The successful state prosecution of the Protestant *Morning Journal*, the most virulent press opponent of Catholic Emancipation, for personal libels on members of the government did nothing to assuage the bitterness of party feeling.

IV

With the passing of Catholic Emancipation the capabilities of Wellington's ministry for either reform or concession were virtually exhausted. The stage was now set for the third act of the constitutional revolution. Emancipation accelerated parliamentary reform partly by removing from politics the issue which for quarter of a century had overshadowed all other domestic questions, partly by completing the disintegration of the old Liverpool party and its natural supporters. 'The Catholic Emancipation', wrote Horace Twiss, 'had riven the Conservative body asunder, and through the chasm the Reform Bill forced its way.' Peel's insistence that he regarded the concession, not as desirable in itself, but only as the lesser of two evils, convinced neither whigs, nor Canningites nor ultra-tories of his integrity. After 1829 Wellington's government rested on an impossibly narrow foundation in the Commons, deficient in ministerial strength and backbench support. The duke, politically unimaginative as ever, had no intention of recapturing support by taking the initiative in parliamentary reform. The mild East Retford bill in 1830, which transferred the seats of that notoriously rotten borough to the neighbouring hundreds rather than to Birmingham, as proposed in the Commons, had to be forced by Peel through the House of Lords against the wishes of his more aristocratic cabinet colleagues who would have preferred no action at all. The plan of a reunion with the Huskissonites, intermittently discussed during 1830, was never taken up by the duke with any conviction. Peel, the only outstanding man in the cabinet of strong reforming outlook, began to feel a prisoner in a ministry whose attitude he found increasingly negative and frustrating.

Though the government was seen to be weak, however, nobody foresaw in the 1830 session that the following year would see a whig ministry and a reform bill. To that extent the 1831 crisis was a fortuitous event. Even the general election of 1830 played no decisive role. Only about a quarter of the constituencies in England and Wales were contested and though the government made on balance no great gains or losses, the House of Commons was too fragmented for any calculation of strength to be of value. It was clear that the electorate had many grievances and wanted many reforms—parliamentary reform, retrenchment, abolition of slavery, cheap bread. Some of the county contests revealed a powerful current against the traditional aristocratic oligarchies. The whigs in the West Riding had to accept the outsider Henry Brougham, the nominee of the urban liberals, who campaigned on the issue of parliamentary reform. The news of the July Revolution in Paris came too late to have any effect on the actual result of the elections; but it provided much discussion in the following months. What could not be doubted was that the electorate was restless and that the new House of Commons would be difficult to manage. But this was not a new phenomenon. Of more practical importance was the King's death which had caused the election. George IV nourished a personal hostility to Lord Grey and would never willingly have asked him to form or allowed him to join the government. His successor William IV, an elderly unpolitical man of mild whiggish views, had no such antipathies—a circumstance which in itself suddenly enlarged the whigs' political horizon.

What precipitated parliamentary reform was the coincidence of a cabinet crisis and the severe economic depression in the country. By the autumn of 1830 it was obvious that the ministry could not go on without reinforcements. The death of Huskisson at the opening of the Liverpool–Manchester railway in September left the prospects for the Canningites as an independent group weak and uncertain. Nevertheless, intermittent negotiations with the elusive Palmerston suggested that he was thinking in terms of a larger liberal coalition than Wellington was prepared to accept. The whig leaders themselves were not averse to joining the ministry but they wanted the invitation to come from Wellington so that they could dictate their own terms. Though as a party they had never been able to agree wholeheartedly on parliamentary reform, and in the mid-1820s had virtually abandoned it, they were now ready to respond to the changed political climate. With Brougham giving them an embarrassingly strong if unofficial lead, it seemed inevitable that they would have to take it up in the new parliament. Simultaneously Wellington was veering to the alternative, and for him more congenial, plan of a reconciliation with the ultra-tories in a common anti-reform front. With dissatisfied tories already discussing in pamphlet literature and *Blackwood's Magazine* schemes of reform which would strengthen the independent gentry and protect the landed interest, Wellington's change of tactics argued a curious ignorance of what was going on in the lower reaches of the political world. Out of it came the celebrated declaration against reform at the opening of parliament in November 1830 which brought about the defeat and resignation of his administration.

Almost up to the last the whigs had been hoping for a coalition. Cabinet politics still seemed of more practical importance than party politics. Lord Grey became prime minister in November 1830 not because he could command a party majority in the Commons but because he was the only man likely to be able to form an efficient cabinet. His administration was still a coalition, even if it did not include Wellington or Peel. The Canningites took all three secretaryships of state together with the presidency of the Board of Control. Offices were given to tories like Anglesey, Wynn, Wellesley and Richmond and offered to others. Before the whigs could become a party of government they had to recruit men of ministerial experience wherever they could be picked up; and they had to rally support in the Commons and in the country by direct concessions to public opinion. Whig political weakness made the Reform Bill a tactical necessity.

For Grey, however, reform was also an act of statesmanship. The antiquated structure of the English electoral system was defensible only if it produced administrations that both worked and were acceptable to public opinion. Once executive government faltered (as Grey thought it was faltering under Wellington) and the system came under hostile or even merely objective scrutiny, its anomalies and abuses were obvious. The aristocracy had adjusted itself to the eccentricities of the electoral constitution until it had become as intimate and comfortable as an old suit of clothes and its oddities praised as possessing rare and subtle virtues. Nor were its defenders without some justification. What is important about any organization is how it works, not how it is constructed. When Wellington in November 1830 said that it would be impossible for anyone to devise such a good legislature as that which already existed, since 'the nature of man was incapable of reaching such excellence at once', he was right in the sense that the parliamentary constitution of 1830 was the product of time, history, the growth of conventions, and the rationalization of defects. It was an institution which nobody would ever have deliberately framed but which did perform the important functions of linking however inefficiently the executive and legislature, representing however imperfectly the great interests of the country, and responding however tardily to important shifts of public opinion—even to the extent of reforming itself when the time came. Treasury boroughs provided safe seats for hardworking ministers; nomination boroughs gave openings for penniless young men of talent; rotten boroughs allowed middle-aged merchants and manufacturers to enter the House; popular constituencies provided a democratic element.

All this was true; but it was not enough to protect a system that had become to a large part of the nation politically unpopular and morally repugnant. The prescriptive authority of parliament had been eroded by half a century of reform agitation; there were powerful classes in the community who felt excluded from the benefits of the system; and by the late autumn of 1830 there were many in the ruling classes themselves who felt not only that reform was inevitable but that, as with Catholic Emancipation, there was more danger in delay than in concession. In addition to uncertainty at the top, there was sullenness and dissatisfaction at the bottom of society. Industry had never really recovered from the 1826 depression. For the Lancashire handloom weavers it was the start of a long, almost unbroken decline in their earning power. There had been scattered industrial troubles most of the year and in the summer Doherty was organizing a national union of cotton spinners to prevent further wage reductions. A slump in manufactures, low wages and unemployment were aggravated by deficient harvests and high cost of food. The price of wheat rose to 72s. 10d. in late August; and though it fell with the harvest, in December it started another

ominous climb which took it to nearly 74*s.* in March 1831. For the
first time in a decade the old links between industrial and political
agitation were being reforged. There were reports of plans to seize
arms and in October 1830 as a precaution the government reinforced
the garrisons of the northern arms depots. Simultaneously disorders
started among the agricultural labourers in Kent which during
October and November spread to Sussex, Hampshire, Berkshire,
Wiltshire and Dorset, in the largest outbreak of rural rioting in
modern British history.

Social discontent fed movements for parliamentary reform. The
circular for the Birmingham meeting at which Attwood's Political
Union was founded in December 1829 declared in familiar radical
language that the distress in the country was due to governmental
mismanagement and could only be remedied by a reform of the
legislature. The rapid support which Attwood attracted was
a measure of the extent to which the artisans and lower middle
classes in the Midlands were already imbued with this Cobbettite
doctrine. Attwood belonged to the respectable profession of banking
and derived much of his success from his insistence on the need for
the middle and lower classes to join together in a peaceful constitutional campaign. His initiative was followed in a number of other
towns, including London where the Metropolitan Union founded
by O'Connell and Hunt in March placed the same emphasis on
economic distress, mismanagement of public affairs, and the need
for social unity. Not all opinion in the capital was so restrained.
By the autumn of 1830 Carlile and other radical orators were
preaching almost nightly at the Rotunda in Blackfriars Road a gospel
of class warfare to audiences who pinned on tricolour cockades and
demonstrated afterwards in the streets. In November the ministers
had to cancel the King's state visit to the Mansion House on Lord
Mayor's Day and only the new metropolitan police prevented an
ugly riot from developing. Cobbett, himself one of the Rotunda
lecturers, was hard at work all through 1830. At the start of the
year he was talking in Yorkshire and Nottinghamshire; in the spring
he made a great circuit through East Anglia and the Midlands; in
the summer he was active in Yorkshire, Lancashire and the north
of England. Unlike most radicals, moreover, Cobbett's influence was
not confined to the towns and the industrial areas. He had a considerable following among farmers, freeholders and village artisans.

Further north there was renewed activity among the Scottish
liberals. In September Graham and Kennedy of Dunure were
planning a separate motion in the House of Commons for Scottish
parliamentary reform. The case for electoral changes north of the
border was overwhelming and success in one part of the field would

encourage attacks elsewhere. Brougham was not the only MP who went up to Westminster with his plans already laid.

All this scattered, but in aggregate, impressive, activity, coming after a session in which the whig Russell, the eccentric tory Lord Blandford, and the Irish leader O'Connell had all brought forward reform proposals, played its part in determining whig tactics at the start of the new parliament. Even the outgoing cabinet, with the exception of the prime minister, told the king when surrendering their seals in November, that some reform of parliament would have to take place. If the occasion was ripe for parliamentary reform, Grey was equally clearly the man whose record entitled him to take the lead. He had been identified with that cause throughout his political career; and though he had often doubted its feasibility, he had never lost faith in its rightness. All the conditions he needed were now present: a favourable public opinion, a receptive legislature, and freedom of action as new prime minister. Long years of reflection had convinced him that if reform was to be the lasting, conservative remedy he envisaged, it would have to come in full and generous measure. His action in entrusting the drafting of the bill to Durham and Russell, the two most prominent extreme reformers among the whigs, indicated a determination to act boldly.

The primary purpose of the Reform Bill introduced by Russell in March 1831 was to rally middle-class support round the aristocratic system, or in the more decorous language of the Reform Bill committee, 'to satisfy all reasonable demands, and remove at once, and for ever, all rational grounds for complaint from the minds of the intelligent and independent portion of the community'. The political advantage was twofold. It would strengthen the constitution by securing the support of what, in a private letter to a colleague, Grey described as 'the real and efficient mass of public opinion ... without whom the power of the gentry is nothing'. At the same time it would detach the middle classes from a dangerous alliance with the lower classes, founded on common dissatisfaction with the aristocratic system. To achieve this the cabinet, particularly in the first Reform Bill, were concerned not so much to remodel the electoral system as to remove the defects and abuses of which the public most loudly complained. The medley of ancient, often oligarchic, borough voting rights were to have a uniform £10 household franchise imposed on them; sixty rotten boroughs were to be abolished; forty-seven other small boroughs were to lose one member. From the pool of seats thus made available the representation was to be improved by allotting thirty-four to the more important unrepresented towns and fifty-five to the respectable but under-represented county constituencies. The expense of elections was to be reduced by dividing some of the larger counties, increasing the number of polling places, limiting the duration of the poll to two days and providing an official register of electors.

Though various afterthoughts and criticisms (notably the refusal of the House of Commons to allow any diminution of its numerical total) led to revision and expansion of this original plan in the second and third Reform Bills, the fundamental pattern of the whig measure remained unaltered. What Grey called the three cardinal principles of reform—the disfranchisement of rotten boroughs, the enfranchisement of new towns, and the common £10 household franchise—formed the core of the 1832 act. The rest was either secondary detail or political compromise. The object of the ministers was to amend and make acceptable the old system, not to design a new one. The aim of reconciling other influential forces in British society to aristocratic government would have been meaningless if they had not at the same time preserved and at some points even strengthened what they regarded as the sound and respectable parts of the system.

Implicit in this concept was the distinction between the 'legitimate' influence of wealth, property and social rank and the 'illegitimate' influence of individual patrons, bribery and intimidation. The borderline between the two was roughly indicated by the original ministerial proposal to extend the county franchise to a variety of leaseholders, who because of the protection of their lease could be presumed to possess a degree of independence, but not to the tenant-at-will who could be turned out at the end of the year. The enfranchisement of the £50 tenant proposed by Lord Chandos was carried against the government by a combination of landlord squires and urban democrats. The ministers were not altogether pleased and the defeat stiffened their determination to leave the urban 40*s.* freeholder as a county and not a borough voter to counteract direct landlord pressure.[1] But the importance of the Chandos clause was exaggerated both at the time and afterwards. Even before the Reform Act it had not been difficult for tenant farmers to acquire

[1] The decision to leave the urban 40*s.* freeholders in possession of their county vote was actually taken by the cabinet four days before the Chandos amendment was carried. The reason was simply that their exclusion would be highly unpopular with government supporters in the towns. In subsequent debate, however, ministers sometimes spoke as if their decision was consequent on the Chandos clause. It may be added that the argument that the whigs were attempting to effect a complete separation of town and country communities, as distinct from a better balance between those interests, finds little support either in the enactments of the bill or in the deliberations of the cabinet. As against the urban 40*s.* freeholder who voted in the county, many small boroughs were enlarged by taking in surrounding rural areas, a circumstance welcomed by Lord Lansdowne as 'infusing landed interest in town elections'. In any case there is the obvious fact that every county contained small towns not parliamentary boroughs which supplied a recognizable urban and often dissenting element to the county constituency. A geographical segregation of town and country was physically and electorally impossibly.

a 40s. freehold qualification. Farming opinion had been politically influential long before 1832 and to ascribe the subsequent electoral strength of the protectionists solely to the Chandos clause would be absurd. It would be equally absurd to view the Reform Act of 1832 as a sophisticated device of the aristocracy to strengthen their hold on the electoral system under the cover of minor concessions to the urban middle classes. Nothing in the public or private utterances of the cabinet justifies such an interpretation; and though the opposition welcomed the Chandos clause, it did not inhibit them from mounting a comprehensive and continuous attack on other parts of the bill.

For the opponents of reform, the issue was not so much one of principle as of degree. With Catholic Emancipation the question had been whether or not; with parliamentary reform it was how much or how little. The whigs declared that a generous reform was necessary; the opposition believed that it was too generous. They argued that the greater weight given to the House of Commons by the bill would upset the balance of the constitution by destroying the discretionary powers of the crown, weakening the co-ordinate legislative authority of the House of Lords, and giving greater influence to the electorate. The task of the executive, difficult enough before, would be even more difficult. But this was not all. By making, however roughly, distribution of population and size of constituency the criteria for change, a principle was being conceded which could only end in a purely democratic system with all that this implied for aristocratic privilege and the sanctity of property. Finally, the bill could in no sense be regarded as the final solution on which the whigs prided themselves. The arbitrary standards and lack of uniformity in the ministerial plan were guarantees that it would not be permanent. The crude pruning of some parts, the clumsy enlargement of others, would produce an electoral structure no more logical and consistent than the old but lacking the authority which custom and usage had bestowed on it. Some of these criticisms were exaggerated, others confuted by events. Royal authority and the power of the Lords had been declining before 1832; they were not killed outright by the bill, though undoubtedly weakened still further. In prophesying that government would become unworkable, the tories did not foresee the rise of organized party which in the end would act as a substitute for the old executive influence over the legislature. But though they tended to exaggerate the speed with which the other consequences they dreaded would come upon them, their basic fears were intelligible and perceptive.

The real criticism of the opposition was that they had no alternative to suggest. Under eminently favourable conditions

Liverpool and Canning had not only kept the old system going but given it the appearance of vigour. It was unrealistic, however, to suppose that these fortunate circumstances of national prosperity and skilful leadership could continue indefinitely. The vast economic and social changes going on in British society made it inevitable that some adjustments would have to be made sooner or later. On this there was no real dispute among intelligent observers. The reluctance of the opposition in the House of Commons in February 1831 to challenge the principle as distinct from the detail of parliamentary reform was proof of this. But it was never clear what kind of reform the opposition was ready to accept; and all the indications before 1831 were that nothing they might have proposed in office would have been adequate. After the *volte-face* over Catholic Emancipation, it was psychologically as well as politically impossible for Peel, if not Wellington, to carry out another reversal of policy, particularly on an issue where what counted was not the principle but the degree of reform. 'I think', wrote Peel to his brother a few days before their parliamentary defeat in November 1830, 'it is better for the country and better for ourselves that *we* should not undertake the question.' Grey's sweeping measure, though it astounded his own supporters in the Commons, was based on hard political sense. Admittedly it did not give the manhood suffrage and annual parliaments demanded by radical reformers. After earnest consideration the cabinet even rejected the ballot. But the scope of the bill, far beyond anything proposed by any responsible politician in the post-war years, captured the imagination of the public and ensured success.

It could be argued, though not proved, that a less extreme bill might have served the same purpose. But given the composition of the Commons elected in 1830 it may be doubted whether any measure could have been devised that would have satisfied both parliament and the country. The hairline majority of one vote on the second reading of the bill at the end of March 1831 was enough to keep the ministry afloat and justify a dissolution. A defeat might have had disastrous consequences. As it was, many expectations were left unrealized and in less than twenty years Russell himself was to raise in another whig cabinet the advisability of further reform. In the incalculable situation in which Grey found himself in 1831 his decision to introduce a large and 'final' measure of reform was a statesmanlike one. His error was that in looking at the national scene, he misjudged the effect on all three branches of the legislature through which his measure had to pass. His patrician aloofness from the grind of parliamentary warfare made it easy for him to see the ultimate objective, less easy to appreciate the immediate difficulties.

A more professional politician might have displayed greater caution, and in the end, been less successful.

In the event the parliament elected in 1830 had to be dissolved and a general election fought on the direct issue of reform (the nearest approach to a referendum that the country had ever experienced) before a majority in the lower house for the bill was secure. The House of Lords, which rejected the second Reform Bill in October 1831, had to be threatened with a mass creation of new peers before it gave way. The King, whose opposition was not to the bill but to the methods used to force the bill through, had to undergo the humiliating experience of taking the whigs back after he had dismissed them because neither Wellington nor anyone else could provide him with an alternative ministry. An eighteen-month political struggle, a dissolution of parliament, coercion of the Lords, unprecedented pressure on the crown, a running accompaniment of popular agitation, and some sporadic but savage outbreaks of rioting in the country—all this had to be endured before the Reform Bill became law. Had Grey been able to foresee all that happened, he would never have embarked on the course he did. But once embarked, he rightly felt that there was more danger in turning back than in continuing. Once the whig plan of reform was made public in March 1831 there could be no retreat. The famous Days of May in 1832, when there was an unprecedented mobilization of public opinion behind the fallen whig cabinet, demonstrated in an impressive fashion the national will. But politically it was unnecessary; the battle for reform was already won. Though it was wildly misinterpreted in the country as an attempt to block reform entirely, William IV's object in asking Wellington to form a ministry was simply to find a means of passing an extensive reform measure without the need to misuse the royal prerogative of creating peers.

For the opposition, however, the manner of passing the bill was as obnoxious and dangerous as the bill itself. They thought that Grey, by the radical nature of his proposals, was not so much following as inflaming public opinion; and that having roused the country, he used the excitement to force the bill through the legislature by grossly unconstitutional means. The disturbances in the provinces when the Lords rejected the second bill in October 1831, in particular the riots at Nottingham and Derby, and the even more dangerous and savage violence at Bristol at the end of the month, added to the emotional feeling that the aristocracy was being overborne by the threat of physical force. In the winter of 1831–2 the country houses of some of the peers and gentry were being fortified and mounted with cannon for the first time since the Civil War. 'Look at any country house which has been built in England for three hundred years,' wrote Hobhouse bitterly in December, 'and you will see that the owners have never dreamed of being obliged to provide against the attacks of a Mob.'

This emotional reaction against the scenes which accompanied the bill inevitably coloured many men's views of the bill itself. Because it seemed to have been carried by quasi-revolutionary violence, it was easy to believe that the actual measure was revolutionary. The exaggerated hopes and fears that surrounded the Reform Bill owed much to the turbulence of its passage. Only gradually was it realized that the act was not the subversive event it seemed in 1831. Its importance was largely psychological: it satisfied a pent-up demand. Bright's subsequent verdict was as percipient as any. 'It was not a good Bill but it was a great Bill when it passed.' The very difficulties and hazards of the long struggle added to the sense of achievement.

Divorced from its contemporary context and analysed dispassionately, the Reform Act represented no more than a clumsy but vigorous hacking at the old structure to make it a roughly more acceptable shape. Even so, it was a great political achievement; and it is doubtful whether any man other than Lord Grey could have done it. A complete recasting of the electoral system would have been impossible in 1832. It was not only beyond the intention but outside the power of the whig cabinet. They lacked the necessary statistical information and experience; and they were working in haste to carry out a political pledge. They did not profess to be logical; they were neither doctrinaires nor democrats.

Inevitably therefore the characteristics of the old system persisted in the new. The old franchise holders, where resident, still exercised their vote and many were still doing so when the second Reform Act was passed thirty-five years later. A lack of balance remained between south and north, county and borough. There were enormous differences in the size of constituencies. It is possible that with the increased party activity and greater number of contested elections after 1832 bribery and corruption actually increased. In the smaller boroughs family and personal control still sometimes decided the outcome of elections; even the newly enfranchised towns were not entirely exempt from this type of special influence. Possibly only about 300,000 new voters were added to the conjectural half million of the old electorate in the United Kingdom as a whole. Of the total number of adult males no more than a seventh (a fifth in England and Wales) possessed the vote after 1832. During the reform debates Lord Durham claimed as one of the great merits of the bill that 'to property and good order we attach numbers'. It was difficult in practice to reconcile this objective with the other principle, on which most members of parliament were agreed, of confining the vote to persons of some education and property. The latter condition was bound to result in a limited electorate since the middle classes themselves were small in comparison to the mass of labouring population. When the cabinet momentarily contemplated fixing the borough household qualification at £20, it was discovered that this would actually reduce the size of the constituencies. As it was, in London and other prosperous towns, the £10 householders included many of the artisan class.

As far as immediate results were concerned, the most revolutionary of the three Reform Acts passed in 1832 was that for Scotland. Ireland had already, in effect, been subjected to two recent parliamentary reforms. The Union Act of 1800 eliminated all the smaller boroughs and only slight changes in the representative system were necessary in 1832. The real issue was over the franchise. The Catholic Emancipation legislation, by abolishing the 40s. freeholders and making the county qualification £10 freehold, had drastically reduced the size of the electorate. Though there could be no going back on such a recent decision, the addition by the Irish Reform Act of various forms of leaseholders enlarged the county constituencies to respectable if not pre-1829 proportions. In the urban constituencies the imposition of the £10 householder franchise broke the corporation monopolies and close nomination system in over half the Irish boroughs. But in the relatively poorer island the £10 household qualification regarded as adequate in England resulted in an undue number of very small constituencies where property and corruption were the decisive influences. Even so, emancipation and reform together made the Irish political system more independent than in the days when Peel as chief secretary had managed the elections for Lord Liverpool.

In Scotland the case was different. 'It is giving us,' wrote Cockburn, the Edinburgh advocate who became the whigs' solicitor general, 'a political constitution for the first time.' It was not surprising that the Scots identified themselves wholeheartedly with the fortunes of the English bill. When it passed its second reading by one vote in March 1831 towns and villages all over Scotland were illuminated and in Edinburgh and Dundee reform mobs celebrated the victory with riot and window-smashing. The combination of narrow oligarchies in the burghs and the 'superiority' system in the counties provided Scotland with a pre-reform electorate of only about 4,500 for its thirty counties and sixty-six burghs—less than the number who voted for Romilly and Burdett in the one constituency of Westminster at the 1818 general election. The post-Union system was in effect little more than a series of virtual pocket boroughs. Except for the retention of the burgh groupings, the whole structure was remodelled by the Scottish Reform Act of 1832. The £10 household franchise was uniformly imposed on the burghs, though this, in the less affluent northern kingdom, failed to produce as large an electorate in the smaller burghs as the Scottish reformers would have liked. The grouping of burghs avoided, however, any unduly small constituency. With an average of over 1,300 voters each the Scottish urban seats could stand comparison with any part of the United Kingdom. In the counties also the new electorate—the £10 property owners, leaseholders and tenants-at-will—did not result in such large constituencies as might have been anticipated. There were a number of reasons for this: the small size of many Scottish counties, the absence of the 40s. freeholders who supplied the bulk of the English county electorate, and the restrictive definition of the new qualifications. With an average of just over 1,100 voters each the Scottish county constituencies as a class were smaller than the burghs. Even the largest Scottish county (Perthshire) was smaller than all but three English counties. The predominance of the landlord influence was therefore assured. The balance was to some extent redressed by the addition of eight to the fifteen pre-1832 Scottish burgh seats. Of the new total of twenty-three seats, nine were given to large individual towns—two each to Edinburgh and Glasgow, one each to Aberdeen, Paisley, Dundee, Greenock and Perth. With this powerful reinforcement of the direct urban interest and an almost fifteen-fold increase of the total electorate to 65,000, a new political era had dawned for Scotland.[2]

The events of 1829–32 in fact worked a greater political transformation for Scotland and Ireland than for England; but the effects on the larger kingdom of this transformation were to be profound. In the post-Waterloo period the most independent and critical parts of the House of Commons were the English county members and representatives of large boroughs. The most consistent supporters of the executive were to be found not only among the MPs for the smaller boroughs, but among the representatives for Scotland and Ireland where a narrower franchise, a poorer community, and a greater hunger for patronage still gave the government of the day considerable influence. After 1832 there was a fundamental change. A large number of English nomination boroughs had been swept away. More significant still, enfranchised Scotland and Catholic Ireland became powerful reinforcements for the general whig–liberal parliamentary strength. As cabinet government gave way to party government, the essential conservatism of England was faced with

[2] See appendix C for the distribution of parliamentary seats before and after the 1832 Act.

the essential radicalism of the other two kingdoms. The Irish threat scarcely needed advertisement; but in a quieter way Scotland presented almost as great a challenge to the traditional English establishment. That stout Scotch tory Sir Walter Scott was expressing at least a grain of truth when he warned a member of the government as early as 1826 of the dangers of allowing wholesale reforms north of the Border. 'Scotland,' he wrote to Croker, 'completely liberalized, as she is in a fair way of being, will be the most dangerous neighbour to England that she has had since 1639.' By 1837, only five years after his death, the electoral alliance between the larger English towns and the radical Celtic fringe, which was to be the pattern of the Gladstonian Liberal party, was already foreshadowed in the party of Melbourne and Russell.

6 Parties and Politics

I

Although the whig ministers hoped that the 1832 act would settle
the question of parliamentary representation, they realized that for
the majority of reformers in the country it was only a means to an
end. The mood of the nation was not one of satisfaction but of
anticipation. Further reforms were under consideration by the
cabinet as early as the autumn of 1832 and, though some members
of the government were uneasy, the House of Commons ministers
for the most part were emphatic that management of the reformed
legislature would require legislative concessions. On the eve of the
meeting of the new parliament in January 1833 Althorp warned
Grey that without popular measures 'the Reform will lead to
Revolution'.[1] For a ministry compelled to continue along the path
of reform there was an embarrassing variety of issues from which
to choose. A tithe war was raging in Ireland; the Irish members
were demanding fundamental changes in the position of the established Church of Ireland; and O'Connell had started a campaign
for the repeal of the Union. English dissenters expected to see the
removal of the last vestiges of their social inferiority. Cobbett was
still pounding away at pensions, sinecures and the national debt.
Working-class political unions, dissatisfied at the failure to get manhood suffrage and the ballot, were putting out broader programmes
of political reform. In urban and industrial districts there was
agitation against the corn laws and church rates. The *Extraordinary
Black Book*, that secular bible of radical reformers enlarged and
republished in 1832, called for a long list of changes in church and
state and reiterated the familiar radical article of faith that all the
blessings the nation should be enjoying, 'the rewards of industry,
science and virtue', had been 'dissipated in iniquitous wars abroad—
at home, in useless establishments, in Oligarchical luxury, folly and

---

[1] *The Holland House Diaries*, edited by A. D. Kriegel (1977), Introduction, p. xxxvii.

profusion'. Optimism went hand in hand with expectation. It was widely held that the days of tory and whig were over and that the old aristocratic factions would be replaced by a government directly dependent on public opinion. The issue was no longer one between reformer and anti-reformer but how to make policy and legislation reflect the great constitutional revolutions of the last five years.

The whigs were thus carried forward by pressures which they could not control. The general election of December 1832 resulted in the return of a great mass of reformers, many of them new, inexperienced men. Nearly half the members of the 1833 House of Commons had not sat in the previous parliament. The attention of the public was concentrated on the votes and speeches of their representatives as never before. Many MPs came up to Westminster already pledged on a number of issues and the flood of petitions when the session started testified to the continuing political excitement in the constituencies. Management of such an assembly was clearly not going to be easy; it would be impossible without a reforming programme of some kind. The dilemma for the ministers was how to satisfy the expectations of the public without imposing intolerable strains on their own hastily patched-up coalition cabinet. As early as October 1832 Grey confessed to Lord Holland that they had been 'on the point of breaking up' over Irish church reform. Nevertheless, he felt he had no choice but to stay in office. If his ministry collapsed, he believed that the immediate successor would be a weak tory government under Peel and Wellington which would soon be driven from office by a triumphant radical party. In the post-1832 political world it seemed more than ever necessary for the whigs to continue their historical function of holding the balance between the aristocracy and the people.

In 1839 Lord John Russell observed to Melbourne that he had always thought that the whigs as a party would be destroyed by the Reform Bill. The counterpart to that piece of retrospective wisdom was Melbourne's remark to Brougham in 1835 that the whigs as a government could not have survived without the Reform Bill. Both comments were probably true. As a political faction the whigs were held together by the Foxite tradition, resentment at their long exclusion from office between 1783 and 1830, a network of family ties, and the social centres provided by a few whig peers at Holland, Lansdowne and Devonshire House, for which no parallel existed on the Tory side. It was not easy, however, to communicate this sense of historic clanship to others. If the whigs were to have a future, as well as a past, a widening of the party base was imperative.

It was not obvious that this was appreciated in the first phase of their recently acquired power. For a couple of years after the

Reform Act they seemed to envisage themselves as benevolent
arbiters rather than as the nucleus of a new popular party. The
government pamphlet *The Reform Ministry and the Reformed Parliament*
that came out in 1833 admitted that the majority in the House of
Commons were 'partisans not of the Ministry or of the Opposition,
but of good government' and that ministers were leaders rather than
masters. It was in other words a government based on opinion and
not party. The dissensions of the first two sessions revealed the strains
on an executive in this position. The whigs at least had the fleshpots
of office to sustain them. The prospects for the opposition seemed
hopeless. Their numbers in the Commons had been reduced to about
150, the lowest they were to record for the whole of the century.
They were the third largest group, fewer than the joint radical-Irish
party which was estimated at 190. In the pessimism created by the
general election Lord Mahon even suggested to Peel that they should
abandon the customary opposition seats on the left of the Speaker
and retire below the gangway. It was only by courtesy that the
opposition could be called a party. They had no acknowledged
leader, no agreed policy, and apart from the Carlton Club founded
in 1832, little in the way of organization. Relations between Peel
and Wellington had reached freezing point. In the Commons Peel
was surrounded by ultra-Protestants who had not forgiven him for
Catholic Emancipation and agriculturalists who ascribed many of
their ills to the return to gold under 'Peel's act' of 1819. Many of
them had helped to vote him out of office in 1830.

It was a mark of the disorganized state of party that tory agriculturalists like Knatchbull of Kent, Vyvyan of Cornwall, and
Chandos of Buckinghamshire found themselves associating with
radicals like Attwood and Cobbett in an attack on the government's
orthodox financial policies. In contrast Peel collaborated with
ministers when in April 1833 a snap motion by an agriculturalist
backbencher to halve the malt tax (entailing a loss of £2½ millions)
threatened to wreck Althorp's budget. Unknown to him Wellington
was simultaneously snubbing overtures made behind Peel's back to
secure the duke's authority for a concerted attempt to bring the
government down on this issue. Nothing, replied the duke tartly to
one tory MP, would induce him to countenance 'breaking down
the existing financial system of the country'. For Peel the support
of men like these was not worth having. The fusion of the
'administrative tories', the inheritors of the old tradition of the 'king's
ministers', and the 'social tories', the inheritors of the old 'country
party' tradition, was not to be accomplished overnight. Though
attempts were made by others to secure some kind of unity, they
came to nothing. Peel made his position uncompromisingly clear.

He would concede nothing in principle, least of all on the financial issue, to obtain the backing of men whose policies he regarded as both pernicious and irresponsible. Like Lord Grey, he believed that if the whigs were driven from office, the result would only be a more radical government. The duty of a genuinely conservative party was to uphold executive authority, protect the whigs from their radical allies, and restrain them from making popular concessions. All this he made the text of his first important speech in the new House of Commons in February 1833, a speech all the more approved by moderate men since it also contained an unequivocal acceptance of the Reform Act and a declaration of his readiness 'gradually, dispassionately, and deliberately' to reform 'every institution that really required reform'.

Nothing happened in 1834 to clarify the confusion of parliamentary politics. The divisions over Irish church reform caused the resignation of Stanley and three other cabinet ministers in May; in July, tired at the endless wrangling in cabinet, Grey himself retired from office. In an attempt to mend the disjointed state of public affairs, the King asked Melbourne, one of the more moderate members of the government, to form a coalition with Wellington and Peel. Melbourne declined, his stated reason being their opposition to measures like the Irish tithe bill and the Irish church commission which he himself regarded as 'vital and necessary'. Conceivably too, he did not relish the prospect of an alliance with his two former chiefs. His refusal killed the chance of a coalition and ensured his appointment as prime minister. Nevertheless, it still seemed at the close of session that a cabinet reconstruction involving a central group of politicians was the most likely road to stable government. With Lord Grey in only semi-retirement, Stanley and Graham detached, Peel independent and unshackled, owing his commanding position in parliament to his own talents rather than to a party, many elements of coalition seemed to be present.

It was this fluid situation which gave crucial importance to the King's dismissal of the whigs in November 1834 when Althorp, by the death of his father Lord Spencer, was removed to the House of Lords. So far from being deliberate or desired, the emergence of a more clearly defined party system after 1834 was simply the instinctive reaction of politicians to events which they had not foreseen and few of them approved. The royal summons to Peel to return from Italy to take over the government in effect also installed him as conservative chief. It was a mark of the rudimentary nature of party organization that William IV in a real sense made Melbourne and Peel the first leaders of the Victorian Liberal and Conservative parties by the simple process of asking them to form a ministry. In November 1834 he had hoped, like his father in 1784, to secure himself against policies to which he objected by bringing in a minister of his choice who might win public approval. Peel, though he thought the King's action premature, followed similarly traditional lines by appealing to the independent and uncommitted elements in the House of Commons to give the King's ministers a fair trial. Paradoxically, however, 1834 proved the point of departure for a new party system which ensured that William IV's dismissal of his ministry was the last act of its kind in the history of the British monarchy.

The label 'conservative' was by that date a well established and convenient general description of all those who wished to preserve the great institutions of the state against radical innovation. But it was a label that covered a wide range of political attitudes from blank reaction to moderate reformism. The significance of the Hundred Days' ministry was that it enabled Peel as prime minister, and by virtue of that office party leader, to impose his own version of conservatism on his followers. The Tamworth Manifesto of December 1834 was a landmark not because Peel was saying anything about himself that he had not said before, but because he made it, as far as any such document could be, the official pronouncement of the party which gathered round him. The issue of such a statement was in itself unprecedented. It was prompted partly by the imminence of the general election which the weakness of the ministerial support in the House of Commons made necessary, partly by the need to dissociate the new government from the Wellingtonian tory image which had been revived by Peel's absence in Italy and the duke's caretaker commission during the first three weeks of its existence. At the start of the manifesto Peel made it clear that he was making a plea 'to that great and intelligent class of society ... which is far less interested in the contentions of party, than in the maintenance of order and the course of good government'. For the rest, he repeated the main points of his 1833 speech, indicated his attitude to current legislative issues, and in general promised 'a careful review of institutions, both civil and ecclesiastical' together with 'the correction of proved abuses and the redress of real grievances'.

Though the conservatives won another 100 seats at the general election of 1835, the solidity and numerical superiority of the opposition made the position of the ministry impossible. After battling adroitly for seven weeks, Peel resigned in April with none of his legislative proposals accepted. Nevertheless the Hundred Days' ministry transformed the formerly disjointed opposition. Peel was now the acknowledged head of his party and, as the countless addresses which followed his resignation testified, by his skill and restraint had impressed himself on the public as a politician of stature unequalled (in the opinion of *The Times* at least) by anyone since the younger Pitt. Fortified by its electoral gains, heartened by its brief possession of office, the Conservative party was now a political fact, not merely a conventional phrase. Though its hastily improvised machinery for fighting the election had been unavoidably defective (it was only able to contest about three fifths of the parliamentary seats), the efforts then made proved the basis for continued recovery. A feature of the election and the ensuing months was the multiplication of Conservative Associations in boroughs and counties all over England. As Bonham, the party's chief electoral manager, wrote to Peel later in the year, 'we had to find candidates, organizers and friends in almost every place. *Now that work is done.*'

If 1834 gave unity and direction to the conservative opposition, by a not uncommon political process it did much the same for their opponents. The dismissal of what was still essentially Grey's cabinet followed by the losses in the general election of 1835 was in many ways a godsend to Melbourne and the whigs. It trimmed the size of the unwieldy 'reform' majority in the House of Commons, and it destroyed the illusion that after 1832 there were only two serious contenders for political power, a moderate whig party on one side and an extreme radical party on the other. The shock of a Conservative ministry in office only two years after the passing of the Reform Act brought the quarrelsome forces of the left to their senses. The Lichfield House compact of February 1835, though at the time no more than a tactical decision by whigs, radicals and O'Connell's Irish to combine for the immediate purpose of evicting Peel, was in fact the point of origin for the Victorian Liberal party. Though the older aristocratic whigs like Grey and Lansdowne loathed any formal alliance with O'Connell, the men who still had their careers to make were less squeamish. Russell, the new leader in the Commons, made it clear that he would take no part in another cabinet as compromising and cautious as that of Lord Grey. Melbourne himself, though scarcely an addict of extreme measure, was sufficiently stung by his unceremonious dismissal to declare that 'this is really an important moment, and a great start'. The foundation of the Reform Club in 1836, designed to supplant both the radical Westminster Club and the whig Brooks's, was a sign of the new party spirit. That the initiative came from the moderate radicals made it all the more significant. It marked the belated realization that in the post-reform political world government by opinion was a pipedream, that power could only be maintained through party, and that party could only exist if there was a measure of organization and discipline.

For the more extreme radicals, the dilemma after 1835 was whether to support the whigs or not. To oppose meant risking the return of a conservative ministry under Peel. To support meant accepting whig limitations on liberal aspirations. A pamphlet by an anonymous radical MP in 1839 entitled *What Ought The Radicals To Do?* had as its significant sub-title *Shall We Overturn the Coach?* What became increasingly evident was that the radicals were not capable of forming a parliamentary party, still less an administration, by themselves. They had no acknowledged leader. In so far as there was a collective radical leadership it rested with a small group of outstanding individuals, apt to disagree among themselves, often 'single-subject men' (as Miss Martineau called them) identified with a particular cause such as financial retrenchment, the ballot, abolition of the corn laws, or education. They were distinguished, as political crusaders are apt to be, more by obsessive zeal than by practical sense, and tended to be as contemptuous of each other in private as they were of the whigs in public. These were the radicals who made a noise and attracted publicity; but the important aspect of parliamentary radicalism in the 1830s was the way in which the more anonymous rank and file reformers were being quietly absorbed into the general following of the whig government. 'Whig in party and Radical in opinion', in Lord John Russell's phrase, these were the backbone of the reform majority. While they favoured such measures as the ballot, shorter parliaments, and church reform (though less decided about reform of the House of Lords), they preferred to support the whig government rather than follow the extreme radical leaders. The electorate seemed much of their opinion. After the 1837 election the number of old-fashioned whigs and ultra-radicals both diminished. As the Liberal party took on a firmer outline, the genuinely independent radicals in the Commons were reduced by 1841 to a mere handful.

The same process of consolidation was at work in O'Connell's Irish party. After 1835 he proved a remarkably loyal ally of the whigs, content to forego office for himself and suspend his campaign for the repeal of the Union until the advent of a conservative ministry. Even if these were no more than clever tactics designed to extract benefit from a friendly government while retaining his long-term objective of repeal as the ultimate strategy, he lost as much as he gained. At the 1832 election his party, fighting as an independent organization, had emerged as the largest in Ireland. The conservatives, who up to 1830 normally won a majority of Irish seats, returned less than a third. In 1835 and 1837, however, when there was close cooperation between the Irish nationalists and the whigs, O'Connell's electoral ascendancy perceptibly weakened. It was true that whig losses in England made his support a parliamentary necessity. But in Ireland the Liberal party was now preponderantly whig rather than O'Connellite. In the remaining years of power whig association and whig patronage continued to eat into O'Connell's parliamentary following. The 1841 election left the liberals the largest single Irish party, closely followed by the conservatives, with O'Connell's Repealers holding only eighteen seats. Long before 1841 the sting had been drawn from both the independent radical and the Irish nationalist parties. A recognizable Liberal party was actually in being.

Within ten years of the Reform Act therefore politics were dominated by two major parties to an extent previously unknown in British history. By 1841 it was common practice for newspapers to classify election results in terms of liberals and conservatives and assess the results in terms of party gains and losses. Party discipline, party influence operated not only at Westminster through the traditional apparatus of whips and patronage secretaries, but in the constituencies through a new network of influences stretching from the central political clubs and the central party election managers and committees, to the provincial party associations and agents. Each party copied the other's methods. The Carlton, Lord Granville Somerset, Bonham and the constituency Conservative or Constitutional Associations were matched by the Reform Club, Ellice, Parkes, Coppock and the constituency Liberal or Reform Associations. Though the rapidly evolved party organizations were not as substantial or authoritative as they sometimes appeared, they still marked a revolution in parliamentary politics.

Once balance had been restored to the House of Commons and the stimulus of party rivalry revived, the development of electoral organization was shaped largely by the technical and psychological consequences of the Reform Act. It was one of the most important and least anticipated results of that historic measure. The actual size of the national electorate was larger. The abolition of many small boroughs and the widening of the franchise ensured that there were few constituencies where it was not advisable to listen to the opinion of the electors. The emergence after 1832 of fresh controversies ensured that there were few constituencies in which the electors were not eager to express their opinions. The accident of four general elections in the nine years from 1832 to 1841 added to popular political interest; such recurrent election excitement had been unknown since the reign of Anne and the old Triennial Act. Technically it was soon appreciated that the yearly revision of the electoral register required the constant attention of members, candidates and agents. Organization was needed to raise the money for these activities. In turn organization produced greater continuity of party effort, led to more contested elections, facilitated the flow of information from the constituencies to the party headquarters and sometimes prompted the provision of candidates by headquarters for the constituencies. Though there were still many independent and unpredictable, not to say corrupt and venal, elements in the electoral system, party leaders after 1834 were provided with more detailed knowledge of the political views and wishes of a wider section of the electorate than they had ever possessed, or needed to possess, before. For the ordinary MP party loyalties and party discipline were more insistent features of parliamentary life. The kind of man who entered the House of Commons was not greatly different from his predecessors of the unreformed era, but he was exposed to greater pressures both from his constituents and from his party.

The rapid growth of a two-party system inevitably affected the character of the parties themselves. The new labels of liberal and conservative in place of whig and tory were outward signs of a real change. Borrowed originally from continental politics, they were used before 1832 to indicate a type or an attitude. After 1834 they became the names of the parties themselves while whig and tory were left as descriptions of types or temperaments. The shift in nomenclature reflected the fact that the parties themselves had become larger and more comprehensive—and more diluted—in both outlook and membership. To secure and retain power in post-1832 politics it was essential for both whigs and tories to widen their social basis, to become national parties rather than aristocratic factions. But in the complex society of early Victorian Britain, a national party had also to reconcile itself to being a composite party with considerable class and regional variations. The Liberal party had its origin in a specific coalition of whigs, radicals and Irish; the Conservative party in an amalgam of the old tory country party and the enlightened administrative tradition of Lord Liverpool. In both cases the precocious party development between 1834 and 1841 allowed little time for those disparate elements to achieve a satisfactory fusion. In an age when it was still conventional for candidates on the hustings to emphasize their personal independence, even the idea of a disciplined parliamentary party was novel, and to both electors and elected not always welcome. The task of party leadership was therefore considerable. If party policy attempted to reflect the divisions of opinion within the party, as the *Edinburgh Review* hopefully claimed that the whig cabinet was doing in 1840, the result was ineffectiveness and drift. If party leaders attempted to impose their views on an heterogeneous following, as Peel did between 1842 and 1846, there was danger of dissension and revolt.

II

What gave reality to the new party system was that it incorporated or at least represented substantial middle-class interests and opinions, as well as those of the governing classes themselves. In turn the different middle-class interests looked to the classes beneath them for reinforcement. A traditional feature of the aristocratic party rivalry was that both sides appealed to public opinion and tried to enlist popular support. It was this which prevented politics from becoming a simple confrontation between the urban middle classes and the landowning gentry. Despite occasional jealousies between rival governing oligarchies in town and country, the primary division in British political society was vertical rather than horizontal. Parliamentary whigs and tories were at the head of national factions which extended deep down in British society. Guizot, the new French ambassador, was struck when arriving in London in 1840 by the extent to which the political aristocracy looked outside its own class for approval and even guidance. 'While preserving its social rank, it is today servant but not master; it is the habitual but responsible minister of public sentiment and interest.'

Public opinion was on most issues divided; without such divisions a party system could scarcely have survived. The whigs were primarily concerned to respond to influences that came to them from their main electoral supporters, the radical electorate of the large English towns, the organized body of English dissent, Scotland and Ireland. The impressive array of reforms which mark the mid-1830s was largely shaped by these pressures rather than by any predetermined whig programme of reform. That they mainly took the form of constitutional measures was in the nature of the situation. The traditional whig emphasis on civil and religious liberty, the void left by the reluctance of Liverpool's government to make organic changes, the expediency of conceding to demands from an expanding middle class for greater social and political equality, the conscious adjustment of other institutions to complement the central reform of parliament—all these circumstances helped to put a recognizable stamp on the post-1832 whig legislation. Of the more important reforms outside this category, the abolition of slavery in 1833 was a popular non-party issue, under official attention long before 1830, supported by the bulk of evangelical, Methodist and dissenting opinion, and hallowed in whig eyes by Fox's abolition of the slave trade in 1806. The succession of legal reforms that carried still further Peel's work of the 1830s, though infused with Brougham's energy

was also in accord with the party tradition started by Romilly and
Mackintosh. The Poor Law Amendment Act of 1834, while owing
much of its detail to the Benthamite intellectual influence of the
administrative experts, was a non-partisan remedy for the long-
standing burden of heavy poor rate and the evils publicized by the
recent agricultural riots in southern England. The substantial
majorities in its favour demonstrated the general conviction of the
legislature that something must be done.

Of the more central reforms aimed at satisfying radical, dissenting
middle-class opinion, one in particular was virtually an appendix
to the parliamentary reform act, in that it was designed to effect
a parallel transfer of political power. The reform of municipal
government in England and Scotland was intended to repeat at local
level what had been done nationally. Although the new parliamentary franchise had broken the direct electoral power of the old
close corporations, enough influence and patronage still adhered to
them to make their destruction a matter of party interest for liberal
reformers as well as arguably and in the long run a condition of more
efficient local government. For dissenters and Roman Catholics 1835
was the logical and necessary complement to the relief legislation
of 1828 and 1829.

Influenced by Jeffrey and Cockburn, their two Scottish law officers,
the government took up the question of Scottish municipal reform
first, partly because the case was stronger, partly because the opposition was likely to be weaker. The self-perpetuating oligarchies of
the royal burghs had long presented to liberal eyes a depressing scene
of corruption and stagnation. The rise of independent middle-class
spokesmen—merchants, lawyers, doctors, editors and university
professors—had produced a burgh reform movement as early as the
1780s. After Waterloo it resumed with the powerful aid of the new
organs of Scottish liberalism: the *Edinburgh Review*, *The Scotsman*, and
local newspapers in such growing towns as Aberdeen and Dundee.
In 1819 Lord Archibald Hamilton had secured a parliamentary
enquiry which proved corruption in several Scottish burghs, including Edinburgh and Aberdeen. Nothing was accomplished, however,
until after the Reform Act when two Scottish municipal reform acts,
for royal and parliamentary burghs respectively, were passed in 1833.
They followed the precedent of the recent parliamentary reform bill
in giving the municipal vote to the £10 householder and setting up
an elective system of burgh government in place of the former self-
electing councils. Though the electoral property qualification disappointed the more democratic Scottish radicals, at least the acts
provided a foundation for more effective and responsive local
administration. Indeed, an earlier act the same session, giving powers

to Scottish burghs to establish a general system of police, virtually required such a reform if its provisions were to be properly implemented. In December 1833 the first popular elections to the new Scottish town councils took place, exactly twelve months after the first popular parliamentary elections. 'These two reforms,' observed Cockburn with satisfaction, 'have changed, and will permanently change, the whole country.'

The English municipal reform bill two years later proved more controversial. It encountered a determined resistance in the House of Lords from Lyndhurst and the ultra-tory peers which threatened to bring on both a constitutional and a party crisis. Dealing with the wider and more complicated English scene the ministers had proceeded more warily, prefacing their legislation with a commission of enquiry appointed in 1833. To deny to those who had been given a share in electing members of parliament the right of voting for their municipal legislators was clearly a political illogicality. But the commission of enquiry based its case for reform largely on the defects and abuses of the existing corporations. Though there were recognized exceptions, as a class the borough corporations were regarded as strongholds of tory anglican power and their patronage as a source of political corruption. The report of the radical-dominated commission painted a black picture, blacker than was always justified. The appointment of a partisan body to find evidence that will justify a predetermined conclusion is not a modern invention.

Nevertheless Peel and Wellington accepted that the case for reform was overwhelming and the bill encountered little difficulty in the Commons. In one respect it proved less alarming than they expected. What they had feared was the creation of a municipal electorate based, as in the Scottish bills, on the parliamentary £10 householder. This in many towns would have produced an oligarchy of middle-class dissenting radicals who already, through their control of vestries and elections of churchwardens, were vigorously waging war against the old tory corporations. The whig proposal to give the municipal franchise to all permanent ratepayers, choosing their representatives for a three-year period, was from the conservative point of view a decidedly better arrangement since it offered a more balanced electoral constituency. A tory-popular party might offset the historic alliance of dissenter and whig. The opposition amendments eventually accepted by the government—property qualifications for councillors, election of aldermen for six years, nomination of borough magistrates by the crown—were probably improvements on the original scheme but did not materially affect its main principles.

On their side the whigs and liberals had little doubt that municipal reform would strengthen them politically. 'Municipal Reform is the

steam engine for the Mill built by "Parliamentary Reform"',
declared Joseph Parkes, the radical secretary of the commission who
later and not accidentally became the chief electoral agent of the
Liberal party. When the first borough elections, fought on strict party
lines, resulted in sweeping successes for liberals and radicals, his
optimism overflowed. 'No more Tory Ministries.... No Conservative majority can ever be got in a British House of Commons....
The greatest political revolution ever accomplished.' Only gradually
were these confident partisan predictions seen to be exaggerated.
But little more than four years later Bonham, the Conservative
electoral agent, was telling Peel that the coming borough elections
would 'prove the truth of my conviction that in England at any
rate the Municipal Reform bill has done hardly any, if any, mischief'.

Administratively the act did little more than impose a uniform
structure of democratically elected councils on the 178 old corporate
boroughs found to exist in England and Wales. Other towns could,
however, apply for incorporation under the act and by the middle
of the century eighteen had done so, including such important
industrial agglomerations as Birmingham, Bradford, Manchester
and Sheffield. Specific clauses in the act required the corporations
to set up police forces to be paid from the rates and gave general
powers for lighting and cleaning the streets. This in itself was enough
to make 1835 an important stage in social development. But otherwise the reformed municipalities were left to their own devices,
answerable only to their ratepayers for the 'good Rule and Government of the Borough'. The controversy in parliament and the country
was almost exclusively political. The interest was in the classes and
parties who were to have the power, not in the civic purposes to
which that power was to be put.

Church reform on the other hand was seen primarily as a matter
of privilege. As an institution the Church of England was open to
two forms of attack: from radicals who saw in it a corrupt corporation with excessive wealth, and from dissenters who saw it as an
ecclesiastical monopoly from whose competition they suffered and
to whose support they were legally bound to contribute. The parliamentary controversy over church rates, for example, was only an
extension of what was in many towns a burning local issue. Ireland
presented a kind of gross caricature of the English scene. When they
came to deal with the acrimonious problem of the church, therefore,
the whig ministry had to face the consequences not only of parliamentary reform but of the new dissenting equality gained in 1828
and the new political power of Irish Catholicism gained in 1829.

The long radical campaign against the establishment and the

wildly exaggerated notions of its wealth led in 1832 to the whig royal commission to enquire into ecclesiastical revenues. Though the object was primarily to ascertain the facts, it was obvious that the information elicited would be the basis of legislation. That there was a case for legislation was admitted by many anglicans. When Howley was appointed archbishop of Canterbury in 1828 he impressed on Wellington the desirability of church reform. A bill for that purpose was actually prepared but put aside with the change of government. Reform of the establishment was in a sense of greater interest to anglicans than to other sections of the public. English dissenters and Irish catholics were less concerned to reform the church than to gain equality with it. In England it was doubtful whether the majority of dissenters were actually opposed to the existence of a state church. What they wanted was the removal of the remaining marks of their historic inferiority; they assumed that in a reformed parliament this would be done. Their demands were for relief not from any penal legislation but from the bias of the law and the constitution. The specific grievances listed by the 1833 United Committee (compulsory anglican rites for dissenting marriages and burials, non-admission of dissenters to Oxford and Cambridge degrees, liability of dissenters for payment of church rates and of dissenting chapels for poor rates) all derived from the historic fiction embedded in the law of the country that the English people and the anglican community were one. Failure to obtain instant redress created both dissatisfaction with the whigs and animosity towards the Church of England and its powerful ally the House of Lords. The demand for disestablishment and the active part played by organized dissent in the 1835 general election were symptoms of rising political hostility.

When, after Peel's Hundred Days, the whigs returned to office under Lord Melbourne, political prudence if not conscientious conviction prompted a fresh attempt to conciliate their discontented dissenting supporters. The 1836 session, which saw the Dissenting Marriages Act, the compulsory state registration of births, deaths and marriages, a tithe commutation act, and a royal charter for the new non-confessional London University, marked the peak of dissenting influence on legislation in the post-reform era. The next few years demonstrated that the limits of concession had been reached. The withdrawal of the 1837 bill to abolish church rates (caused as much by the lukewarmness of anglican whigs as by the efforts of the opposition), the dropping of the appropriation clause from the Irish tithe bill in 1838, the defeat of the whig education plan in 1839, were proof that the political value of the whig-dissenting alliance was nearly exhausted. Consciousness of their declining influence drove the dissenters back on a policy of self-help.

In the 1840s the growth of Voluntaryism—reliance on private effort and hostility to government interference—marked a retreat from orthodox politics. By 1847 the gulf between the whigs and their traditional dissenting allies was wider than it had been at any time in the post-war period.

In Ireland the attempt at religious reconstruction came close to wrecking the whigs entirely. Church reform, like other measures such as corporation reform, was part of the whig concept of justice for Ireland, though their need for O'Connell's support in the Commons explains the persistence with which they struggled on with their load of unfinished Irish legislation between 1837 and 1839. Reforms regarded as necessary for England and Scotland could hardly be denied to the other island; but the conditions in Ireland were so different, the issues so fundamental, that Irish measures usually generated an intensity of controversy unknown in English affairs. The appropriation issue, for example, which technically concerned the right of parliament to appropriate part of the revenues of the Church of Ireland for other than church purposes, raised instantly larger questions—the autonomy of the church, the legitimacy of establishments, the Protestant ascendancy, and even the Union itself. Step by step the whig ministers found themselves drawn into a more formidable Irish programme than they had ever envisaged. The tithe war and the desperate plight of the anglican clergy in Ireland, as well as pressure from the Irish MPs at Westminster, made some constructive policy necessary. Orderly government without a degree of coercion was administratively impossible; but for liberals coercion without concession was politically impossible. Balanced uneasily between repression and reform, the whigs discovered in the Irish church question a Pandora's box of all the evils that could afflict a party of liberal aristocrats trying to satisfy popular, radical demands.

The Irish church bill introduced by the whigs in 1833 abolished ten bishoprics and effected various other reforms. It was saved from certain defeat in the Lords by dropping the notorious clause 147, involving the principle of appropriation, halfway through its legislative passage. In that emended form it received Peel's general blessing in the House of Commons. But the ministers themselves had been deeply divided. When the appropriation issue came up again in connection with the Irish tithe bill it caused the resignation of Stanley, Graham, Richmond and Ripon (formerly Lord Goderich), helped to bring about Grey's retirement six weeks later, and formed the primary objection to Russell's promotion to the leadership of the House of Commons which was the occasion for William IV's dismissal of the whigs in November 1834. Of all the proposals put forward by government in the 1830s it was politically the most lethal.

The amputation of the conservative wing of the cabinet in 1834, however, left the more radical ministers with a clear field. Appropriation became the rallying point for the mixed forces of the left—whigs, liberals, radicals, dissenters and Irish—which found themselves in temporary opposition in the winter of 1834–5. It was the issue on which they finally drove Peel from office in April 1835. But the price paid for that victory was a heavy one. It led to a direct confrontation with the Lords; and while that struggle raged, all other Irish legislation was held up. Worst of all, it was an issue that divided the cabinet and failed to obtain permanent ministerial support. After the 1835 session Lansdowne openly and Melbourne tacitly were ready in cabinet to drop appropriation. Grey's son Howick, who had all the Grey love of principle and more than his share of family cantankerousness, was understandably moved to enquire what right they had in that case to turn Peel out. It was not, however, until 1838 that Russell signified the government's readiness to abandon the issue; not until 1840 that the Irish municipal reform act finally wound up the whig programme of Irish legislation. They had done much for Ireland; but in the process they had exhausted themselves, sacrificed much goodwill among their English supporters, and laid themselves open to the charge of conceding everything to retain O'Connell's support. They were not the first nor the last nineteenth-century administration to learn by hard experience that justice for Ireland frequently brought injustice from England.

It would, however, be an exaggeration to ascribe the decline of the whigs solely to their association with O'Connell. The inescapable limitations on their power and the character of whig leadership also contributed. One formidable obstacle was the House of Lords. The great reform battle had frightened but not intimidated the peers. Indeed their fears probably stiffened their resistance. When Wellington in August 1833 could agree with his chief whip that 'there will be no blow-up, no bloodshed [but] that all our ancient institutions will be destroyed by due course of law', it was not surprising that the more hot-headed peers were prepared to make a last-ditch stand. If any politicians had been intimidated, they were members of the whig cabinet like Grey, Melbourne, Holland, Lansdowne and Palmerston, who would accept almost any provocation from the House of Lords rather than risk a repetition of the 1832 crisis.

The provocation was certainly great. It was not merely that the Lords rejected, mutilated or delayed some of the government's most important measures. The majority of them were also clearly acting as a political party opposed to the ministry of the day and using their coordinate legislative powers to overrule both the executive and the majority in the Commons. This was a new and disturbing constitutional consequence of the Reform Act. Before 1830 the traditional role of the upper house had been to act as virtually an adjunct of government, occasionally blocking unwelcome legislation that had got through the Commons but almost invariably reflecting the wishes of the ministers of the crown. Though over Catholic Emancipation the dangers implicit in a disagreement in principle between the upper and lower houses was beginning to be realized after 1825, it was not until the reform crisis that the independent legislative powers of the House of Lords became a political issue. After 1832 the continued obstruction of government measures in the upper house, reaching its climax over municipal reform in 1835, placed the whigs under a serious handicap. Despite the efforts of Wellington and Peel to restrain the tory peers from abusing their powers, reform of the House of Lords became one of the great radical demands of the mid-1830s. For many of them it seemed that the 1832 Reform Act would prove ineffective without a similar remodelling of the upper chamber.

Even if the cabinet had been prepared to coerce the Lords, however, it was doubtful whether they could impose their will without a direct appeal to the electorate; and the discouraging fact was that every general election after 1832 saw a decline in liberal strength. Though a political deadlock seemed to have been reached after 1837, it was not one that the whigs could solve by the mere process of dissolving parliament. Moreover, while there was resentment against the use the Lords made of their constitutional powers, there was no real feeling against the aristocracy as an institution in middle-class English society. The inevitable waning of the 1831 reform enthusiasm, the resumption of normal electoral influences, the discontent caused by many of the whig reforms, anglican fear of dissent, English dislike of O'Connell, agricultural suspicion of radical free traders—all conspired to pen the whigs within the narrow constitutional framework through which government still operated. The whigs were far from wielding sovereign power. In the mixed and balanced constitution which was still regarded by many as a safeguard for liberty, no such absolute power existed. The wonder is not that the whigs did so little but that they achieved so much. They would have achieved even less had they not been assisted by the sense and moderation of the Conservative opposition under Peel. It was Peel who 'threw over the Lords' in 1835 and cooperated with Russell in a compromise over the municipal corporations bill which the tory peers in the end had to accept, Peel in 1837 who persuaded Wellington to accept Stanley's plan of dropping general opposition to the government's package of Irish legislation in return for abandonment of appropriation. Though the whigs took the initiative in legislating, much of what was actually achieved represented a compromise agreement between the two main parties.

For Melbourne compromise, if not always welcome, was at least usually acceptable. The cynical, disarming frankness which was half his charm concealed a curiously detached, self-protective personality. Though he could show considerable energy, even ruthlessness, when it was necessary to get rid of troublesome colleagues or keep his cabinet together, his interest was always practical, and his energy short-lived. On larger issues he was politically as well as temperamentally indifferent. He did what had to be done, but he did no more than was necessary. As chairman of a quarrelsome cabinet he was admirable; as leader of and inspirer of an immature political party he was fundamentally miscast. The main measures passed during his ministry originated under his predecessor; he had little interest in enlarging that programme. 'More, or as much, has been done in the last nine years of change,' he wrote characteristically in 1838, 'than from the Restoration to 1830. Whether all of it has been wise is another matter.' What new impulses were felt in the cabinet came mainly from Lord John Russell, the new Leader of the House of Commons. A curious and uneasy blend of patrician whig and popular statesman, Russell was even so better fitted than any of his colleagues to be leader of the new Liberal party. But the unkind nickname of Finality Jack which he acquired in these years indicated how far the passivity of the cabinet after 1837 acted as a brake on his political instincts. Nevertheless, the decision to make the corn laws and ballot open questions and the reorganization of the cabinet in 1839 were largely due to his promptings; as was the attempt in 1841 to turn the budget into a genuinely radical measure. Russell's defects were a certain littleness of mind and a temperamental infirmity of purpose—qualities which grew more pronounced after his second marriage in 1841. His misfortune was that in the decade when he was at the height of his powers, he was not in command of the party.

Paradoxically, therefore, in proportion as the Liberal party began to take shape, its parliamentary strength diminished and its sense of purpose waned. The one issue which might perhaps have revived the party was a fresh instalment of parliamentary reform. By 1839 the liberal *Morning Chronicle* was calling on the government to rally reformers by declaring in favour of triennial parliaments, ballot and household suffrage. The previous year, on Grote's ballot motion, nearly two hundred regular supporters of the ministry voted for it against a motley majority composed of some sixty official whigs and the full strength of the Conservative opposition. When the ballot was made an open question the following year the number in its favour rose to 217, including seventeen members of the government and court. A party so frustrated by its leaders could scarcely be expected to show continuous enthusiasm. For the whig cabinet on the other hand, quite apart from personal views on the ethics of the ballot, the perennial problem was whether it was worth risking another constitutional crisis with the House of Lords in order to enlarge their popular support. To guide and moderate public opinion was one thing; to put themselves at the head of a democratic 'movement' was another. Not many whigs had a taste for perpetual agitation.

Melbourne's difficulties were therefore real. Yet he seemed unduly content to accept the limitations of his position. The accession of Victoria in 1837, while giving him a pleasant personal reason for staying in office, diverted an increasing amount of his interest from the cabinet to the court. When colonial crises in Canada and Jamaica blew up in 1838 and 1839, the ministry appeared to lack toughness and resilience. In May 1839, with some radicals abstaining and a few voting with the opposition, the government's majority on the Jamaican Assembly bill sank to five and Melbourne resigned. It was a hasty and hardly justified decision, made even worse by his return to office a few days later when Victoria quarrelled with Peel over the appointment of new ladies of the Bedchamber. A desire to support the impetuous young queen when (as Melbourne at least realized) she was constitutionally in the wrong, made nonsense of the cabinet's previous conclusion that they lacked the strength in the House of Commons to continue. More than anything else, the last two ineffective years of whig rule from 1839 to 1841 appeared to justify the well-known jibe of Leader, the radical MP for Westminster, that O'Connell ruled Ireland, Sir Robert Peel ruled England, the whigs were content with office and patronage without power, the leader of the opposition with power without office or patronage. Dissenters had been alienated, radicals disillusioned. The whigs seemed to have lost the will as well as the capacity for further liberal advances. The sudden ministerial conversion to free trade and tariff reform in 1841, though it roused the flagging enthusiasm of some of their followers, failed to convince the country. The last spasm of whig reforming energy came too late.

III

'You are supported,' Peel told his followers in May 1838 at the great Conservative party banquet in Merchant Taylors Hall, 'by the Clergy, the magistracy, the yeomanry, and the gentry of the country, as well as by the great proportion of the trading community.' The emphasis was perhaps deliberate, certainly significant. The foundation of the conservative recovery in the 1830s was the alliance between the church and the land; and of the two, it was the church which was initially the more important partner. Middle-class politics in the post-reform decade are unintelligible except in terms of the religious animosities which divided British society. From 1831 to 1852 the sectarian struggle seemed to be increasing rather than diminishing. Growing dissenting hostility to the establishment was matched by growing anglican disillusionment at the consequences of reform. Liberal Protestants who had optimistically persuaded themselves that Catholic Emancipation would end the Irish problem were dismayed by the immediate transfer of O'Connell's apparently inexhaustible energies to a campaign for the repeal of the Union. Anglicans faced with mounting radical and dissenting criticism, demands for the removal of the bishops from the upper house, disestablishment, and confiscation of church property, began to see in the constitutional revolution of 1828–32 a fatal surrender which had merely put power into the hands of their enemies. The Irish church legislation brought forward in 1833 and 1834 seemed the start of a general despoiling of the establishment at the hands of a secular parliament that had ceased officially to be either anglican or even Protestant. It was not a coincidence that the 1833 session, which saw the passage of the Irish church bill and the disappearance of ten Irish bishoprics, heard the opening shots of the Oxford Movement.

Keble's famous assize sermon in July on *National Apostasy* was the first public protest to come from the group of Oxford high churchmen who were to become known as the Tractarians. It was a protest not only against the erastianism of the reformed legislature but against what they thought was the equally dangerous liberal reformism of many bishops and anglican laity. In September appeared the first three *Tracts for the Times* which by their passion and novelty helped to create a sense of 'the church in danger' stronger than had been known since the days of Queen Anne. In their search for a principle on which to base a defence of the church, the Tractarians were driven back on the high anglican doctrine of the continuing Christian

church in which the Reformation was only an episode and establishment an historical accident. This was going further and faster than
most anglicans approved or intended in 1833. A more popular and
representative reaction to radical and dissenting threats was the
address of the clergy (with some 7,000 signatures) to the archbishop
of Canterbury in February and a second from the laity (signed by
some 230,000 heads of families) in May 1834. This impressive
mobilization of feeling, demonstrating a strength unknown even to
anglicans themselves, powerfully affected the political situation. In
many respects it was the start of the anglican recovery; in some
respects of the conservative recovery also. 'The revolutionary temper
of the times,' wrote Dean Church, the historian and contemporary
of the Oxford Movement, 'had thrown all Churchmen on the
Conservative side; and these addresses were partly helped by political
Conservatism, and also reacted in their favour.'

If the problem was how to save the church from its enemies, the
solution in the view of liberal anglicans, both lay and clerical, was
for the church to reform itself. The defect of evangelicalism
was that its emphasis on individual salvation weakened its concern
for the church as a corporate body; the danger of Tractarianism
was that its emphasis on spiritual independence questioned to the
point of repudiation the value of the establishment itself. The
traditional stabilizing force of the *via media anglicana* still existed,
however, despite the absence of any distinguishing party label. As
early as 1832 the two great church reformers, Archbishop Howley
and Bishop Blomfield of London, had began their partnership;
consultations within the hierarchy on church reform had taken place;
and the idea of a mixed body of clergy and laity to work out a
common policy was gaining adherents. The failure of the whigs to
bring forward any constructive proposals in their first two years of
power after 1832 left the field to their opponents; and when Peel
came into office in November 1834 he sensed that the time was ripe
for action.

The Ecclesiastical Commission of 1835 set up by royal prerogative
stood as the one permanent achievement among the wreckage of
Peel's parliamentary programme in the 1834–5 ministry. It was
arguably the most important single measure affecting the Church
of England in the whole nineteenth century. If any two men could
be said to have saved the church from its enemies, they were Peel
and Blomfield. Growing radical and dissenting hostility made church
reform inevitable; Grey's Church Revenues Commission of 1832 had
prepared the ammunition. Peel's object was to reconcile the church
to reform by placing the responsibility for uncovering defects and
proposing remedies on the church itself. The machinery he provided

was a mixed commission of bishops, eminent anglican laymen and senior cabinet ministers, charged not only with enquiring into the organization of the church but with preparing bills for parliament embodying their recommendations. Consciousness of the exposed position of the establishment and of the favourable opportunity provided by a friendly government ensured the support of most of the bishops. Before Peel left office the first epoch-making report of the Commission was laid before parliament containing proposals for parochial and diocesan reorganization and the creation of two new bishoprics. The initiative had been captured; and when the whigs returned to office they had little choice not only to continue the Commission on a permanent basis but to accept the general principle that all ecclesiastical legislation presented to parliament by the government should originate with the Commission. Three senior whigs—Melbourne, Russell and Lansdowne—took the place of the outgoing conservative ministers (Peel, Graham and Wynn) on the Commission and found themselves, the first two perhaps with no great enthusiasm, participating in the work of reform. With that, the safety of the establishment was assured.

By 1838 the continuing activities of the Ecclesiastical Commission, the relief legislation for Dissenters in 1836, and the anglican victory over church rates in 1837, had shifted the battle between church and dissent away from expropriation and disestablishment to the more marginal issue of national education. It was a predictable development. Education was the only large and expanding field of competition between the two where no permanent boundaries had yet been fixed. In 1833 the government had started a system of grants to aid the two chief educational agencies, the anglican National Society and the dissenters' British and Foreign Society. At £20,000 the grant was not large; and there were criticisms both of the practice of giving assistance in proportion to local efforts (which favoured the wealthier anglican community) and of reliance on voluntary, sectarian agencies to meet a national need. The radical Central Society of Education founded in 1836 pressed boldly for a state system of secular education. But this, in a country where the majority of educated people regarded the churches as the proper supervisors of education, and properly supervised education as the only safeguard of religion and morals, was scarcely a practicable aim at that time. The whigs in 1839 proposed a compromise designed to assist their political protégé, the British and Foreign Society. The state grant was to be raised to £30,000; funds were to be allotted equally between the two main societies; money was to be made available to populous districts according to need; 'normal' (teacher-training) schools were to be set up on a non-confessional basis; and the whole apparatus was to be supervised by a committee of the Privy Council.

Compromise though it was, the scheme introduced three new features: equality of treatment for dissent; greater state control; and the beginnings of secular undenominational instruction. With some misgivings on the last two points, dissenters gave the scheme a general welcome for the sake of the first. To anglicans, however, every part of the plan was open to objections. To them it seemed a three-pronged weapon designed to deprive the church of its historic task of super-intending the main educational activities of the nation. Long before the proposals reached parliament a storm of public protest broke over the government. When the matter was discussed in the Commons the ministerial majority fell almost to vanishing point. In the House of Lords an address to the crown against the scheme was carried by an immense majority; and the archbishop of Canterbury recom-mended clergy to refuse all state grants until the proposal for school inspectors unauthorized by the diocesan bishop was abandoned. After a prolonged battle behind the scenes the ministers finally capitulated. The unpopular normal school proposal had been abandoned before the parliamentary debates had even started. The plan of state inspectors was now dropped, episcopal control reaffirmed, and the old system of allotting grants restored. The completeness of the victory marked the high point of anglican recovery after the depression of the 1828–32 period. It was in the heady mood of confidence inspired by this triumph that the young Gladstone published in 1839 his book on *The State in its Relations with the Church* in the exalted hope of bringing the whole nation back to the anglican communion.

Few sensible Anglicans shared Gladstone's fervent dream. Never-theless a feature of the anglican attitude in 1838–9 was that it was constructive as well as negative. 'It won't suffice to abuse the Government plan,' Peel had sensibly observed in November 1837. Part of the strength of the opposition was that even before the long-advertised whig scheme materialized, there were counter-proposals on the anglican side. A group of distinguished young conservative MPs under the leadership of Acland conceived the idea of turning the somewhat moribund National Society into an active agency for diocesan and parochial reform; and early in 1838 they successfully pressed on the leaders of the church a plan of education which included diocesan training colleges for teachers and a system of middle-class schools. The first diocesan training college in fact was opened at Chester in 1839 and within the next six years another twenty-one were founded.

This tide of anglican confidence, still running strongly in 1841, powerfully reinforced the political recovery of the Conservative party. Another current, totally different in character and attracting less national publicity, was setting in the same direction. As early as the general election of 1832 fears were expressed by some agricultural constituencies that in the reformed parliament the corn laws would be one of the first objects of attack. It did not happen, partly because the 1828 corn-law revision had gone some way to satisfy free traders, partly because good harvests and low food prices between 1832 and 1837 deprived the repeal movement of any urgency. The annual average price of wheat in these six years was never above 60s. and in 1835 fell as low as 40s. It was a feature of all corn laws, however, that whatever the state of the market either consumer or producer had a grievance. Farmers were discontented at low prices and their political fears were sharpened by the activities of some of the government's own supporters. Reform or abolition of the corn laws was still the professed object of most political radicals. The substitution of a small fixed duty was part of Grote's election platform, for example, when he successfully contested the City of London in 1832. Two years later Hume formally proposed in the Commons a motion for a fixed duty as a first step towards complete free trade in corn. Poulett Thomson, the whig vice-president of the strongly liberal Board of Trade spoke in its favour and several junior ministers were in the substantial minority which voted with Hume. Even Althorp, the leader of the House, confessed that he personally was in favour of a change in the law.

While farmers were being kept on the alert, more opportunities were coming their way to express their views. The movement for more scientific farming which had as one of its by-products the foundation of the English (after 1840 Royal) Agricultural Society, resulted in the 1830s in the formation of innumerable local agricultural societies and farmers clubs. Sometimes, as with the Buckinghamshire Association founded by that self-appointed champion of the agricultural interest Lord Chandos, they represented a deliberate attempt to organize support for such objects as the repeal of the malt tax. But even when started for the laudable purpose of improving farming methods, such societies had a disconcerting habit of turning into centres of protectionist agitation. Not all the gentry welcomed this semi-political activity among their tenants and the encouragement it gave to 'a feeling of consequence above their rank' as one old tory squire put it.[2] But farming opinion could not be safely ignored. Accustomed as they were to following their landlords on purely political issues, on matters which directly affected them like

[2] *Dyott's Diary*, edited by R. W. Jeffery (2 vols, 1907) II, p. 388.

rent, tithe, malt tax and corn laws, farmers had views of their own.
Few county MPs were immune to their pressure; few could be
indifferent to their votes.

In the years immediately after the Reform Act the agricultural
interest in the House of Commons was still a cross-bench grouping
in which whigs and tories worked together on behalf of their rural
constituents. It was a whig MP, Ingilby of Lincolnshire, who proposed the reduction in the malt duty in 1833 which so embarrassed
his leader Althorp. But as with each general election the number
of whig county representatives declined, the 'country party' changed
its character. From being a backbench alliance against the two front
benches, it became a separate interest within the Conservative party.
This concentration of agricultural strength within one party was
one of the significant developments of the 1830s. The potential danger
to party unity and ministerial policy was demonstrated as early
as Peel's 1834–5 ministry. Lord Chandos, who with his father the
duke of Buckingham represented the last of the old 'Grenville connection', refused to enter the cabinet without a pledge of some concession on the malt tax and in March made an independent attempt
to secure its abolition. Though Peel was irritated by this gratuitous
threat to his fragile administration, on this occasion the party rallied
round him and with the assistance of the liberal opposition Chandos's
motion was decisively negatived. Even so, it secured two hundred
votes and the 'agricultural Fanaticks' as Lord Granville Somerset,
the party's chief of staff, styled them, continued to be a source of
anxiety to the conservative managers.

By 1841 the consolidation of the agricultural interest within the
Conservative party was almost complete. The results were ironic.
In the 1820s whigs and radicals had done their best to stimulate
independent political action by the farming community against Lord
Liverpool's government. That community now regarded the Conservative party as its natural political champion in the legislature,
whigs and radicals as its natural enemies. In 1831 the reformers had
won all but six of the eighty-two English county seats then in existence. In 1841 the conservatives won all but twenty-three of the post-
Reform Bill total of 159 English and Welsh county seats. In the 1820s
Peel, with the rest of Liverpool's colleagues, had been accustomed
to regard the 'country members' as an independent, respectable but
sometimes obstreperous interest largely extraneous to the government. In 1841 they provided a fundamental element in the party
to whose victory at the polls he owed his position as prime minister.

Despite the renewed strength of anglicanism and the solid weight
of the agricultural interest, however, it is unlikely that without Peel
the Conservative party would have come to power in 1841. It was

the first general election in British history in which an organized opposition, previously in a minority in the House of Commons, defeated the government of the day. It was the only time this happened between the first and second Reform Acts. It was the only election in those thirty-five years in which the Conservative party obtained a majority. Given the intrinsic whig–liberal bias of the reformed system, the strong middle-class dissenting electorate in the larger English boroughs, the inherent radicalism of Scotland, and the liberal–national alliance in Ireland, it is difficult not to conclude that what made the margin of difference in favour of the conservatives in 1841 was the quality of its leadership over the previous half-dozen years. In proportion as the economic and social state of the country worsened after 1837 and the whigs seemed floundering in a sea of difficulties, the prospect of having Peel as prime minister grew more attractive to moderate, middle-of-the-road electors. The greatest intangible advantage enjoyed by the Conservative party in the 1841 general election was the widening conviction that Peel would administer the country's affairs better than his opponents.

There was an urban as well as a rural conservatism and it was here perhaps that Peel's leadership made its decisive contribution. Though the party gained a further twenty-nine county seats in 1841, this would still have been inadequate had it not been for the forty-four conservative members returned for the large towns with electorates of over 1,000, including four seats won in London and Westminster for the first time at any general election since the Reform Act. It was in constituencies like these that the shift of public opinion could most clearly be discerned. Peel's reputation had been built up more as a national than as a party leader. He had made no promises; he had entered into few commitments. There was no second Tamworth Manifesto. The Conservative party, observed *The Times* in a leading article after the election, would come into power not as the result of any pledge or programme but 'solely because the nation places confidence in their capacity'. It is doubtful whether the protectionist farmers of the counties were quite so confiding. But as an expression of the educated, middle-class, urban opinion which *The Times* usually reflected, it was probably correct.

In the preceding ten years Peel had devoted most of his energies to winning this confidence in himself and in his party. As parliamentary leader (and it is often forgotten that he was one of the most successful opposition leaders of the century) the main tasks he set himself were to build up a following in the House of Commons, strengthen the growing ties with Stanley and Graham, the ablest of the whig seceders of 1834, assist Wellington in preventing tory hotheads in the Lords from precipitating a constitutional crisis, and

by Fabian tactics (as Graham called them) first to contain and then
to wear down the liberal majority. But parliamentary tactics alone
would probably not have been enough. Equally important was the
fact that outside parliament he made use of every opportunity that
came his way to enlarge the party's reputation for sense and
moderation, and to expound his views to the wealthy, educated,
urban middle-classes whose support was essential if the Conservative party was ever to gain a majority. His plea to such men was
that if they had supported the Reform Bill in 1831, they should now
join in making the reformed constitution work peacefully and
efficiently and prevent any further slide towards radical democracy.

Along with the basic themes of law, order, and defence of the great
institutions of the country, including the established churches of
England and Scotland and the House of Lords, he preached the
Tamworth gospel of progressive improvement, the enlargement of
the party's social base, and the importance of party organization
in the constituencies. To those who attached importance to social
mobility and opportunities for wealth, talent and intelligence, he
pointed to himself, the son of a cotton spinner, as proof that there
was no natural barrier between the Conservative party and the
middle classes of society. Some of this was no more than a reiteration
of the principles that had guided Lord Liverpool's administration.
But in addition he was calling on the more conservative elements
in the community to enlist in a specific political party. To aim, as
Liverpool's government in the 1820s had been content to do, merely
at the approval of the respectable public was no longer sufficient.
Peel's experience in 1835 had demonstrated that the House of
Commons was so dominated by faction as to be impervious to any
plea for disinterested support. Except among the small group of
Stanleyites there was not even a pretence on the part of the House
of Commons in 1835 at giving him as newly appointed minister of
the crown the 'fair trial' for which he asked and before 1830 would
undoubtedly have got. His appeal was therefore transferred from
the Commons to the electorate. The Tamworth Manifesto was the
opening shot in an electoral campaign which was sustained until
1841.

It is difficult now to recapture the impact of that manifesto partly
because the circumstances that gave it force and colour have long
disappeared, partly because so much of it has been incorporated in
standard Conservative philosophy. But at the time it conveyed a
novel and attractive doctrine. It offered a safe mean between the
radical movement on the one side and negative tory reaction on
the other. It provided a refuge for those who disliked English
democracy, Irish nationalism, and whig compromise. It promised

to the timid and unpolitical firm and efficient government. It offered to the young and idealistic the challenge of adapting the ancient institutions of the past to the new wants of the present. This 'moral Conservatism' was to be one of the great distinguishing features of Peelite politicians. It was this which enabled Peel to gather round him not only the surviving members of the Liverpool administration and disillusioned whigs like Graham and Stanley but enthusiastic young men of the post-1830 vintage like W. M. Praed, Gladstone, Lincoln, Eliot, Cardwell, and Sidney Herbert. One of the secrets of the conservative recovery in the 1830s was that it was capturing the younger generation. As early as 1837 the radical *Westminster Review* was commenting on the drift of even members of traditional whig families at public schools and university towards conservatism.

IV

The epoch-making decade of whig rule came to a close in the general election of 1841. Before it ended there was a significant widening of the gap between the two parties on a matter which until then had scarcely been a party issue at all. Despite the activities of individual whig free traders and economists, the whigs collectively had not been a specifically free-trade party. In response to radical pressure for 'cheap government', the ministry had reduced as far as possible direct taxation; and their consequent increased reliance on indirect taxation made it impossible for them to experiment in Huskissonian fashion with any substantial tariff revisions. Financially in fact they left themselves with no room for manoeuvre; and when an economic depression started in 1837 the vulnerability of their financial position was exposed. There was no budget surplus in 1837 and in the following three years there were annual deficits. In 1840, in an attempt to halt the slide into ever deeper insolvency, they actually increased both direct and indirect taxation. Only when this failed to produce a surplus did Baring, the chancellor of the exchequer, have recourse to the policy, recommended by the recent radical-dominated Committee on Import Duties, of reducing duties in the hope that increased consumption would produce a higher tax yield. Baring singled out timber and sugar for the experiment; but it was Russell's addition of the old radical device of a moderate fixed duty on corn in place of the 1828 sliding scale that turned the budget into an electioneering instrument. Technically, it was merely the substitution of one form of protection for another. Practically, however, it raised the issue of free-trade against protection, and ensured that beneath innumerable hustings in 1841 the 'Big Loaf versus Small Loaf' banners were an evocative popular symbol.

In the protectionist agricultural constituencies the whigs had little left to lose; it was in the large towns that they hoped to gain. For Peel and the Conservative opposition, however, the transformation of the corn law question into a party issue brought short-term advantages and long-term liabilities. Since the 1837 election the topic had been brought annually before the Commons by the aristocratic radical C. P. Villiers, MP for Wolverhampton, who made it his personal crusade. A growing opinion among the Liberal rank and file, as well as the free-trade sympathies of some of his own colleagues, extorted from Melbourne a reluctant permission for the issue to be treated as an open question. In 1839 Villiers's motion for a committee of enquiry secured nearly 200 votes, including those of an impressive number of ministerial whigs, Russell and Palmerston among them. Meanwhile industrial depression and rising food prices stimulated the agitation out of doors. In 1838 the Manchester Anti-Corn Law Association was founded, the most famous but not the only nor the first of such societies; and the national Anti-Corn Law League was established in Manchester the following year. After almost a decade of public indifference, a new phase had started in the long campaign against the corn laws which had been carried on intermittently ever since 1815. The conservative opposition, cast now in the role of chief guardian of the agricultural interest, had repeatedly to define and defend its position.

As far as Peel was concerned, the defence of agricultural protection in the years 1838–41 rested on specific, practical grounds. He did not think that agricultural distress in itself justified legislative interference. He did not think that the landed interest was entitled to regard itself as a privileged class for which the rest of community should be taxed. But he stressed the special burdens on the land— tithe, county rate, poor rate and land tax—the undesirability of sudden changes in great national economic interests, and the fact that not only agriculture but industry as well still enjoyed substantial tariff protection. As for the existing 1828 corn law, he gave no pledge to maintain it in detail if he came into office, though he expressed a steady preference for a sliding scale over the fixed duty which became official whig policy in 1841. Taking up Liverpool's favourite theme of the interdependence of agriculture, industry and commerce, he argued that the justification for protection was not the special interests of the farming community but the benefits it brought to

the community at large. It was consistent with this basic attitude
that he said on several occasions that if it could be proved that the
corn laws adversely affected national prosperity, in particular the
condition of the working class, he would be ready to amend and
if necessary repeal them. Finally, he said emphatically and
repeatedly, that if he took office, he would be guided by his own
view of national needs. He would never be the instrument of policies
with which he did not personally agree.

With all these reservations, however, it remained true that he
supported the principle of protection enshrined in the corn laws and
argued that what he variously described before the 1841 election
as 'a liberal protection' or 'a just and adequate protection' for
agriculture was in the national interest. Nobody doubted at the time
that he and his party were pledged to maintain, if not the 1828 act,
at least a corn law of some kind. Nor is there any reason to dis-
believe that for Peel in these years the only problem was to decide
on what precisely was implied by the terms 'just' and 'adequate'
in relation to agricultural protection. The reservations he made
about his freedom of action as minister were genuine expressions
of his general beliefs on the nature of governmental responsibility,
and were addressed as much to his backbenchers as to his opponents.
But he did not at that time anticipate any clash between those beliefs
and the maintenance of some protection for corn.

Melbourne, bearing the burden of office, was pressed more
hardly on the issue. Indeed the real analogy is between Melbourne
in 1841 and Peel in 1846. Since 1838 Melbourne had struggled to
avoid taking up the corn question as government policy. Intellectually he doubted in his gloomier moments whether the property
and institutions of the country could survive free trade in corn.
Politically he thought, as he wrote to Russell in 1839, that abolition
could only be carried 'by the same means as we carried the Reform
Bill, and I am not for being the instrument of another similar performance'. Making the issue an open question in 1839 was for him
a safety-valve for the unrest in the party, not a preliminary to the
acceptance of free trade. Taxed in 1841 with unpardonable incon-
sistency in supporting a change in the corn laws after his strong
language earlier against any alteration, he defended himself with
the argument (not unlike that which Peel was to employ five years
later) that his views had always been based on 'particular and
temporary grounds' and that 'undoubtedly I have changed the
opinion which I formerly held, grounded as that opinion was on
purely temporary interests'. The difference between the two leaders
in 1841 was simply that Peel, swayed by the needs of his party in
opposition, placed a greater emphasis on one aspect of the problem

than his general intellectual approach entirely justified; while Melbourne was led by party expediency to assent to a proposition of which he was not intellectually convinced. For both the growth of the party system which gave them supreme office was another addition to the innumerable limitations with which the exercise of political power is invariably attended.

7 The 'Condition of England' Question

I

The harsher economic climate of the first four years of Victoria's reign contributed to the decline in whig popularity even though the problems raised were outside the field of party politics and only rarely figured in debates at Westminster. Some years before the general election of 1841 the realization was growing that there was a social question to which middle-class sectarian and party conflicts had little relevance. 'A feeling very generally exists,' ran the opening sentence of Thomas Carlyle's famous pamphlet on *Chartism* in 1839, 'that the condition and disposition of the Working Classes is a rather ominous matter at present; that something ought to be said, something ought to be done, in regard to it.' When intelligent and socially conservative members of the educated classes considered the state of industrial England and Scotland, two reflections usually occurred to them. One was the instability of a society where thousands of men, cooped up in mean houses and narrow streets, without savings, adequate poor relief or even gardens of their own in which to grow food, could be thrown out of work or put on reduced wages at a moment's notice because of trade depression. The other was what seemed to them the artificiality of a system where the traditional framework of social life—community sense, acceptance of rank and inequality, reciprocal feelings of duty and deference, the practice of religion, charity and neighbourliness—had been replaced by the indiscriminate massing in particular areas for purely economic reasons of people whose only link with their employer was the cash nexus.

The comparison, conscious or unconscious, was always with the older, rural Britain of a pre-industrial age. As with most stereotypes of this kind, it contained a large measure of self-deception. There was little in the contemporary state of rural society to justify any favourable contrast between the poorer classes of the countryside and those of the towns. During most years between 1815 and 1830 it would not have taken much to drive the rural labourers of the overpopulated, Speenhamland counties of southeast England to riot and arson. Low agricultural wages and even lower parish dole for the unemployed, substantial reductions after Waterloo in the scale of family allowances given by the poor law authorities, kept them on a bare subsistence level. The final demoralization came with the widespread practice, by farmers seeking to cut their costs, of throwing large numbers of men on the parish during the winter months when work was slack. The growing use of threshing machines contributed to this standing evil of winter unemployment since on large arable farms hand-threshing formerly constituted as much as a quarter of the total work. For men trapped in this situation a poor farming season came as a double hardship, reducing the amount of harvest work and sending up the price of bread.

The run of bad harvests between 1816 and 1818 had produced the East Anglian riots. The run of bad harvests between 1828 and 1831 was marked by even larger rural disturbances. After two cold, wet years it only needed one successful example to start a wave of rioting in the southeastern counties at the onset of the third lean winter of 1830. The trouble began with the failure of the hop harvest in Kent. Unemployed labourers attacked threshing machines and disturbances went on almost unchecked throughout September. Their example was soon followed in neighbouring counties. Sussex was affected early in November; Hampshire, Berkshire and Wiltshire in the second half of the month. By this time the central authorities had bestirred themselves and though the outward wave of unrest penetrated westward into Dorset and Gloucester and northward to Buckinghamshire, Bedfordshire and East Anglia, by December it was all over. A considerable deployment of troops had been thought necessary to restore order in the worst affected counties; and the alarm created in the minds of the propertied classes was reflected in the appointment of special commissions to try the large number of labourers who had been arrested in Berkshire, Hampshire, Wiltshire, Dorset and Buckinghamshire.

Though there was some evidence of radical propaganda at work in Kent, in the central southern counties the riots had been born of hardship and poverty, prompted by news of disturbances elsewhere, and directed with naïve hope towards limited, practical ends. Almost everywhere the two principal objects were the same: the destruction of all forms of farm machinery that replaced manual labour, and the extortion of a higher rate of wages. There was a leaven of artisans among the rioters—carpenters, masons and the like—but the bulk of the men were ordinary agricultural labourers, many of them impressed from farms and cottages as the mobs went

round from village to village. The ringleaders usually carried
weapons such as axes, hammers and iron bars, but these were solely
for breaking machines. A feature of the disturbances was the absence
of cruelty and vindictiveness. Not a single life was lost among the
gentry, farmers, constables and military who came face to face with
the rioters. Indeed only one man in all England died in the 1830
riots—at Hindon in Wiltshire in a clash with yeomanry.

The magistrates and gentry on their side showed some sympathy
with the men. The lenient attitude of the bench in East Kent was
blamed by some for contributing to the spread of the disorders. In
other riotous counties the magistrates, acting either collectively for
their divisions or as individuals in their parishes, often recommended
a higher rate of wages for farm labourers and higher poor-law
allowances for children. To the Home Office, forced to remind
magistrates that their powers of fixing wages had expired in 1813
and that the duty of protecting property applied even to threshing
machines, this indulgent attitude was a source of disquiet. The
ponderous machinery of justice, once set in motion, was not so
merciful. Of the nearly 1,000 persons tried before the special commissions, over a third were summarily dismissed, over 200 formally
sentenced to death, and eleven left for execution. Following intense
pressure through newspapers and local petitions eight were reprieved
and three finally hanged, one at Reading and two at Winchester.
Contrasted with the sentences carried out on the Luddites and East
Anglian rioters some fifteen years earlier, it was a relatively light
retribution. That public opinion was uneasy was a measure of the
growing humanitarianism of the age. The crushing and unprecedented feature of the judicial punishments, however, was that
(including those tried before ordinary courts) over 450 were transported to Australia in addition to almost as many who served short
sentences at home. Though within half a dozen years of their arrival
all the transported men received pardons, few ever returned. It was
to be another two generations before the riots and the wholesale
reprisals which followed were effaced from rural memory in southern
England.

By comparison the case of the Dorchester labourers (as they were
known to contemporaries) in 1834 was of minor importance. Its place
is in the hagiography of the trade union movement rather than the
history of the agricultural labourer. Though the local magistrates
wrote to the home secretary in alarmist language of the spread of
unions in Dorset, they could adduce singularly little proof. The fact
that George Loveless, the leading spirit in the pathetic little
labourers' association, had to obtain his knowledge of union rules
and procedure from correspondence with Leeds and London suggests

that it was a completely pioneer effort. Trade unions themselves were not illegal but the six Tolpuddle men, who tried to form a union of agricultural labourers, in their ignorance had infringed acts of George III relating to the administration of secret oaths. This technical offence gave the opportunity to the alarmed Dorset magistrates, supported by Melbourne, to make a warning example. The sentence of seven years transportation passed at Dorchester assizes in March 1834 by an inexperienced judge on a strained linking of two separate statutes brought about a sharp public reaction. The Grand National Consolidated Trades Union, whose emissaries had encouraged the forlorn Tolpuddle venture, staged a massive demonstration in London and though the six convicted labourers were hastily despatched to Australia, the continued public agitation, led by political radicals and trade unionists, in the end was successful. The remainder of the sentences was respited by Russell in 1836 and by 1838 five of the six had already returned home.

In April 1838, ten years almost to the day before a rather better known Chartist demonstration over the same route, they were rapturously feted in London with a great procession of the London trades from Kennington Common through Westminster to Copenhagen Fields, with a band playing 'See the Conquering Hero Comes' as they passed the Home Office. The trade union movement had been provided with more deserving 'martyrs' than the 'Glasgow thugs' of 1837. In fact the last ripples of the Dorchester case merged into the beginnings of Chartism. A pamphlet *The Victims of Whiggery*, written allegedly by George Loveless, was often quoted at Chartist meetings and its author was elected delegate to the Chartist Convention though he never took his seat. It asked one question at least which went to the root of Chartist feeling. 'When will they attempt to raise the working man to that scale in society to which he can lay claim from his utility?' Ironically, for the Tolpuddle men the dream came true. The Dorchester committee that raised subscriptions on their behalf was able to place five of the men on small farms in Essex, though they later migrated with their families to Canada. The sixth preferred to return to his native Dorset. Set against the fate of the forgotten rioters of 1830 their lot might have been thought enviable.

Neither the 'Tolpuddle martyrs' nor the 1830 riots did much to change the condition of the country labourers in southern England. Some hundreds of threshing machines had been destroyed and for a number of years afterwards farmers were afraid to reintroduce them. But for the most part they soon brought the men's wages back to their former level and it was the new poor law of 1834 that was to be the main influence in eliminating winter unemployment.

Even sympathetic gentry, clergy and magistrates found it difficult to do much in the face of the prevailing system; and once the danger was over, public concern was diverted to the wider issue of the Reform Bill.

In the countryside itself sullenness and ill-feeling continued. The rural incendiarism that had both preceded and accompanied the disturbances, though rarely the work of the rioters themselves, persisted as an ugly if fitful sign of the conditions which led men of poverty to take vengeance for real or imagined wrongs on men of property. But except for such unusual outbreaks as the epidemic of rick-burning in Norfolk and Suffolk in 1843–4, its history is to be found only in court records and the local press. Even in the latter perhaps it was deliberately underemphasized. 'In London,' wrote Somerville bitterly in 1843 when giving a description of the state of the agricultural labourers in Berkshire and Oxfordshire, '...only a small portion of the rural fires are reported; the directors of insurance companies have been taught practical philosophy, and know that publicity makes crime contagious. The provincial newspapers agree with them.'[1] When the Anti-Corn Law League journalists (of whom Somerville was one) came to enquire into the real situation in the English countryside in the 1840s, they did not lack material for their attacks on the landed interest.

II

The validity of the whig claim to have detached the middle classes from lower-class radicalism was never more clearly demonstrated than in the years 1831–6. Left to themselves the small knot of men who formed a link between the age of Peterloo and that of the Chartists—James Watson, Benbow, Cleave, Lovett and Hetherington—like other working-class leaders in this period spent their energies on a succession of short-lived organizations with grandiose objectives incapable of realization in their own or perhaps any other imperfect human society. The achievement of parliamentary reform was followed by a collapse in the membership and finances of the London National Political Union. The more extreme National Union of Working Classes, founded in 1831 on the fragments of a smaller Owenite association, for a short time became the residuary legatee of working-class political interest. After the

[1] Alexander Somerville, *The Whistler at the Plough* (Manchester, 1852), p. 129.

failure of the banned Cold Bath Fields meeting in May 1833, designed to prepare the way for a national convention, it also rapidly declined. In 1835 it merged with the Radical Association founded by Feargus O'Connor only for this in turn to be absorbed by the London Working Men's Association under Lovett and Hetherington.

This procession of transient, shallow-rooted political organizations was evidence both of the lack of any large political issue that would enlist mass support and of the persistence with which a relatively restricted group of committed radicals in London continued to work for a wider measure of parliamentary reform than the whigs had provided in the 1832 act. Some new ideological elements were, however, beginning to emerge. Though superficially the NUWC, for example, offered little more than the traditional mixture of Painite, French Revolutionary, democratic politics and Cobbettite attacks on the corruption and extravagance of government, it was from the start also infused with economic and social ideas derived from Owen and Hodgskin, in particular the theory of labour as the true source of wealth, the need for a more equitable distribution of national resources, and the possibility of economic cooperation among the poorer classes themselves. The standard working-class dogma remained that social ills were due to bad government and their remedy lay in a democratic reform of parliament; but it was reinforced by the new semi-socialist notion that the working classes created the nation's wealth and that this wealth should be divided among those who created it. This blend of political and social doctrines pointed to two enemies, the government and the rich. The identification was made all the easier by the widespread conviction among lower-class radicals that the effect of the 1832 Reform Act was merely to put government under the domination of the urban middle classes.

Not all proletarian radicals pursued this theory to its logical conclusions; but these novel social ideas, however crudely disseminated, probably assisted the mushroom growth of the Grand National Consolidated Trades Union. Lovett at least attributed the decline of the NUWC to the superior attractions of the GNCTU, founded largely under Owen's influence in 1834 to regenerate society by a comprehensive organization and representation of the united working classes. The years between 1829 and 1835 saw the efflorescence of utopian trade unionism as well as utopian political unionism. The perhaps over-publicized GNCTU was only the most ambitious of a number of attempts to realize working-class ambitions through national organization. Doherty's Grand General Union of cotton spinners, intended to cover England, Scotland and Ireland, ran its brief course from 1829 to 1830. A National Association for the Protection of Labour (1829–31), designed heroically to enrol all the unions of the different trades in Lancashire and the Midlands, had an almost identical career. A general Builders' Union centred on Birmingham appeared in 1832–4; and there were many others. At the same time favourable industrial conditions, especially in 1833, led to greater activity by the craft unions and a series of strikes and lockouts in the Midland industrial districts. These were conditions which favoured Owen's brief, dramatic but largely meaningless irruption into the world of trade union politics.

Like some of its predecessors the London-based GNCTU indulged in apocalyptic and menacing language better calculated to alarm and anger employers than bring immediate practical rewards. It was not surprising that some manufacturers took drastic action to deter their work-people from joining it. Its inflated membership figures meant little since there was no system of regular subscriptions. The more important established trade unions held aloof; and what little strength it had was wasted in petty strikes. By August 1834 the dream had vanished and Owen turned to other things. When the industrial depression of 1837–42 came, only the smaller craft unions based on the better-paid and better-organized aristocrats of labour were able to survive into the 1840s. The industrial proletariat was still too split up by regional, social and occupational differences for mass organization to be possible.

In other, more restricted fields, however, middle-class sympathy and leadership continued to be of crucial importance. The early factory acts were a case in point. Long before the Manchester Anti-Corn Law League began its attack on the landed aristocracy, the condition of the workers in the textile factories, particularly the children, had attracted the interest of a miscellaneous array of reformers—medical men, clergy (especially anglicans and Primitive Methodists), country squires, a few tory and radical manufacturers, trade unionists and several conservative MPs. After the passage of the elder Peel's act of 1819, regulating the employment of children in cotton mills, the momentum had been maintained by reforming mill-owners like John Wood of Bradford and Doherty, the cotton spinners' leader. Two more acts introduced in 1825 and 1829 by the radical J. C. Hobhouse testified to the principle if not yet to the effectiveness of parliamentary intervention. Oastler's famous letter to the *Leeds Mercury* on 'Yorkshire Slavery' in October 1830 heralded a new intensive campaign in which short time committees among the operatives, encouraged and often financially assisted by tory and radical gentry and manufacturers, appeared all over the textile districts of England and Scotland.

Oastler, the main organizer, orator and propagandist of the move-

ment, was a tory anglican land agent. Sadler, their first House of
Commons spokesman, was a tory evangelical linen merchant with
strong Methodist sympathies who had been brought into parliament
by the duke of Newcastle to oppose Catholic Emancipation. The
short-time delegates (predominantly from Lancashire and Yorkshire), who met at Bradford in 1833 to consider the situation caused
by Sadler's parliamentary defeat in 1832, authorized their secretary,
a local tory evangelical parson, G. S. Bull, to find a successor; and
it was Bull who finally secured the services of Lord Ashley, an
anglican, Conservative MP for Dorset and heir to the earldom of
Shaftesbury created in the seventeenth century. Though the movement remained eclectic, its principal character from the start was
that of a tory–radical alliance, in which anglicans and operatives
made common cause against whigs, liberals and orthodox dissenters.

The motives of the participants were inevitably mixed and not
always disinterested. Tory romantics, including literary men like
Southey, Wordsworth and Coleridge, were instinctively opposed to
anything that seemed to them a destruction of traditional society
by the godless and ugly worship of industrial mammon. The clergy
were conscious of the hollowness of any attempt to give moral and
religious education to children who spent most of their working lives
in the mill. The unions hoped for the employment of surplus male
operatives and a general reduction of hours without loss of earnings,
if restrictions were imposed on child labour. Indeed, in 1837 the
operatives' short-time committees were prepared to extend children's
hours from eight to ten if this could be made the standard working
day for all. The reforming manufacturers not unreasonably thought
that in a harsh, competitive world no real reform was practical unless
it was imposed by law on all millowners.

What carried reform, however, was the publicity provided by the
newspaper discussions and the report of Sadler's 1832 committee,
reinforced by religious and humanitarian feeling in the country once
the facts became known. There was much opposition to intervention
both from manufacturers and in parliament. The ministers themselves were lukewarm and took refuge in a royal commission. But
when Benthamites like Chadwick and economists like McCulloch
were convinced by the evidence that there was an irresistible case for
legislative interference, some action was inevitable. Even a strict
individualist, *laissez-faire* adherent had to admit that children could
scarcely be regarded as free agents, capable of deciding on their own
economic interests. Accordingly the government factory act of 1833
forbade in textile (other than silk) mills the employment of children
under nine; restricted the labour of those between nine and thirteen
to nine hours in any day or forty-eight in any week; and of those

under eighteen to twelve hours in the day or sixty-nine in the week. Four inspectors with magisterial powers were to supervise the operation of the act.

Industrial inspection was not unknown in the textile areas but the 1833 centralized inspectorate with regular reporting to the secretary of state formed an important administrative innovation. After 1833 the factory reform movement tended to disintegrate— partly because of the attractions of other movements; partly because of the further unrealistic demands of some of the men (followers of Owen's National Regeneration Society) for 'ten hours pay for eight hours work'; partly because of divisions between the newer and older leaders. Nevertheless, a permanent legacy remained: the clear-cut principle of the ten hours day advocated by Oastler and Sadler in the 1831–2 agitation, the nucleus of national organization, and the awareness of the public that there was a 'factory question'.

Overlapping, and to some extent weakening, the ten hours movement in the mid-1830s was the other emotional issue of the new poor law. For many of the country gentry the 1830 riots had destroyed the last remnant of belief in the old system of parochial assistance. If the great burden of poor rate could not even guarantee social order, there seemed an overwhelming case for reform. In 1831–2 expenditure on poor relief had reached £7 millions, the highest level since the bad years of 1817–20. It was not perhaps an excessive amount for a country as rich as England; but it absorbed nearly 80 per cent of the money raised by local rates, and compared with the central expenditure by the state for normal government purposes (exclusive of debt charges) in the same year of £19 millions, it seemed to contemporaries a vast sum. A disproportionate amount of it, moreover, was expended and therefore raised in southern and eastern England as against Wales and the northern industrial areas. In Scotland, with a different system more parsimoniously administered, the expenditure on poor relief per head of population was perhaps as much as eight times less.

The royal commission set up by the whigs in 1832 put the blame squarely on the 'Speenhamland' abuses of the old poor law. It prescribed as remedies the abolition of the rate in aid of wages, the discontinuance of assistance to the able-bodied outside the workhouse (the 'workhouse test'), the institution of a rigorous and discouraging workhouse regime (the 'less eligibility' principle), and the creation of a central commission to superintend a national, uniform system of poor law administration. Since the bill introduced in 1834 was primarily concerned with the administrative structure of the new system rather than with the policy it was to administer, it was not easy for parliamentary critics to concentrate their attacks. But the

cabinet itself had at first been uneasy at the drastic nature of the proposals and strong objections were soon raised in public by such influential organs as *The Times* and the tory *Quarterly Review*. At a lower level of society sinister rumours began to circulate that the new workhouse 'Bastilles' were to be run on prison lines, that the Malthusian and Benthamite Poor Law Commissioners believed in depopulation as the only effective cure for poverty, and that the new poor law was only a halfway house to the abolition of all forms of outdoor relief. These wild exaggerations increased the popular fears and prejudices which surrounded the enforcement of the act. At the heart of the controversy was, however, a real social issue. Outdoor relief had been a safeguard in time of unemployment: its existence guaranteed a minimum standard of living for the poor. If you abolished the right of the poor man to call on society for assistance in time of need, wrote Cobbett in the last pamphlet of his long pamphleteering career, *The Legacy to Labourers* (1835), 'you do all in your power to break up the social compact'.

Though dislike of the measure was widespread, there were striking regional variations in the nature and extent of the opposition encountered by the commissioners when from 1835 on they tried to put it into operation. In the Speenhamland, low-wage area of England, the southern, southeastern and eastern counties, a few members of the upper classes, especially clergy, wrote critical letters to *The Times* or, like the Reverend F. Maberley in East Anglia, organized local protest meetings. There was also some sporadic resistance from the labourers themselves. But with the lessons of 1830 still fresh, the demonstrations, stonings and rioting invariably stopped as soon as police and military were brought in. By the end of 1836 most of this area was reorganized and the new guardians were beginning to apply the official policy. They were considerably aided in this task by the good harvests and general prosperity of the 1835–6 years, and in some districts by the additional employment available on the new railway lines being built at this time. Only in Cornwall did the commissioners run into a stubborn pocket of resistance from the elected guardians who refused to put up new workhouses or discontinue outdoor relief. In Wales, though there was little violence, the opposition was more baffling. There was profound antipathy to the English centralizing bureaucrats in London and a determined refusal to abandon such traditional Welsh practices as sending money to poor parishioners who had migrated elsewhere. Though the framework of the new unions was established by 1837, magistrates, gentry, established and dissenting clergy, as well as the mass of ordinary people, combined to elect anti-poor law guardians who openly flouted the instructions and regulations given to them by the zealous and not over-tactful assistant commissioners. In the face of this non-cooperation by almost the entire Welsh population, the commissioners in London were forced to compromise for fear of exposing their complete helplessness.

It was in England north of the Trent that the most open and violent resistance manifested itself. For the most part the old poor law authorities there had conducted their affairs tidily and economically. They disliked the prospect of that 'centralization' and subordination to London which was the constitutional objection to the bill most strongly voiced when it went through parliament in 1834. They felt with justice that the new system had been designed to deal with southern, rural problems that were irrelevant to their own local conditions. The twin evils in the south had been the regular and protracted winter unemployment and the systematic exploitation by farmers of the rate in aid. In the industrial districts of the north and Midlands wages were considerably higher. The problem came when a manufacturing slump put thousands of men simultaneously out of work. No workhouse test could be applied in that situation, as the commissioners themselves realized when they lifted the prohibition on outdoor relief at Nottingham for almost twelve months in 1837–8 because of the general distress among the hosiers.

What finally wrecked their general policy in the north was the start of the great industrial depression in 1837 at the precise moment when they were extending their operations into the Yorkshire and Lancashire textile areas, still seething with the union activity and factory reform agitation of the preceding few years. All the materials for instant protest were at hand. Most of the short time committee leaders became anti-poor law militants—Oastler, Fielden, Bull and Stephens—and were joined by Feargus O'Connor for whom the agitation was a heaven-sent opportunity to establish himself as a popular figure after his break with the London radicals. The new law was held up as yet another example of the readiness of the whigs to surrender to the interests of the manufacturing middle classes. In many places the poor law entered into municipal politics as a class and party issue between liberals and dissenters on one side, a tory–radical alliance on the other. The attempts of the poor law assistant commissioners to set up the new administration met with harassment, boycotting, obstruction and rioting. Military and detachments of metropolitan police were called in; in Bradford at one point the troops had to open fire.

Yet by 1839 the anti-poor law movement had almost completely collapsed. For this there were several reasons. Despite the efforts of Earl Stanhope and the Metropolitan Anti-Poor Law Association, there had never been much prospect that it would become a national agitation. Even in Yorkshire and Lancashire the leadership soon disintegrated. Sincere moderate social reformers like Parson Bull were alienated by mob violence and the bloodthirsty language of men like O'Connor and Stephens; the unfortunate Oastler, dismissed from his stewardship at Fixby, entered a debtor's prison in 1840. As a natural result, the anti-poor law feeling was increasingly absorbed into the wider movement of Chartism. The main reason for the transient nature of the campaign, however, was that the issue was soon seen to be unreal. It was significant that the main excitement was before, and not after, the establishment of the new unions. Once they had been set up, the northern labourers found that little had changed. After all the initial clamour, there seemed little to quarrel about. In the northeastern industrial areas of Durham and Northumberland, where there had been no great disturbance, the administration of the new poor law seems in fact to have been more lenient and humane than the old.

It was the difference between the theory of the law and its practical enforcement. Clearly the early rioting and the continued stubbornness of the local guardians in Yorkshire and Lancashire taught the commissioners in London a salutary lesson. Though their secretary Edwin Chadwick had regretted the inadequacy of the powers given to the central commission and still put his trust in the Benthamite principles of the 1834 report, his superiors increasingly distrusted his judgement and excluded him from policy decisions. Independently of the parliamentary weakness of the government, and the vulnerability of an unpopular state department that lacked a political chief to defend it in the House of Commons, the commissioners had justifiable doubts of their own. They showed remarkable tolerance and flexibility in dealing with the recalcitrant northern areas and when the industrial depression was prolonged into the 1840s they gave up any attempt to enforce a common national policy. Outdoor relief continued as the main method of assistance and in the north there was hardly a pretence of building new union 'houses'. In the spring of 1844, ten years after the passing of the act, 84 per cent of those who received poor relief still received it outside the workhouse. It was not until after the middle of the century that the new Poor Law Board, which had replaced the old commission in 1847, made an attempt to impose a labour test order on the unions in south Lancashire and the West Riding; and the renewed opposition they encountered soon led to another series of compromises.

Even in the more deferential rural south the continuing low wages of the agricultural labourers made it almost inevitable that humane poor law guardians should resort to concealed but illicit forms of outdoor relief. Ostensibly 'special' payments—before and after pregnancy, during illness, on account of some real or imputed disability, to assist the parents of a crippled or diseased child, or to cover the costs of a funeral—were often simply covert means of supplementing wages for the very poor. A well informed country parson in Dorset, which had some of the lowest-paid peasantry in the kingdom, wrote roundly in 1846 that 'the New Poor Law has only worked well where it has worked in opposition to the chief principles of its founders, in defiance of the rules of the Commissioners'.[2] Without this connivance by sympathetic local authorities the plight of the poor in some rural areas, attempting to live as wage-earners on less than the poor law commissioners allowed for the upkeep of a pauper in the workhouse, would have been desperate. These were the classes for whom the fear of 'the Union House' was always present, even though it was more of a threat than a reality.

In effect the position of equilibrium reached in the mid-1840s remained. Even more decisive perhaps than the threat of popular resistance was the degree of provincial autonomy represented by the elected boards of guardians with their *ex officio* JP members. It was this practical safeguard that ensured that no 'centralized' bureaucracy could ride roughshod over local feeling. The gentry and clergy in the rural districts, the middle classes in the towns, found that whatever the regulations prescribed, in practice they could administer the new poor law much as they thought fit, with almost as much power and patronage as before. The cost of poor relief certainly dropped. In the first quarter of 1844 it was 30 per cent less per head of population than in 1831–2. In such a happy situation there was little likelihood, despite the sustained and violent agitation carried on by *The Times*, and occasional workhouse scandals, that ministers or parliament would abandon the 1834 act. Reforms of a limited but useful nature had been put through, especially in the rural districts; but it was generally recognized that in the industrial areas the problem of mass unemployment was virtually outside the scope of any poor law principle that could be devised. As against Chadwick's scientific but unimaginative administrative theory, the governing classes had come down tacitly but overwhelmingly on the side of compromise, commonsense and humanity.

[2] *Letters to S.G.O.* (the initials used by Sidney Godolphin Osborne, rector of Durweston 1841–75, in his frequent letters to *The Times*), edited by Arnold White (2 vols, 1890), p. 24.

III

Between 1837 and 1843 a large part of the aspirations and discontents of the manufacturing population was drawn into the movement known as Chartism. It was a deceptively simple label. From small and identifiable origins Chartism widened into a heterogeneous mass of activities which make broad generalizations dangerous and neat analysis impossible. Chartism floated, as it were, on a conglomeration of working-class movements with different objectives, different philosophies, different grievances and different leaders. The 'Charter' provided nothing new in the way of political thought; and less than is commonly assumed in the way of united action. Underneath were still the old complicated phenomena of classes, trades and regions, mass meetings, religious revivalism, the popular press, physical violence and constitutional agitation. It is only the verbal substitution of 'the Charter' for the more familiar 'parliamentary reform' that hides the fundamental continuity between 1816–20 and 1837–42. Many features of the post-Waterloo period reappeared: the caps of liberty, the tricolour flags, the calling-up of the yeomanry, the extensive military preparations, the use of spies and informers, the trials and arrests, the fears and alarms of the magistracy. What was new perhaps was the greater sophistication and better organization of the radical leaders, the longer experience and greater restraint of the central authorities.

The London Working Men's Association which drew up the Charter was formed in 1836 by an intellectual *élite* of London artisans following the success in the same year of the long campaign against the high stamp duty on newspapers. After the disappointment of 1832 there was a conscious desire to emancipate themselves from middle-class leadership. This, however, was not easily achieved. The decision to proceed by way of parliamentary petition led to involvement with radical MPs like Roebuck and Leader. The campaign for support in the provinces led to association with such bodies as Attwood's Birmingham Political Union which had a strong middle-class element. Yet the aims of those who composed the Charter were not class aims. They thought the organization of society faulty, government corrupt, legislation biased and popular education defective. But they did not want to attack property or restrict liberty. They were essentially reformists, not revolutionaries. They were sober men, dedicated to moral and educational improvement and aware of the long tradition of political radicalism that stretched back through Cobbett and Hunt to Cartwright and Paine.

Essentially therefore all they were doing was to restate the classic theme that social evils were due to bad legislation and curable by parliamentary reform. In this lay the instant appeal of the Charter to the people and organizations in the provinces, the old political unions, the radical clubs and working men's associations, to whom the doctrine and programme had long been familiar. All six points of the Charter—universal suffrage, no property qualification, annual parliaments, equal representation, payment of members, and vote by ballot—had been in the Westminster programme of 1780 and had been the stock-in-trade of radical reformers ever since. To Cooper, attending his first Chartist meeting in 1840 as reporter for the *Leicestershire Mercury*, the lecture he heard was 'simply the recital of the old programme of the Duke of Richmond, and his friends, at the close of the last century' which had been his political creed ever since his radical childhood at Gainsborough. It was precisely this lack of novelty that made it easy to enlist mass support for the Charter; conversion was unnecessary. After the collapse of utopian trade unionism, the narrow and already disintegrating movement for factory reform, the brief resistance to the new poor law, a fresh campaign for the old fundamental radical programme had many attractions. The Chartists themselves recognized the continuity between their movement and that of the pre-1830 reformers. They celebrated the anniversary of Peterloo and O'Connor laid the foundation stone for the Hunt memorial in the Ancoats chapel at Manchester in 1842.

Not surprisingly Chartism was at first a broadly based, anti-aristocratic movement that enlisted support from both skilled artisans and the middle classes. The radical reformers, who parted company with the 'moderate liberals' in asserting the need for a further instalment of parliamentary reform, could see in the campaign for the Charter an alternative road of advance. Attwood's Birmingham Union collaborated enthusiastically with the London WMA in the series of mass meetings which launched the Charter on the national scene in 1838. More assistance was forthcoming from the two great northern political unions formed at Leeds and Newcastle in June of that year. Despite the disavowals of some Chartist leaders like O'Connor, the trade unions, initially at least in England and throughout the years 1838–43 in Scotland, gave encouragement, provided many local leaders and officials, and some financial help. At the mass demonstration on Kersal Moor near Manchester in September 1838, the largest of its kind that year, the procession of trades outnumbered that of the political unions.

This alliance, invaluable in the early days of the Chartist movement, became less prominent as time went on. From 1839 the growing violence of Chartist propaganda caused a certain uneasiness. The craft unions had no desire to risk their status or their funds by becoming involved in illegal political activities; and they resented encroachments on their own sphere of influence. When the local Chartists at Sheffield called for a general strike in 1842, the secretaries of seven trade unions publicly dissociated themselves and their organizations from their action. It was perhaps significant that in Scotland, where the Chartist movement was controlled by the moderates, there was a more solid record of trade union collaboration, from the great Glasgow meeting organized by the trades of the city in May 1838 to the demonstration in favour of O'Connor and Duncombe at Aberdeen in 1843, when a procession was held by the 'incorporated trades' headed by 'the United Bakers in full regalia, and dressed in suits of rich pink muslin, and wearing splendid turbans'.

Methodism, particularly Primitive Methodism and the New Connection, was another movement which assisted the rapid spread of Chartism. Besides the well known Methodist firebrand J. R. Stephens, a number of other Chartist leaders were Methodists or had been reared in Methodist homes. The politico-religious sermons of Thomas Cooper, journalist and Sunday School teacher, were a feature of Chartist meetings in Leicestershire, John Skeffington, a prominent Chartist at Loughborough, was a Primitive Methodist itinerant preacher. Another was Joseph Capper, an old Mow Cop convert of 1807, who stood trial for sedition and rioting in Staffordshire in 1842 and received two years imprisonment. A fourth was George Russell of Warwick, Chartist, hymn-writer and temperance-advocate. Chartist organization in the Midlands, Lancashire, Yorkshire, the northeast and the West Country, was a conscious imitation of the old Methodist techniques of classes, leaders and camp meetings. There were even singing processions with Chartist hymns, the words often a direct adaptation from the Methodist hymnbook and sung to familiar chapel tunes. Chartist meetings were held in Methodist chapels and Chartist crowds were addressed by innumerable 'Reverend Mr's' even if their clerical title could not always bear close examination. For many Methodists, both laymen and preachers, Chartism was a practical expression of Christian teaching. Such phrases as 'Jesus Christ was the first Chartist' and the well known line of hymn, 'The Charter springs from Zion's hill', illustrate the extent to which popular Christianity and political reform were interwoven. It was true that in the movement as a whole there was also an anti-clerical, anti-establishment current; and some of the Chartist intellectuals were Owenite socialists and agnostics. But Christian Chartism was a more genuine vernacular expression for the rank and file of the movement than the secular ideals which after 1848 developed into the international socialism of Harney and Ernest Jones. Together with 'Temperance Chartism' and 'Educational Chartism' it was part of the idealistic fervour for self-help and self-improvement which gave Chartism much of its dignity and moral strength.

Between 1838 and 1842 Chartism attracted a number of leaders of varying and sometimes discordant outlook, many of whom had encountered frustration or failure in other forms of public activity. The sober printer Hetherington had made his reputation in the long battle for the unstamped press. The idealist, persevering Lovett was the leading organizer of the LWMA. Vincent, with his oratory and good looks a natural demagogue, was another though more youthful product of the LWMA. The Reverend J. R. Stephens, as notorious as O'Connor for his violent, crowd-stirring oratory, had been expelled from the Wesleyan Connexion in 1834 because of his attacks on the established church. Bronterre O'Brien, known to the movement as 'the schoolmaster', though he would have preferred to be regarded as the English Robespierre, was a graduate of Dublin University and sometime law student of Gray's Inn who after 1830 had been drawn into radical journalism. The would-be Marat of the English Revolution was George Julian Harney who exercised his restless, bitter talents indiscriminately in journalism, platform speaking and organization. He was a London orphan from a poor home, for a time shopboy to Hetherington, who had been imprisoned three times before he was twenty for his activities in the illicit, unstamped press movement. Frost, a kind of Cobbettite Welshman, had a stormy and embittered career in local politics behind him when he joined the Chartists. Feargus O'Connor, Irish politician and barrister, elected MP for Co. Cork in 1832 and 1835 but later unseated for lack of property qualifications, found in Chartism the opportunity which eluded him in parliamentary politics where he was overshadowed by his party leader, Daniel O'Connell.

The combination of genuine idealists, ambitious intellectuals and rootless demagogues in a familiar phenomenon in any large popular movement. But the scattered, regional nature of Chartism made the organization seem at times little more than a confederacy of districts under their local chieftains: Lovett among the respectable London artisans, Harney with the impoverished domestic workers of Spitalfields, Thomas Cooper in the old Luddite counties of Leicestershire and Nottinghamshire, Vincent with his enthusiastic female audiences at Bath, the sober and respectable tea-merchant James Moir at Glasgow. The only Chartist who secured real dominance as a national figure was Feargus O'Connor. He achieved this largely by violent strength of personality and use of unscrupulous methods. The same combination of qualities won for his newspaper the *Northern Star* a position of undisputed primacy among the Chartist periodicals. Physically and mentally he resembled his former leader Daniel O'Connell which explains the intense dislike between the two men and O'Connell's gradual alienation from a movement which he had at first supported. O'Neill Daunt's description of O'Connor could equally well apply to the other great Irish agitator: 'a bold face, a burly figure and a reckless, daredevil air of defiance ... [with] an insatiable passion for notoriety'. Nor was O'Connor without the legal caution and basic prudence which made O'Connell so difficult an opponent to pin down.

There is a certain irony in the fact that an industrial proletarian movement found its only acknowledged national leader in a member of the gentry class who claimed descent from the kings of Connaught and whose only original contribution to Chartism was his plan to settle workers on the land in a series of Irish-type peasant communities. But he had all the demagogic attributes: an imposing appearance, a clarion voice that reminded people of Henry Hunt, an Irishman's ready tongue, and a facility for suiting himself to the mood of his audience. In the heady atmosphere of the northern camp-meetings, with the darkness and hum of voices, the thousands of pale upturned faces, the lurid glare of torches, the occasional crack of a pistol, the dimly illumined banners with their deathshead devices, the roars of approval, the ripple of laughter at some jest, he found his reward and satisfaction. The tempestuous rhetoric he poured out on such occasions was probably not taken seriously by either orator or audience. On O'Connor's part, if he was not merely surrendering to the atmosphere of the meeting, it was calculated bluff designed to intimidate the authorities. To his passionate, unlettered hearers, accustomed to the perfervid contemporary language of both platform and pulpit, the violence of his oratory came as an assurance of his sympathy and understanding, rather than as a direct incitement to forcible action. In this lay O'Connor's greatest strength and his greatest contribution to the movement.

Nevertheless, Chartism remained a heterogeneous affair. Though it drew some support from factory operatives, its more natural breeding-ground was among the overcrowded, underpaid workers concentrated in districts using the older, simpler manufacturing techniques, like the hosiers of Leicester and Nottingham, the woollen weavers of Wiltshire and Somerset, the silk weavers of Bethnal Green and Spitalfields, or in small single-industry towns such as Paisley and Stockport that could be brought to a standstill by a slump in one particular branch of manufacture. Large towns like London,

Manchester, Birmingham and Leeds were less affected, partly because their more mixed society shielded them against total economic disaster, partly because they possessed a strong tradition of middle-class radicalism. A distinction must be drawn, moreover, between support for the Charter and participation in the more aggressive tactics of the Chartists. The analysis of the signatures on the Chartist petition of 1842 showed London at the top of the list with 200,000 followed by Manchester with 99,000, Newcastle with 92,000 and Glasgow district with 78,000. The nearest to these were Bradford district (45,000), Birmingham (43,000) and Leeds (41,000). But readiness to sign was not necessarily an indication of readiness to become involved. Such a socially respectable town as Brighton produced over 12,000 signatures, Worcester 10,000 and even more surprisingly Cheltenham nearly 11,000.

In Wales, where religious nonconformity was joined to agrarian discontent, Chartism in the early stages was as much rural as industrial. It was a couple of years before the coal and iron districts of Monmouth and Glamorgan, with their bad social conditions and influx of rootless immigrants, joined the movement. The manufacturing area round Glasgow, on the other hand, was from the start a centre of Chartist activity. The Birmingham Political Union and London WMA launched the national reform campaign with a mass meeting at Glasgow in May 1838 and this was followed by intensive propaganda among the working population of the central industrial belt. Chartism in Dundee, for example, began with the visit later the same month of a Birmingham delegation consisting of Messrs Collins, Muntz and Douglas.

Much of this early Scottish prominence in the movement was ascribable to the excitement in local trade union circles created by the recent trial of the Glasgow cotton spinners. The cotton spinners' union there had long possessed a sinister reputation for its brutal treatment of 'nobs', the name for workmen who refused to contribute to the support or to obey the orders of the union. Several had been murdered in the 1820s and during a strike in 1837 another 'nob' had been shot in the streets. The trial of five union officials on a number of charges, including murder and arson, in January 1838 was followed with intense interest in both kingdoms. J. R. Stephens and Feargus O'Connor both came up to Scotland, the one to denounce the manufacturers and the other the judges. The unions campaigned vigorously on the prisoners' behalf and petitions were sent to parliament from innumerable manufacturing centres. After a protracted trial the jury by a majority found the defendants guilty on the minor charges only and they were sentenced to seven years transportation. Cockburn, who had no doubt about the murder

charge, thought that the case had been mishandled by the crown
and that some of the jurymen as well as witnesses had been intimidated. The evidence threw a lurid light on the terrorist methods
employed by the union but direct evidence for the serious
charges was difficult to obtain and the sentences were out of proportion to the offences on which the men were technically found
guilty.

Despite this sinister start the Chartist movement in Scotland was
conspicuous for its moderate tone, its general preference for 'moral
force', and the emergence of a form of popular 'Christian Chartism'
that disturbed both the established and secessionist Presbyterian
churches. After the early impetus of the movement had carried it
to Edinburgh, Dundee, Paisley and Aberdeen, the organization fell
back into the hands of the central committee for Scotland set up
in August 1839 which was dominated by the Glasgow men. Their
main object was to keep the movement away from the English
extremists and more in touch with middle-class radicals south of the
border like Hume, Roebuck and Sturge. But lacking an outstanding
leader, circumscribed by lack of money, and weakened by the efforts
of O'Connor to draw over to himself the loyalty of the Glasgow
spinners, the movement declined rapidly after 1842. Its active
members turned instead to more congenial outlets such as cooperative societies, trade unions, temperance advocacy or suffrage
reform.

Regionalism, discordant personalities, local and class rivalries were
obvious weaknesses of Chartism. Clashes of policy derived more from
these features than from any considered principles of strategy.
Though there was talk of 'moral force' and 'physical force' Chartism,
there was rarely any clear-cut divisions among the leaders on that
issue. To a large extent, indeed, the issue was unreal. Moral-force
advocates were usually aware of the value, even the necessity, of
threatening speeches and demonstrations to persuade the governing
classes to accede to their demands. The physical-force party proclaimed the justice of violence but almost always stopped short of
practising it. All Chartist leaders sooner or later were brought up
against the question of 'ulterior measures': in other words, what
was to be done if agitation, demonstrations, and petitioning did not
succeed? But the dilemma was never solved. Most of them were
equivocal or inconsistent on this vital matter, allowing time and circumstance to colour their actions and words. The most 'physical
force' Chartist of all, judged by his deeds, was John Frost who led
the march on Newport in November 1839 which resulted in the death
of some two dozen Chartists at the hands of a company of the 45th
Foot. But the evidence in this confused affair suggests that Frost was

more a pathetic victim of his own past, borne along on a current he was too weak or too vain to resist.

Certainly there was much talk of fighting—too much to offer the likelihood of much action. Speakers, newspapers and handbills called on the people to procure arms and be ready to march when the signal was given. There was evidence of weapons like pikes being manufactured and the accumulation of small stores of arms. Most of these were probably pikes and knives, though some Chartists were able to purchase muskets and many seem to have possessed pistols. At Manchester the Chartists were even said to be in possession of five brass cannon. Gunpowder enjoyed a brisk sale in some parts. At Nottingham homemade fireballs, more frightening than lethal, were actually seen by General Napier. In Yorkshire a treatise on street-fighting by an Italian revolutionary named Macerone was reported to be in circulation and a Polish major contributed an article on military science to the *London Democrat*. In most of the larger manufacturing districts there were reports, duly conveyed to the Home Office, of men being drilled secretly at night.

Of actual planning for an armed rising, however, there is little hard evidence. The Whitsunday week of 1839 was widely expected to produce a general uprising; but though there were many Chartist demonstrations, all passed off in relative calm. The only circumstantial, though secondhand and retrospective accounts of a deliberate attempt to organize a simultaneous rebellion in several parts of the country came in connection with the Newport rising. Even these are open to criticism on many details. At most it can be accepted that the angry determination of the south Wales Chartists to attempt a forcible release of Vincent from Monmouth gaol in the autumn of 1839 was known to Chartists in Yorkshire and Lancashire, and that there was talk of staging simultaneous demonstrations in the north and Midlands. If there was a more serious and extensive plot, it can only be assumed that those involved lacked the nerve to put it into execution when it came to the crucial point. In the event Frost's ill-fated attack on Newport on the eve of Guy Fawkes Day 1839 was the signal for nothing except a determined effort on the part of respectable people in south Wales, including the anglican and most dissenting churches, to get rid of Chartism for ever. Reports continued to come to the government of a plan for a general rising in December but other than an armed attack on the town hall at Sheffield in January and a simultaneous demonstration at Dewsbury, the winter of 1839–40 was marked by the activity of the authorities rather than by insurrectionary movements among Chartists.

Once the initiative had passed from London to the provinces, however, the growing violence in language, outlook and action of the Chartist leaders alienated middle-class radicals and probably many of the moderate-minded artisans. The withdrawal of the Birmingham Political Union men from the first Chartist convention in the spring of 1839 was a significant event but there had been signs of disagreement long before. When Chartist crowds sang

> By pike and sword your freedom strive to gain,
> Or make one bloody Moscow of old England's plain,

middle-aged householders and family men could hardly be expected to sympathize. The *Northern Star*, with its aggressive proletarian language, fostered the growing class division. Cooper at Leicester in 1841 was struck by the 'fierce and open opposition' of the working men to their employers compared with the warmer social relations of his early life in Lincolnshire. In Scotland the usually moderate *Chartist Circular* began a leader in January 1841 with the words 'the middle classes are the real tyrants of society' and argued that the aristocracy could only impose repressive legislation such as the new poor law because of the support of the £10 householders. It was this class antagonism which conditioned the attitude of many Chartists to the Anti-Corn Law League. They approved the end but not the means. The employers, they thought, were pursuing a single and selfish class objective, whereas once the Charter was obtained, corn laws and all other 'exclusive legislation' would disappear automatically. On the other hand, some working-class men who had imbibed a smattering of economic theory thought also that low food prices would only mean low wages; for handloom workers this had often seemed to be the case. In the early years Chartism was far from being a free-trade movement. Especially in the north there was a strong protectionist strain in the membership which was reflected in the views of some of their leaders, notably O'Connor with his rural background, his land scheme and his partiality for agricultural tariff support.

Nevertheless, it was equally true that not all working men were Chartists and 'repeal of the Corn Laws' was an old radical cry. In the early stages of the movement Chartist and League lecturers were trying to recruit support from much the same class of people, and using much the same violent, popular language. The deliberate invasion and wrecking of League meetings by Chartists in some areas was a recognition of a dangerous rival. Though some of the operative Anti-Corn Law Associations were obviously subsidized by rich manufacturers of the main Manchester League, there was probably from the start a genuine element of working-class support for the repeal of the corn laws. Simultaneously, as in the 'Leeds new move' of 1840, there was a feeling among some of the traditional middle-class radicals that a joint campaign for electoral reform might draw the violence from the Chartist movement. Theoretically there existed an alternative strategy of uniting middle- and working-class agitation in a common cause against the aristocracy. Miall's new periodical the *Nonconformist* published a series of articles on this theme in the autumn of 1841, though moved probably more by fears of revived anglicanism than by purely political ambitions. It was certainly true that all four elements in this possible confederacy—Chartism, the League, dissent and middle-class radicalism—were in need of allies. When Sturge started his complete suffrage movement in 1841 even Cobden thought that it would be 'something in our *rear* to frighten the Aristocracy—and it will take the masses out of the hands of their present rascally leaders'.

But Miall's ambitious attempt to mount a simultaneous campaign for parliamentary reform, disestablishment and repeal of the corn laws never got beyond the Birmingham meeting of April 1842 when Sturge, Miall, Bright and various Chartist leaders like Lovett and O'Brien sat together on the same platform. The disturbances of the following summer put an abrupt end to this utopian, grand-national-consolidated partnership of anti-aristocratic forces. The more the Chartists exhibited the aggressive proletarian nature of their movement, the more the middle classes doubted their fitness to exercise the parliamentary franchise. Even the well-meaning Leeds Parliamentary Reform Association went no further than a household franchise; and the Chartists would accept nothing less than manhood suffrage. For a growing number of the liberal middle classes even the milder proposal was too much. The unhappy Leeds association found itself attacked by O'Connor's *Northern Star* on the one hand and by Baines's influential *Leeds Mercury* on the other. It is the common lot of peace-makers to please neither side. But clearly one of the effects of Chartism was to dampen liberal enthusiasm for a further instalment of parliamentary reform. It was not for nothing that the whigs had passed their reform act in 1832.

IV

Though Chartism in one sense was only a continuation under another name of the old radical reform movement and was to last in some shape or other into the 1850s, what gave it contemporary importance was the great industrial depression from 1837 to 1843.

The force and intensity of Chartism at its peak came from men who knew that they were painfully worse off than other classes in society and were not prepared to reconcile themselves to that condition. Hungry bellies filled the ranks of the Chartists; the return of economic prosperity after 1843 thinned them. The chronology of effective Chartism is also that of the worst industrial depression which the country endured during the nineteenth century.

The railway and shipbuilding boom that helped to bring prosperity to the mid-1830s broke in 1836. The coalmining, cotton and woollen industries, having expanded rapidly in the early years of the decade, found the home market now unable to absorb their products. By the following spring distress was beginning to be felt in all the main areas where Chartism was later to flourish—south Lancashire, the West Riding, the Midlands and western Scotland. The publication of the Charter in May 1838 was followed by a series of mass meetings in Scotland and England, and the election of delegates to a national convention. To unemployment and reduced wages there had by then been added another hardship. This was the year of the worst harvest since 1816; and that of the following year was hardly better. The price of wheat reached 77s. a quarter in August 1838, a level above that at which the 1828 act allowed foreign bonded grain to come on the market at a nominal duty. But though prices fell temporarily, they rose again until they reached 78s. in December and remained near or over 70s. for most of the following year. Early in February 1839 the first Chartist Convention met in London, moving to Birmingham in May. In July the House of Commons rejected the first Chartist petition; the plan of a general strike— the 'Sacred Month'—broke down; and in September the Convention disbanded.

At the start of 1840 Chartism, after Frost's failure in south Wales and the arrest of many of its leaders, seemed to be losing ground. But the industrial depression was deepening all the time. The severe financial crisis of 1839 was followed by some of the worst years ever experienced in living memory. In April 1839 Napier found that the best handloom weavers at Nottingham could only earn 5s. a week, insufficient even to find a man in food, let alone clothes, fuel and lodging. At Leicester a year later Cooper was startled to find that the average earnings of a stocking weaver when fully employed were 4s. 6d. a week. Factory workers in the Lancashire and Cheshire cotton industry, on short time, lowered wages, or totally unemployed, were scarcely better off. Though they earned good money when in full employment, few of them made any provision for hard times. At Stockport, where by July many of the town's 8,000 unemployed had left to search for work elsewhere, seventeen mills were closed and others working half-time. More than half the master manufacturers were said to have failed since the start of the slump.

By 1842 the sheer weight of prolonged unemployment, particularly in the textile areas, was beginning to break down the resources of both poor law and private charity. At Leeds the number of families relieved by the workhouse board had risen from over 2,000 at the end of 1838 to over 4,000 at the start of 1842. The local authorities calculated that about 20 per cent of the population were on poor relief. 'Four years of unrelieved depression have brought this Borough into a state more lamentable than the oldest Inhabitant can remember.' From Paisley in Scotland a memorial to the government stated in February 1842 that 17,000 persons were 'enduring a gradual starvation with exhausted resources, and manifestly impaired health and strength on the part of the people, and with failing funds on the side of the Relief Committee'.[3] Meanwhile the run of bad harvests continued. The price of wheat was over 72s. all through August 1840 and after the usual fall in winter and spring, when the new harvest grain came on the market, again rose to touch 76s. in August 1841.

It would have been remarkable in these circumstances if the Chartist protest had not continued. 'Chartism,' Carlyle had written a couple of years earlier, 'means the bitter discontent grown fierce and mad, the wrong condition therefore or the wrong disposition, of the Working Classes of England.' As long as bad conditions existed, discontent would persist. In 1840 there were signs of renewed activity in the various Chartist areas of England, following the example of the Universal Suffrage Central Committee in Scotland founded the previous autumn. The general object was to establish the movement on a sounder organizational basis. The national conference at Manchester in July and the creation of the National Charter Association were among the fruits of this revival. After the failure to impose their will on the legislature in 1839, the strategy now was one of peaceful persuasion. For that purpose the emphasis was on lectures, pamphlets, the coordination of the many local Chartist bodies, and the gathering of funds. The second Chartist petition, presented to the Commons in May 1842, was the culmination of this second phase. Its vast tail of signatures, said to be over three million, was a reflection of the organizational effort put into it. For this O'Connor, released from gaol in the summer of 1841, could fairly take much credit. There was, however, a price to pay for his energetic, vain and intolerant leadership. It brought a breach both with Lovett's National Association for the Improvement of

---

[3] Brit. Mus. Add. MSS. 40612 fos. 105, 114.

the People and with the moderate Chartist movement in Scotland;
and it gave an aggressive and insulting tone to the second Chartist
petition. At a time when Sturge's suffrage campaign and the Anti-
Corn Law League were offering rival outlets for working-class
discontent, the Chartist movement was becoming little more than
a narrow O'Connorite organization.

The inevitable rejection of the Chartist petition in the spring of
1842 marked the end of Chartism as a movement of any real
importance. The interest of its remaining dozen years of life is largely
in its internal history, including O'Connor's utopian land settlement
scheme. The sudden reappearance on the national stage in 1848
only served to demonstrate its fundamental ineffectiveness. The
significance of the failure of the second petition in 1842 has, however,
been obscured by the widespread industrial disorders later the same
year in which many Chartist leaders were implicated but for which
they were not responsible. By the early summer of 1842 distress, low
wages and unemployment had brought the central industrial districts
of England to a state of desperation. In Lancashire and Yorkshire
gangs of workless men went round, often armed with sticks and
iron bars, demanding relief and overawing people by their numbers
and appearance. Incidents began to be reported of attacks on provision shops and clashes with police and yeomanry. Further south
attempted reductions of wages by colliery-owners in Staffordshire
led to strikes and lockouts. By the end of June the lockout was
general and crowds of bludgeon-carrying miners, several thousand
strong, began to appear in the neighbouring counties of Cheshire
and Lancashire, demanding food and money, attacking town
constables, and forcibly stopping any small pits they came across.
Early in July wage reductions by a number of manufacturers led
to a great turnout of cotton weavers at Stalybridge and Ashton near
Manchester.

By August the current of industrial unrest was mounting in
volume and violence. Crowds went round stopping mills, drawing
plugs from the steamengine boilers, and preventing any men from
working. Manchester itself was invaded by large mobs from the
surrounding mill towns, and factories were attacked. The news of
the rioting in Lancashire and Cheshire provoked disturbances further
afield. In the third week of August there was a turnout of some 6,000
operatives in Leeds. In Leicestershire, beginning with the colliers
in the western districts of the county, the strikes spread to the
stockingers of Loughborough and finally to the glove-makers of
Leicester. By this time the whole central industrial area of England
within the quadrilateral bounded by Leeds and Preston to the north,
Leicester and Birmingham to the south, was in a state of upheaval.

The main purpose of the strikers was to enforce a rise in wages by stopping all machinery and turning out all the operatives. But forcible action on this extensive scale inevitably overflowed at times into more violent actions and attracted a fringe of more irresponsible and rascally participants. Prisons, town halls, police stations, law courts, railway stations, workhouses, private dwellings of magistrates and clergy, shops and bakeries were attacked and ransacked as well as mills and collieries. More distant still, and on a smaller scale, there were strikes and disorders on Tyneside and in south Wales. In Scotland wage reductions, actual or threatened, had led to similar disturbances earlier the same month. There were strikes in Glasgow and more violent outbreaks among the colliers of Airdrie and the weavers of Dunfermline which necessitated the intervention of the military before order was restored. But Chartist influence was negligible. The legendary 'March to Forfar' of the Dundee Chartists which took place belatedly on 23 August proved a complete fiasco, some 300 tired, hungry, turnip-stealing Chartists being charitably fed by the local inhabitants before they were returned home.

Before the disturbances in England Chartist and League lectures had been busy in the main Midland area, using inflammatory language and placards to stir up the workers. But in no case do the Chartists seem to have instigated the strikes or rioting. It was a purely economic movement of protest, though local Chartists often tried to exploit the situation in their own neighbourhoods once it developed. In many places meetings of operatives passed resolutions not to return to work until the Charter was the law of the land. A Chartist conference had been arranged in Manchester on 16 August though it did not fully assemble until the following day. By that time the violence had reached its peak and was about to subside. Carried away by the scenes most of them had witnessed, the Chartist delegates resolved to support the industrial movement as a means of securing the Charter. There was wild talk of fighting and the fiery young Scots-born Lancashire delegate McDouall secured the issue of a proclamation calling for a general strike and placing the decision with 'the God of justice and of battle'.

But the committee had been divided and uneasy. O'Connor had obvious misgivings though he characteristically sided with the majority. Within a few days he equally characteristically attacked McDouall in the *Northern Star* for dangerous recklessness and urged a return to peaceable methods. Chartist mythology, so far from claiming credit for the 1842 disturbances, subsequently attributed them to a sinister conspiracy of League millowners (the 'Plug Plot') to bring about a general stoppage of work in order to coerce the government into repealing the corn laws. In the arrests which

followed the rioting a number of Chartists were included, among
them O'Connor, Cooper and Hill (the editor of the *Northern Star*),
while McDouall only avoided capture by taking refuge in France
for a couple of years. For a time the crown lawyers pondered the
feasibility of a general indictment against the Chartist prisoners for
conspiracy and a special trial at bar before the Queen's Bench. In
the end the difficulties and dangers of this course produced more
prudent second thoughts. The Chartists were not singled out for
political martyrdom but left to stand trial with the hundreds of
ordinary rioters. Most of them received comparatively light
sentences and O'Connor on a technicality escaped entirely. In Scotland five leaders of the Dundee Chartists arrested after the Forfar
march were sentenced at the High Court of Justiciary to four months'
imprisonment in January 1843 and a sixth was released. So far from
being authors, beneficiaries, or even victims of the 1842 riots, the
Chartists were little more than incidental casualties.

V

For the authorities, concerned with the primary task of preserving
order, discrimination between industrial discontent and political
agitation called for tact and judgement. At the start of the Chartist
campaign in 1838 the whig ministers, conscious of their historic
tradition of civil liberty, were anxious not to appear repressive. The
private view of the Home Office was that much of the trouble was
due to the refusal of the employers to pay adequate wages. Napier,
briefed in London in March 1839 before taking up command of the
Northern District, found among the Whitehall officials a considerable
degree of ignorance about what exactly was going on in the disturbed
districts and a certain distrust of the efficiency of the local magistrates.
What government and senior army officers, as in the pre-1830
years, were particularly concerned to avoid was any armed confrontation which might lead to large civilian casualties. Peterloo was
not easily forgotten on either side. Napier and his successors, Warre
and Arbuthnot, followed a general policy of making a deterrent show
of force at the various danger-points, avoiding as far as possible the
employment of small detachments in vulnerable situations, and
drawing up careful plans for emergencies. The relatively peaceful
state of Ireland allowed reinforcements to be brought in from the
other island when necessary and the new London to Birmingham
railway, followed by the opening of the Grand Junction line linking

it with Manchester in 1837, facilitated rapid troop movements. Between 1839 and 1842 some 10,000 regular troops could usually be concentrated when required in the Northern District.

The more threatening appearance of Chartist meetings in the winter of 1838–9 led the whigs, after their initial hesitation and real or assumed nonchalance, to reinforce the Northern District and to encourage magistrates to take a stiffer line with Chartist meetings. Many delegates to the first Chartist convention, the heads of the Political Unions at Manchester and Newcastle, and a large number of the rank and file were brought to trial. Of the more prominent men O'Connor, Stephens (though he denied being a Chartist), Lovett, Vincent, McDouall all received terms of imprisonment ranging from twelve to eighteen months. Their more unfortunate followers, often convicted on charges of drilling or possession of unlawful arms, did not escape so lightly: a number were transported. Police bills were introduced for the creation of local forces at Birmingham, Bolton and Manchester under commissioners of police directly responsible to the Home Office. But ministers were unwilling to ask for any extraordinary repressive powers. Not long before the Newport rising in November Campbell, the whig attorney-general, claimed that the government had been successful in putting down Chartism without bloodshed by legal and constitutional means. This premature boast subsequently brought him some ridicule but at the time he was only reflecting the general feeling of optimism among the ministers.

The criticism of the whigs is that perhaps they underestimated the danger and assumed too lightly that Chartism was simply the product of political agitation. The replacement of Russell at the Home Office in August 1839 by the indolent, inefficient Normanby was further evidence of their unwillingness or inability to grapple with the realities of the situation. Peel made no such error when he appointed Sir James Graham to the home department in 1841. Graham, who had made his mark as a reforming head of the Admiralty under Grey in 1830–34, was probably the firmest, most conscientious administrator of all his colleagues. Anticipating a winter of distress and riot he set to work at once to infuse energy and purpose into the whole unwieldy chain of command at his disposal, from army commanders and lords lieutenant down to the local magistrates and constables. Between February and August 1842 he never absented himself one day from his office. When the trouble started in the summer he immediately reinforced the troops in the disturbed areas and urged the magistrates to mobilize their local resources, maintain a good intelligence system, suppress large meetings of any character, and prevent isolated bands of rioters from

entering the big towns. General Warre, the commander of the
Northern District, who was felt to be insufficiently energetic, was
virtually superseded by Lieutenant-General Arbuthnot who was
given command of all the affected areas, Midlands as well as north.

At some points the military found it necessary to open fire and
at Burslem, Blackburn, Preston, Salford and Halifax a number of
rioters were killed or wounded. Two policemen died at Manchester
and many others, together with soldiers and individual magistrates,
were wounded, mainly by stones. What was remarkable, however,
was the small number of casualties. For this there was a variety of
reasons. Mindful perhaps of Peterloo or guided by common prudence,
magistrates with only a handful of men at their disposal in the early
stages made little attempt to stop the violence. Only when reinforced
by large numbers of special constables, army pensioners, yeomanry,
and above all regular troops, did they take vigorous action to prevent
disorder and disperse the mobs. Even then the military seem to have
been careful not to use their weapons except when actually attacked.
For their part the rioters, when faced by a determined show of
strength, often broke up and fled without even token resistance.
Napier in 1839 had remarked on the cowardice of the crowds of
demonstrators; there were similar instances in 1842. Many of the
rioters, and often those foremost in actual looting and destruction,
were young men between sixteen and twenty-five, some hardly more
than boys, often accompanied by girls who cheered them on and
carried stones in their aprons to supply them with ammunition.
This was hardly the stuff of revolution. On the other hand there
were instances when older workmen enrolled as special constables
or helped to defend their employers' mills against attack.

The judicial consequences of the riots were relatively restrained.
Many rioters were arrested on the spot and others, including a
number of Chartists, rounded up afterwards. The most fortunate
were those who came up for trial in the ordinary way at the York
assizes or the Salford sessions court in September. Light sentences
of two to six weeks for the most part were meted out at the first,
from a few weeks to two years at the second. The bulk of the
prisoners, however, amounting to several hundreds, were tried by
special commissions sitting at Stafford, Chester and Lancaster. At
Stafford, where the largest number stood trial, fifty-four were
sentenced to transportation, 146 to varying terms of imprisonment, eight discharged and fifty-five acquitted.[4] In all about 700
rioters were brought before the courts in Cheshire, Lancashire,
Yorkshire and Staffordshire and a total of eighty transported.

[4] *Annual Register 1842*, p. 163. Other accounts give slightly varying figures.

Though the number convicted was comparable to that of the rural rioters a dozen years earlier, on this occasion there were no executions and those transported were less than a fifth of the total of agricultural rioters sent overseas after 1830.

The conservative government had shown more energy and strictness in repressing the disorders than their whig predecessors. On the other hand they were more sensitive to the social problems that lay behind the rioting. Their concern for law and order was accompanied by an equally strong concern to remove the causes of the disorder. At the start of the disturbances Graham had told Peel that the masters were more to blame than the men. General Arbuthnot was instructed not only to avoid any appearance of intervention to make the men return to work but to urge employers to meet the legitimate complaints of their work-people. The distinction between civil disorder and what Peel called 'just and peaceable demands for a rise of wages' was central to the thinking of the ministers in 1842. Nor did their concern disappear when the danger subsided. When drawing up plans after the riots for the future employment of army pensioners as auxiliary police, the home secretary emphasized the need for a wider policy of improving the condition and temper of the working classes. 'We must augment the means of education,' he wrote to Peel on 8 September 1842, 'we must keep down the price of articles of first necessity; we must endeavour to redress the wrongs of the labourer; we must mark an honest sympathy with his wants; and while we uphold the authority of the law with firmness, we must temper it with mercy.' Meanwhile a letter had come from the prime minister asking Graham to enquire into the grievances of the coalminers in the disturbed areas. 'I strongly suspect the profits in many of these collieries,' wrote Peel, 'would enable the receivers of them to deal with much more liberality towards their workmen than they do at present.'[5]

The real culprits, in the eyes of the government, were the radical urban magistrates, many of them members of the Anti-Corn Law League, who had threatened before the riots to remain inactive until the corn laws were repealed; the incendiary orators of both Chartist and League organizations; and behind them all, the ringleaders of the League itself. To discipline individual JPs or even to stiffen them with professional stipendiary magistrates, was not however an easy matter, particularly for a conservative government dependent on the goodwill of the country gentry who furnished the bulk of the magistracy. In the end Graham had reluctantly to abandon both possibilities. The League was a different matter. As with the Chartists,

[5] Graham Papers (2 September 1842) slightly paraphrased in C. S. Parker, *Sir Robert Peel from his Private Papers* II, p. 543. Peel was in Scotland with the Queen at the time.

there was a widespread belief among conservatives in the country
that the riots had been deliberately instigated by the League millowners to bring pressure to bear on the ministers. An exact apportion-
ment of blame, however, was not easy. The first trouble among the
colliers at Longton in June started at a tory-owned mine; and the
wage reductions at Stalybridge which began the cotton workers'
turnout in July were made by the great tory manufacturers Messrs
Lees. Yet the League leaders had advocated in public and discussed
seriously in private just such a policy; and the action of some of
them during the actual disturbances had been at least equivocal.

Though the Home Office diligently collected information,
however, it was soon realized that there was no evidence that in a
court of law would convict the League, any more than the Chartist
Convention, of actually causing the outbreak of violence. But there
was some justification for thinking that the League organization with
its journalists and itinerant orators had a large share of moral
responsibility for stirring up the masses in the industrial districts
during the preceding weeks. It was this which formed the argument
of the famous article on 'Anti-Corn Law Agitation' concocted by
Graham and Croker, with a final revision by Peel, which appeared
in the *Quarterly Review* in December 1842. In denouncing the League
as a subversive, immoral and unconstitutional body the ministers
went as far as they could. Their object, however, was not merely
to strike back at a dangerous opponent but to weaken the influence
of the League on the working classes—a point which Peel emphasized
more than once. It should be brought home to the operatives, he
wrote, how the League had first encouraged them to use physical
force and then, when the riots started, abandoned them to the
penalties of the law. Like Liverpool in 1817 and 1819 Peel was
concerned to separate political agitation from economic discontent.
Of the two great movements with which he had to deal the League,
by reason of its intelligence, wealth and respectability, seemed more
culpable than Chartism—and to the government a greater political
threat.

Chartism, on the other hand, as some Chartists themselves
admitted, was primarily a 'knife and fork question'. The six points
of the Charter offered no immediate cure for what was fundamentally
an economic grievance; nor could its sweeping doctrinaire programme be carried by any means that were political possibilities in
the years of the Chartist agitation. Secure in the support of the
respectable middle classes, parliament regarded unmoved a document which contrived simultaneously to be impracticable, irrelevant,
and insulting. Even if the Chartists represented, which was doubtful,
a majority of the working classes, mere numerical strength would

not have sufficed. As the veteran radical agitator Francis Place wrote in February 1842, 'the Chartists ... can never have the least chance of carrying the Charter, neither numbers nor anything which they can do, could in any conceivable case, carry the Charter.' All that the Chartist movement achieved in that direction was to postpone for a generation the likelihood of a second instalment of parliamentary reform. It was as a social protest, stirring both the fears and sympathies of the rest of the community, that Chartism was successful.

8 Peel's Decade

I

Peel became prime minister because he was leader of a party which had won a majority of some eighty seats in the House of Commons. Though he recognized his debt, he was not disposed to allow the party to dictate policy. Like most of his immediate predecessors in office—Pitt, Liverpool, Canning and Grey—he regarded himself as minister of the crown whose duty it was to govern the country according to his judgement of what was in the national interest. Prince Albert had already smoothed away the difficulties over court appointments that had caused the 1839 fiasco. In the next few months his influence and Peel's tactful handling reconciled Victoria more quickly than she would have admitted to her new prime minister.

The administration he formed was one of the strongest of the century. The duke was given office without portfolio, setting the Foreign Office free for Aberdeen. The two prized converts from the whigs, Stanley and Graham, were given the other secretaryships of state. Ripon and Haddington represented the old Canningite connection; Chandos (now duke of Buckingham) and Sir Edward Knatchbull were brought into the cabinet to please the agricultural interest. There were also a number of younger men who were to leave their mark on nineteenth-century administration: Gladstone at the Board of Trade, Lord Lincoln at Woods and Forests, Herbert at the Admiralty and Eliot in the Irish government. Before the ministry ended the first three were promoted to the cabinet and another able young man Edward Cardwell had been brought into the Treasury as financial secretary. Peel himself, at the age of fifty-three was at the height of his political and intellectual powers. His reputation had grown steadily since 1834; after 1841 he was to dominate politics, in or out of office, for the remainder of his life.

His first and most pressing problem was finance. There had been national deficits for three years running and the whigs had been forced to go to the country in 1841 because the House of Commons had expressed no confidence in their latest budgetary attempt to regain solvency. If Peel was to demonstrate his administrative superiority he had to do it in the field of finance; there was no other way. He had, almost certainly, made up his mind for some time that when he returned to power he would reintroduce the income tax. Equally characteristically he felt under no necessity to advertise this intention in advance. It was the one great unused financial weapon at his disposal, a weapon which the Wellington cabinet had come almost to the point of accepting in 1830 and which the whig cabinet had unanimously refused to consider when proposed by Althorp in 1831. Even in 1841 Stanley and Graham had enough whiggishness left to take fright when Peel suggested that it should be one of the first acts of the new government. There were enough survivors of the Liverpool era, however, to support the prime minister —Ripon, Goulburn (the chancellor of the exchequer), Herries (though out of office) and even the duke himself.

Once the decision was taken, other consequences followed. If the expensive machinery of the income tax was to be set up once more, it seemed pointless to brave the political unpopularity involved unless a substantial amount (Goulburn mentioned £5 millions) was raised which would not only absorb the whig deficit but yield a handsome disposable surplus. In turn a surplus, while justified by the temporary emergency nature of the tax, would for political and social reasons best be devoted to reducing taxation on consumer goods. This, as Goulburn wrote to Peel as early as July 1841, would win the approval of 'the working classes at least'. The decision to reimpose the income tax, therefore, led naturally to a review by Peel, Ripon and the Board of Trade of the tariff system, which had hardly been touched since the days of Wallace and Huskisson.

In turn any large recasting of the tariff system could hardly fail to bring up the question of the corn laws. The whigs, by proposing in 1841 to lower duties on sugar, timber and corn, had directed public attention to these three primary commodities. Over sugar there were technical difficulties connected with competition from slave-grown produce and the economic plight of the British West Indian colonies following the abolition of slavery. But no tariff reconstruction could easily avoid timber; and as for corn, Villiers's campaign in the 1830s, the new Manchester Anti-Corn Law League, and the 'cheap bread' cry at the general election of 1841, made it certain that the corn laws would be at the centre of any public debate on tariffs. Whatever was thought about the principle of protection for agriculture, experience had shown that the 1828 corn law was unable to maintain the steady price level that would satisfy both farmers and consumers. It was assumed by most intelligent observers that

Peel would make some change in the system. For the prime minister there was the further consideration that together tariff reform and a reduction of corn duties, promising cheaper living and encouragement to trade, would help to make the income tax more acceptable.

After prolonged discussions during the autumn of 1841 a scale was drawn up which imposed a duty of 20*s.* on foreign wheat when the price of home wheat was 51*s.* a quarter, dropping to a nominal 1*s.* when the domestic price rose to 73*s.* Other modifications were introduced designed to diminish market fluctuations and prevent fraudulent manipulation of the market averages on which the sliding scale operated. Tariffs on other cereals were reduced proportionately. The degree of protection given was greater than the prime minister privately thought necessary to provide the farmer with adequate compensation for his rent, capital investment and local rate burdens. Even so, the new bill made drastic reductions in the duties imposed under the 1828 act. Between 59*s.* and 60*s.*, for example, the previous duty of 27*s.* 8*d.* was cut by more than half to 13*s.* Peel had to consider not only what was theoretically desirable but also what he could persuade first his cabinet and then his party followers to adopt. As it was, the duke of Buckingham, who preened himself on being 'the farmer's friend', eventually resigned, though assuring his leader that he would support the government on everything except corn—the one thing on which his vote was valuable. Conservative MPs in the lower house proved more amenable. The corn bill was the first major measure to be introduced in the new parliament in February 1842. It was a wise tactical decision. A party meeting on the opening day of the main debate showed that while they would have preferred a higher degree of protection, even the representatives of the agricultural counties were prepared to support the bill.

The initial excitement was out of doors. In the course of 1841 the Anti-Corn Law League had been strengthening its Manchester base and elaborating its tactics. The Chartist threat in its home town (and elsewhere) had been countered by organizing 'operative free-trade associations' and coming to an understanding with Daniel O'Connell and his Repealers. One product of this were the gangs of Irish who could beat the Chartist demonstrators at their own game and prevent the disruption of League meetings. The *Anti-Corn Law Circular* was given the more propagandist title of the *Anti-Bread Tax Circular.* Equally propagandist, a conference in Manchester during August 1841 of mainly dissenting ministers of religion, carefully stage-managed by the League, issued a strong condemnation on moral and humanitarian grounds of the system of agricultural protection which (it was alleged) restricted the nation's food supply in the

interests of the landed classes. Similar meetings were subsequently
held in other towns, including a very successful one at Edinburgh
in January 1842. Socially and politically it was not difficult to draw
the dissenters (though not Wesleyan Methodists) into the free-trade
movement. All their historical instincts placed them in opposition
to the anglican landed gentry. The Unitarian minister W. J. Fox,
for example, lecturing in his chapel on 'Aristocratical and Political
Morality', had as far back as 1835 described the corn laws as
existing for no other reason than that 'a privileged class is created
and vested with the powers of legislation'.[1]

Nevertheless, the unofficial alliance with dissent formed in 1841
not only powerfully reinforced the petitioning and electoral resources
of the free-trade movement but infused its propaganda with that
moral emotionalism in which the early Victorian public found a
peculiar satisfaction. At the general election the League, despite
some disappointments, was encouraged by the return to parliament
of a number of its candidates, including Cobden himself; and an
Anti-Corn Law Conference in London was arranged to coincide with
the opening of the parliamentary session in 1842. On the day when
Peel announced the ministerial plan a crowd of Leaguers, foiled in
their attempt to take possession of the lobby, stationed themselves
outside the House and greeted the entering members with shouts
of 'No Sliding-Scale' and 'Total Repeal'. Free-trade petitions, many
of them from well drilled dissenting congregations, poured into the
Commons. When the details of the new corn bill became known,
protest meetings were held up and down the country; in a number
of places in England, Wales and Scotland effigies of the prime
minister were publicly burnt.

Meanwhile the rest of the government's plans were unfolded.
In March came the announcement of the income tax. At 7*d.* in the
pound, and with more concessions to low incomes and farmers than
Pitt's wartime measure had allowed, its yield was estimated at only
£3·7 millions. The rest of the £4.3 millions needed was made up
by a variety of miscellaneous taxes. But the secret had been well
kept and the surprise was total. The whigs had thought that Peel
would never dare to reintroduce the tax in time of peace and their
confusion was obvious. Some at least of them were compelled into
an unwilling admiration at his political courage. In his speech the
prime minister made a direct plea to the wealthy classes to take on
their shoulders the task of rescuing the country from its financial
troubles rather than impose fresh burdens on 'the comforts of the
labouring classes of society'. Some landowners thought the tax would

[1] *Morality and Classes of Society* (1835), Lecture 2, p. 29.

ruin the landed interest. Cobden and Bright asserted that the manufacturing interest was being sacrificed for the sake of the aristocratic
oligarchy. But opinion in the country was more favourable, or at
least less hostile, than the cabinet had feared. Politicians, especially
the whigs, had assumed for so long that it would be impossible to
reinstate the tax that they had perhaps lost contact with changing
public opinion. The Chartists welcomed the income tax as a measure
of social justice; and the cynical Melbourne disconcerted his whig
colleagues by observing that any middle-class meeting to protest
against it would risk being swamped by a lower-class vote in its
favour.

Even among potential income tax payers dislike was tempered
with satisfaction at the new tariff proposals. Duties were reduced
on a wide range of imports (some 600 in all, including timber, a
primary material for house building) involving a loss to the revenue
of about £1·2 millions. The object, Peel emphasized to the Commons,
was to reduce the cost of living for every class in the community.
Whatever the argument might be over any particular reduction, the
general effect would be to 'make a considerable saving in the expenses
of every family in the kingdom'. After their own 1841 budget the
whigs were in no position to offer any general opposition. The
difficulties for the government came, not altogether unexpectedly,
from their own party. The farmers had not been happy over the
new corn bill and in some strongly protectionist counties like
Lincolnshire, Buckinghamshire and Essex, the local MPs had been
made to feel their constituents' displeasure. When the new tariff was
debated many of the agriculturalist members, whether anxious to
placate their electors or indisposed to make any further concessions
to the ministers, raised objections over farm produce. Since Peel
adamantly refused to make any modifications, W. Miles, member
for East Somerset, moved in May an amendment to the clause
admitting foreign meat and cattle (formerly prohibited) which would
have had the effect of raising the duty proposed. The amendment
was defeated by 380 votes to 113. But almost half the majority was
composed of opposition free traders and among the minority were
eighty-five of Peel's own party.

It was the first split in the conservative ranks—not serious perhaps
but certainly symptomatic. During the rest of the summer, while
unemployed colliers and cotton weavers rioted in the Midlands,
Leaguers and Complete Suffragists agitated, and thousands lived on
poor relief and charity in such towns as Greenock, Paisley, Leeds
and Stockport, the grumbling of the agriculturalists continued. They
distrusted the evident free-trade tendencies of the government and
accused Peel of truckling to agitation. To the complaints that filtered

through to him from the body of the party the prime minister returned sharp answers. For Peel both problem and solution seemed clear. Without an improvement in social conditions disorder would continue. For good or ill Britain was fast becoming an industrial, urbanized nation whose teeming millions depended on the wealth produced by trade and manufacture. No nostalgic regret for the passing of a deferential rural society could alter that inexorable development. Poor relief, private charity, emigration, were palliatives, but only palliatives. What was needed was the production of more wealth. Government could not increase wages; but by encouraging commerce and industry it could diminish unemployment, and by lowering the cost of living it could make wages go further. 'We must make this country a *cheap* country for living,' he wrote in August as the rioting in the country was moving to a climax. Under the impact of the distress and violence of 1842, the worst year of social disorder that century, the academic free-trade ideas he had imbibed as a young man were hardening into passionate conviction.

It took, however, more than riots in the manufacturing districts or government-inspired articles in the *Quarterly Review* to shake the protectionist convictions of the English farmers. As the price of wheat fell from over 65*s.* a quarter in July to 54*s.* in September and 46*s.* 10*d.* in December, their fears mounted. Stanley's Canada corn bill in the following session showed how sensitive they were. In 1842 the colonial secretary had virtually promised the Canadians free entry of their corn into Britain if they could provide safeguards against the illicit inclusion of American corn. This they had done and although the government was conscious of the uproar that would be caused, they honoured the pledge in 1843. As soon as they heard of the cabinet's intention the agriculturalists in several districts held county meetings to protest against this apparent move to weaken even the modified protection offered by the act of 1842. In some instances the county MPs involved even pledged themselves to oppose the bill. Stanley, however, was able to justify his bill by the principle of imperial preference which had a respectable lineage going back beyond Huskisson to the 1815 corn act. A meeting of government supporters on the morning of his introductory speech heard explanations from Peel and Stanley which seemed to satisfy them. Though various amendments were proposed, most of them came from the whig benches. This possibly helped to consolidate conservative support and the bill went through both Houses with a minimum of embarrassment to the government. Only about two dozen conservative MPs went so far as to vote against their leaders and probably some at least of these only did so to appease their rural constituents.

For the agricultural electorate, however, the Canada bill brought a further loss of confidence in the ministry. In the course of 1843 the Anti-Corn Law League, in the naïve belief that the tenant farmers were the economic victims of landlord oppression who were ripe for conversion to free-trade, extended its campaign to the rural areas. This attack from without, couched in the usual vituperative language of the League lecturers, stung the farmers into the organization of an 'Anti-League'. With waning faith in the ability or willingness of their parliamentary representatives to stand up for their interests, they embarked on a more explicit political movement than had been known among them since the days of Webb Hall. Initiated largely by Robert Baker, a tenant farmer in Essex, an Essex Agricultural Protection Society was founded in December 1843 with the object of uniting the farmers and freeholders in self-defence against the League and of securing greater publicity for the protectionist case. It was the signal for a wave of farmers' meetings in other counties and within a few months there were nearly a hundred similar societies in existence, mainly in southern and eastern England. Influenced by this strong manifestation of feeling and perhaps by a desire to retain aristocratic leadership, a number of peers and protectionist MPs, headed by the dukes of Richmond and Buckingham, formed a Central Agricultural Protection Society in February 1844 on which the farmers, who had been contemplating a central body of their own, were given representation. Though specifically renouncing political activities, and less vociferous than the provincial societies, the Central Society nevertheless set the seal of social approval on the farmers' Anti-League. Meanwhile, even among the politicians of the parliamentary party who held aloof from the movement, feeling was hardening against any more concessions to their leader's free-trade liberalism.

II

In 1843 there was little likelihood of any further action by the government to jangle the nerves of the agriculturalists. The success of the government's 1842 budget still hung in the balance. Various factors, among them the great manufacturing depression and unavoidable lateness in setting up the machinery for collecting the income tax, delayed financial recovery. In 1843 there was yet another deficit of £2 millions in place of the modest £½ million surplus that had been envisaged. Nevertheless, the cabinet was not unduly discouraged. It was now clear that in a full year the income tax was going to yield considerably more than had been estimated and already there were signs that the worst of the depression was over.

In the absence of any government initiative, there were plenty of other topics to engage public attention. Frightened by the events of the previous autumn and conscious how near they had come to actual illegality, the leaders of the Anti-Corn Law League had learnt their lesson. Though the fear of criminal prosecution did not disappear until 1843, it helped to settle the internal disputes over tactics and strategy. From the end of 1842 the League leaders concentrated on organization, fund-raising and recruiting. Their object now was to bring influence to bear within the House of Commons and build up electoral support for the next general election. In 1843 they moved their official headquarters to London to emphasize their status as a national movement, although the efficient office organization located in Newall's Buildings in Manchester continued to be the real directing centre. It was some time, however, before the violent language and actions of the 1841–2 period were forgotten; and the old animosities were never far below the surface. The assassination of Peel's secretary in January 1843 by a crackbrained Scots mechanic in mistake for Peel himself was followed by a sharp scene in the Commons when Cobden charged the prime minister with direct responsibility for the disturbed state of the country and Peel denounced the personal menaces of the League. Subsequent debates in the House demonstrated a growing tendency for free traders to attack the landed aristocracy and for agriculturalist MPs to retort in kind on manufacturers and factory owners.

Industrial distress and disturbances had evidently done little to dampen class and sectarian animosities. The fate of Graham's factory bill the same session was further proof of this. The failure of the whig educational scheme in 1839 seemed to demonstrate that few people wanted secular education and no system would be acceptable to parliament that did not assign a leading role to the established church. Graham's bill of 1843 to regulate the employment of women and children in factories attempted to make effective the deadletter clauses of the 1833 act by setting up state schools for children working in factories or coming from poor families. Though there were arrangements for separate religious instruction for non-anglicans, the schools were to be under general anglican control. To nonconformists this seemed a plan to set up state-subsidized recruiting institutions for anglicanism in precisely those areas where dissent outnumbered the establishment. The current controversy over the Tractarian movement, and fears of Romish tendencies in the Church of England, were further reasons (particularly powerful among Methodists) for nonconformist distrust. The Wesleyans threw their formidable resources behind the protest campaign launched by the Three Denominations; and though the House of Commons, sympathetic to the object of the bill and distrustful of the apparently automatic production of dissenting petitions, gave it a second reading, it was obvious that it would never work in the face of the intense hostility it had created. The dissenting success in securing the withdrawal of the bill, following the similar anglican victory of 1839, offered a clear moral. 'The Dissenters,' wrote Lord Ashley, 'and the Church have each laid down their limits which they will not pass, and there is no power that can either force, persuade, or delude them.'

While education remained a sphere in which the legislature was unable to prevail against organized sectarian opinion, the year 1844 saw the government reaping a delayed reward in its own field of finance. With the economic recovery the budget presented by Goulburn in April showed that both customs and income tax had yielded more than forecast and that expenditure had been less. The massive surplus of over £4 millions was enough to absorb the deficit of the previous year and leave a small credit balance. The financial work of the session was rounded off by the Bank Charter Act, designed to stabilize banking credit by enforcing a stricter relationship between paper money and gold reserves. It put the coping-stone on 'Peel's act' of 1819 and was the basis of the country's currency policy for the next eighty years. The ease with which it went through parliament was an impressive tribute to the prime minister's reputation for financial skill.

Over Graham's revised factory bill, however, the cabinet was plunged into a severe parliamentary crisis which was all the more disconcerting because of the political cross-currents which produced it. Early in the 1844 session Graham reintroduced his bill, shorn of the contentious educational section. The technical clauses of the measure, framed on the advice of his factory inspectors, were in many respects the more important contribution to the small but growing body of industrial legislation. Two years earlier, in 1842, Ashley had secured an act forbidding the employment in the coalpits of women, girls and boys under ten or of boys under fifteen for supervising machinery. According to the 1841 census women and girls only constituted 2 per cent of the total underground workforce in the mines and allowing for defective returns, particularly in Scotland, perhaps did not exceed 5 per cent in fact. Their employment had been generally on the decline since the eighteenth century and in some important areas like the northeast had completely disappeared.

Nevertheless, the evidence of the royal commission on which Ashley based his bill disclosed such a revolting picture of cruelty, degradation and sexual indecency in those pits where they still worked that a wave of public indignation drowned both the doctrinaire opponents of intervention and the more reasonable criticisms of those who tried to bring some statistical balance into the emotional controversy.

Graham's 1844 bill owed as much to the precedent of Ashley's act as to the factory act of 1833. All children under nine were as a class excluded from employment in factories. By fixing the maximum working day at twelve hours for women, as well as for young persons under eighteen, a new category of protected adults was established; and the fencing of certain types of dangerous machinery was made compulsory on employers. These were significant principles. In addition the hours for factory children were reduced to six and a half a day to allow time for schooling; the duration of the working day for factories was restricted; and the powers of factory inspectors considerably strengthened. The importance of these provisions was, however, obscured by the controversy over hours for adults. The twelve-hour norm had been recognized in a long line of factory acts stretching back to 1802 and had been upheld by the whigs in the 1830s. In preparing his bill Graham had secured the general agreement of the employers to the restrictive clauses in return for an explicit understanding that the twelve-hour working day would remain untouched. In March, however, Lord Ashley, who had refused to take office in 1841 because of his commitment to the ten hours movement, carried an amendment against the government reducing the hours to ten.

Both sides realized that what was effectively at stake was the maximum working day for men as well as women. On the government side, in addition to the moral pledge to the manufacturers, there was the conviction (fortified by the views of their factory inspectors and accepted in principle by their opponents) that a loss of working hours would reduce productivity and result either in unemployment or lower wages. At a time when British industry was just beginning to recover from the depression of 1837–42, this was not a prospect which Peel viewed with any pleasure. Cotton accounted for 80 per cent of British exports and its prosperity was vital for trade recovery. It seemed to him that a section of the Commons was discriminating unreasonably against the cotton manufacturers simply because the factory system, unlike agriculture and almost all the rest of industry, was peculiarly exposed to criticism and publicity. The political parties in the House of Commons were hopelessly split on the issue. Some whigs, including their former chancellor of the exchequer Francis Baring, joined with radicals like Bright and Warburton in supporting the government. Some conservative MPs, genuinely in sympathy with the paternal evangelical toryism represented by Lord Ashley, followed the impulses of humanity against considerations of economic policy. Some of the tory gentry voted with them out of hostility to the League and the Manchester manufacturers as a class. Lord John Russell and other official whigs who had opposed Ashley's ten hours' campaign in the 1830s when in office, now discovered persuasive reasons for supporting him in opposition.

In the end the government had its way but only by forcing the Commons to rescind their earlier vote and using the ultimate threat of resignation to bring its wayward supporters to heel. The strain on party loyalty was all the more ominous since within a month Peel found himself in almost an identical position over sugar duties. Sugar was to British imports what cotton was to its exports. It was the most valuable of the dutiable commodities entering the country, a considerable item in the cost of living, and a significant source of revenue for the government. The ministerial plan introduced in 1844 was designed to pave the way towards cheaper supplies of foreign sugar without ruining the West Indian planters or giving encouragement to slavery. In June an unusual, but not altogether accidental alliance, between liberal free traders who wanted to admit all foreign sugar regardless of origin and conservative protectionists who objected to a decrease in imperial protection, brought about a government defeat.

It was not that the danger had not been foreseen. The day before the crucial vote Peel convened a party meeting to explain government policy. But it was obvious that the protectionists, led by Philip Miles, the member for the great port of Bristol, were not going to be converted. It was, reported the prime minister grimly, the most unsatisfactory meeting he had ever known. But the extent of the defeat, by twenty votes in a well attended House, was shattering and Peel's first instinct was to resign. In the end more prudent counsels prevailed. A private meeting of some 200 conservative MPs passed a motion deploring talk of resignation and expressing gratitude for the past services of the ministry. A few days later the decision of the House was reversed by an amendment moved by Peel in an icy speech which could have done little to ensure success. In fact he anticipated another defeat and his own consequent resignation. But Stanley came to the rescue with a soothing speech; the whig opposition abstained from an official whip; and the government had its way.

The effect on party morale, however, was disastrous. Peel and several of his colleagues felt that they had a right to expect more loyalty as a government over policies which they put forward for the approval of the legislature. A large number of their supporters, while ready to keep them in office, believed that they had a perfect right to vote against them on matters where the interests of themselves or their constituents were involved. That Peel twice in one session should force them to reverse their votes struck some of them as a form of thinly veiled dictatorship. Both leaders and led in fact claimed a large degree of independence. It is arguable that only on those implied conditions could the parties of the 1830s have been built up. But the relationship called for tact and management; and in 1844 Peel mismanaged the situation as badly as any in his long career. Overwork, disillusionment, the strains of office stiffened the autocratic tendencies in his nature, making him increasingly indifferent to party claims and the party's future.

The estrangement between Peel and his party deepened in 1845. The occasion was Ireland, that ungovernable island which was the bane of every nineteenth-century British government and the destroyer of not a few. The dangerous repeal movement of 1843 had been halted by the banning of the Clontarf meeting and the subsequent arrest of O'Connell. But this for Peel was only the beginning, not the end. 'Mere force, however necessary the application of it,' he wrote, 'will do nothing as a permanent remedy for the social evils of that country.' Ireland therefore joined social and financial policy as the trilogy which he saw as his main tasks in the final years of his administration. There seemed two obstacles to good government there: bad relations between tenant and landlord, and bad relations between the British government and the Catholic middle classes. The exploration of the first problem was delegated to the mixed, non-party Devon Commission of 1843. A series of impressive memoranda to the cabinet in the spring of 1844 outlined the prime minister's views on the other half of the programme. At the heart of his proposals were the plans to make provision for private endowment of Catholic clergy and use the resources of the state to offer better education at university level for Irish Catholics, including a reform of the impoverished clerical seminary at Maynooth.

It was this last which provoked uproar in Protestant Britain. At the end of 1844 after initial difficulties the cooperation of the Irish bishops was secured for the Charitable Trusts Board, designed to facilitate endowment of Catholic chapels and benefices. In 1845 the next great measure, the Maynooth bill, proposed a special building grant of £30,000, an increase in the existing annual grant from roughly £9,000 to £26,000 and an effective system of inspection. The principle of state support for Maynooth College was as old as the act of parliament which set it up in 1795. The increase was substantial, though hardly more than its needs. But what was important was the changed state of British public opinion. Anti-Catholic feeling had hardened dangerously since 1829. There were several causes for this: disillusionment at the failure of Emancipation to pacify Ireland; the violence of O'Connell's campaign to repeal the Union; and widespread alarm at Tractarian progress in the Church of England. In 1844 a book by a leading Oxford Tractarian, W. G. Ward's *Ideal of a Christian Church*, had argued paradoxically that only the Roman Church satisfied ideal Christian requirements while claiming that men like the author could remain in the Church of England without renouncing a single Roman doctrine. The formal condemnation of the book and the deprivation of Ward's degrees by Oxford University in February 1845 was the signal for the departure from the establishment of a number of Tractarians, including Newman who was received into the Roman Church in October 1845.

The crisis at Oxford increased the alarm and indignation of evangelical Protestantism at Peel's Maynooth proposals. The prime minister had few illusions about the probable reception of his plan in the country. When trying to dissuade Gladstone from resigning on the issue in January 1845, he remarked calmly that the bill would 'very probably be fatal to the government'. But even he perhaps had not fully anticipated the nationwide opposition to his proposal which developed during the next few months. In many respects, both in the fundamental issues raised and in the effect on the government's traditional supporters, it resembled the Catholic Emancipation crisis of 1829 with Peel once again at the centre of the storm. The double principle of religious endowment by the state and encouragement to Romanism touched some of the deepest passions in contemporary Protestantism. The fiercely anti-Catholic evangelical Anglicans and Wesleyans joined with the anti-establishment Congregationalists, Baptists and Scottish Free Churchmen to oppose the bill. A central Anti-Maynooth Committee was set up to organize the agitation and over 10,000 petitions, containing more than a million and a quarter signatures, poured into parliament in the first four months of the session.

The Maynooth bill went through, as Catholic Emancipation had done in 1829, with large cross-bench majorities. The Commons were always less prone to religious hysteria than the great British public. The union of official men, liberal conservatives, erastian whigs and Irish Catholic nationalists was too strong for the ultra-Protestants and doctrinaire radicals. But though the government and the legislature were able to enforce their will in what was primarily a matter of Irish policy, the effect of the great Maynooth agitation was far-

reaching. The voluntaryist party among the dissenters, already dis-
enchanted with political parties, were alienated still further from
their historic whig allies. The concept of a united liberal party, which
had not appeared unreal between 1835 and 1839, now seemed more
chimerical than ever. For the moment liberal Peelites and liberal
whigs were driven together under flanking attacks from dissenting
voluntaryists and anti-Catholic anglicans.

Inside the House much of the debate had turned, not on the
principle of the bill, but on the record of the prime minister who
proposed it. All the old charges of 'betrayal' over Catholic
Emancipation were brought out once more. Peel defiantly answered
his critics by claiming for himself and his government the right to
do what they thought was necessary in prevailing circumstances
'without reference to the past and without too much regard for what
party considerations must claim from them'. The party answered
by splitting 159 to 147 in favour of the bill on the second reading,
149 to 148 against it on the third. Following on the divisions over
factory hours and sugar duties the previous session, this fresh
disruption was devastating. Graham and Aberdeen could not have
been the only conservative politicians who believed that the
consequence of Maynooth, as of Emancipation, would be the
disintegration of the party.

Some observers felt that the revolt of the Conservative party over
Maynooth would not have been so great had it not been for the
resentment of the agriculturalists at the continued free-trade policies
of the government. In 1845 general economic prosperity and the
healthy state of the national finances had enabled Peel to plan a
further advance. His free-trade budget of 1842 had been a large-scale
experiment, with its undoubted risks covered by the insurance of
the income tax. The budget of 1845 was a grander but safer
operation, based not only on the government's accrued surplus of
£5 millions but on the proved efficacy of free-trade policy. In the
long run it now seemed demonstrably true that a reduction of tariff
duties would lead after an interval to increased consumption and
this in turn to a recovery of the lost revenue. What Peel proposed,
in the budget which he himself introduced in February 1845, was
to renew the income tax for another three years and in return devote
all the surplus revenue to another sweeping reduction in tariff rates.
After allowing for a modest £1 million naval rearmament programme and various other extraordinary expenses, the available
surplus amounted to £3·4 millions. Of this £3·3 millions were to
be returned to the public in the shape of lower sugar duties (accounting for one third of the total), the abolition of all export duties on
British goods, and free entry for more than half the over 800 different

articles of import still carrying duty, including cotton and other raw materials for industry.

Because it was unattended by controversy, the importance of the 1845 budget has not always been given the attention it merits. It was a far more extensive free-trade exercise than that of 1842. The remission of revenue was almost three times as great and the duties on many articles were abolished completely instead of being merely reduced. As a financial operation, moreover, it was a resounding and instant success. When Goulburn presented his estimates to parliament the following year he was able to report that the surplus, instead of the estimated £700,000, was over £2½ millions. Buoyant trade figures had absorbed nearly a third of the tariff cuts; internal revenue from stamp duties and the post office was over £½ million up; and though £1 million of excise duties had been swept away, the decrease on the year was only £200,000. The financial solidity of the government in 1845 enabled Peel in 1846 to produce his third and last great free-trade budget in which duties amounting to over £1 million were taken off, an amount almost equal to that of the great budget of 1842. In all, between 1842 and 1846, the work of transforming Britain into a free-trade country was largely accomplished, leaving only a remnant to be done by Gladstone in 1853 and 1860. Budgets do not excite the interest of posterity. But Peel's work and its results did not go unappreciated by the great mercantile and manufacturing classes nor by the mass of the people who consumed the cheap butter, cheese and meat that was beginning to come into the country in increasing quantities.[2]

Merely from the point of view of balancing the budget, the tariff revision of 1845 was in a sense unnecessary. What Peel was doing was inviting the wealthier classes to make their contribution for yet another period in return for another long stride down the road of commercial and industrial expansion. To that appeal the House of Commons was more than ready to respond. Though the whigs denounced the renewal of the income tax, they were not prepared to vote against it. The only sour note came from behind the government front bench. Nothing had been done for agriculture; it had not even been mentioned. It alone among the great interests of the country, as more than one county MP pointed out, received no compensation for the continued burden of the income tax. The tory agriculturalists had other occasions on which to express their grievances. Even if they lacked personal incentive, there was pressure from the Central Protection Society and its local branches. In the course of 1844, moreover, the backbencher Disraeli, denied office in 1841, had started his vendetta against the prime minister, using

[2] See J. H. Clapham, *Early Railway Age* (1926), p. 499.

his remarkable satiric talent and appealing to a wider audience than the 'Young England' coterie had ever afforded. Few politicians trusted Disraeli: they knew too much about him. But he was bold and amusing; and much that he said was balm to the discontented and inarticulate country squires.

Peel himself was well aware of the mixed motives behind the conservative revolt over Maynooth, including disappointed ambition in some and wheat at 46*s.* a quarter (in March it actually touched 45*s.*) in others. What he resented was that the positive achievements of his ministry apparently counted for nothing with many of his nominal followers. Trade and industry were in a flourishing state, the working classes better off, Chartism dead, the League driven back into constitutional courses, the church stronger than ever (except for its own internal quarrels), demands for parliamentary reform no longer heard, the finances of the state put on a firm basis, the revenue buoyant, amicable relations restored with France and the USA. 'But,' he wrote ironically in May 1845, 'we have reduced protection to agriculture, and tried to lay the foundation of peace in Ireland; and these are offences for which nothing can atone.' Though there was justice in his complaint, it was not a mood which argued well for the future. Yet for the moment he was invulnerable. Secure in the general support of the public and the personal confidence of the crown, he dominated the political scene. It was a paradox springing from the narrow electoral basis of parliament that Peel was regarded as the indispensable national statesman by masses of unpolitical people who took little interest in the League or Anti-League, Maynooth or Anti-Maynooth, at the very time when his parliamentary position was full of difficulty. Within the confined atmosphere of the House of Commons the relationship between him and a large section of his party was brittle with distrust. 'Everybody expects that he means to go on,' wrote Greville ruminatively at the end of August 1845, 'and in the end to knock the Corn Laws on the head, and endow the Roman Catholic Church, but nobody knows how or when he will do these things.'

III

Six months later the Conservative party broke up on the central issue of the corn laws. The event which precipitated the crisis was the Irish potato disease. Even while Greville was writing his sardonic prophecy, Peel and his home secretary were anxiously discussing the

unseasonable weather, the prospect of a poor harvest, and the
appearance of a dangerous and unknown disease of the potato crop
both in England and on the continent. By the third week of
September the ministers knew that the disease was present in Ireland;
by the middle of October they knew that they were in the presence
of a great social calamity. For the bulk of the Irish peasantry the
potato was the staple article of diet. A failure of the crop, which
in England and Scotland brought only high prices and hardship
for the poor, in Ireland meant disaster. The experts Peel sent across
reported that at least half the Irish potato crop was ruined, that
more would rot in the storage pits, and that the harvest would
probably be affected by the same disease the following year. By
November the public alarm was acute. In Ireland there were calls
for official action and in England the Anti-Corn Law League
demanded the opening of the ports for the free entry of grain.

To Peel and Graham it seemed clear that the potato disease spelled
the end of the corn laws. Even if food could be brought in from
abroad, the Irish peasant living on a subsistence economy had no
money with which to buy it. Peel, who as Irish secretary had lived
through one Irish famine in 1817, had no illusions as to the consequences. A great scheme of national relief at the taxpayers' expense
would have to be organized if widespread starvation and disease were
to be prevented. The general shortage of foodstuffs in Europe would
ensure that prices would remain high. Could the British taxpayer
be asked to contribute a million or more to feed Ireland and still
tolerate the existence of the corn laws? The alternative was suspension
for a limited period or abolition. To suspend the corn laws would
be to admit the League's argument that their presence aggravated
scarcity and their removal would promote plenty. The length of the
suspension was unpredictable, but almost certainly would be longer
than a year. Resumption of the law, when it came, would provoke
a violent political conflict fought on class lines, possibly in the very
year 1847 when a general election was due.

In a series of emergency cabinets from the end of October to the
first week of December Peel tried to convince his colleagues that
a drastic modification of the corn laws was unavoidable. They were
ready to sanction the immediate measures Peel and Graham had
already taken: instructions to the lord lieutenant to set up relief
organization, the secret purchase of £100,000 worth of maize from
the USA, and a search for possible sources of food in Europe. But
though this constituted in Peel's eyes a recognition of the coming
disaster, the cabinet still hung back from the crucial decision. They
all felt that to open the ports, even for a limited period, would be
tantamount to repealing the corn laws. On 6 November Peel put

before them a specific proposal to suspend the corn laws by order in council, call parliament together to sanction that step, and announce their intention of bringing forward a new corn bill after the Christmas recess. Only three of his colleagues—Aberdeen, Graham and Herbert—supported him. The rest either opposed in principle or felt that the absolute necessity of such a reversal of party policy had not yet been demonstrated.

It was to give time for the waverers to convince themselves that Peel delayed a final decision until December. The delay worsened the position of the government without securing the unanimity which was its only justification. At the crucial meeting on 4 December Stanley and Buccleuch indicated that they would resign rather than consent to the gradual extinction of the corn duties which Peel had in mind. By that date Lord John Russell, reacting impulsively to the public excitement, had already announced in his *Edinburgh Letter* of 22 November his conversion to total repeal and called on the nation to bring pressure to bear on the government to abolish the corn laws. Though, characteristically, he had consulted none of his party nor reflected very carefully on the possible political consequences for himself, the leader of the Liberal party in the Commons had in effect put himself at the head of the national movement hitherto monopolized by Cobden and the League. Peel's contention in cabinet that, whatever they did to meet the crisis in Ireland, they would have to face the political implications for the corn laws in England, had been vindicated earlier than he could have expected. Any concession ministers now made would appear to be dictated by pressure from without. On 5 December the cabinet concluded that the loss of Stanley and Buccleuch would make it impossible to carry Peel's bill and the prime minister announced that in those circumstances he felt it his duty to resign.

From the beginning of the crisis Peel and Graham were clearly convinced that the corn laws were doomed. Other men in their position might have looked for expedients or compromises. The most that Peel conceded was a period of eight years during which the corn duties would be progressively reduced until they became extinct. The instant certainty that famine meant repeal could only have come to men who were already intellectually convinced that the corn laws could no longer be defended and that their disappearance was only a matter of time. To Peel the success of the 1842 budget had proved experimentally the validity of the free-trade theory. There had been an increase in consumption and a reduction in the cost of living. Cheap food did not, as economists had once argued and some still feared, go hand in hand with low wages. On the contrary lower prices had been accompanied by full employment and a restoration

of social order. After the 1845 tariff changes corn was in a position
of isolation as the only primary article enjoying a high degree of
protection; this in itself constituted a political danger. To maintain
the corn laws against the trend of national economic policy was to
lend credibility to the arguments of the League that they were continued only because the class which benefited from them had a
monopoly of government and legislation. Under cover of the repeal
campaign the League was already attacking the position of the
aristocracy, the Church of England, the army, navy and colonial
establishments, and the whole structure of parliamentary government. They were doing it, moreover, not cynically but with all the
conviction and passion which the early Victorians were apt to import
into their public controversies.

For the aristocracy to tie its fortunes to the fate of the corn laws
was, in Peel's eyes, an unnecessary and suicidal act of folly. Neither
their parliamentary supremacy nor their economic basis depended
on a continuance of laws which had conspicuously failed to give
satisfaction either to growers or consumers. Peel's 1842 act had
proved the best technical solution so far devised. Between 1843 and
1845 the annual average price of wheat varied only between 50s. 2d.
and 51s. 3d. But the low price was largely due to a run of good
harvests and the annual average concealed monthly fluctuations
ranging from 60s. to 45s. No law could command the climate or
put a stop to the remorseless growth of the British population. The
corn laws were both ineffective and in the long run untenable.

Peel, like many other practical landowners, had for over a decade
held the view that the prosperity of British agriculture depended
not on the artificial prop of high tariffs but on the greater productivity that could only come from more intensive cultivation and more
modern methods. The scientific farming to which the Royal Agricultural Society was dedicated, rather than the Central Agricultural
Protection Society, represented the road of progress. For at least a
couple of years the cabinet had been aware that for the prime
minister the only alternative to the 1842 act was total repeal. That
alternative had already been taking shape in his mind as a practical
possibility. There is no reason to doubt his statement to Prince Albert
in December 1845 that he had intended to announce to the party
his conversion to repeal and seek support for it before the general
election of 1847. The Irish potato blight only precipitated a decision
already in contemplation.

The only question in December 1845 was whether the corn laws
would be repealed by Peel or by Russell. Lord John had his chance
and turned it down. It was an unheroic but not unreasonable
decision. The whigs were in a minority in the Commons, in a

considerable minority in the Lords. Their record in opposition had been full of hesitations and internal divisions. Whatever new lights their leader had seen, they were not united or enthusiastic over corn. While Russell and most of his senior colleagues accepted Peel's promise of general support as satisfactory, some did not. Lord Lansdowne, a reluctant convert to repeal, stood out for large compensations to agriculture. The final unnerving complication was Grey's refusal to enter the cabinet if Palmerston went back to the Foreign Office. After eleven days of discussion the distraught Russell abandoned the Queen's commission, to the evident relief of many leading whigs. Peel to his deep satisfaction found himself charged with the national duty of putting an end to the corn laws. It was an illuminating contrast.

In the changed circumstances all the members of Peel's old cabinet except Stanley rejoined him. Protectionism was dead; the choice seemed between themselves and an alliance of Cobden and Lord Grey. Peel held out no assurance that his tenure of office would be a long one, but that seemed irrelevant in the face of the immediate task confronting them. What Peel proposed to do was to make one last round of tariff changes in which corn would at last be treated as an ordinary commodity. 'Let us,' he wrote to his chancellor of the exchequer, 'leave the tariff as nearly perfect as we can. . . . Let us put the finishing stroke to this good work.' Whether the device of wrapping up the repeal of the corn laws in a general tariff reconstruction was the best parliamentary tactics is open to question. Though it restored logic and consistency to the government's economic policy, it weakened the connection between the Irish famine and repeal, and gave colour to the charge that the government had intended all along to repeal them. Perhaps it did not matter; whatever Peel did, his opponents did not allow the central issue to be obscured. The danger was the other way round: that the value of the budget as a whole would be lost from view in the conflict over corn. When at the end of January he unfolded his plans to the Commons, they included in fact the abolition or reduction of duties on a large range of articles, many of them foodstuffs of common consumption like sugar, cheese, butter and dried fish. But his audience, like most of the public, had ears only for the one subject of corn. On this he proposed simply a progressive lowering of duties over the next three years until in 1849 they ceased entirely. In compensation he offered loans to agriculture and various forms of relief for county rates.

The anticipated battle broke out immediately. There were a number of resignations from the royal household and the lower ranks of the administration. Some conservative MPs who indicated their intention of supporting the government were told by their constituents or their patrons to resign. The Central Protection Society, meeting in London during the excitement and speculation of December, had already dropped its rule of non-intervention in parliamentary elections and called on its members to bring pressure to bear on their local members. In the weeks preceding the opening of the session protectionist meetings were held all over England to promote petitions to parliament and exact pledges from constituency MPs against repeal. It was this angry determination by the outraged agriculturalists, expressed through their representatives, especially those sitting for counties and small rural boroughs, that was the main cause of the disruption of the party in 1846.

The emergence in the early weeks of the session of Bentinck, a friend of the duke of Richmond and younger son of the duke of Portland, added prestige and determination to the protectionist party. To Bentinck the prime minister was a dishonest jockey who had cheated his backers and had to be barred from the course for the rest of his life as a lesson to others. His chief lieutenant Disraeli, with greater intelligence concentrated on Peel's flagrant disregard of party claims and party loyalty. But the savage tenacity of the one, the brilliant sarcasms of the other, and their increasingly personal attacks on the prime minister, widened the emotional gap between Peelites and protectionists without always enhancing their cause. Even their alliance with the Irish nationalists over the arms bill, which the distracted state of Ireland had forced the government to introduce, could only delay, not avert the inevitable free-trade victory. The depth of division among the conservatives was shown on the second reading of the tariff bill at the end of February when 231 members of the party voted against the government and only 112 with. On the third reading in May the figures were roughly similar. In all, allowing for tellers and absentees, the conservative chief whip estimated that only 117, or less than a third of the parliamentary party, still stood behind their leader.

With almost the whole strength of the liberal opposition behind repeal, however, there was no danger of defeat in the Commons. The danger lay in the House of Lords where in May a number of whig peers were toying with the idea of an alliance with the protectionists on the basis of a small fixed duty. Russell put a stop to that by summoning a meeting at which he told the dissident whig peers that he would be no party to any amendment to the corn bill and that if the government resigned on the issue, they would have to look elsewhere for a leader. With that the last threat disappeared and the charmed life which Peel's minority government had been leading since the start of the session was nearly over. Foiled in defeating the corn bill, Bentinck was now set on revenge. A ministry with little more than a hundred firm supporters in the Commons could clearly not survive for long. If the government had not been defeated on the Irish arms bill, they would have been vulnerable on other issues such as the postponed sugar duties on which the whigs had already threatened opposition. In neither case was Peel disposed to make concessions merely to postpone the inevitable. The end came in the early hours of 26 June when by a careful contrivance of the opposition, the Irish bill was defeated in the Commons a few hours after the corn bill passed its final reading in the Lords. Less than a third of the conservative protectionists voted with the whigs and Irish; nearly half supported the government. But with other conservatives abstaining, Bentinck's reduced squad of seventy-four was enough to bring victory to the opposition.

The following Monday, 29 June, Peel announced his resignation. His last speech as prime minister was remembered for two things —the tribute to Cobden as the real author of repeal, and his wish to be remembered with goodwill in the homes of the poor. The first was perhaps a gesture of reconciliation; but it was resented by both friends and opponents, and was better left unsaid. It was moreover not true. If there was agreement on anything, it was that only Peel could have secured the abolition of the corn laws at that time. His influence as the outstanding statesman of his generation and his initiative as prime minister were essential. The famous peroration was dismissed by Greville as 'claptrap about cheap bread'; but there can be no doubt that it touched the hearts of those of Greville's countrymen who did not share the advantages of his birth or fortune.[3] For Peel the corn laws had become part of the 'condition of England' question. Their repeal, as he said more than once during the corn law debates, was the most conservative act of his life. He told the Commons in January at the very start of the controversy:

> I have thought it consistent with true Conservative policy, to promote so much of happiness and contentment among the people that the voice of disaffection should no longer be heard, and thoughts of the dissolution of our institutions should be forgotten in the midst of physical enjoyment.

Though he certainly believed that free-trade in corn would alleviate the lot of the working classes in time of scarcity, he did not attach to the abolition of the corn laws the magical effects which the League orators sometimes predicted. More important in his view was the knowledge that their repeal would remove a feeling of class injustice and demonstrate to the voteless and unpropertied masses that a

---

[3] Charles Greville, political diarist, racehorse owner, and clerk to the Privy Council, was a descendant of the fifth Lord Warwick and a nephew of the duke of Portland.

legislature of landowners was not indifferent to their wants. Only so could the aristocratic system in which Peel believed hope to survive in mid-Victorian society.

That it would do so, he was quietly confident. As early as August 1847, in a letter to Prince Albert on the future of British politics, he observed that while there were signs of democratic leanings in the larger constituencies and no lack of ambitious popular politicians, yet the repeal of the corn laws had removed the one great issue on which such forces could come together. For the moment there was no question, not even parliamentary reform, which would excite the public mind. As long as the House of Commons took a lead in promoting rational improvement and efficient administration there would be little danger from political agitation. In any case, 'the quiet good sense and good feeling of the people of this Country will be a powerful instrument on which an Executive government may rely'. In his view the political system as it existed after 1832 was a trustee-ship exercised by the aristocracy on behalf of the nation at large. The danger was that either the aristocracy would not recognize its trusteeship or that the terms of the trust would not be understood. Given continuing wisdom and restraint within the political oligarchy, however, he thought after 1846 that the worst of the class conflicts that had racked British society since Waterloo were now over. For him the repeal of the corn laws, as the Reform Act had been for Grey, was essentially a preserving measure.

IV

The consequences of the repeal of the corn laws dominated British politics for another half-dozen years. The whigs found themselves the possessors of power for which they were unequipped either by clarity of policy or unity of party. They were a government by default. This initial disadvantage, which need not have been permanent, was perpetuated by the deficiencies of their leader. Russell's ineffective-ness in the December crisis was a warning that his promise as leader of the House of Commons in the 1830s was not going to be fulfilled as prime minister in the 1840s. The famous *Punch* cartoon of January 1846[4] showing him in buttons and livery being interviewed by the Queen—'I'm afraid you're not strong enough for the place, John'—reflected a view among the public that never quite disappeared. It was Russell's fate always to be overshadowed by a bigger man

[4] Reproduced in H. C. F. Bell, *Lord Pamlerston* (2 vols, 1966) 1, p. 364.

than himself. In the 1830s it had been Melbourne; in the 1850s and 1860s it was Palmerston; in the 1840s it was Peel.

Though the savagery of the protectionist attacks in the 1846 session made Peel momentarily contemplate retirement, in the end he stayed in politics. But he publicly and repeatedly disclaimed any intention of leading a party or taking office again. Instead he consistently used his influence to keep the whig ministry in office as the only men capable of providing stable government and preserving the fundamentals of Peelite policy. Between 1846 and 1850 he held a unique position in public life. He was the friend and confidant of Prince Albert who sought his opinions on foreign and (more embarrassingly) on domestic affairs. The new chancellor of the exchequer Charles Wood showed a deferential anxiety to obtain his advice. Clarendon, the whig lord lieutenant, was so impressed by one of Peel's speeches on Ireland in 1849 that he asked for a personal interview and subsequently persuaded the prime minister to introduce a bill embodying some of Peel's proposals. He was more than once recalled from Drayton to add his strength to the government side and over the repeal of the navigation acts, which only went through the upper house by ten votes, he was even requested to use his authority with the Peelite peers. In more than one debate his speech in defence of government policy left nothing for Russell, the nominal leader of the House, to say. From his example, his speeches, and his private counsel the government derived invaluable strength.

Yet paradoxically his presence in public life contributed to the unsteadiness of parliamentary politics. An ex-prime minister of Peel's standing (Greville opined that on any popular vote he would sweep the country), especially when surrounded by a devoted and ambitious group of younger followers, can scarcely revert to the role of a private MP. As Stanley observed in 1849, 'he *must* be *a* Leader, in spite of himself'. In the four remaining years of his life Peel made it difficult for anything like a proper two-party system to re-emerge. Many, perhaps most, people expected that one day he would return to office. The Peelites, alienated from the protectionists and contemptuous of the whigs, looked forward to a coalition of moderates in which their reluctant leader would be forced by circumstances to play the central role.

The protectionist wing of the party, on the other hand, seemed to have neither immediate strength nor long-term prospects. Though Stanley had been conscripted as their leader, he had played a singularly passive part in the corn law debates. He wished to leave the way open for an eventual reunion of the party, and his relationship with the irascible, unrelenting Bentinck was for that reason alone studiously cool. As the only man among them who had held high

office, he was painfully conscious of the intellectual poverty of those
who looked to him to lead them back to power. The disruption of
the Conservative party had left the numerical majority on one side,
the brains and experience on the other. Bentinck himself was more
popular with farmers and freeholders than with the country gentlemen. The tory backbenchers did not share his tolerant views on
Catholics and Jews (it is easy to forget that Bentinck was originally
a Canningite whig) and they disliked his erratic and violent
behaviour in the Commons. It was not difficult for the protectionist
whips to get rid of him at the end of 1847. The absence of men
of talent and the void in the leadership in the lower house enabled
the suspect Disraeli to demonstrate his indispensability. But he in
turn found the protectionists a difficult pack with which to hunt.
For a man of his flexible mind and intense ambition it was
increasingly unsatisfactory to belong to a party with one idea. But
though by 1850 he could say cheerfully that protection was not only
dead but damned, his party chief was not prepared to abandon the
issue on which they had broken with Peel until the sense of the
country had declared specifically against it.

There was thus no feasible alternative to a whig government
though this in itself did not assist Russell to stamp his authority on
either parliament or his party. His historic family connection and
his occasional flashes of real fire and eloquence in the Commons
formed his chief assets. But his lack of constructive policy and
administrative talent soon became obvious. Even his renewed interest
in parliamentary reform seemed to be caused more by a nostalgic
longing for a repetition of the triumphs of 1831–2 than a realistic
assessment of the requirements and possibilities of the moment. In
1846–7, so far from reverting to the task left unfinished in the 1830s
of building up a broadly based Liberal party, he thought that the
moral of post-reform politics was to avoid extremes. His overtures
to Cobden in 1846 and 1847 were vague and ineffective. His several
attempts to bring some of the younger Peelites into the cabinet,
though genuine, were ignominiously rejected. The general election
of 1847, which weakened the protectionists, left the Peelites largely
intact, and strengthened the liberals, seemed on the surface to consolidate his position. The reality was less comforting. Though the
mass of liberal MPs just outnumbered Peelites and protectionists
combined, the extreme and independent radicals had increased their
numbers at the expense of more orthodox party men. The dependable
strength of the government was less than a majority of the whole
House. It was not an impossible position, given the goodwill of the
Peelites; but government on a knife-edge called for greater skill than
Russell was able to provide.

Part of the weakness of his parliamentary position arose from the educational controversy of 1846–7 which further strained the already frayed ties between the dissenters and the whig party. The educational committee of the Privy Council, urged on by their energetic secretary James Kay (the Chadwick of the educational world), proposed to change the basis of school grants in order to encourage the training of pupil-teachers and raise the status of the teaching profession. But the scheme involved an extension of governmental inspection and the principle of professional examinations. To dissenters, embittered by the great religious and educational conflicts of the previous ten years, it seemed yet another attempt to enlarge the sphere of the state and promote the authority of the established church. While the National Society, with some reservations by the high church party, welcomed the proposals, the main body of dissenters plunged into heated opposition. A conference of delegates in April 1847 not only condemned the whig plan but called on liberal electors to support at the forthcoming general election only those candidates who stood for complete religious liberty. A dissenting electoral committee was set up to organize parliamentary opposition; the Anti-State Church association, founded by Miall in 1844, worked hard on behalf of voluntaryist candidates in the provinces; and even the Protestant Deputies in London aligned themselves with the movement of protest. When the elections were over, the voluntaryists claimed successes for twenty-six of their candidates and a further sixty MPs pledged against the government scheme.

Between education, Maynooth and free trade, the general election of 1847 was one of the most shapeless of the century. Fewer seats were contested than in any election except one between the first and second Reform Acts. It was a battle of causes rather than of parties. Influential dissenting periodicals like the *Eclectic Review* branded whigs and conservatives as a single, undifferentiated aristocratic interest; Peelites found themselves damaged by their Maynooth rather than by their free-trade label; liberals and conservatives in many constituencies worked together to return the same candidate; radical educationalists quarrelled with dissenting voluntaryists; erastian cabinet ministers took comfort in the support of the bishops. The noisy, untidy conflict helped to disintegrate party without securing the objectives of the voluntaryists. The government persisted with its plans, raised the educational grant to £100,000, and negotiated special agreements with the Wesleyan Methodists and a section of the Congregationalists. But while the bulk of the nonconformists satisfied their consciences by holding aloof from the state educational scheme, they also forfeited any chance of securing whig concessions on such matters as church rates and made talk of disestablishment mere rhetoric.

A further source of disunion was provided by the extreme parliamentary radicals under old leaders like Hume and new ones like Cobden and Bright. Though the role of the Anti-Corn Law League during the 1846 crisis had not been passive, it had been essentially a subordinate one. Its leaders had agitated for instant repeal; they had threatened the protectionists; but in the end it had been Peel and not the Leaguers who swept away the corn laws. The trial of strength at a general election for which they had been assiduously preparing never took place. In July 1846 the League itself had been dissolved.

The responsibility of the League for the repeal of the corn laws became one of the legends of middle-class ideology in the prosperous, free-trade decades of the later Victorian era. But for the moment repeal left its leaders with an appetite for politics without a recognizable role and the Liberal party in general with only a tenuous bond of unity. The dangers of the situation were shown in April 1848 when some fifty or sixty radical MPs under Cobden and Hume constituted themselves as a separate party with a programme of financial retrenchment and parliamentary reform. The endemic vices of excessive individualism and quarrels over policy prevented a true radical party from emerging. But the existence of a critical, discontented, dissident group among the nominal liberal supporters helped to paralyse still further Russell's government. Their nuisance value was particularly marked over financial matters where the traditional radical demand for government economy and low taxation was supported by the protectionists who calculated that if ministers could be forced to abandon the income tax they would be obliged to restore revenue-producing import duties, including one on corn. Already in February this tactical alliance had defeated the government's proposal to meet defence expenditure by raising the income tax from 7*d.* to 1*s.* and from that point the finances of the Russell administration could only be shored up by shifts and expedients.

Not surprisingly the more important legislation of the 1846–52 period owed its origin to chance forces or the momentum of administrative developments within individual departments rather than to any coherent whig programme. The disruption of party alignments allowed, for example, a ten hours bill (introduced by Fielden, the Quaker cotton manufacturer, in the absence from the Commons of Lord Ashley) to be passed in 1847. Russell and his colleagues, though not enthusiastic, were tied by their previous record and the protectionists were always prepared to vote against

Peel and the Manchester men. In addition much of the genuine fear that reductions in hours would mean reductions in profits had died down, and with a slump in the cotton industry most factories were already working short hours. The act, despite its name, did not in the event result in a strict ten hours' day, either for factories or individual workers. Loose drafting and managerial ingenuity allowed a system of relays to be devised and when Ashley secured an amending act in 1850 he had to compromise on ten and a half hours for protected persons and, in practice, for the men.

Another important piece of social legislation, the Public Health Act of 1848, though an important milestone in the history of sanitary policy, municipal government and state regulation, derived less from any intrinsic interest of the government than from Chadwick's inexhaustible energy and an inherited departmental concern. There was little enthusiasm in the cabinet and the public was largely indifferent until the cholera epidemic of 1848 brought the subject up in a singularly practical manner. Free-trade measures fell more directly into the arena of party politics, though there was usually a safe majority for them in the Commons if not the Lords. In 1849 came the largely symbolic repeal of the navigation acts. They had been so eroded by the legislation of the previous thirty years as to be little more than an encumbrance to colonial interests and a source of friction with foreign powers. Otherwise little was added to the work of Peel's administration; the danger was that some of it might be destroyed. The income tax remained in a vulnerable position, exposed to attacks from both radicals and protectionists. Even the corn laws, suspended in 1846 but not legally expiring until 1849, could not be regarded as an absolutely closed issue. But friendly collaboration between Peel and Wood, the whig chancellor of the exchequer, carried the government safely through the financial crisis of 1847; and though there were disquieting rumours in the winter of 1849–50 that ministers were contemplating the reintroduction of a small fixed duty on corn, Peel was quickly reassured through indirect channels that the government had no intention of reversing the decision of 1846.

Nevertheless the ability of the administration to survive seemed increasingly to depend on a succession of temporary alliances with one or other of the remaining four groups in the Commons— Peelites, protectionists, radicals and Irish. The situation could clearly not last indefinitely. Though Peel was unwavering in his support, he seemed to some of his more restless and ambitious followers like Gladstone to be a mere prisoner of whig policy. The Peelites in consequence began to lose all appearance of being a united party. Over a number of issues they voted on different sides.

In February 1850, for example, on a motion by Disraeli to relieve
the landed interest by removing part of the burden of poor rate,
thirty-five Peelites voted with the protectionists as against twenty-
seven who joined Peel in supporting the ministers. As John Young,
the Peelite chief whip, warned Peel, a large number of MPs would
'rally round you personally, or any organization distinctly formed
under your auspices and guided by your advice, but they will not
make sacrifices and risk their seats night after night and year after
year for those whom they cannot help regarding as political
opponents.'

Peel, however, was not to be moved from his chosen path. Though
later in the same session he voted against the government in the
debate on Palmerston's foreign policy, it was only because the
challenge was one he could not decently avoid and victory for the
ministry a foregone conclusion. His feeling after the debate was one
of sober satisfaction that he had been able to speak out at last on
a subject from which for political reasons he had previously
abstained and that the whig government was still safe. Four days
later he was dead and with him the greatest prop to Russell's
ministry was abruptly removed.

The contrast between the narrow context of parliamentary life
and the wider British society which Peel had made it his business
to understand was shown in the country's reaction to his death. Out
of office, without an organized party behind him, he was still
regarded by the majority of the press and the public as the greatest
statesman of the day whose eventual return to office was among the
certainties of politics. The disruption of 1846, in an age which
attached less importance to party ties and party fortunes than was
common later in the century, seemed to them a matter of little
concern compared with his record of national achievement. Among
the mercantile, manufacturing and professional classes of the north,
for example, the reputation he had made with the corn law and
budget of 1842 had been crowned by the repeal of the corn laws
in 1846. The two greatest liberal newspapers in the provinces, the
Manchester Guardian representing the cotton masters and the *Leeds
Mercury* representing the woollen manufacturers, both gave him
enthusiastic support, as did significantly the two leading northern
conservative newspapers, the *Manchester Courier* and the *Leeds Intelli-
gencer*.[5]

But it was not only the mass of the middle classes but a large
section of the working classes who made him their hero after 1846.
His accidental death in 1850 reinforced their keen sense of the
sacrifice he had made in renouncing the leadership of his party for

[5] See Donald Read, *Press and People 1790–1850* (1961), pp. 190–98.

the sake of abolishing the corn laws. 'He fell from official power into the arms of the people,' wrote one popular journalist. The crowds of ordinary London working people who kept vigil outside his house as he lay dying, the Birmingham factory hands who subscribed their pennies for a monument to his memory, the Wiltshire labourers who bought cheap prints of his portrait to hang up in their cottages, all testified to the hold he had on the ordinary people of Britain.

Peel had consciously set out to justify aristocratic rule and close the class divisions in his country. His popularity in the last four years of his life was a measure of the success he achieved. Other circumstances besides free-trade tariffs and financial reform had fostered national recovery after 1842, including the boom in railway construction and a run of good harvests. The corn laws never had the economic importance, for good or bad, usually attributed to them. It was as a political symbol that they loomed large in public consciousness. From 1815 through post-war radicalism, Peterloo, Chartism and the League, they had stood as the supreme example of class legislation. For that reason their repeal was also a symbol. That it was followed by several years of good harvests and low prices was a piece of good fortune. What mattered was that a parliament of landowners had made a great social concession for the good of the country as a whole. The failure of the 1848 Chartist demonstrations, both in London and the provinces, and the social solidarity that ensured that failure, seemed to most observers to be a vindication of what providentially had been done only two years' earlier. Peel himself thought so. 'It was that confidence in the generosity and justice of parliament,' he told the Commons in 1849, 'which in no small degree enabled you to pass triumphantly through that storm which convulsed other nations.'

Different men had different explanations for the change that seemed to be coming over British society as the middle of the century grew near; but it was rare for there to be no mention of Peel's work in their lists of preferred reasons. 'We may now thank God that the Reform Bill has been passed and the Corn Laws repealed,' wrote one Warwickshire squire[6] in April 1848 after the Chartist demonstration in London passed off quietly. Three years later Shaftesbury (as Ashley had now become) wrote to Lord John Russell from Manchester. 'Chartism is dead in these parts; the Ten Hours Act and cheap provisions have slain it outright.' That great organ of middle-class opinion *The Times* summed it up in 1852 with a single authoritative sentence: 'In one sense we are all Peelites.'

[6] W. S. Dugdale of Merevale Hall, JP and MP for North Warwickshire 1832–47 (from private diary).

9 The Decline of Party Politics

I

The great debate on foreign policy in June 1850 marked a silent shift in the balance of power within the cabinet. Palmerston, junior minister for many years under Perceval and Liverpool, follower of Canning, belated convert to reform in 1830, had never fitted comfortably into the whig political tradition. As foreign secretary between 1830 and 1841 he had struck an independent line of his own and in 1840 almost broke up the Melbourne cabinet by his readiness to risk war with France during the Middle East crisis. In opposition between 1841 and 1846 his campaign against Aberdeen was supported neither by aristocratic whigs who approved the *entente* with France nor by radicals who approved the restoration of peaceful relations with the USA. When he returned to the Foreign Office in 1846, he seemed to politicians of all parties (including his own), by the provocation of his acts and the brusqueness of his language, to be adding to the tensions of a Europe soon to be shaken by the revolutions of 1848.

The Don Pacifico incident of 1850 was important not for the dubious figure of the Portuguese Jew whose exorbitant claims against the Greek government the royal navy had been instructed to uphold, but for the general issue of Palmerston's diplomatic methods. The debate was staged by the government as a demonstration of House of Commons' confidence in reply to the vote of censure carried by Aberdeen and Stanley in the House of Lords. The result was a rare but resounding victory for the ministry, partly because its existence was seen to be at stake, partly because the radical MPs as well as more orthodox government supporters rallied round the Palmerstonian banner of patriotic opposition to the European autocracies. It was not merely that Palmerston's attitude was in accord with the instinctive reactions of a large part of his fellow countrymen. What was equally compelling was the grand, confident style in which he proclaimed his sentiments. For the rank and file of the party it was exhilarating to have a man who could display such powers of popular leadership and win such a great parliamentary triumph. It was not an experience which often came their way with Lord John Russell. The celebration dinner (at which no other cabinet minister was present) given to Palmerston by 250 members of the Reform Club was a significant event both in Palmerston's career and in the history of the mid-Victorian Liberal party.

For Russell, on the other hand, the episode had been a personal disaster. For a long time the prime minister had been dissatisfied with Palmerston's handling of foreign affairs without knowing either how to control him or how to satisfy the bitter complaints of the court. Prince Albert with his continental background had greatly reinforced the traditional interest of the crown in foreign affairs; and both he and Victoria had as much cause to complain of Palmerston's offhand treatment as the cabinet. Between the royal couple at Windsor and the foreign secretary in Downing Street Lord John had been in an unhappy situation. By the start of 1850 he was already discussing with the Queen the replacement of Palmerston at the Foreign Office by himself. The Don Pacifico debate, however, made it impossible to remove his dashing and undisciplined colleague from the department he had made so peculiarly his own. It had been a triumph not so much for the government collectively as for Palmerston personally. With his great 'civis Romanus sum' speech (the only outstanding piece of oratory in his whole career), he had emerged as a popular national figure indispensable to any future Liberal administration.

This recently acquired reputation was reinforced by more durable assets. Palmerston was a tough, resilient, self-confident man who exploited the press more assiduously and skilfully than any other contemporary politician and was backed by a clever and ambitious wife. In domestic matters it did him no harm that he was essentially conservative. He had been one of the least enthusiastic reformers in Lord Grey's cabinet and had disapproved of Russell's conversion to the repeal of the corn laws in 1845. But foreign affairs absorbed his main energies. Up to 1841 he took little interest in what was being done in other departments of the government and resented any interference with his own. After June 1850, however, he realized that if he could retain the approval of the liberal English middle classes he could afford to ignore the criticisms of the aristocratic leaders of the party with which he had thrown in his lot. The support of the liberal backbenchers and the newspaper-reading public was a firmer foundation for parliamentary power than the fading family connections of grand whiggery. Palmerston was not by nature an excessively ambitious man, otherwise he would scarcely have spent nineteen years in the minor office of secretary at war between 1809 and 1828. But he liked power, he needed his salary, he enjoyed office. He knew he was a better man than Russell and after 1850 he was moving into a position of advantage, even if he was not yet acceptable as leader of the party.

If anything was wanted to assist Palmerston's rise to power it was the course of self-destruction on which Russell embarked within a few months of Peel's death. In November 1850 he wrote his notorious *Durham Letter* condemning a recent papal brief establishing a Roman hierarchy with territorial titles on British soil for the first time since the Reformation. Russell's extravagant phraseology ('mummeries of superstition' being only one example) was inspired more perhaps by fear of the Tractarians within the church than by papal encroachments from without. Coming four weeks after the papal brief and the pastoral letter of Wiseman, the newly appointed archbishop of Westminster, the *Durham Letter* was hardly the product of impulse; nor had the government been without some diplomatic warning of the Pope's intentions. The suspicion must remain that there was a measure of calculation in the *Letter* and that it was an attempt to exploit the Protestant excitement engendered by this act of 'Papal aggression'. The word 'mummery' had already been used in a *Times* leader on the subject. Calculated or not, the *Durham Letter* alienated the Peelites and affronted the Irish Catholic MPs. The ecclesiastical titles bill, introduced to give retrospective legitimacy to the prime minister's protest, went through the Commons with large majorities. But it did not help Russell as party leader to have his division lobby momentarily swelled by Protestant protectionists from the opposite benches. What was more important was that the opponents of his measure were almost entirely men who in happier circumstances might have been supporters of the ministry—Irish nationalists, Peelites and leading radicals like Hume, Cobden, Bright and Roebuck.

As prime minister Russell still had a residuary authority, even though he was making it a wasting asset. His position would have been stronger had he been an efficient head of cabinet. In fact he had shown himself to be administratively worse than Melbourne. With disunity and lack of purpose evident at the top, confidence steadily drained from the bottom of the party. The effect was seen in the shrinking number of liberal MPs who turned up to important divisions and debates, and in the fretful temper of the prime minister himself. Early in 1851, in a largely deserted House of Commons, the government was defeated by a miserable 100 to 52 votes on a radical motion to extend the county franchise, and Russell abruptly resigned. A similar motion had been defeated in 1850 with the help of protectionists and Peelites. On this occasion they marked their increasing indifference to the fate of the ministry by abstaining. It was a trivial pretext for resignation made worse by the anticlimax which followed. Stanley, after several days' enquiry, decided that he had not the men in his party fit to form an administration. 'These,' he is recorded by Disraeli as saying impatiently to his chief whip, 'are not names I can put before the Queen.' Though Victoria and Albert favoured a coalition of Peelites and whigs, the Peelites would not join Russell as long as the ecclesiastical titles bill was pending. But for this unhappy measure the coalition of 1852 would have arrived a year earlier.

As it was the whig cabinet was obliged to resume office, weaker and more pessimistic than ever. The last screw in the coffin of the old whig party was Russell's action in removing Palmerston from the Foreign Office in December 1851. The occasion was Palmerston's approval of Louis Napoleon's *coup d'état* in France, conveyed personally to the French ambassador but concealed from the cabinet when the following day they decided to instruct the British ambassador in Paris to remain neutral. It is possible that Russell's renewed preparations for a parliamentary reform bill in the autumn contributed to Palmerston's uncompromising readiness to quit the government rather than acknowledge that he had offended in any way. In any case the administration was visibly crumbling. The defeat on the militia bill the following session on an amendment moved by the ex-foreign minister was enough to bring it to the ground.

By 1852 it seemed clear to many observers not only that Russell would never again head an administration but that the old whig party had outlived any useful function. As early as 1846 Lord Clarendon had written trenchantly that 'as a political party it is thought to be nearly effete, and as the means of governing, a matter of history rather than of fact'. In the intervening six years the last opportunity to revive and expand the party had passed away. The problem was to find an administration that could take its place. The disintegration of the liberal wing in politics left the protectionists as the only coherent if minority parliamentary group; and Stanley, now Lord Derby, showed more appetite for office than in the previous year. But his failure to recruit Palmerston left him with that obscure and inexperienced set of men who went down to history as the 'who? who?' cabinet, from the deaf old Wellington's repeated question when the list was read out to him in the House of Lords. Any hope of bringing the Peelites back into a reunited Conservative party depended on the government's readiness to abandon protection. Lord Derby thought it a point of honour to wait until a general election decided the issue. Disraeli, as chancellor of the exchequer, showed himself less sensitive. His free-trade and income tax budget statement (Disraeli's 'eulogy on Peel') ensured that the party fought the general election of that year in a state of intellectual and moral confusion. It failed to get a majority despite a desperate and somewhat disreputable use of government influence in the dockyard constituencies which did nothing to enhance its reputation.

Nevertheless, the protectionists for the first time gained ground in the constituencies while both whigs and Peelites (though the latter term was ceasing to have much precise meaning) suffered severe losses. In the face of common danger the two opposition groups during the autumn moved closer towards that alliance which Russell's No-Popery bill had rendered impossible the previous session. In December Gladstone tore Disraeli's budget to pieces and the House of Commons by a majority of nineteen declared against the government. Protectionism as a practicable policy was finished and the manner of its demise showed the blindness of the course into which the party had been led in 1846. To retain the principle of protection meant that they were unlikely in any foreseeable future to get power or attract men of ability; to abandon it meant a certain loss of identity and self-respect. It was an intolerable dilemma for any political party; yet it was another fifteen years before it could be resolved.

Both old whiggery and 'country party' conservatism were in fact anachronisms, as not only Peel and Russell but, in their different ways, both Liverpool and Canning had long ago realized. The aristocratic governing classes had to come to terms with British society as it existed; they could not survive on nostalgia for their own past. In the circumstances of 1852 this could only mean one thing: a union of Peelites and whigs, including Palmerston. Although his 'tit for tat with Johnny Russell' over the militia bill had encouraged speculation that he would join the protectionists, it is doubtful whether even this would have saved the Derby ministry. In any case Palmerston was too realistic and, despite his sixty-eight years, too careful of his own future to desert the party in which he had served for more than two decades. Russell was now out of his way, even if he himself was not yet able to step into the vacancy. The Queen sent for Aberdeen and Lansdowne, the elder statesmen of the two parties. Gouty, seventy-two-year-old Lord Lansdowne was ill and in any case was disinclined to take office. Aberdeen, only a month away from his sixty-ninth birthday, went alone. He returned with a commission to form a government. Since neither Palmerston nor the Peelites would serve under either Russell or Derby, it was in fact the only solution. The party alignments which had dominated politics since 1828 were no longer capable of fulfilling their primary function of providing an administration. The central government of liberal–conservatives and conservative–liberals, for which many hoped after 1846, had materialized at last, though without the commanding figure of Peel and under the man who was temperamentally one of the least forceful of Peel's senior colleagues.

'England does not love coalitions,' said Disraeli dismissively when about to be defeated by one in the Commons in December 1852. It would have been truer perhaps to say that politicians do not love coalitions, as Disraeli himself had discovered when hunting desperately for alliances with Peelites, radicals and whigs in the preceding half-dozen years. There are too few posts for all the claimants; too many compromises on policy; too many old animosities to be smoothed over. Compared with their numbers in the Commons the Peelites in the Aberdeen coalition, like the Canningites in 1830, obtained a disproportionately large share of higher offices. As finally settled the cabinet consisted of six Peelites, six whigs and one radical. But the forty or more Peelite MPs, only about half of whom were survivors of 1846, held the balance of power and their leaders brought a much needed addition of prestige and talent which was not susceptible of arithmetic calculation. There was, however, a deeper reason why Aberdeen stood firm against the protests of Lord John Russell that the complexion of the ministry was 'too Peelite'. At the start he took the view that his administration should be not a simple whig–Peelite coalition but a 'liberal Conservative Government, in the sense of that of Sir Robert Peel'. The whigs he invited into the cabinet, as Russell and his wife were jealously quick to note, included no strong adherent of Lord John and several (such as Lansdowne, Palmerston, and Charles Wood) who were his critics. What Aberdeen clearly hoped was that such an administration, by reason of its moderate Peelite character, would attract support from the loose fringe of conservative MPs who were neither committed protectionists nor confessed followers of Peel. In the event a further three dozen conservatives did in fact frequently vote with the government during the lifetime of the coalition.[1]

There were therefore important differences in the way in which the coalition was viewed by Aberdeen and Russell. Aberdeen set out to construct an integrated government from the materials available to him. It was a perfectly correct constitutional attitude, though lacking a certain political realism. To Russell the coalition between himself and the prime minister was an alliance of equals—

[1] See J. B. Conacher, *The Aberdeen Coalition* (Cambridge, 1968), p. 6, n. 2.

a view which would have been more tenable had he not been partially repudiated by his own followers and already had in Palmerston a serious rival for the leadership of the whig–liberal party. Though Palmerston's acceptance of office counted as a success for the coalition, if only because it denied him to the opposition, his presence in the cabinet was a calculated risk. He thought little of Russell and ostentatiously demonstrated his independence of his former leader. At the same time he despised Lord Aberdeen and was convinced he could manage foreign policy, and probably the cabinet too, better than the prime minister. It was these latent discordances, rather than any refusal of Peelites and whigs to work together, that was the fatal flaw in the Aberdeen coalition. In fact, though the cabinet was frequently divided on policy, the divisions were not on party lines. The difficulties were essentially personal rather than political. What destroyed the coalition's chances of settling down as a workable team was the triangle of incompatible personalities represented by Aberdeen, Russell and Palmerston—the present, past and future prime ministers.

The situation, difficult enough, was further complicated by Aberdeen's assurance to Russell, during the negotiations which preceded his entrance into the ministry, that when the time was ripe, he would retire and Russell would succeed him. Ripeness of time in this context could be interpreted in many ways. It would clearly involve the consent of the Queen and also perhaps of the rest of the cabinet as well as a suitable occasion for the change. The initial vagueness was made worse by Russell's erratic behaviour. In addition to the leadership of the Commons he also took the Foreign Office, since recent events had disqualified Palmerston for that post. But he did so only on a temporary basis, with the proclaimed intention of giving it up not so much if but when the work became too great for him. Within a few months in fact he made way for Clarendon and by the end of the session he felt that the time had come for him to succeed to the premiership. For Aberdeen, despite his personal readiness to give way to his impatient whig colleague, it was less obvious that the fitting moment had arrived. Gladstone was strongly opposed to such a step; the Queen and Albert decidedly reluctant to sanction it. The deterioration in the Middle East situation provided everybody who needed it with a cogent argument against a change of leadership at that stage.

Russell's resentment at this delay in fulfilling the bargain underlay most of his subsequent actions as member of the Aberdeen cabinet. Partly to find work for him to do, partly because of genuine Peelite sympathy with his ideas, Aberdeen agreed to allow a cabinet committee to consider plans for parliamentary reform. This in turn provoked Palmerston whose behaviour became as vague and exasperating as that of Russell. In December 1853 he resigned, ostensibly on the issue of reform, but skilfully contriving to mix up his domestic anti-reform views with his attitude on the Eastern Question. It is more than possible that he overreached himself and never intended to do more than frighten the cabinet into an abandonment of the reform issue. The press, however, (except for *The Times* which was probably being fed with inside information by the Foreign Office) chose to interpret his resignation as a dismissal and connected it with the Middle East crisis and the alleged pro-Russian sympathies of the court. The younger Peelites, fearful of a hostile demonstration in the Commons, and unwilling to leave Russell without a counter-poise in the cabinet, persuaded Aberdeen to take Palmerston back. It was not a very happy calculation of events and personalities. With the increasing certainty of war, Russell's reform bill was soon relegated to the limbo of postponed policies; and his restless urge to assert himself inevitably found an outlet in foreign affairs, where he generally aligned himself with Palmerston against Aberdeen. Palmerston, in fact, who on any rational calculation should have been discredited by the resignation episode, found his position in the cabinet strengthened and his standing with the public immeasurably raised. As Macaulay commented in 1849, 'what a knack he has for falling on his feet'.

II

In March 1854 the war with Russia towards which the cabinet had been drifting since the summer of 1853 became a reality.[2] Few conflicts between Britain and a major power have been entered into with such indecision. It is arguable that had either Aberdeen or Palmerston been in sole charge of British diplomacy during the previous fifteen months, war would have been averted. Aberdeen would have been successful because of his patience, his conciliatory methods, his sincere desire for peace, and his friendly relations with the Tsar Nicholas. More doubtfully it could also be contended that Palmerston would have achieved the same result by a different road. His mere presence at the Foreign Office would have acted as a warning beacon to Russia; his audacity and resource would have enabled him to secure a diplomatic victory without resort to force.

---

[2] The diplomatic events leading up to the Crimean War are dealt with in chapter 10.

As it was, there were too many ministers anxious to take a hand.

Indeed there were altogether too many ex-foreign secretaries in the cabinet for comfort. Lord Clarendon arrived at the Foreign Office in February 1853 to find the Middle East crisis already taking shape, and himself surrounded by senior colleagues who had once sat at his desk and still thought they had residuary rights to it. Aberdeen's long experience under Wellington and Peel was given further weight by the traditional prime minister's right to supervise foreign policy. Russell, leader of the House of Commons and spokesman for the government on foreign affairs in the lower house, regarded himself as having a peculiar right to be consulted. Palmerston treated his successor in a friendly avuncular fashion but was not prevented by his duties at the Home Office from taking a proprietorial attitude towards the ramshackle building in Downing Street which he had dominated so long and quitted so recently. The virtual assumption by the two whig ministers of co-equal authority with the foreign secretary had a further disastrous effect. When the advice of Russell and Palmerston was not followed, both of them (but particularly Russell) could feel in a sense free to disown responsibility for what ensued.

Not surprisingly British diplomacy in 1853–4 bore the hallmarks of a committee product: compromise, delay, short-term views, half-hearted action. The pacific measures of Aberdeen were stiffened by Palmerston and Russell to the point where they lost their conciliatory character. The more incisive proposals of Palmerston were watered down by his more nervous colleagues so as to destroy their intimi-datory effect. It was not a division between a war and peace party, but a fundamental disagreement on the best way to save peace and avoid war. But Aberdeen's characteristic desire to keep his cabinet united merely meant that the policy actually followed (more accurately, the series of cabinet reactions to events in the Middle East) had no merit except that of being a mean between rival views. Everyone had their say and nobody had their way.

As time went on the cabinet as a whole seemed paralysed by a sense of their inability to control events. It was symptomatic how often they used the ominous word 'drift'. 'We are drifting fast towards war,' wrote Aberdeen in June 1853; and again in July, 'we are drifting hopelessly towards war.' 'Everything seems drifting towards war,' Clarendon told his wife in September. The duke of Argyll spoke in October of a 'drift of circumstances'. Clarendon even told the House of Lords in February 1854 that 'we are drifting towards war'. It was a confession of weakness that was intensified by the pressure of public opinion without. In the sharp words which Argyll, the youngest member of the cabinet, addressed to his colleagues in

October 1854 after hostilities had commenced, ministers were 'afraid of public opinion, because we do not try to lead and guide it'. The war party in fact existed in the press and public, not in the government. Stirred by the Russian invasion of the principalities of Moldavia and Wallachia in July 1853, British feeling was raised in November to a pitch of hysteria by the so-called 'massacre' of Sinope, a one-sided Russian victory over the Turkish fleet after the two powers had finally gone to war. All through 1853 the bulk of the national press, including proletarian newspapers like *Reynold's Weekly News*, had been following an increasingly violent anti-Russian and pro-Palmerston line. Even *The Times* and the *Morning Chronicle*, which had been pacific, anti-Turk, and sympathetic to Aberdeen, slowly succumbed during the year to the overwhelming popular current.

Though Palmerston did not discourage, there was little need for him to foment a bellicose feeling so widespread and spontaneous. While his main press connection was with the *Morning Post*, the conservative and much of the radical press applauded every apparently anti-Russian move and jingoistic speech. The temporary resignation of Palmerston, known to the public in the middle of December, showed the national mood at its silliest and most excited. Prince Albert, who as the presumed tool of the European autocracies had been blamed for Palmerston's dismissal in 1851, was now held responsible for his resignation in 1853. There were reports that the Prince had been arrested on a charge of high treason and a crowd actually gathered to see him being taken to the Tower of London. 'Better that a few drops of guilty blood should be shed on a scaffold on Tower Hill,' wrote one radical newspaper hysterically, 'than that the country should be baulked of its desire for war.' While the most unscrupulous attacks were launched by the radical *Daily News* and *Morning Advertiser*, the Conservative press, notably the *Morning Herald* and *Standard*, carried on the campaign with criticisms of the Prince's alleged unconstitutional interference in politics. When the opening of parliament took place at the end of January 1854, though the crowd applauded the Queen, they kept their loudest cheers for the unlikely figure of the Turkish ambassador.

War, in fact, was something on which the British public had set its heart and the fault of the Prince was that he momentarily appeared as an obstacle between the people and its desire. 'Never in the history of this country,' declared that popular family paper, the *Illustrated London News* on 31 December 1853, anticipating the actual event by three months, 'was a war undertaken under more inspiriting auspices, and with so little opposition or demur from any portion of the people.' In April 1854 in Manchester, only a dozen years after the Grenadier Guards had marched through the town with fixed bayonets and ball cartridges to overawe the 'Plug Plot' rioters, a cheering crowd lined the streets to watch the Royal Fusiliers entrain for Southampton. 'One could have walked over the heads of the people, who were wrought up to such a pitch of excitement as almost amounted to madness,' recorded Sergeant Major Gowing, who despite being the son of a Baptist minister had patriotically enlisted in the ranks of that regiment only three months' earlier.[3] The month before, when a battalion of the Guards left London for the front, the crowd had bought up all the oranges from the stalls along their line of march to give to them as they went by.

The mood of bellicose enthusiasm in 1854 has no simple explanation. Forty years of European peace since Waterloo, the growth in material prosperity, the decline of internal social conflicts, and an easily provoked national pride, all helped to create the psychological background for a popular war. Equally important was the immaturity of public opinion on matters of foreign policy, the most remote and specialized aspect of the old system of aristocratic government. Traditionally it had been the preserve of a few initiates and shielded to a large extent from the pressures of parliamentary politics. Public attention was directed more towards occasional crises and dramatic episodes than to any general understanding of the principles on which the conduct of British foreign policy was based. The growth of a popular press, often conducted by singularly violent or irresponsible editors, and the complacent assumption that 'public opinion' had a kind of overriding wisdom and authority of its own, had resulted in an increasing stridency of expression without a corresponding growth in intelligent understanding. The public excitement at the time of the Tahiti incident in 1844, the Don Pacifico affair in 1850 when the votes and popularity were with Palmerston, the reason and argument with his critics, had been warning signs of a growing danger to British diplomacy.

For contemporary Victorians the Middle East crisis offered an array of evocative issues. The old radical dislike of the European autocracies made it easy for some sections of the public to regard the war with Russia as the climax of a long struggle in Europe between liberalism and nationalism on the one side, despotism and imperialism on the other. In its crudest personified form the conflict could be presented in terms of the 'Russian Bear' against the 'Sick Man of Europe'. The equally sentimental enthusiasm of the 1820s for the struggle of Christian Greeks against their brutal Moslem overlords seemed to have been conveniently erased from public memory. On the wilder shores of evangelical Christianity the growing cult

---

[3] T. Gowing, *A Soldier's Experiences* (Nottingham, 1889), p. 11.

of millenarianism made it tempting for its votaries (which included Lord Shaftesbury) to see in the great Middle East upheaval that pouring out of the 'last vial' of the Apocalypse and long-awaited return of the Jews to their native Palestine, which was to herald the approaching end of the world. For more sober-minded Christians the war presented itself not only in the 'Right against Wrong' formula of the *Punch* cartoon of April 1854 but as a mobilization of national will, energy and self-abnegation that would overcome material ambitions and social differences. At a meeting in Birmingham to support the 'Patriotic Fund', Dr Miller, the anglican rector of St Martin's and R. W. Dale, the young Congregational minister of Carr's Lane, both spoke from the same platform in a demonstration of Protestant unity. Dale used the occasion to point out how war could bring together different parties and churches, and demonstrate that the country was prepared to sacrifice the blessing of peace for the sake of mercy, justice and truth. Even that quiet and saintly anglican theologian F. D. Maurice could write to his friend Charles Kingsley in July 1854: 'I do hope something from the war in spite of all the feebleness with which it is prosecuted and with which we feel about it; but chiefly as a sign of what God is doing. It is more like a commencement of a battle between God in His absoluteness and the Csar in his than 1848 was.'

Given this fervent, moralistic attitude to the war, it is not surprising that most assumptions about its duration and intensity were wildly unrealistic. Some, looking back to the precedent of the Napoleonic Wars, thought that the struggle against the even larger Russian empire would inevitably last for many years. Others believed that the alliance of Britain and France, together with the superior technical efficiency of the west, would bring about a rapid overthrow of the backward Muscovite state. But there was general agreement among the educated public on one thing: that the war would be a 'great war' and its outcome likely to shape the future of Europe for the next generation. It was a war, observed the *Annual Register*, 'which may change, ere it closes, the destinies of the civilized world'. This exalted view of the Russian war, together with the months of mounting anticipation, explains much of the public reaction when the military news from the Middle East began to tear away the web of optimism, sentimentality and ignorance created by press and public opinion.

After the departure in the spring of the troops for the Black Sea and the fleet for the Baltic, little seemed to happen until the landing in the Crimea and the battle of Alma in September. This was followed by the bloodier battle of Inkerman in November and the protracted siege of Sebastopol which went on until September of the following

year. By the start of 1855 the early mood of patriotic unity had
turned to one of unpatriotic attacks on the government and the
army command. *The Times*, then perhaps at the height of its influence
with the educated public, from December 1854 took the lead in a
violent campaign against Lord Raglan in the Crimea and the general
war administration at home. But the greater part of the British press
joined in the wave of recrimination; and the contemporary adulation
of 'public opinion' made it impossible to check its excesses even in
matters of military security.

The uncensored frontline despatches of the journalists in the
Crimea, particularly those of *The Times*' correspondent W. H. Russell,
brought home to the Victorian civilian public in a sensational
manner the realities of war. The unfortunate Raglan was the first
and last British general in the field to exercise his command under
the scrutiny of a group of uncontrolled, ignorant, and sometimes
vindictive unofficial eye-witnesses. The inevitable consequence was
the spread of alarm and anger at home, and the provision of valuable
intelligence to the enemy abroad. The press, however, was not the
only culprit. The flow of complaining letters from disgruntled
officers at the front in the early months (something from which
Wellington had suffered at the start of the Peninsular campaign)
affected a large and influential section of society. By the time parliament reassembled in January 1855 the British public was demanding
a scapegoat and the House of Commons, weak and demoralized,
was in no state to resist.

The first and least surprising defection was that of Lord John
Russell. By December 1854 he was putting the whole blame for the
conduct of the war on Aberdeen and declaring that he would resign
after Christmas. It was the fifth or sixth time since the start of the
coalition that he had raised the question of his retirement; but this
time he put his threat into execution. When the Commons met on
23 January, Roebuck gave notice of a motion for a committee of
enquiry into the conduct of the war. The same day Russell sent in
a formal letter of resignation and, in view of the defeatist attitude
of some of the other whig members, the cabinet decided to retire
from office. The Queen, showing more toughness than any of her
ministers, refused to accept their resignations and wrote a stinging
rebuke to Russell. But this only delayed the inevitable. On 29 January
Roebuck's motion was carried by an overwhelming vote of 305 to
148. It was the end of the Aberdeen coalition but not, as Palmerston
warned the Commons, of coalition government. Once more the old
political minuet was performed. The Queen sent first for Derby who
abandoned his commission when he found that neither a hesitant
Palmerston nor any of the leading Peelites would join him. She then,

on Lansdowne's advice, went through what Prince Albert dis-
paragingly called the 'ceremony' of asking Russell to form an
administration as a means of opening his eyes to the realities of his
position. As had been calculated, he promptly discovered that no
politician of standing (except the cynical Palmerston) would agree
to serve under him. Finally the slightly shop-soiled commission was
placed in the hands of Palmerston who succeeded with some difficulty
in reassembling the old government with the omissions of Aberdeen
the discredited prime minister, Newcastle the discredited secretary
for war, and Russell who was discredited on all counts.

In promoting Palmerston's elevation to the premiership Victoria
and Albert showed considerable magnanimity. But they shared the
view of the public that of all the coalition ministers Palmerston with
his characteristic energy and resource was best fitted for the leadership of the war effort; and they hoped that the continued alliance
with the Peelites would provide him with both a safe majority and
such restraining influences as might be needed in addition to the
sobering responsibilities of supreme office. In the event Palmerston,
since he could not prevent, decided to accept the appointment of
the Roebuck committee; Graham and Gladstone then resigned,
taking with them Herbert and Cardwell. Their objections on constitutional grounds to such an enquiry at such a time were not without
substance. But it would have been better to have acquiesced, like
the thicker-skinned Palmerston, in something that could not be
prevented and in the end turned out to be of little political or even
military significance. What was perhaps of equal importance in
deciding their action was that Gladstone and Graham in the first
place had only reluctantly joined Palmerston under pressure from
Aberdeen and Herbert. They were possibly not sorry to have a
colourable excuse for backing out. As Victoria wrote tartly to her
uncle, 'the good people here are really a little *mad*.' Russell, sent
to Vienna on a diplomatic mission to prevent any mischief-making
at home, then accepted cabinet office. But as soon as he was back
the revelation of his apparent readiness to accept soft peace terms
raised a parliamentary storm which ended in a second resignation.
Diplomacy apart, the shabby role he had played in the fall of the
Aberdeen coalition marked him out as the most appropriate Jonah
to cast into the angry political waters.

Palmerston himself had been lucky, as he had been on several
occasions before in his long career. By the time he became prime
minister the worst was over. The efforts of the Aberdeen ministers
at home and of the military authorities in the Crimea were beginning
to bear fruit and Palmerston's contribution to victory was only
marginal. But to the British public, despite his seventy-one years,

he conveyed an impression of activity and resolution; and appearances were important. The Palmerstonian myth was less powerful
in the Commons where the prime minister continued to face difficulties and criticisms from both the official opposition and the 'peace
party' of Manchester radicals and Peelite ex-ministers. Though the
news from the front was occasionally disappointing, however, it was
soon clear that the war was being won. The British public indeed
would have liked the war to have gone on longer, the victory made
more emphatic, the peace terms more stringent. The first news
of peace negotiations was met with disappointed criticism in the press.
When in the spring of 1856 the war finally ended, the usual
celebrations were held not so much because there was any real
satisfaction at the close of hostilities but because it was a traditional
occasion for public entertainment. The Crimean War, after only two
short years, ended as it had begun, on a note of anticlimax. In its
annual review at the close of 1856 *The Times* commented curiously
that 'one thing we have certainly all but forgotten, as if it had never
been, and that is the war which was still convulsing and draining
all Europe at the beginning of this year'.

While it lasted, however, particularly in the first six months of
1855, it had uncovered some peculiar aspects of mid-Victorian
society. The extraordinary constitutional crisis of February 1855,
when politician after politician refused to assist in forming a government and the Queen observed ironically to Clarendon that she
seemed the only person in politics who could not resign, offered
an exhibition of factious, selfish and jealous personalities at their
worst. 'I am ashamed of the figure which the first men in England
have made during the last month,' wrote Sir Charles Wood
indignantly after the resignation of the Peelites. Men whose memories
went back to the period before the Reform Act were convinced that
the war had demonstrated the inaptitude of parliamentary methods
for the conduct of a great state. But it was not only individuals but
the system that was questioned. The military deficiencies exposed
during the first Crimean winter lowered British prestige abroad and
provoked bitter recrimination at home. Some thought there was too
much democracy in government, some too little. Some blamed party
politics, some the weakness of coalitions, some the decay of local self-
government and the rise of 'centralization', bureaucracy and the 'red
tape' mentality. What was undeniable was that in place of the
balanced patriotic society which many had imagined at the start
of the crisis had come tension, uncertainty and frustration.

Perhaps the most significant circumstance was that for a large part
of the press, and the middle-class public whose moods it expressed,
the war had cast serious doubts on the continuing ability of the

aristocratic system of government to serve the complex, advanced society which had come into existence since 1815. The attacks on aristocratic rule launched in the Commons by A. H. Layard, the radical ex-archaeologist and diplomat, and the Administrative Reform Association which enjoyed a meteoric career in the summer of 1855, reflected a wider unease in British society. It was a characteristic conviction of the public that what governmental institutions lacked were precisely the qualities of business efficiency and technical skill which had given Britain its commanding place in the world. At the end of 1854 *The Times* had argued that 'the first duty of the nation is ... to bring the efficiency of its military departments up to a level with the management of private enterprises'; and once started, criticisms were not confined to the service departments.

The most alarming feature for the governing classes, however, was that middle-class resentment against aristocratic rule was so close to the surface of society that it only required the initial frustrations of war to bring it into the open. Greville in February 1855 confessed that for the first time in his life he was seriously alarmed at the state of public affairs. 'The press, with *The Times* at its head, is striving to throw everything into confusion, and running amuck against the aristocratic elements of society and of the Constitution.' To such men the Crimean War was a sharp reminder that aristocratic rule existed, if not on sufferance, at least on conditions. What was less obvious, in the medley of discordant criticisms, was that there was no obvious alternative to the aristocratic system. It had been a crisis of confidence, not a movement of revolution; and the crisis soon passed.

III

The parliamentary history of the post-Crimean period was a mirror-image of the previous decade. The years from 1846 to 1855 had seen Russell's long whig ministry followed by two short-lived administrations under Derby and Aberdeen. What happened between 1855 and 1865 was the reverse of this pattern: two short ministries under Palmerston and Derby followed by a long one under Palmerston. This pattern was not accidental. Throughout the whole nineteen years the permanent parliamentary majority was made up of liberals of various shades from whigs and Peelites to extreme radicals. What prevented that majority from sustaining an unbroken series of liberal administrations were two separate sources of weakness. One was the political incapacity of Lord John Russell in the face of the growing challenge of Palmerston. The other was the erratic behaviour of the Peelites who, as somebody unkindly observed, seemed perpetually offering themselves for sale and then buying themselves in again. Both problems were most acute between 1850 and 1859 when there were five different administrations and three general elections within eight years. As long as these two sources of liberal disunion existed, there were periodic breaks in the continuity of liberal administration. When these breaks occurred, the conservative opposition came in as understudies to hold the stage before an indifferent audience while the regular cast conferred angrily behind the scenes. The solidity of Palmerston's second ministry between 1859 and 1865 simply reflected the circumstance that a solution had at last been found for both the Russell and the Peelite problem.

In the immediate post-war years Palmerston's position looked superficially strong. He had the prestige of victory, even if the abrupt end to the fighting after the fall of Sebastopol came as something of a disappointment. The wars with China (1856–8) and the Indian Mutiny (1857–8) seemed continuing reasons against a change of government. Nevertheless he was faced in the Commons with the hostility of Russell, most of the leading Peelites, and the Cobden-Bright radicals, as well as of the official conservative opposition. It was this combination which inflicted a technical defeat on him over the lorcha *Arrow* incident which had provoked the hostilities with China. Palmerston's prompt appeal to the country in the general election of 1857 was rewarded with a majority of about eighty-five over all his opponents, which was reckoned to be the largest since the reform majority of 1833. It was far from being a disciplined majority, however, and it was soon clear that the election had done nothing to end the basic instability of the Commons. Over the next few years the votes which decided the fate of administrations and the dissolution of parliaments were rarely shaped by the nominal issues at stake. Majorities in divisions were composed to a large extent of men to whom the matter in dispute was less important than the result. Factious votes were justified by disingenuous arguments in support of dishonest resolutions. What lay behind this occasionally unedifying spectacle, however, were certain important realities; and until these were recognized, no stable government was possible.

In the forefront was the antagonism between the two 'dowager prime ministers', neither of whom could easily be brought to yield precedence to the other. Russell was not without some advantages over his older rival. He was still the hereditary chieftain of the whig clan; on many aspects of liberal policy he had the support of the Peelites; and he was capable of redeeming by a dashing parliamentary performance his recurrent errors of tact and judgement. In the eyes of many observers, however, he had forfeited his claims to the leadership of the party by his foolish and petulant actions between 1850 and 1855. Among the observers were Victoria and Albert. The disintegration of the party system had inevitably led to an increase in the influence of the crown on domestic politics. Albert's intelligence and assiduity made the monarchy a formidable critic of cabinet policy; and though he never pushed the authority of the crown beyond the constitutional limits of the time, he and Victoria were more than ready to play their part. In view of the courage, commonsense and patriotism of the royal couple, it might have been better for the country had that part been larger. Though they disliked Palmerston's provocative handling of foreign affairs, they came to recognize his resolution, honesty and political judgement. Russell, on the other hand, who had been their ally against Palmerston in the 1840s, had been relegated to second place under Aberdeen and forfeited his last claim to royal respect by his part in destroying the Aberdeen coalition in 1855. In their turn the Peelites, by deserting Palmerston at the outset of his ministry and joining the peace party, had done much to quench the royal partiality which had been transferred to them after Peel's death.

All this strengthened Palmerston's standing at court and with the bestowal of the Garter in April 1856, the old soreness between the prime minister and the monarchy seemed to be healing over. Nevertheless, Palmerston's jaunty inactivity at the start of the Indian Mutiny annoyed the Queen and Albert; and the pessimistic utterances of the foreign secretary Lord Clarendon, in whom they had greater confidence, increased their fears and displeasure. The installation of the second Derby ministry, following Palmerston's defeat over the Orsini conspiracy bill in 1858, was therefore less disagreeable than it might have been, particularly since protectionism had now been quietly abandoned. When the following session the conservative reform bill was defeated, they encouraged Derby to try a dissolution rather than resign. The result of the general election, however, made the formation of yet another administration inevitable. Already in 1857 the Queen had sounded Clarendon on the possibility of his becoming prime minister should Palmerston's health or age make it expedient to replace him. Clarendon wisely discouraged that notion and urged instead the claims of Russell.

When Derby resigned in June 1859, however, the royal couple sent for Lord Granville. It was the first serious mistake the monarchy had made since Victoria's marriage. Like Clarendon, 'Pussy' Granville was a pleasant, slightly vain man with some experience of office and unimpeachable whig aristocratic connec-

tions. It was clear that his only chance of success lay in persuading
Russell and Palmerston, both old enough to be his father, to join
his ministry. But while the two whig leaders were prepared to serve
under each other, neither would agree to be third in a triumvirate
headed by Lord Granville. In the end therefore the Queen had to
choose between the two dowagers. It was an eventful decision. In
sending for Palmerston she ended the struggle for the leadership
which had for so long weakened the Liberal party.

What made possible the reconciliation between Russell and
Palmerston was the chastening experience of being in divided
opposition from the spring of 1858 to the summer of 1859. In the
previous session, with neither Russell nor the Peelites anxious for
the return of Palmerston, and many liberal MPs disinclined to face
the expense of another election, the paralysis of the liberals was
obvious to all. In the absence of any great issue—and after 1852
great issues were conspicuous by their absence—what was needed
was some deliberate pledge of union similar to the Lichfield House
compact which had preceded Peel's defeat in 1835. The great liberal
meeting in Willis's Rooms on 6 June 1859, which united whigs,
moderate liberals, Peelites and radicals, was in its way a refounding
of the Victorian Liberal party. An influential part in preparing for
the meeting had been taken by Sidney Herbert, the most level-
headed and loyal of the Peelites; and the Peelites in general contributed to the consolidation of the Liberal party to an extent that was
out of all proportion to their voting strength. By 1857 the body
of Peelites in the Commons were so wasted in numbers and so
divergent in their votes that no sensible political critic persisted in
talking of a Peelite 'party'. The general election of that year completed the process of attrition and forced on their leaders, now
officers without even a bodyguard, a reconsideration of their
political prospects. Their assets were their talent, experience and
prestige. Most of them wanted reunification with the liberals.
Herbert, Aberdeen and Graham believed in fact that the crucial
choice had already been made in 1852, but Gladstone equally clearly
did not. In any case their dilemma was the same as for many liberals.
While Herbert and Cardwell leaned towards Palmerston, the inclination of Aberdeen, Graham and Gladstone was towards Russell.
Yet old associations and personal friendship still held them together;
and their support was indispensable for any liberal reconstruction.
It was axiomatic that the 'broad basis', on which Russell and
Palmerston were agreed, must include the Peelites.

When Palmerston finally formed his administration in 1859, the
two senior Peelites, Aberdeen and Graham, were too old for office.
But he put three of Peel's 'young men' of the 1830s in the cabinet—

Herbert, Newcastle (formerly Lord Lincoln) and Gladstone—and appointed Cardwell Irish Secretary. The most noteworthy, and for the evolution of the Liberal party in the nineteenth century the most momentous, appointment was that of Gladstone. He had played a leading part in the destruction of the conservative ministry in 1852 and his great budget of 1853 had been regarded at the time as consolidating the position of the Aberdeen coalition. One of the few financial experts in parliament and a formidable debater, he remained, in Greville's colloquial expression, 'the great card of the pack', until the war came to push his financial policy into the background and himself ultimately from office. In the years from 1855 to 1859, however, it was far from clear where Gladstone would finally pitch his political caravan. If his free-trade views and zeal for retrenchment endeared him to the radicals, his high church convictions, his lack of enthusiasm for parliamentary reform, his Oxford University connection, and his own frequent assertions seemed to identify him with the conservatives. He had collaborated with Disraeli in attacking Palmerston's government; he had twice been offered a place in Derby's cabinet in 1858. On the second occasion both Graham and (eventually) Aberdeen[4] had counselled acceptance, on the not unreasonable grounds that since he was bound to return to the Conservative party sooner or later, he had better do so at once.

They were not alone in this belief. The same month Greville recorded his opinion that Gladstone's 'natural course is to be at the head of a Conservative Government'. Gladstone, however, refused Derby's offers, ostensibly because he could not join without his friends. This no doubt was one reason. Another was the uncomfortable circumstance that many conservative backbenchers regarded him with a distaste amounting to loathing. There was also what he described long afterwards as his 'strong sentiment of revulsion from Disraeli personally'. What he was less able to admit as a motive was the question of the leadership of the Conservative party after the retirement of the sixty-year-old Lord Derby. It was clearly, however, a matter which affected the actions of both Gladstone and Disraeli at this critical point in their careers. Disraeli was ready to surrender the lead in the Commons to either Palmerston or Graham since their active life in politics on any reasonable actuarial calculation could not last much longer. He was not prepared to be displaced by Gladstone who was five years his junior. Nevertheless, Gladstone's acceptance of the mission to Corfu the same year was taken as proof of his continued desire to cooperate with

[4] Though Aberdeen had at first agreed with Gladstone that on balance the weight of argument was against acceptance, he was later apparently convinced by Graham's letter in a contrary sense. See C. S. Parker, *Life and Letters of Sir James Graham* (2 vols, 1907) II, p. 350.

Lord Derby and in the crucial no-confidence division of June 1869 he voted on the conservative side.

Herbert believed that Gladstone, in his usual tortuous way, was secretly relieved at the result of the vote which set him free to accept Palmerston's offer of the chancellorship of the exchequer and thus join the new administration in company with his friends. Gladstone's ideal ministry—Derby as prime minister, Palmerston as a member but not in the Foreign Office, Disraeli dethroned from the leadership of the Commons—was not and probably never had been practicable politics. To hold aloof any longer would have jeopardized Gladstone's whole future; and the momentary coincidence of sympathies between himself, Russell and Palmerston over the Italian question was a convenient intellectual bridge across which to pass back into the liberal camp. It was a personal rather than an ideological choice. The Peelite programme to which Gladstone still clung—peace, sound financial policy, administrative reform, and resistance to unnecessary organic changes in the constitution—was one to which Palmerston could only be regarded at best as a 50 per cent subscriber. On the other hand, while Derby seemed sympathetic to Gladstonian and Peelite principles, the experiences of the 1858–9 administration suggested that Disraeli was prepared on any advantageous occasion to outbid the liberals for the radical vote if by so doing he could retain office.

Whether the recruitment of Gladstone in 1858 would have enabled Derby's ministry to consolidate its power is doubtful. The Conservative party was already deeply divided and Gladstone's accession would have caused even greater disunity. Electorally the return of agricultural prosperity had washed away most of the old protectionist feeling and the general election of 1857 had witnessed for the first time since 1832 a substantial whig recovery in the county constituencies. Politically many of the country gentry preferred Palmerston to Derby, and perhaps even Russell to either Disraeli or Gladstone. Some of them had disapproved of the opposition vote on the *Lorcha* incident and thought that the Conservative party had behaved in a factious manner. Derby's attempt to make an electoral pact with the Peelites in the 1857 election had completely misfired. It was rejected by Sidney Herbert and was unpopular in Derby's own party, so much so that Lord Malmesbury thought that the mere report of a coalition had done 'irreparable mischief'. In Wiltshire Sidney Herbert found that the enthusiasm for Palmerston at the election was greater among old-fashioned tory families than among professed liberals. They shared Palmerston's lack of enthusiasm for free-trade, Gladstonian finance and Russellite reform; and they liked his patriotic foreign policy.

In the House of Commons many conservative MPs had voted with the government on the Orsini conspiracy-to-murder bill in March 1858[5] and after 1859 there was a noticeable reluctance on their part to do anything that would bring about the fall of Palmerston's ministry. Many of those who faced Palmerston in the House were in spirit behind him. The party truce after 1859 was endorsed by Lord Derby and, whatever his inner feelings, Disraeli had to accept the situation. He was not head of the party and could not even control that section of it which sat in the Commons. There was still a great deal of what Greville in 1860 described as the 'hatred and distrust of Disraeli' in a large section of the Conservative party. So marked was the discontent in that year that Disraeli even offered to resign from his position. He was (perhaps without undue difficulty) prevailed upon to remain but the incident emphasized the limits of his influence. At no time between 1859 and 1865 was there much inclination among the tory backbenchers to replace Palmerston by the man who for want of a better was their official Commons leader.

IV

Clarendon called Palmerston's 1859–65 ministry 'a great bundle of sticks'. The cabinet included aristocratic whigs, Peelites, and two radicals in the persons of Milner Gibson and C. P. Villiers. Its following in the House of Commons ranged from traditional whig squires through a nondescript mass of liberal landowners, lawyers, and business men to a small rump of old and new radicals. It seemed another Aberdeen coalition but with a more radical flavour and there were many who prophesied that it could not last. Yet it held together without undue strain for six years and would have lasted longer had it not been for Palmerston's death.

One major reason for its success was the quiescence, in a political sense, of Lord John Russell. Technically Palmerston could be criticized for putting him in the Foreign Office, where his lack of judgement and habit of lecturing European governments were peculiarly unfortunate, instead of in the Home Office where his genuine reforming instincts might have provided the administration with a dash of progressive legislation. But this is to argue out of context. The Foreign Office was the price exacted by Russell for

---

[5] 112 conservatives voted with Palmerston as against 146 (including Disraeli) who voted with Peelites and liberals to evict the government. R. Stewart, *The Foundation of the Conservative Party* (1978), p. 317.

joining Palmerston and from the prime minister's point of view the arrangement had much to recommend it. To many government supporters Russell's periodic fits of reforming energy had been more alarming than inspiring. After 1859 the Foreign Office both absorbed his erratic energies and allowed Palmerston to exercise a real if tactful control over his inexperienced colleague.

Russell, whose views on foreign affairs were little more than an echo of Palmerston's, was happy in the illusion of power and activity. With both Palmerston and Gladstone overshadowing him in the House of Commons, his interest in domestic policy soon waned. His reform bill, which had been one of his conditions for resuming office, died of inanition in the summer of 1860, unmourned even by its parent. In 1861, having inherited a small Irish estate from his brother he went to the House of Lords as Earl Russell. By 1863, when he adjured liberals during a speech in Scotland to 'rest and be thankful', he seemed to have relapsed into complete Palmer-stonianism. There were of course disadvantages. Russell's defects as a foreign secretary reinforced those of Palmerston and much of the energies of the rest of the cabinet, aided by the brisk expostulations of Victoria and Albert, had to be spent in restraining the reckless-ness of what the Queen in 1864 called 'those two dreadful old men'. But though the conduct of British diplomacy suffered, their alliance at least provided the basis for the government's parliamentary stability at home.

Russell's abandonment of parliamentary reform in 1860 was a tacit recognition of the declining interest in the subject. His advocacy of reform before the war and the criticism of parliamentary government during it had left politicians with a feeling that something would have to be done. At the same time the old fears of extending the franchise beyond the limits of 1832 were lessening. The loyalty of the mass of the population at the time of the last great Chartist scare in 1848; the mood of class and national unity induced, however temporarily, by the Great Exhibition of 1851; the patriotic spirit exhibited during the Crimean War; the growing popularity of the monarchy—all these signs seemed to indicate that the class and political divisions of the previous generation were healing over. In 1858 the warm welcome received by the Queen in Birmingham suggested to the patrician but not unobservant Greville that the masses were fundamentally attached to the crown and that there might be some sense in the argument that there was less danger in giving power to the people than to the middle classes. Universal suffrage might be an inoculation against bourgeois jealousy of the aristocracy.

Against this comfortable hypothesis was the statistical fact that any large extension of the franchise to the working classes would give them a numerical majority in many constituencies and perhaps in the electorate as a whole. If the enfranchisement of the people meant the practical disfranchisement of the minority of wealthier classes, the issue became one of the political balance of power within the state. In that case the aristocracy and the middle classes would find themselves on the same side. Stanley, the son and heir of Lord Derby, expressed it crudely but honestly when he said to Bright in 1855, 'you don't want to be governed by your operatives any more than we by our labourers'. Bright was not the most suitable recipient for such blunt wisdom; but others of his class and standing were. It was easy to see that much of what passed for moderate liberalism among the monied classes in the towns was already a form of disguised conservatism. The contemporary attraction of pure democracy, which supported a despotic emperor in France and a republic in America, was not obvious to mid-Victorian society. 'Although a well considered measure for the enfranchisement of the aristocracy of the operatives would be entitled to favourable consideration,' pronounced *The Times* judiciously in 1861, 'the deliberate opinion of England revolts more and more against the political supremacy of the multitude.'

The question of parliamentary reform between 1856 and 1860 was characterized therefore by two inconsistent features. One was that both parliamentary parties appeared to believe that readiness to support a reform bill was the mark of an enlightened political outlook which would endear them to the public. The other was an instinctive preference for extending the franchise laterally rather than vertically in order to preserve the social balance. Not all politicians believed that these two features could be reconciled. The realistic Palmerston thought that franchise reform would divide both his parliamentary party and the middle-class electorate on which it depended. It was only under pressure from his cabinet that he made a tepid reference to the question in his election manifesto at Tiverton in March 1857. He was not against reform in the abstract; but he held the traditional view that the vote was a trust and that it should only be given to men of some intelligence and understanding. This definition did not exclude what was usually described as the 'superior artisans' but it placed a clear limit on the extent to which the franchise should be extended in a downward direction.

When the conservatives took office in 1858 there was general agreement among them that reform should not be left as a liberal monopoly. There were obvious difficulties in this decision for a ministry that was nominally conservative; but the bill produced in 1859 seemed a reasonably safe proposal even though it brought about the resignation of two cabinet ministers, Walpole and Henley. It showed its tory origin by retaining the borough £10 franchise, excluding the urban 40s. freeholders from the county vote, and enlarging the electorate in the rural constituencies where the social control of the landed interest might be expected to continue. It also made a gesture towards the creation of a larger, more independent electorate by proposing a number of what Bright derisively christened 'fancy franchises', for which clergy, doctors, schoolmasters, university graduates, government pensioners, fundholders and possessors of £60 in the savings bank would all qualify.

The fate of the bill, however, depended not on its merits, which were arguable, but on the extent to which it could be made to serve the ends of the parliamentary parties. In the country at large there was remarkably little feeling. *Punch* in March 1859 had a cartoon showing Disraeli, Bright and Russell, armed with great iron goads marked 'Reform', all trying to prod the somnolent British lion into showing some kind of interest. Inside parliament the Reform Bill was primarily viewed either as a device for maintaining ministers in power or as an opportunity for evicting them. The opposition amendment, deploring interference with the county franchise and demanding changes in the boroughs, was ingeniously framed to enlist the support of conservative–liberals who thought the bill went too far and radical–liberals who thought it did not go far enough. Russell was determined not to let the credit for parliamentary reform be wrested from his hands; Palmerston did not particularly dislike the bill but voted for the amendment; Gladstone was against the amendment though he did not like the bill. His eloquent but not very relevant defence of pocket boroughs in the course of the debate was not the least of the oddities of the occasion.

What was clear was that though House of Commons members might agree in principle on the need for reform, they were not going to agree on the details of any specific reform bill. While they claimed to be answering a public need, it was not obvious that they had any clear knowledge of what the public really wanted. Increasingly 'parliamentary reform' seemed a mere political shibboleth to which all parties paid lip-service but on which none (except perhaps Bright and a few radicals) had any serious convictions. Russell's antiquarian insistence on presenting his own subsequent reform bill in 1860, on the exact anniversary of his introduction of the first Reform Bill in 1831, merely emphasized the unreality of the question. Its moderate provisions, reducing the franchise in the boroughs to £6 and in the counties to £10, together with a small redistribution of seats, were met not so much with hostility as with indifference. Nobody opposed it but nobody wanted it. The whole issue had become both flat and false. It remained so for most of Palmerston's last administration.

The real division in the cabinet was not between Palmerston and Russell over the question of parliamentary reform but between Palmerston and Gladstone over the question of finance. It was a struggle not merely between parsimony and extravagance, a peace policy and a war policy, but over a fundamental feature of national development. The irony was that in that struggle Gladstone was fighting against the tendencies of the age and the seventy-six-year-old Palmerston was on the side of the future. At the centre of the debate was the income tax. After Peel's death the whole position of that great financial engine was in doubt. Sir Charles Wood had constructed his budget in 1851 on the assumption of its permanence, only to encounter the refusal of the House of Commons to extend it beyond one more year. It was renewed by Disraeli for another year the following session but when Gladstone presented his budget in 1853, the tax had already legally expired. In view of the mounting opposition it was questionable whether it could be restored. Gladstone's great feat was to disarm the critics of the income tax by demonstrating on the one hand the impracticability of immediate abolition and offering on the other a well organized scheme for its progressive reduction and final disappearance in 1860. Meanwhile, with a comfortable surplus in hand, he used £1½ millions of revenue to repeal the duties on over 120 articles of import and reduce them on over 130 in a classic free-trade operation.

The Crimean War shattered the 1853 programme. Income tax was immediately doubled to 1s. 2d. and soon raised by another two-pence to 1s. 4d., a level at which it remained until 1858. Even so, the coming of peace left the country with an increased debt and, in Gladstone's opinion, a tolerance of high spending from which it never recovered. Nevertheless, if the British public no longer clamoured for 'cheap government', it had still not rid itself of the traditional dislike of taxation. The higher rate of income tax, the 'war ninepence' as it was called, presented an immediate target and in 1857 a formidable agitation developed both in and out of parliament. In the Commons Russell, Gladstone and Disraeli, all for the moment in opposition, pressed not only for a reduction in the income tax but a return to the 1853 programme of complete abolition by 1860. Sir George Lewis's budget of 1857 produced therefore a lively discussion of fundamentals. Was expenditure to be decided by the requirements of policy, or was policy to be adjusted to the limits of permissible expenditure?

The reduction of the income tax to its pre-war level of 7d. did not entirely answer this question. Disraeli, faced as chancellor of the exchequer in 1858 with the financial consequences of both the China War and the Indian Mutiny, did his best to maintain his commitment to the policy of ending the income tax in 1860. He lowered the rate to 5*d.* even though this entailed an abandonment of the Sinking Fund contributions and left a deficit of nearly £5 millions for his successor. Gladstone in 1859 was obliged to raise the income tax again to 9*d.* with a supplementary budget later in the session to deal with the outbreak of the third China War. The following year came the first great tussle over finance between Gladstone and the prime minister. On the one hand there was Palmerston's coastal fortifications programme which was to cost £9 millions spread over three or four years; on the other the loss in revenue resulting from the chancellor of the exchequer's own liberal acts, the free-trade treaty with France negotiated by Cobden, and the abolition of the paper duty, the 'tax on knowledge' in traditional radical language. Gladstone met the problem with a characteristic blend of courage, resource and eloquence. He raised the income tax to 10*d.*, its highest ever peacetime rate, and in the fifth and final great tariff-reform budget since 1842 virtually swept away the surviving remnants of the old protective system. The total number of dutiable articles was reduced to fifty, only fifteen of which made any substantial contribution to the revenue. It was a great personal and parliamentary triumph. Faced in 1860 with the highest expenditure (nearly £73 millions) ever known in peace, he persuaded the House of Commons to accept an increase in taxation and a major tariff reconstruction that ranked in importance with his budget of 1853.

His success, however, had only been secured at the cost of strained relations within the cabinet. Gladstone had to meet the hostility not only of the prime minister but of his friend and fellow-Peelite Sidney Herbert, the secretary for war. When the Lords rejected his paper duties bill he received little sympathy or support from his leader. A constitutional crisis was only averted the following year because the upper house accepted the budget (including the postponed repeal of the paper duties) when it came up to them as a single comprehensive bill. The struggle inside the cabinet went on for another twelve months. Gladstone, though almost isolated in the cabinet, fought with his usual emotional vigour and tenacity, even to the point of threatening resignation. In the seventy-eight-year-old prime minister he met a will as tough and resourceful as his own. In the end it was a compromise; but for a time the likelihood of Gladstone's departure from the government seemed very real and very dangerous. He had a strong personal following among the more radical MPs; and a combination of Gladstone, Bright and Disraeli might have been enough to bring down the ministry. These were the years when Disraeli, unconscious of his future as an imperial statesman, coined the phrase 'bloated armaments' and denounced defence expenditure with all the moral severity of the Manchester School. His difficulty was to make his followers support that line of attack. In June 1862, for example, a parallel move by radicals and conservatives to oppose the government over expenditure collapsed ignominiously when Walpole, mover of the conservative amendment, much to Disraeli's annoyance withdrew it after Palmerston announced that he would treat it as a vote of confidence.

After 1862 the tension relaxed, though fundamental differences of outlook on finance and defence policy were always there. In January 1865 Gladstone recorded that the cabinet discussions on naval estimates were 'almost as rough as any of the roughest times'. Nevertheless, he could feel with justice that he had erected a few dykes against the rising tide of government expenditure. Naval estimates decreased after 1861, army estimates after 1863. Both were still higher than in 1853 but less than in the middle period of Palmerston's administration. Meanwhile the revenue had proved remarkably buoyant despite all the tariff cuts that had been made. The deficit of 1861 was turned into a small surplus in 1862 and a large one in 1863. The £3·7 millions of the latter year was the first real, uncommitted surplus since 1845; and this was followed by a similar balance in 1864. The tea and sugar duties were reduced; the income tax brought down to 7d. in 1863, 6d. in 1864 and 4d. in 1865, the lowest point at which it had ever been levied. To Gladstone this was a glimpse of the promised land where income tax should be no more. He still had on his conscience the pledge of 1853 to abolish the tax by 1860; and taught by his experiences under Palmerston he was coming to the conclusion that the income tax was not only fiscally objectionable but morally wrong since it made it fatally easy for governments to raise large sums of money for warlike purposes.

Palmerston, on the other hand, who had whiggishly opposed the income tax in the early forties, was now one of its ardent supporters. He was not enthusiastic about the successive reductions in the rate to a mere 4d. since he felt that this might be taken as a sign that the cabinet hoped to abolish it altogether. To Gladstone he dexterously used the Peelite argument that it was a socially equitable tax, bearing exclusively on the middle and upper classes. It is difficult to believe, however, that he saw no connection between adequate expenditure on national defence and the retention of the income tax as a permanent institution. His conviction was that if the country wanted security, as well as such social objects as education, it should be ready to pay for it.

As interpreter of the national mood Palmerston was unequalled in British politics in the last half-dozen years of his life. In 1859 *The Times* observed that no one had taken the place of Peel and Wellington in public estimation. But over the next few years, as Palmerston consolidated his ministry after the rapid changes of the previous decade, public confidence in the prime minister grew steadily. If there was no enthusiasm, at least there was a readiness to be guided by him. In the absence of great issues and clear party distinctions, it was to a particular man rather than to particular measures that the British electorate looked for assurance. 'Lord Palmerston,' wrote *The Times* approvingly at the end of 1861, 'in truth, represents the precise state of the national mind in opposing unnecessary changes without setting up resistance as a principle, and in countenancing all foreign approximations to the political theories and system of England.' But even in foreign affairs the country was content with attitudes rather than action. The Crimea had spoiled its amateur taste for war; and though the Indian Mutiny, with its horrors graphically recounted in the press, evoked a savage cry for vengeance, the outcome was no more than a deeper determination to maintain British rule in the sub-continent. For the rest, as long as British prestige was upheld, the public was ready to be a spectator of the momentous events abroad which followed the ending of the 'forty years' peace' after Waterloo. The Italian War of Napoleon III, the Polish rebellion, the American Civil War, the Prusso–Danish war of 1864 reinforced the British sense of security at having at the head of its affairs a man who could be trusted to watch over British interests in this new world of change and conflict. There was little need for excitement at home when there was so much excitement abroad.

Palmerston's popularity owed more perhaps to a happy co-incidence of circumstance and character than to a conscious affinity with the prosperous mid-Victorian society over which he presided. His appeal was not to the intellect or the morality of the English people but to their instincts. Nevertheless, he was too shrewd a politician not to cultivate his public reputation. He kept on good terms with the press; with his vivacious wife he entertained princes, ambassadors, radical journalists and Polish refugees. His evangelical appointments to bishoprics, like Bickersteth at Ripon and Villiers at Durham, were appreciated by the nonconformists and Methodists of the industrial districts. His genial preference for wealth rather than lineage in the matter of honours enabled him to gratify the manu-facturing class by elevating Edward Strutt,[6] grandson of the great

---

[6] Though the cotton mills of Messrs Strutt continued to dominate the economic life of the Derbyshire town of Belper in the middle of the century, Edward Strutt was a typical

cotton spinner Jedediah Strutt, to the House of Lords and reward philanthropic factory owners like Baxter of Dundee and Crossley of Halifax with baronetcies. Lower down the social scale he showed a natural touch in dealing with the masses as well as the classes; and it did him no harm that he was believed to have attended the great Sayers–Heenan prize fight in 1860 or that he defended the sport afterwards in the House of Commons in words that might have come straight from Cobbett. He was the first prime minister regularly to undertake a round of speaking engagements in the provinces during the summer vacation. While his natural arena was the House of Commons, he was always conscious of a larger English society, though it was not perhaps that of Shaftesbury or Bright. To the end he was a supremely professional politician and it was a measure of his success that he never appealed in vain to the British electorate.

In the Commons and in the cabinet he was faced with a more critical audience. At Westminster his main strength was that most MPs would have been reluctant to have him replaced by any of his possible rivals. But they saw him at close quarters and knew his worst as well as his best qualities: his slapdash manner, his insensitivity to the feelings of others, his unscrupulous tactics and sometimes brutal language. Palmerston was a rough fighter, not always either honest or nice in his methods. Like the sportsmen of the Regency period to which he belonged, he always played to win. He was not without principles, even genuinely liberal impulses, but they came from the heart rather than the head. Beyond all else, he was a realist in politics. His main purpose after 1859 was to keep his administration in being. To that end he tolerated strange bedfellows. He put radicals in both the upper and lower reaches of the government and even offered a cabinet post to Cobden. He also knew when to yield. As Argyll sensibly observed in 1858, 'comparing Lord John with Lord Palmerston, the latter is, in very many respects, the safer man of the two, inasmuch as he is more amenable to the opinion of his colleagues.' The buccaneer of British politics in the middle decades of the century ended his long career as the conciliatory statesman bent on keeping together the assorted 'bundle of sticks' that had been tied together in Willis's Rooms in 1859.

It would be wrong, however, to suppose that his last administration was devoid of any achievement except survival. In some areas like

third-generation product of an established industrial family. Educated at Cambridge and Lincoln's Inn, he became liberal MP for Derby (1832–47), Arundel (1851–2) and Nottingham (1852–6) and was appointed chancellor of the Duchy of Lancaster in the Aberdeen coalition. The family were also considerable landowners in the county.

education the work was preparatory rather than enacting. The two great royal commissions, the Newcastle Commission on elementary education which reported in 1861 and the Clarendon Commission on public schools which reported in 1864, were signposts for the future rather than signals for immediate parliamentary legislation. It was the same with the reform of the civil service. Under the impact of wartime criticism the Trevelyan–Northcote report of 1854 led to the preliminary establishment of the Civil Service Commission in 1855 to supervise entrance examination requirements for the civil service. But no major changes were made in the actual methods of staffing and promotion within the separate departments until after 1870. The work of the Commission between 1855 and 1870 was to strengthen the case for major reform rather than to effect any radical alterations.

In terms of useful legislation, however, this was far from being a barren period. Among its more notable achievements were the Joint Stock Companies Acts of 1855–6, facilitating the formation of limited liability companies; the consolidating Companies Act of 1862, which laid the foundation of modern company law; the Divorce Act of 1857, allowing divorce for the first time by ordinary processes of the civil courts; the reform of the poor law in 1865, which virtually ended the old restrictions on settlement; the great series of six acts consolidating and reforming criminal law in 1861; and the Bankruptcy Act of 1861 relieving private debtors. The famous Victorian banker Lord Overstone had no doubt an incomplete view of the needs of his own society; but he was clearly expressing a general sense of satisfaction with the steady 'progress of the nation' when he wrote in November 1865 that 'the Legislation of the last thirty years is the best which the world has ever seen'.[7]

Nevertheless, beneath the apparently tranquil surface of the Palmerstonian political world other currents were flowing. The revival of Miall's old Anti-State Church Society in 1853, under the less aggressive title of the Liberation Society, was followed by a sustained campaign for the removal of such remaining dissenting grievances as chapel registration, admission to universities, and above all church rates. There was assiduous lobbying of MPs and much circulation of literature at general elections, though the effect on Westminster was not easy to assess. The greatest success came in

[7] *Correspondence of Lord Overstone*, edited by D. P. O'Brien (1971) III, p. 1095. His family was a good illustration of the fluidity of British nineteenth-century society. The founder of the family fortunes was Lewis Loyd Jones who started his career as a humble Unitarian teacher and supply preacher, married a banker's daughter, turned his father-in-law's firm into one of the leading private banks of the day, and died worth £1½ millions. His son, Samuel Loyd Jones (Eton, Cambridge, MP for Hythe, a government borough, 1819–26) left a fortune of over £5 millions. The great banking expert of the period, he was created Baron Overstone in 1860.

an old, unhappy age of domestic conflict rather than to the
ʿosperous high noon of Victorian society.

It was true that Bright in many ways was looking backwards
ther than forwards. He was not primarily a democrat and certainly
ɪt a champion of working-class aspirations. He thought in moral
ɪd political, not social and economic terms. His enemy was
ivilege; democracy was only a weapon to destroy it. He had no
ɑl conception of what democracy would bring in its train;
ɑlmerston had some inkling. When Gladstone made his famous
ɪclaration in May 1864 that every man not incapacitated by
ɪrsonal unfitness or political danger was 'morally entitled to come
ɪthin the pale of the constitution', the prime minister told him it
ɑs a speech to be expected of Bright rather than from a member
the Treasury bench. Though Gladstone's language was character-
ically equivocal and he expressed surprise at the sensation he had
used, he admitted privately to Palmerston that his words consti-
ted at least a declaration that the working classes should be
franchised to some extent when the time was favourable. His
ɪdience, and the press in general, took it to mean more; and one
wspaper percipiently observed that the speech had placed Glad-
ɪne 'at the head of the party that will succeed the present
Iministration'. His Lancashire tour that autumn did nothing to
minish this growing opinion.

By 1865 Gladstone stood almost alone, ready for a new point of
parture. Nearly all his contemporaries and seniors among the
ʿelites had vanished. Aberdeen and Dalhousie had died in 1860,
ɪdney Herbert and Graham in 1861, Canning in 1862, Newcastle
1864. St Germans, after his resignation from the lord lieutenancy
Ireland in 1855 in sympathy with his fellow-Peelites, retired to
ɪ shelter of a court appointment. Only Cardwell, who succeeded
ɪwcastle at the Colonial Office, was left of the former band of
ɪelites to whom the Palmerston administration owed so much.
ʲher ties which bound Gladstone to his past were also snapping.
the Oxford University election of 1865, when for the first time
ɪ innovation of a postal vote enabled the mass of country clergy
swamp the London barristers, politicians and resident fellows who
ɪally decided the result, Gladstone was defeated by a Conservative
ɪndidate. Nominated for South Lancashire he opened his election
ɪmpaign with the well known words, 'I am come among you
muzzled.' Within a few months, however, an even greater muzzle
ɪs removed; in October 1865 Palmerston died. 'We are breaking
ɪh the old generation,' wrote Bright grimly. Most educated
ɪglishmen felt the same; but they were not all so confident of the
ɪure as John Bright.

1858 with the passage through the Commons
church rates; but even this was defeated in
further unsuccessful attempts in subsequent
gradually slackened. Nevertheless, the campaign
out wider consequences. It brought religious ques
disestablishment of the Church of Ireland, befc
helped to create among nonconformist liberal vo
of opinion in favour of further relief legislation.
to capture the interest of that formidable but un
the chancellor of the exchequer. In 1863 Gladst
behalf of dissenters in the matter of separate bui
mid-1860s, at the initiative of two influential
C. N. Hall and Henry Allon, he was meeting
ministers like Binney, Dale and Spurgeon; and as
he told Bright that when the Liberal party wa
the Irish church would be one of the great pro
solution. A year later, in the spring of 1865,
about the Church of Ireland in an otherwise m
a thrill of apprehension among his clerical con
University.

This was not the only direction in which Glad
his liberal education, or, as more cynical observ
it, making a bid for popular electoral support. F
apparently not unsympathetic to the view that
to fear the working classes and that 'something
should be done towards their enfranchisem
working-class and trade union deputations over h
bank and small annuities bills confirmed his fav
In March 1864 he was confiding to Bright that t
parliament had treated the people badly on r
question should be brought up again. The choi
significant. Bright's great northern campaign
reform in 1858 had won him a loyal following a
working classes but had signally failed to attra
What he had set out to do was to reforge the o
middle- and lower-class radicalism. His public
deliberately recalling memories of Peterloo, the
the class attacks of the Anti-Corn Law Leagt
middle class as well as aristocratic opinion. Den
in the upper house as 'of monstrous, nay, ever
of the whole conduct of diplomacy since 1688 a
of outdoor relief for the aristocracy' and of the
as squandering the fruits of industry 'in every c
which a Government could possibly be guilty

10 Safeguard and Security

I

Britain in 1815 was a satiated power. The objects of its diplomacy were to obtain security in Europe, to safeguard its possessions overseas, and to promote freedom of commerce everywhere. The ideal of universal free trade (the doctrine of the strong industrial country) was given a characteristically moral content as the foundation of international harmony. The guiding principles followed by British policy were containment and order, not conquest and expansion. It was only a superficial paradox that minor hostilities were usually taking place somwhere along the vast perimeter of British imperial possessions throughout the period. Small campaigns and punitive expeditions seemed an inescapable burden of empire. But they were mainly necessitated by the difficulties and tensions that inevitably arise when a powerful, technically superior civilization is in constant contact with weakness and barbarism. The only imperial frontier where Britain had to deal with an opponent of comparable stature was in North America. But there the unresolved Canadian–USA boundary problems were settled by judicious concession over the Maine–New Brunswick line in 1842 and judicious firmness over the British Columbia–Oregon line in 1846.

Foreign policy in the real sense was a question of Europe. It was a Europe still dominated by courts, dynasties and diplomats rather than peoples, parties and opinions. With this society the British aristocracy had close personal ties. The intimacy of the European diplomatic system did not, however, lessen the significance of the issues involved; nor did it mean that there was a lack of fundamental principle in the British attitude towards Europe. It was true that successive foreign secretaries in this period carried on their work without looking for advice from their permanent civil servants and showed considerable variations in the style of their diplomacy. Nevertheless there was a continuous tradition, from Pitt and Castlereagh through Canning and Palmerston to Clarendon and Russell, which underlay all their work.

The classic British concept of Europe in the first half of the nineteenth century was simple. At either extremity were the two great aggressive military states of France and Russia. Between them lay the weak central area: a fragmented Germany, a multiracial Austrian empire, a partitioned Poland, and a divided Italy. The most serious danger to the stability and peace of Europe was likely therefore to come from the two formidable powers to the east and west; the equilibrium of Europe could best be preserved by strengthening the middle. The threat of French hegemony dated back to Louis XIV even though it had been most devastatingly realized under Napoleon. The arrival of Russia as a dominant power in European politics was more recent. But Pitt in the Oczakov incident of 1791 had already sounded the alarm. Jenkinson, the future Lord Liverpool, made his maiden speech in the Commons on the theme that while in the past the balance of power in Europe had been mainly endangered by France, 'a power had succeeded to France, no less deserving of attention from its restless politics and ambitious views—this was Russia.' To those who could remember the closing years of the Napoleonic Wars (as every British foreign secretary up to 1865 could except Lord Granville) the presence of the Old Guard at Moscow in 1812 and of the Cossacks at Paris in 1815 were dramatic reminders of the military potential of both states.

The Vienna settlement of 1815 had, as far as France was concerned, been constructed in accordance with these principles. An enlarged Prussia, rewarded with Saxon territory and given a forward position on the Rhine, constituted the main obstacle to French expansion north of the Alps. Austria, with its Lombardy–Venetian possessions in Italy, stood sentry south of the Alps. Outworks to this line of defence were furnished by the new kingdom of the Netherlands on the northern frontier of France and the kingdom of Sardinia–Piedmont to the southeast. Russia, however, with the great salient of the puppet Polish kingdom thrust forward between East Prussia and Austrian Galicia, had secured a strategically powerful position in eastern Europe. From the British point of view, moreover, the Russian menace extended beyond the European frontiers to the overland route to India through the Red Sea. India itself was exposed to Russian penetration in Persia and Afghanistan. The enormous expanse of the Russian empire, half-European and half-Asiatic, had no natural counterweight other than geographic obstacles, no political counterweight other than the British Empire. Without British seapower behind it, the newly created state of Norway and Sweden was only a diminutive guardian of the outlet from the

Baltic. In the Balkans, and across the Straits which formed the only passage from the Black Sea to the Mediterranean, the barrier was the Ottoman Empire with its effete dynasty, its paralytic administration, and its restive tributary states. With the Vienna settlement, the importance of Turkey began to be increasingly appreciated by European diplomats and in the end its existence became even for many liberals a European necessity.

To strengthen the middle and keep in check the two great flanking powers was therefore the basic principle of British policy. Prussia, Austria and the Ottoman Empire were essential for stability and order in Europe, their preservation therefore a primary British interest. But the application of this principle necessarily varied with shifting circumstances. To have followed in mechanical fashion a fixed concept would have been to fall into the same trap that Metternich fell into when dealing with Germany. The European state system was not a rigid, unalterable entity but a collection of societies marked by the usual attributes of evolution and change, not to speak of ambition, selfishness and miscalculation. The union of Sweden and Norway was never more than nominal; the kingdom of the Netherlands did not last fifteen years. Prussia and Austria entered on a bitter rivalry for the leadership of the German Confederation; Sardinia under Cavour embarked on a policy of aggrandisement which involved war with Austria and alliance with France. Austria refused to make those timely external concessions and internal reforms which in British opinion would have strengthened her for her indispensable European task. The cunning and cynical rulers of Turkey in self-defence tried to play off one European power against another. The two 'aggressive powers' of France and Russia at different periods made serious and rational efforts to obtain the friendship and alliance of Britain. The new forces of liberalism and nationalism which found uncritical approval in England not infrequently showed themselves more corrupt, unstable and bellicose than the old autocracies which they had overthrown.

The neat British formula for the European states system was therefore continually being distorted by the pressure of events. In following its basic principles British diplomacy had in practice to pick a way through a maze of contemporary and temporary issues. Not surprisingly it often seemed, and sometimes was, little more than an improvised and hesitant response to unexpected situations; and it not infrequently involved illogical and apparently contradictory attitudes. Nevertheless, its fundamental objectives were clear to all British foreign secretaries from Castlereagh to Clarendon; and beneath obvious but superficial differences of manner and matter they followed a remarkably consistent tradition. Not until the

Bismarckian revolution in central Europe between 1864 and 1870
did the fundamental assumptions of the classic British policy of 1815
disappear.

II

The problem for Castlereagh in the post-war years was not the
likelihood of an immediate collapse of any part of the European
structure erected with such care and difficulty at the Vienna Congress, but the need to keep in harmony the victorious allies of
1814–15. The most creative and imaginative of nineteenth-century
British foreign secretaries, he had an aristocratic scorn of popular
movements, was indifferent to public opinion, and was unmoved by
abstract theories. His civilized outlook and serene intelligence—'just
and passionless' in Caulaincourt's phrase—made him value peace,
order and freedom above everything else in international life. His
chief aim after 1815 was to ensure that the problems of the great
powers were solved by discussion rather than by conflict. While
imbibing many of Pitt's ideas on the future shape of Europe, he
discarded Pitt's idealistic concept of mutual guarantees, and the
institution of some form of public law in Europe, as probably impracticable and certainly dangerous. Though the Vienna settlement
was signed as a single instrument by all the powers, and to that
extent all were implicated in its enforcement, there was no specific
commitment to guarantee the maintenance of every part. To defend
the general integrity of the treaty and preserve the 'just equilibrium'
in Europe, Castlereagh relied on more practical devices: the per-
petuation of the Quadruple Alliance between Britain, Russia, Austria
and Prussia, and periodic consultations between the great powers.
Article IV of the alliance, drafted by Castlereagh himself, provided
for regular meetings of the signatories to discuss common interests
and consider any measures that might seem necessary from time to
time for the 'repose and prosperity of Nations and for the maintenance of the Peace of Europe'.

There were two early modifications to this central system, one
acceptable to Castlereagh, the other less so. The restoration of the
Bourbon monarchy, the absence of vindictive peace terms, the early
evacuation of the armies of occupation made it easy to admit France
into the general 'concert of Europe'. At the congress of Aix-la-
Chapelle in 1818 France was invited to join in a five-power convention providing for the settlement of mutual problems by peaceful

negotiations. The other diplomatic accretion to the Quadruple Alliance was the Russian-inspired 'Holy Alliance' of the three eastern powers. Though handled by Castlereagh with the public courtesy due to an ally, it was not a paper to which the Prince Regent in Britain could subscribe as head of a parliamentary state. Even association with the eastern autocracies damaged the reputation of Castlereagh and Wellington in the eyes of British liberals and added to the post-war unpopularity of Liverpool's government. In fact Castlereagh firmly rejected, in 1818 as in 1815, proposals from the Tsar for mutual guarantees of the existing European dynastic system and state frontiers, and joint action to resist aggression or revolution. Even apart from the theoretical objections to such wide commitment, the nature of the British constitution (as he and Wellington constantly pointed out) made it impossible for any British ministry to undertake precise, contingent responsibilities. Diplomacy by conference, not rule by congress, was Castlereagh's ideal. He opposed the formalism of holding meetings at fixed intervals and resisted attempts to define more closely the nature and purpose of the 'concert of Europe'. When disturbances in Germany and revolts in southern Europe—Spain, Portugal, Italy and Greece—brought Austria and Russia together, Castlereagh refused to regard their meeting at Troppau in 1820 as a full meeting of the allies.

His famous state paper of May 1820 was a direct repudiation of the Tsar's attempt to transform the congress system by infusing into it the principles of the Holy Alliance. It rejected categorically the right of the great powers to supervise the internal affairs of smaller countries or erect some form of international government; and it argued that the Quadruple Alliance would best be preserved by limiting rather than extending the range of joint action. The British government had its own public to consider. Even the strongest administration could not go to war against the will of parliament and public opinion; and in the age of Peterloo Liverpool's administration was far from strong. British action abroad, it reiterated, must always depend on circumstances and be subject to the limitations imposed by the parliamentary constitution. It was a classic enunciation of British foreign policy in the nineteenth century.

Nevertheless, though Castlereagh fought against the congress system as envisaged by the Tsar, and in latter years even by Metternich, he never abandoned the idea of diplomacy by conference. When the interests of Britain became involved in the question of Greek independence and the rebellious Spanish colonies in 1821, he decided to attend in person the Congress of Verona the following year. The instructions he drew up, originally for himself but later passed on to Wellington, made it clear that he was not prepared to sanction, if diplomacy failed, any forcible intervention in either country, and that he did not rule out ultimate recognition *de facto* of successful revolutionary governments. The ostentatious withdrawal from the policy of the eastern autocracies carried out in 1822 by Canning was started by his predecessor. For all his civilized ideals, Castlereagh was a realist. Over South America, for example, he took the view that the issue of the Spanish colonies lay solely between the Spanish government and Britain, and that their recognition was only a matter of time. Before his death he had already acknowledged their belligerent status. It was only to contemporaries that the change at the Foreign Office in 1822 seemed crucial.

Canning, his inferior in European statesmanship, was strong where Castlereagh was most vulnerable—in his relations with British public opinion. By his open breach with the Holy Alliance, his unprecedented series of speeches on foreign affairs to audiences outside the House of Commons,[1] and his disconcerting habit of publishing current diplomatic documents, Canning conveyed the impression of a switch of direction in conscious deference to liberal opinion. This in reality was hardly justified. Canning merely accelerated the process of detachment from the eastern powers initiated by Castlereagh; and he looked to public opinion less as a guide to policy than as a support against his critics in parliament, the cabinet and at court. For Canning popular liberalism was something to exploit rather than to follow.

The Spanish and Greek revolutions with which Canning had to deal between 1822 and 1827 illustrated the varying nature of British influence. Like Castlereagh he strongly opposed the French intervention in Spain sanctioned at Verona but in practice he could do little more than protest and threaten. French action could not be halted except by force and for force on that scale the Liverpool government was neither militarily nor politically prepared. Canning's policy of bluff merely alienated opinion in governing circles; and popular enthusiasm was no substitute for support from cabinet and parliament. In the event French military presence in the peninsula between 1823 and 1827 brought little reward. Though Spanish internecine conflicts made intervention easy, Spanish national pride ensured that little tangible benefit accrued to the intervening power. The real question was the fate of the Spanish colonies where British seapower put Canning in a commanding position. Even so, he approached the problem with a caution that reflected the unease in the cabinet at any action that might appear to encourage rebellion against legitimate authority. As George IV unkindly

---

[1] Not only in his constituency of Liverpool but in London, Bristol, Plymouth and Harwich in the years 1822–6. H. Temperley, *Foreign Policy of Canning 1822–27* (1925), pp. 512–13.

reminded his ministers, the state of Ireland hardly justified an attitude of moral superiority.

In 1823 Canning's overture to the USA for a joint declaration against French interference in the Spanish colonies broke down on American distrust. The 'Monroe doctrine' promulgated by the president of the USA in December 1823 demonstrated the American preference for independent action. It condemned any further colonization or interference in the American hemisphere by European powers; but without the shield of British seapower the statement was an empty gesture intended largely for a domestic audience. The decisive event was the final and reluctant decision of the British cabinet in 1824, after the failure of one final effort at direct negotiations with Spain, to recognize the independence of Buenos Aires, Colombia and Mexico and make trade agreements with their governments. Other issues apart, it was of importance for British commerce to have an open door to South America; and the merchants of London and Liverpool had already been pressing for a regularization of relations.

By 1825 the chaotic politics of the Iberian peninsula had thrown up an even more pressing problem. The political independence of Britain's oldest ally Portugal, with its Atlantic coastline and harbours, was as important a strategic interest to Britain as the Low Countries. The Portuguese alliance largely counterbalanced the Franco–Spanish alliance; and the fear after 1823 was that French military support might encourage traditional Spanish designs on the smaller kingdom. For some years the internal state of Portugal caused anxiety in London. The death of the Portuguese king in 1826, and the precarious position of the regency during the minority of the young queen Maria, finally brought matters to a head. Britain, which had already in 1825 secured the recognition by the Portuguese government of Brazilian independence, in 1826 received a formal request from its ally for assistance against Spanish efforts to organize armed resistance to the regency on Portuguese soil. It was not the first such request Canning had received; but on this occasion the case seemed urgent and the treaty obligation incontestable. The prompt despatch of a military force to Lisbon in December 1826 brought the required result without a shot being fired. The Spanish government was given a sharp lesson that British influence was not confined to the occasional warship in the Tagus; and the belligerent Spanish colonies in South America were correspondingly heartened. The Portuguese expedition was the occasion for Canning's famous House of Commons speech of December 1826: 'I called the New World into existence to redress the balance of the Old.' The phrase was memorable; but it was mere rhetoric. Neither then nor at any other time in the

nineteenth century was either north or south America in a position
to alter the balance of power in Europe. What Canning had wanted,
and what he had obtained, was the preservation of Portuguese
independence and the denial of the former Spanish colonies to
France. The preceding sentence in the same speech—'I resolved that
if France had Spain, it should not be Spain with the Indies'—was
a more apt description of his achievement.

To liberal opinion at home and diplomatic opinion abroad
Canning's dramatic action and defiant speeches in 1826 seemed to
make Britain under his leadership, as later under Palmerston's, the
symbol of resistance to the European autocracies and encouragement to revolution everywhere. It was an exaggerated reputation.
Canning had acted under treaty obligations, for a precise and limited
object, in conditions of maximum military security. He was not an
unqualified supporter of liberalism and free institutions throughout
Europe. His preferred path was a typical English compromise, as
he himself put it, 'between Jacobinism and Ultraism'; and he was
under no illusion that popular government was a guarantee of pacific
policy. Indeed he thought that it was something of an advantage
to have Europe under less enlightened systems, since this provided
a greater contrast to Britain's unique position as a parliamentary
constitutional monarchy. Similarly he no more believed in a policy
of isolation for Britain than Castlereagh had done. The difference
between them was that Canning had a greater distrust of congresses
and held that Britain should only intervene on the continent on
important issues and with decisive force. Under his flamboyant
liberal guise, Canning was an acute, cautious, and conservative
foreign minister.

His basic moderation was observable in his policy over the Greek
revolt of 1821–7. This, rather than Spain or Portugal, was the real
European crisis during his foreign secretaryship. Castlereagh had
refused to lend assistance to the Greeks in the struggle against their
Turkish overlords. He was distrustful of Russian motives in the
Middle East, the one area where Muscovite policy was likely to
depart radically from the conservative principles of the Holy Alliance; and he regarded the Ottoman Empire realistically as a
'necessary evil', the only territorial barrier to Russian expansion into
the Mediterranean. His policy in 1822 was to effect a reconciliation
between Russia and Turkey before proceeding to any discussion of
the Greek revolt; and he was in any case determined to keep out
of any direct intervention by the European powers. Canning followed
the same course when he refused the Tsar's proposal for a special
congress on the Greek question. It was true that he recognized the
belligerent status of the Greek rebels in 1823 but this was scarcely

avoidable in the state of British feeling. To the classically educated classes in Britain the Greek revolt conjured up images of ancient Athens, of Demosthenes and Pericles, of democracy and culture threatened by tyranny and barbarism. Philhellene societies were started; subscriptions were raised and loans floated from which few of the enthusiastic shareholders ever recovered their money. The whigs formed a Greek committee; volunteers departed for the Middle East; and Byron atoned in the public eye for his disreputable life and immoral verses by dying at Missolonghi in the spring of 1824. One of the most enthusiastic anti-Turk and pro-Russian whigs, Lord Holland, was later to declare his regret 'as a citizen of the world' that the Russians did not take this opportunity to capture Constantinople.

The cabinet, not being able to afford such gratuitous idealism, found the problem less simple. They were reluctant to sanction any weakening of the Ottoman Empire, equally anxious to ensure that if Turkish rule in the Balkans did collapse, Britain would be in a position to influence the settlement that must follow. In the circumstances neutrality seemed the only safe immediate policy. The crucial development came in 1825 when the quasi-independent pasha of Egypt, Mehemet Ali, came to the help of his nominal overlord with his more efficient army and navy and occupied the Morea. Canning's principal object was to prevent a Russo–Turkish war and on the accession of the Tsar Nicholas at the end of the year, he sent Wellington to Moscow as his special envoy. Since he distrusted international conferences and yet could scarcely hope to oppose Russia singlehanded, the only course open to him was to join Russia in forcing on Turkey a settlement that could be given some wider diplomatic guarantee. The acceptance by Russia of this policy enabled the new tsar on the one hand to settle his outstanding Balkan territorial disputes with Turkey through the convention of Akerman (October 1826) and on the other to join Britain and France in the Treaty of London (July 1827). The three signatories agreed to offer mediation in the Turco–Greek conflict and in any event to insist on an armistice, to be secured if necessary by force. It was further decided that while Greece should remain under Turkish suzerainty, it should become a self-governing state with frontiers to be settled later by the contracting powers.

It was Canning's last diplomatic achievement and was only a limited success. War had been averted, the congress system and the Holy Alliance circumvented, a settlement concluded by direct negotiations between England, Russia and France. But the policy of neutralization by association had its dangers. While the Greeks accepted a cease-fire the Turks refused. The Cradock mission to

Egypt to dissuade Mehemet Ali failed; and the instructions issued
to Admiral Codrington, the British commander in the Mediterranean,
to prevent further hostilities between Greeks and Turks were meaningless unless they implied a right to use force. The Treaty of London
led directly to the destruction of the Turco–Egyptian fleet at
Navarino in October 1827, ten weeks after Canning's death. For
the Wellington ministry, to whom Turkish military strength was an
essential element in the European balance of power, the official
reference to Navarino as 'this untoward event' in the king's speech
at the opening of parliament the following year was a resigned
understatement. George IV's remark that Codrington, who received
the GCB, deserved a rope rather than a riband, was a more un-
inhibited expression of the views prevalent in conservative circles.
As it was, Britain lost control of the eastern situation and the Treaty
of Adrianople in 1829, which ended the renewed hostilities between
Russia and Turkey, owed its relatively moderate terms to Russian
realism rather to British or Austrian influence. Though the British
government accepted the principle of complete independence for
Greece, the fear that it would become a mere tool of Russia produced
a grudging attitude towards the extent of its boundaries as finally
laid down by the London protocol of 1830.

III

The year 1830, marked by revolutions and rebellions in France,
Belgium, Poland, Germany and the Papal States, began a new
phase in the relations of the European powers. A common internal
danger brought together the three eastern powers whose former
solidarity had been shaken by Russian policy in the Near East; while
in the west there began an uneasy but significant *rapprochement*
between France and Britain. The Münchengrätz meeting of the two
emperors in September 1833 symbolized the first; the *entente cordiale*
the second. The understanding between the French and British
governments was usually incomplete and never cordial; but it was
based on certain hard realities. The new Orléans dynasty, like Louis
Napoleon's popular dictatorship twenty years later, was of undis-
guised revolutionary origin. It looked back for its justification beyond
the Bourbon restoration to the events of 1789–1814, and proclaimed
the right of the French people to self-determination. For Louis
Philippe, as for Louis Napoleon, the moral of the first French
Revolution was that no French government, least of all one which

was suspect to the legitimist monarchies of eastern Europe, could afford to incur the permanent emnity of Britain. From the British point of view, the friendship or neutrality of France ensured invulnerability in any European conflict, since of all the great powers France alone was in a position to threaten the security of the British Isles. For both countries these practical considerations acted as a standing check on their recurrent animosities and conflicting policies. Though it was not easy to discern at the time, the 1830 revolution started a new era in Anglo–French relations.

The Belgian question admirably illustrated the changed situation. The revolt in 1830 was a disturbing event to the British government since it was the first breach in the defensive system erected against France in 1815. Wellington and Aberdeen, however, took the practical view that there was no more chance of reversing events in the Netherlands than in Paris. Instead they concentrated their efforts on bringing hostilities to an end and discouraging both Prussian and French intervention. Faithful to Castlereagh's principle of diplomacy by conference, and to his own strong European sense, Wellington proposed a continuation of the London conference on Greece to deal with Belgium; and over the next few years Palmerston, as foreign secretary in Grey's ministry, ably continued the policy of his predecessor. Though the astute Talleyrand tried every trick in his considerable repertoire to gain concessions for France, including the secession of Luxemburg and the choice of a French prince for the new state, there was never any real prospect that the new and precarious French government would risk an outright breach. The final result was a complete success for British diplomacy and, given the irreparable disruption of the Kingdom of the Netherlands, what seemed the best practical substitute for it that could be devised. Belgium was neither partitioned between Holland and France nor allowed to become a French dependency. The neutralization of the new state ensured that it would act as both a barrier to French expansion and a buffer on its open northern frontier. The form of the Treaty of London (November 1831), which was signed by all five great powers, meant that the main participants in the Vienna settlement endorsed this first major modification of their earlier work.

Over the Belgian issue Britain was in a uniquely strong position. The Netherlands were geographically close and vulnerable to British naval pressure, the *parvenu* French government was politically insecure, Russia and Austria temporarily distracted by their own internal difficulties. Prussia, the only Holy Alliance power with a direct interest and physically able to intervene, was far inferior in strength and influence to its partners. Such a fortuitous set of circumstances was unlikely to recur. The initiative assumed by the western powers was prolonged for a few more years by the Quadruple Alliance of 1834 between Britain, France, Spain and Portugal. Though nominally designed to support the constitutional governments in the Iberian peninsula under their two young queens, in effect it was a counterpoise to the Münchengrätz powers who notoriously favoured the male pretenders in both kingdoms. 'A capital hit and all my own doing,' was Palmerston's version; but the effects were evanescent. The reality of the alliance depended on Anglo–French understanding and within a few years this was undermined by a renewal of the Eastern Question.

The main problem here was the war between the Egyptian pasha, Mehemet Ali, and the Porte which threatened a collapse of the central Turkish empire and the virtual certainty of Russian intervention. Already in 1833 an appeal from the Sultan for help had brought a Russian naval squadron to Constantinople and the signing of the Treaty of Unkiar Skelessi pledging the two states to mutual assistance. Palmerston suspected the ultimate Russian design was the partition of Turkey. In reaction to the theory of the inevitable death of the Ottoman Empire he became a forceful exponent of the view that, so far from being the sick man of Europe, all the Ottoman Empire needed was external security and a few sensible internal reforms. 'All that we hear every day of the week about the decay of the Turkish empire, and its being a dead body or a sapless trunk, and so forth', he wrote in 1839, 'is pure and unadulterated nonsense.' The logical consequence of this attitude was the conviction that Mehemet Ali must be prevented from conquering the territory and undermining any further the authority of the Sultan. This, however, was a policy which aligned Palmerston with Russia and separated him from the French who increasingly favoured Mehemet Ali as a counterweight to Russian influence in the eastern Mediterranean.

Like Canning over the Greek question in 1825 Palmerston in the late 1830s moved slowly and with some reluctance towards an understanding with Russia as the best method of maintaining the traditional balance of power in the Middle East. In fact, some years previously the Tsar Nicholas and his advisers had themselves come to the conclusion that Russia had more to gain by the continued existence on her southern border of a weak Turkey than from any attempt to precipitate its collapse. It was already obvious that, for example, a Russian occupation of Constantinople and Russian control of the Dardanelles would range all Europe against her, including the Austrian Empire. The Münchengrätz conference in 1833, at which the two eastern powers pledged themselves to cooperate in the event of a Turkish collapse, had been a Russian gesture of reassurance to Vienna. The death of Mahmud II in 1839 and the accession of Abdul Medjid, a boy of sixteen, made the need for international action even more urgent. Russian cooperation was therefore not difficult to obtain and the Tsar himself took the initiative with the despatch of the Brunnow mission to London the same year. The Quadruple Alliance of July 1840 between Britain and the three eastern European powers had as its primary object the forcible restraint of Mehemet Ali. In November the surrender of Acre to a combined British–Austrian–Turkish fleet was followed by the confirmation of Mehemet Ali's hereditary pashalik of Egypt in return for an abandonment of his Syrian conquests. The final Straits Convention in 1841, to which Turkey as well as the five European powers subscribed, prohibited the passage of the Dardanelles to foreign warships in time of peace, thus effectively replacing the Treaty of Unkiar Skelessi.

It was a settlement entirely in accord with traditional British interests; but it had been gained at the cost of a dangerous rupture with France. The underlying resentment of the French government at Palmerston's rough language over Belgium had been increased by friction over affairs in Spain. In the Spanish civil war which had started in 1834 both countries indirectly intervened with arms and volunteers in support of different political parties. The breach was completed by the disagreement over Mehemet Ali, the French *protégé* whose cause had been promoted by the French admiral in the Levant. Unable to win French backing for a policy of restraining Egypt, Palmerston retaliated by deliberately and offensively excluding France from the 1840 Quadruple Alliance, thus leaving her in total isolation. It was the start of a prolonged crisis which brought Anglo–French relations to their most dangerous point since Waterloo. To excited French opinion the 1840 treaty seemed a conscious revival of the 1814 alliance against France; and the atmosphere of 'encirclement' was made worse by the despatch of the British fleet to Alexandria and an outburst of German patriotic sentiment along the Rhine frontier. Palmerston's own insulting tactics and language had contributed to the tension. If the Anglo–French *entente* was worth preserving (and in the whig cabinet a majority, including Lansdowne, Holland, Clarendon and Russell, thought it was) Palmerston appeared to be jeopardizing it in a singularly insensitive manner. For a time the danger of war seemed real; and the credit for preserving peace belonged more to Victoria, Louis Philippe and the indefatigable Leopold of Belgium (the uncle of one and the son-in-law of the other) than to the unrepentant and cocksure foreign secretary in Downing Street. The real criticism of Palmerston was not his objective, which was admirable, nor his judgement of what was possible, which was usually borne out by events, but the provocative and sometimes almost brutal methods he employed—methods which in 1840–41 disquieted even the governments of Austria and Prussia which were not usually sympathetic to France.

The *entente* was restored, partly by Louis Philippe's prudent decision in October 1840 to replace the bellicose Thiers by the Soult–Guizot ministry, partly by the change of ministry in Britain the following year and the appointment of Aberdeen to the Foreign Office. The visit of Victoria and Albert to France in the autumn of 1843 was the first of several meetings between the British and French royal families; and Louis Philippe and Guizot were quick to proclaim to the world the *entente cordiale* so happily re-established between the two countries. Despite disquiet at French expansionist policy in Algeria, the attempt by a French admiral in 1843 to annex Tahiti, and the arrest and deportation of the Methodist missionary and ex-British consul Pritchard in 1844, Peel and Aberdeen ensured that the *entente* remained intact during the Conservative ministry of 1841–6. At the second meeting at the Château d'Eu in 1845, when the future of the Spanish princesses was discussed, Aberdeen was assured by the king and Guizot that no French prince would be allowed to marry the queen of Spain's sister until the queen herself had married and produced children to inherit the throne. Since the Neapolitan Bourbon prince favoured by the French as the husband of the queen was rumoured to be impotent, this seemed a sufficiently satisfactory guarantee.

The simultaneous marriages of the queen and her sister in October 1846, following the change of government in Britain, seemed a direct and inexcusable breach of this understanding. Palmerston's curiously maladroit mention of a possible Coburg candidate for the Queen's hand had been probably more the occasion than the cause of the French decision. But he had clearly been anxious to demonstrate his independence of Aberdeen's policy and rebuild his influence in Madrid, while the French were filled with dislike and distrust of their old enemy now reinstated in the Foreign Office. So far from damaging Palmerston, however, the French action was universally condemned in Britain as a piece of cynical perfidy. The revolution of 1848 and the fall of the Orléans dynasty soon robbed the Spanish marriages of any political significance; but the episode was symptomatic of the difficulties which Palmerston's reputation in Europe was creating for British diplomacy. Even if Prince Albert's remark to Russell in 1850 that England was 'generally detested, mistrusted and treated with indignity by even the smallest Powers' was a prejudiced half-truth, it was still a perceptible disadvantage for a state which relied more on prestige and influence than the deployment of military force.

Nevertheless, the difficulties in Anglo–French relations could not be ascribed solely to Palmerston. At most he inflamed an already sensitive relationship. His own simple explanation for French hostility to Britain was that they could never forget or forgive Trafalgar or Waterloo. Certainly Palmerston himself never forgot them; but many other people, even the pacific Aberdeen, thought that war between Britain and France would probably take place sooner or later. When Louis Philippe's son the prince de Joinville in 1844 and the English General Kennedy in 1859 wrote pamphlets on national defence policy, both took it for granted that the basis for their arguments must be a war between their respective countries. The naval rearmament and coastal fortification programmes on which both states spent so much money in the middle decades of the century were meaningless except in terms of a potential Anglo–French conflict. Yet Palmerston, with his proverbial luck, within a few years saw to his pleasure the Orléans monarchy replaced first by a republic and then by the Bonapartist pretender Louis Napoleon. Not all foreign secretaries have their failures so rapidly and completely expunged.

Palmerston's approval of Louis Napoleon's *coup d'état* in 1851 was mainly prompted by his fear of a restoration of the Orléans dynasty. Within less than three years, however, the two countries were allies in the Crimean War. This first armed conflict between the great powers since 1815 arose from a situation which European diplomats had feared ever since the Congress of Vienna. At one end of Europe was the Tsar Nicholas, secure and autocratic at home, increasingly impatient and headstrong in his attitude towards Turkey, contemptuous of the new French plebiscitary emperor in Paris. At the other was Napoleon III, sensitive about his *parvenu* origin, and conscious of the need to justify his name and his throne to clerical and militarist circles in France. At the same time the two great conservative powers in Europe were at a disadvantage—Britain because of the party instability which had brought the Aberdeen coalition to office, Austria because of the shock of the 1848 revolutions on her territory, the forced but resented dependence on Russian aid in 1849, and the recent challenge of Prussia for the leadership of the German Confederation. For the first time since Waterloo Europe seemed dominated once more by the two great military powers on either flank.

Paradoxically it was the appointment of the pacific Aberdeen as prime minister which began the slide towards war. The significance to Russia of this event lay in the discussions with Peel and Aberdeen which took place when the Tsar had visited England eight years earlier. Nicholas believed that in the Nesselrode memorandum of June 1844 he had come to a written understanding with Britain to take joint action should the demise of the 'Sick Man of Europe' appear imminent. The most illuminating passage in the document was perhaps the assertion at the end that Russia would be able to obtain the assent of Austria to any Anglo–Russian agreement on Turkey and that in the face of Anglo–Austro–Russian solidarity France would be obliged to conform. Since the memorandum upheld the principle of maintaining the Ottoman Empire as long as possible and proceeding only on the basis of international agreement, Aberdeen was happy to accept it as a statement of the Russian viewpoint. For the Tsar, however, it constituted a kind of permanent agreement and by 1853 he felt that the time had come to translate it into action. At the start of the year he spoke to the British ambassador of 'the dying bear' and of the need to make timely dispositions if a European war was to be avoided. He clearly wished to work in harmony with Britain; but Russell, now at the Foreign Office, was reluctant to anticipate such a cataclysmic event and unwilling to make separate agreements. The Menschikov mission to Constantinople to demand a Russian protectorate over the Christian subjects of the Porte and a defensive alliance between the two powers demonstrated both growing Russian impatience and a misunderstanding of the changed relationships in western Europe. It brought an immediate reaction from France and Britain. A French fleet was despatched to the Aegean and Russell sent the masterful Russophobe Stratford Canning to Constantinople with powers to summon the British fleet from Malta to the Straits if necessary. Even so, the cabinet still envisaged its role as that of peacemaker, preferably in conjunction with Austria, and hoped that diplomatic protests, backed by a show of naval strength, would be adequate.

The summer of 1853, which saw the Russian occupation of the Rumanian principalities of Moldavia and Wallachia as a hostage for the fulfilment of their demands, was marked by an intense diplomatic search for a compromise settlement of the dispute. The Vienna Note produced by the conference of ambassadors in Austria, calling on Turkey to honour its previous engagements in respect of Christian subjects, was accepted by Russia but rejected by the Porte with (it was thought) the encouragement of Stratford Canning. When it appeared, however, that the Russian government had placed a different interpretation on the Note than that intended by the conference, Palmerston and Russell began to adopt the attitude that Russia could not be allowed to coerce Turkey. Aberdeen, who at one point had wished to recall the suspect Canning, was now defeated on the even more vital matter of naval dispositions. In September, in violation of the Straits Convention of 1841, the British Mediterranean fleet was ordered to the Dardanelles. At this crucial point when the Tsar, as he made clear to the western representatives at Olmütz, was seeking to extricate himself from his increasingly dangerous isolation, the Porte took heart from the Anglo–French action and assumed a more intransigent posture. In October Turkey sent an ultimatum demanding the evacuation of the Principalities and within a fortnight the two powers were at war.

One of the more curious features of the policy of drift and compromise which characterized the diplomacy of the cabinet in London was that no warning had been given, either to Turkey that Britain would remain neutral, or to Russia that Britain would intervene, in the event of hostilities between those two countries. Aberdeen's desire to resume negotiations on the basis of the Olmütz declarations, and to refuse aid to Turkey except on those conditions, was overruled by the cabinet, as was Palmerston's proposal to send the fleet into the Black Sea with orders to detain Russian warships. Instead the cabinet made the evasive decision to allow the fleet to move into the Black Sea for 'strictly defensive' purposes. This was perhaps the event which more than any other finally decided British entry into the war since it put British policy at the mercy of uncontrollable developments several thousand miles away. The Queen, who with Albert had shown herself more clearsighted than any of her ministers, fastened on the weakness of the British position when she wrote tartly to Clarendon on 11 October that 'we have taken on ourselves in conjunction with France all the risks of a European war, without having bound Turkey to any conditions with respect to provoking it.' The entry of the fleet into the Black Sea in January 1854 under pressure from France and public opinion at home, followed successively by a warning to Russia to desist from any further naval action and a Franco–British demand for the evacuation of the Principalities, placed Britain clearly on the side of Turkey. Nicholas, angry at Austrian deviousness and ingratitude, even more angry at Aberdeen's weakness and Palmerston's hostility, was now in a mood of exalted national patriotism which was the emotional counterpart of inflamed public opinion in France and Britain. The hapless British cabinet, having gone so far, felt it could not at this eleventh hour withdraw its support from Turkey. In February diplomatic relations with Russia were finally broken off and in March the western allies declared war.

IV

Of all the great powers Britain was perhaps least prepared for war against a major European opponent. Not the conservatism of the service chiefs but the parsimony of the British public had been the main destructive influence. Wellington's superb army of the Peninsula, which took twenty years to build up, had long been dismantled, its organization discarded, its lessons forgotten. Even the navy was only a hollow shell of the great fleet that had served Barham and Nelson. Of the ninety ships of the line in 1813, only thirteen were in active service in 1817. Even so, the contraction of the navy continued after 1832. In 1844 there were only nine capital ships in commission, three acting as guardships at home, one off Ireland, one in the Mediterranean, one in the Pacific, one off India, and two returning home to be paid off. When the war scare with France blew up in 1840 England was almost completely unguarded. Most of the British naval strength was stationed off the Syrian coast to check the Egyptian advance on Constantinople. The only capital ship available in home waters was HMS *Collingwood* (eighty guns) which was under orders for the Pacific. She was consequently detained by the Admiralty at Spithead to protect Portsmouth and the Solent, although her crew included 200 merchant seamen who had no experience in handling big guns.

The navy possessed a mass of ships dating from the Nelson era, but most of these were laid up in harbours and dockyards, inadequately maintained and often mere hulks rotting at anchor. A similar but human deadweight was present in the form of the hundreds of ageing admirals and captains on half pay, most of whom had received their promotion to post-rank (the established rank of captain at which promotion became automatic) before the end of the Napoleonic Wars. Promotion to flag-rank was by seniority and there was no way of compulsorily retiring officers of post-rank and above. In 1851 there were still a hundred admirals on the active list, all but six of whom had gained post-rank before 1815.

The central administration of the navy, however, had been put on an efficient basis by Sir James Graham when he was First Lord in Grey's administration of 1830–34. His reforms had the gratifying feature in parliamentary eyes of combining improvement with economy. The old divided control and semi-independent boards were swept away and all powers vested in the Board of the Admiralty. Under its collective control were five new departments, each with its own responsible superintendent, usually one of the sea-lords. It was an effective system which in essentials remained intact for the remainder of the century. The real defects of the navy were those which only a more generous spending policy could have put right: the shortage of modern vessels and trained lower-deck crews. Although between 1816 and 1850 the total number of seamen in the navy, including Royal Marines, was never more than 45,000 and at times as low as 23,000, the service was unpopular and good recruits had to find. Reliance on the press-gang, and engagement of men for the period of a ship's commissioning only, meant that in peace several months might be spent in assembling the crew for a large battleship and another six before the motley collection (two thirds usually merchant seamen) settled down as a disciplined fighting complement. Not until 1853 was the principle of continuous service introduced for the lower-deck, too late to be of consequence for the Crimean War.

More progress was made with the modernization of ships. Steamships for special duties were purchased in the 1820s, the first iron frigate acquired in the mid-1840s, the first screw propellers before the end of that decade. Many old sailing ships were converted and on the eve of war the *Agamemnon* (1852) became the first capital ship designed for screw propulsion. Though mechanization was slow, other European powers were equally dilatory; and in naval strategy comparability was everything. In fact the ships which Graham brought together for the Baltic expedition in March 1854 all had steam as well as sail, and all but three screw propellers. Its technical modernity contrasted oddly with its heterogeneous crews. The immediate resources of the navy had been exhausted in bringing the Black Sea fleet up to strength and the Baltic squadron was manned by elderly seamen-artificers from the royal dockyards, naval veterans from the coastguard service, and the sweepings of the London streets.

The officer ranks were characterized by a shortage of experienced juniors and a superfluity of aged admirals. Dundas, the commander in the Mediterranean on the outbreak of hostilities, was in his seventieth year. Napier, the youngest senior admiral available for the Baltic, was sixty-eight. Both men showed their age in the timidity of their operations. The problem was almost as acute in the army. In both services the upper ranks were choked with a mass of Napoleonic War veterans whose claims could not easily be passed over. Raglan, the commander of the expeditionary army, was sixty-six. He had last seen action at Waterloo and had never held an independent field command. But of the group of distinguished senior officers considered for the post, he alone was under seventy. Of the six divisional commanders, all but two were over sixty. The much criticized army practice of purchasing commissions at least allowed some men to command a regiment before they were too old for active service. In the artillery and engineers, where it did not exist, the senior officers were noticeably more elderly. General Burgoyne, the chief engineer, was seventy-two and many of the artillery regimental commanders found it difficult to stand up to the rigours of the campaign. The failure of both services to live up to the expectations of the public at the start of the war was at least partly connected with the age of its more senior men.

The prime cause of the British military deficiencies was, however, the forty years of parliamentary cheese-paring after Waterloo. Sidney Herbert was one of the few politicians to admit the truth when he said to the Commons in December 1854 that the 'stereotyped system of economy in military affairs' that limited the British war effort at the start of the Crimean campaign was 'the fault of all Parties, all administrations, every Parliament'. After Waterloo the peace establishment had been fixed at 147,000 but this was steadily reduced over the next twenty years by the irresistible public demand for further economy. By 1821 it was down to 110,000 and in the mid-1830s, which saw the lowest expenditure on the fighting services between 1815 and 1865,[2] it was down to about 100,000. In general, during the forty years from Waterloo to the Crimea, the army establishment fluctuated between 110,000 and 140,000. Of this total about a quarter was usually stationed in Britain, a slightly smaller number in Ireland, a slightly larger number in the colonies and about 30,000 in India.

The demoralizing effects of prolonged economy were detectable throughout the army. To transport men about the globe, even in the coffin-ships usually hired for that purpose, cost money. Regiments sent to India and the colonies were therefore relieved as infrequently as possible. The official rule of five years at home and ten abroad was in practice never realized. Some regiments remained away for as long as twenty years; twenty-five was not unknown, and fifteen common. Except in India commanders were never able to acquire experience in handling large formations and the opportunities at home were no better. Units stationed in Britain had as their primary task the training of recruits and provision of drafts for overseas, together with police duties against smuggling in the coastal districts and riot in towns and industrial areas. In time of general disturbance, as in 1817–19 or during the Chartist troubles, their strength was always insufficient for the calls made upon them and the authorities had to resort to the volunteer, part-time yeomanry and a temporary mobilization of army pensioners.

[2] £11·7 millions in 1835 as compared with £71 millions in 1814 and £16 millions in 1820 and 1845.

The demands of a state which waged minor wars all over the world on a reduced peacetime establishment, and for a long time refused to sanction the creation of a national police force at home, left the army with an almost impossible task. As an army in the continental sense in fact it did not exist. It lacked trained staff officers, essential ancillary services, and sufficient reserves. The army supply corps (waggon-train in older parlance), field hospitals, and ambulance service Wellington had built up in the Peninsula were abolished after 1815. The militia was disbanded except for a small holding staff on the strength of regular regimental headquarters. The long-service engagement period of twenty-one years was reimposed though this, while producing excellent non-commissioned officers, meant that time-expired men were usually too old for recall to the colours.

The organization controlling the army still awaited the military equivalent of Sir James Graham. Professional conservatism and parliamentary jealousy of independent military authority had produced an array of parallel agencies remarkable even in early nineteenth-century British administration. Control of the land forces of the crown, including militia and pensioners, was divided between no less than eleven different authorities. Of these the most important were the secretary of state for war and colonies, responsible for general policy; the secretary at war, responsible for financial disbursements; the Horse Guards or office of the commander-in-chief; the Home Office which controlled yeomanry, militia and regular units used for internal security duties; the Board of Ordnance, in charge of munitions, engineers and artillery; and the Treasury, which was responsible for pay and commissariat. The defects of the system were patent and successive commissions of enquiry in 1837 and 1849 had made proposals for the rationalization and consolidation of this disjointed structure. But nothing was done, partly at least because of the opposition of Wellington who had an eighteenth-century horror of political interference with the army. Marginal reforms took place of which the militia act of the Derby government in 1852, authorizing the establishment of 80,000 men, was the most important. Half the recruits enlisted during the Crimea came from the militia. Technically the one great innovation was the Minié rifle, adopted with admirable promptitude in 1852: it had only been invented three years earlier. The duke of Wellington witnessed trials with the new weapon, which fired a heavy conical bullet at an effective range of 500 to 800 yards, as compared with the 90 to 200 yards of the old Brown Bess musket; and its general introduction was his last important decision as commander-in-chief. In the Crimea four of the five infantry divisions were armed with the Minié and the ability of the British troops to defeat brave and numerically superior masses of Russian infantry was largely due to this weapon.

Though defective in many respects, the army which went to the Middle East in 1854 was at least more efficient than it had been at any time since the post-Waterloo reductions. Though the cavalry, as in Wellington's day, was less skilled than its European counterparts in manoeuvring and reconnaissance, the artillery and engineers were probably as good as any; and the infantry had not lost their traditional toughness and discipline. The primary deficiencies were in trained staff, transport, supply services, field and base hospitals, and reserves. The expeditionary force was made up of units available at home together with the garrisons of various Mediterranean stations who were replaced by militia volunteers from England. Once wastage by disease, and to a lesser extent from battle casualties began, it was never possible to reinforce as rapidly as the French with their system of compulsory military service; and the drafts from home of mainly young men showed themselves alarmingly vulnerable to illness and wounds. The government made no attempt to introduce conscription and in any case the problem was training rather than recruitment. At the start of the campaign the original British expeditionary force of 27,000 was almost equal to the 30,000 French. By the end of the war the purely British contingent, though it had increased to 60,000, was little more than half the size of the French. The Foreign Enlistment Act passed at the end of 1854 had made possible, however, a reinforcement of a further 7,000 German and Swiss volunteers who had received military training in their own countries. These, together with some 20,000 Turkish troops paid by the government, brought the total force under British command to about 90,000.

The strategy of the war was as improvised as the diplomacy which led up to it. In August 1854, after their failure to capture the Turkish fortress of Silistria, the Russians evacuated Moldavia and Wallachia. These Turkish provinces were then occupied, with allied consent, by Austrian troops. The Franco–British–Turkish forces at Varna further south, already suffering from cholera (brought from France) and amoebic dysentery (as at Gallipoli in 1915), were thus left without an objective. A wedge of Austrian-held neutral territory interposed between themselves and the nearest Russian troops. The position of Austria was in fact the hinge on which the whole conduct of the war turned; and what decided Austrian policy was not its basic hostility to Russian expansion in the Balkans nor the friendly solicitations of the western allies but the equivocal attitude of Prussia. Only four years earlier at Olmütz the challenge of Prussia for the leadership of Germany had been crushed in a humiliating fashion. The memory still overshadowed the relationship between the two German powers. In the face of Prussian refusal to join the anti-Russian alliance Austria felt unable to take the risk of war and in the end adopted a position of armed neutrality which pleased neither side. The Russians kept an army corps on the Austrian frontier as a defensive precaution throughout the war; and the western allies were faced with the choice of either letting the war peter out at that stage or discovering an alternative strategy. The Crimean campaign was in effect a hastily devised punitive expedition to inflict sufficient damage on Russia to make possible an acceptable peace. The objective was the fortified naval base at Sebastopol and the Russian Black Sea fleet it sheltered. It was in fact virtually the only military objective open to the allies in the summer of 1854.

The attraction of this target was obvious both to cabinet members and to the London newpaper editors, the strategic disadvantages less considered by civilian minds four thousand miles from the scene of the conflict. The Crimea, a lozenge-shaped peninsula not unlike the Isle of Wight in general outline (and on the conventional small-scale map of Russia apparently not unlike in size), is in fact a deceptively large piece of territory. The suggestion of the cabinet that the whole peninsula might be cut off from mainland Russia by a small Turkish force stationed across the Perekop isthmus to the north ignored several relevant facts. The coastal waters at that point were too shallow for warships to give any support; in addition to the four-mile front across the isthmus at its narrowest part there was a parallel connecting causeway further to the east which would have to be guarded; the defending force would have to be supplied over a hundred miles of bad roads from the allied base outside Sebastopol; and as a preliminary a superior Russian army would have to be driven from an area equivalent in English terms to one stretching from Kent to Glamorgan, and from Dorset to Warwickshire. Even the more limited object of capturing Sebastopol at the southern tip of the peninsula was a hazardous project. It involved landing an army on open beaches and taking up a position between a numerically stronger Russian force to the north and a defended town to the south. It was not surprising that the allied generals undertook the task reluctantly and only at the bidding of their political masters. They knew little of the topography and resources of the Crimea and reports of the number of Russian troops stationed there varied considerably. The government's optimistic estimate of 40,000 was in fact about half the true figure. On any reasonable military assessment the Crimea campaign might well have turned into a combination of the disease-ridden Walcheren expedition of 1809, Wellington's first unsuccessful attempt to capture Badajoz,

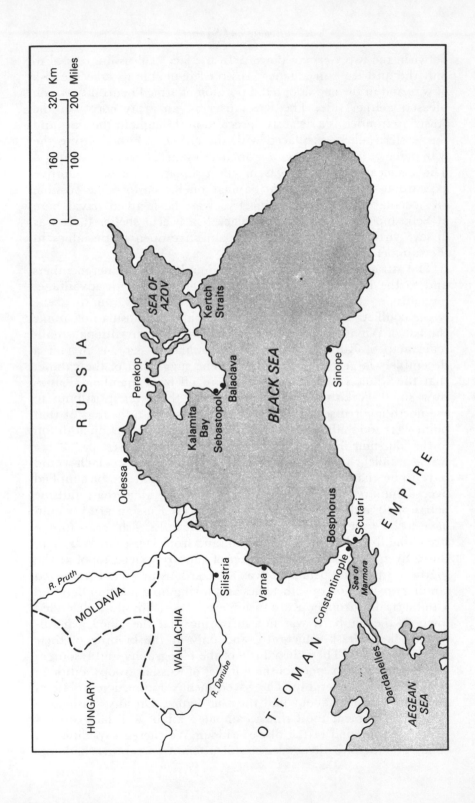

and the evacuation from Corunna. As it was, for long periods the allied troops on the bare heights above Sebastopol were themselves beleaguered by the Russian army. Sebastopol was never properly invested; its garrison was in constant touch with the main Russian forces; and at the battle of Inkerman they formed the right wing of the Russian front.

At the landings in mid-September twenty-five miles north of Sebastopol at Kalamita Bay (Calamity Bay to the irrepressible British soldiery), the British took the left-hand beaches. This original disposition was decisive for the rest of the campaign. Wheeling south the British contingent was on the outer flank, between the French troops and the Russians, and remained in this exposed position in the march across the northern front of Sebastopol to the heights above Balaclava. In consequence the British army took the brunt of the first three battles—Alma, Balaclava and Inkerman—while the French took the leading role in the siege and capture of Sebastopol. After Alma, fought within a week of landing, the crucial decision was made not to attempt to take Sebastopol by a *coup de main*, but to move into an orthodox siege position on the south of the town, using various landing sites on the coast as supply bases. Although the original concept of a limited autumn campaign—a swift descent, capture and destruction of the naval base, and immediate withdrawal —was not officially abandoned until after Inkerman on 5 November, in fact the allied armies had committed themselves by this decision to a protracted winter siege. Whether Sebastopol could have been taken by immediate assault is open to argument. What is certain is that once the opportunity was missed, the professional skill of Todleben and the tenacity of the Russian garrison forced the allied troops into an entirely different campaign from that originally envisaged.

As the numerous Alma Terraces and Inkerman Arms of Victorian England attest, the Crimean War caught the imagination of the British public as no other war between 1815 and 1914.[3] But the subsequent picture of the war in the public mind was highly selective. The 'thin red line'[4] of the 93rd Highlanders at Balaclava neither incurred nor apparently inflicted any casualties. The reprehensible and useless charge of the Light Brigade at the same battle was remembered; the tactically important and equally courageous charge of the Heavy Brigade forgotten. The achievement of that masterful but slightly neurotic lady Florence Nightingale at Scutari became immortal; Mary Stanley's hospital at Kulali and her readi-

---

[3] It was even responsible for the adoption of Alma as a girl's name.

[4] W. H. Russell's phrase was in fact 'that thin red streak topped with a line of steel'. *The War from the Landing at Gallipoli to the Death of Lord Raglan* (1865), p. 227.

ness to brave Miss Nightingale's displeasure by sending her nurses to the Crimea is mentioned only by the professional historians. The 'Crimean winter' became a by-word, although the Crimea is a health resort where the vine and tobacco plant are cultivated, and the winter of 1854–5 was not particularly severe. Until mid-November the weather was mild and by early February the wild crocuses and hyacinths were beginning to bloom again. The real period of distress and hardship for the British troops lasted only two months, from mid-November to mid-January. It was caused by two circumstances: the inadequacy of the harbour of Balaclava which had been allotted to the British as a base, and the great storm of 14 November which wrecked the transport-ships lying offshore. Because there was insufficient room in the little cove at Balaclava, vessels had to wait their turn to come in to unload; and the policy of an early assault followed by immediate evacuation gave priority to guns and ammunition over stocks of fodder, clothes and medical supplies. These and other long-term necessities were left in the twenty-one supply ships that were wrecked in the storm. Only a miracle of improvisation could have atoned for this disaster; and Filder, the elderly commissary-general sent by the Treasury to organize the supply services on the bureaucratic assumption that food, forage, horses, carts and drivers could be hired locally, was in no position to work miracles. But in January a start was made in repairing the damage. Food, clothes, and hutting materials poured in; in March a railway line from Balaclava reached the plateau above Sebastopol; and by April the army was re-organized, reclothed, rehoused and well fed.

The increasingly sharp complaints and criticism arriving at Raglan's headquarters from the cabinet in the early months of 1855 were largely based on false or out-of-date information. Many of the ministerial suggestions for improvement were obvious or unnecessary and sometimes professionally offensive. With no confidence in Raglan but afraid to recall him, the ministers criticized his subordinates instead. They encountered courteous but firm disagreement. Raglan, for all his age, his long years of office routine at the Horse Guards, and his lack of experience in active command, was probably the best man that could have been selected for his difficult post. He was a reticent, modest, even-tempered man whose defects were the qualities of his virtues. He was temperamentally incapable of the flamboyant leadership that might have made an instant impression on the troops under his command and he tended to issue requests rather than orders to his senior commanders. He lacked the theatricality and ruthlessness that often mark a successful general; but his judgement was generally good, his courage and devotion unquestioned, and his tactical sense remarkably keen. His unconventional forward command-position at the Alma and his bringing up of two heavy 18-pounder siege-guns at Inkerman had decisive effects on the two battles. His worst mistake, the bloody and unsuccessful attack on the Redan in June 1855, was committed in a chivalrous attempt to assist the French offensive which was running into difficulties. His own instinct had been for an immediate assault on Sebastopol after the battle of Alma; but Canrobert, the French commander, was opposed to it and Burgoyne, his own chief engineer, also advised against. Commanding the smaller army, Raglan was never in a position to insist on his views. Indeed, his instructions from the government explicitly laid down that, except in trivial operations, there must always be agreement and joint action with his ally. Nevertheless, his fluent French and irresistible charm of manner enabled him to maintain excellent relationships with all three successive French commanders in circumstances which could hardly have been more difficult.

Sebastopol eventually yielded on 8 September 1855, ten weeks after Raglan, weakened by overwork and anxiety, had died of cholera. By that time the army had been brought to a high pitch of efficiency. A land transport corps, a sanitary corps, and an ambulance and works department had been created, a hospital set up at Balaclava, and a telegraph cable laid from Varna which kept the army headquarters in touch with Constantinople. In the seven months between the fall of Sebastopol and the formal declaration of peace in March 1856 the six infantry divisions and one cavalry division, now living in hutted camps, were exercised first by battalion and then by brigade and divisional staffs until they became the best trained and equipped British army since the Peninsula—and for the first time superior in material and in administration even to the French. At home too the war had forced changes which in peace had been postponed. Between June 1854 and May 1855 the secretary-ship for war had been separated from that of colonies and the secretaryship at war amalgamated with it. The reorganized war department took over control of supply and transport from the Treasury, militia from the Home Office, munitions, equipment, engineers and artillery from the Master-General of the Ordnance, the army medical corps from the Medical Board and uniforms from the Board of General Officers. Only the commander-in-chief, in charge of discipline, promotion and training, remained independent; and even he owed a general responsibility to the secretary of state.

Carried through hurriedly and piecemeal, under the pressure of public opinion and without guiding principle other than securing greater centralization, these sweeping innovations were nevertheless more important for the army as a whole than the subsequent

Cardwell reforms of the Gladstonian era. They were followed by other improvements between 1856 and 1868. One effect of the Crimean War was that the British public was noticeably more ready to accept the army as a necessary and valuable institution. It had even been revealed to some of them that the army private was a being not entirely destitute of a certain delicacy of feeling. The obscene language in the hospitals at Scutari and Kulali which shocked the lady volunteers came not from the soldiers but from the hired nurses brought out from England. After the war the army reaped the benefit of this enhanced public esteem. On the initiative of Palmerston and Herbert the establishment was raised in the early 1860s to between 215,000 and 230,000 men, though it was rarely able to recruit enough to bring its numbers up to authorized strength. A number of reforms in training, equipment and barrack amenities were put through, together with an expansion and re-organization of the militia. By 1865, except for the purchase of commissions and long-service recruiting, there was little left of the old army of Moore and Wellington.

The navy too felt the impact of change. The absence of a visible opponent and the limitations of a sea power operating against shore defences reduced its role during the war to little more than that of an armed transport and escort fleet. Nevertheless, only complete command of the sea had made possible the risky expedition against a Russian naval base 4,000 miles away. When peace came the technical lessons of the war were rapidly applied. The recruiting problems encountered in 1854 led in the following decade to the enlargement of the Royal Marines and Coastguards, the establishment of training ships for boys, and a corps of Royal Naval Volunteers. In 1860 the *Warrior*, the first sea-going armoured warship, was launched, capable of destroying single-handed the entire fleet that fought at Trafalgar. The rifled, breech-loading gun was introduced and a number of wooden ships adapted as ironclads. One of these, the *Royal Sovereign* in 1864, equipped with armoured revolving gun-turrets, was the first ship of the line to dispense with sail altogether. The navy had finally turned its back on the age of Nelson and started the long process of experimentation which produced the Grand Fleet of 1914.

V

The Crimean War, which started a revival of British naval and military strength, marked the beginning of a decline of British influence in Europe. The paradox can be explained partly by the damage to British prestige caused by the much publicized defects and disasters of the first Crimean winter, partly by a lack of elasticity in the ageing Palmerston's conduct of diplomacy. More decisive still perhaps was the change in European politics which began with the revolutions of 1848. Superficially that dramatic year seemed a moment of triumph. With England thronged with illustrious refugees —Louis Philippe, Guizot, Princess Lieven, Prince and Princess Metternich, Prince William of Prussia, many of them old enemies of Palmerston—the foreign secretary could have been forgiven for feeling a sense of personal vindication. In fact the end of the old regime in Europe signalled danger for Britain. Canning had been right: his country had more standing in old congress Europe, as the one liberal constitutional monarchy among the timid conservative autocracies, than in the post-1850 Europe of rising national ambitions. Napoleon III, Cavour, Garibaldi, Bismarck and von Roon were an ill exchange for Louis Philippe, Guizot and Metternich. Increasingly mid-Victorian Britain seemed a peaceful civilized refuge from which the inhabitants looked on, half-fascinated, half-repelled, at the momentous changes taking place on the continent.

The Crimean War halted any further danger from the Eastern Question for about twenty years. During that time the two problems that dominated European politics were the movements for the unification of Italy and Germany. In both countries the effective starting points had been the revolutions of 1848. Palmerston had looked with satisfaction on the upsurge of Italian nationalism in 1848–9 since he believed that it would be an advantage for Austria to shed her Italian commitments and concentrate on the task of developing the rest of her vast territories. Italy, he wrote in June 1848, was for Austria 'the heel of Achilles, and not the shield of Ajax'. On the other hand he had no special desire to see a united Italy and he refused to give any encouragement to Piedmont. All he wanted was a quick end to the fighting and the restoration of peace before France was tempted to intervene. The victories of Radetzky ended the comfortable British anticipation of a North Italian buffer-state under Piedmont intervening between Austria and France, and Palmerston's protests at Austrian reprisals were contemptuously rejected. At Vienna there was considerable resentment at Palmerston's attitude and an understandable if unjustified tendency to ascribe all their troubles in the peninsula to British incitement. Yet, difficult as it was for Austrian diplomacy to recognize, Palmerston's basic attitude was pro-Austrian. 'The political independence and liberties of Europe are bound up ... with the maintenance and integrity of Austria as a great European power,' he told the House of Commons in July 1849. 'Anything which tends ... to weaken and to cripple Austria ... must be a great calamity for Europe.' He both shared and voiced the indignation of the British public at the brutal repression of the Hungarian revolution; and he supported Turkey's refusal to hand over Kossuth and other Hungarian and Polish refugees. Yet he had deplored the original rising in Hungary as a further weakening of the Austrian Empire and along with Wellington and Aberdeen had encouraged Russia to intervene to put down the revolt.

The fear of France which conditioned his attitude in 1848–9 emerged with greater force after the Crimean War. Not the least of the many curious aspects of that conflict was that the peace settlement witnessed a rapid rapprochement between the two main belligerents. French public opinion, unlike British, had been in favour of an early end to the fighting and Napoleon was anxious to isolate Austria in preparation for his Italian plans. It was not a difficult diplomatic manoeuvre to accomplish. Austria, which had played a leading part in forcing the Russians to accept the peace terms (including the neutralization of the Black Sea), was already regarded by Russia as an enemy. But the rift between Britain and Austria meant that Palmerston too was isolated. He had to accept the presence of Prussia at the peace conference in Paris which set the seal on French prestige; and his wish to leave the divided principalities under Turkish suzerainty was overruled in favour of an arrangement which ultimately led to the creation of Rumania as an independent state. Though Napoleon, as always, was concerned to retain British goodwill, the Rumanian issue laid bare a fundamental difference between the two countries. Napoleon's instinctive desire to support emergent European nationalities clashed with Palmerston's traditional principle of erecting barriers to Russian aggression. A series of small, weak, independent Christian states like Greece and Rumania would, in his judgement, almost inevitably fall under Russian domination.

It was a clash between the principles of 1815 and those of 1848; and it is not surprising that French overtures for joint action on the Italian problem evoked little response in London. In turn Napoleon became more reticent and more secretive. By the start of 1859 it became clear that he was planning war against Austria and his attempt to get a Prussian as well as the Russian promise of neutrality alarmed both the Foreign Office and the court. Nevertheless, with British public opinion strongly sympathetic to Italian aspirations, there was little any British government could do except remain neutral. The replacement of Derby's conservative administration by Palmerston's in June 1859 seemed to weaken the Austrian and strengthen still further the Italian predilections of the government. In reality, however, British policy was still trapped in the old dilemma, between its wish to see Austria strong and its conviction that the Austrian position in Italy was a source of weakness, between abstract benevolence towards Italian aspirations and practical fear of the disruptive consequences for Europe of a Franco–Austrian war. With much in common Britain and Austria were both isolated and without friends, each unable to assist the other. In April 1859 Austria rounded off her catalogue of errors with an ultimatum to Piedmont which brought war with France. Britain, hesitant and undecided, watched from the sidelines. The peace of Villafranca in July, hastily concluded by the two emperors after the bloody and indecisive battle of Solferino, left the Italian situation still fluid. As in 1849 the British effort was directed towards ending the hostilities and persuading the combatants to withdraw. What the Foreign Office really wanted was to prevent any substantial French aggrandisement. While the views of Palmerston and Russell wavered between alliance with France to force Austria into a quick settlement, and general encouragement for spontaneous Italian liberation movements, events in Italy took their own course.

Distrust of France was the one firm feature of British policy towards Italy; over the question of political unity it was much more uncertain. In 1860 Russell and his chief were still not thinking in terms of a unification of south and north Italy. Palmerston was prepared to support the king of Naples if he gave guarantees of reform; Russell was ready to assist Austria to retain Venetia. Both notions were quietly discarded as events made them obsolete; but it was only at the last moment that Russell changed his mind about joint Franco–British naval action to prevent Garibaldi from crossing to the mainland in the summer of 1860, and not until 1861 that the principle of a divided Italy was abandoned. In the end a united peninsula, even at the unwelcome cost of the cession of Savoy to France, seemed the best practical arrangement for the balance of power in Europe. But it was a conclusion at which British policy arrived only after a series of shifts and improvisations. Subsequent British popularity among Italian liberals was based on appearances rather than actions. The British government had not foreseen or done much to bring about the end result; it merely capitalized on events.

The outcome of the war, which left Austria isolated and discredited, was neither the object nor in the interest of Britain. Yet Palmerston, for all his conviction of the importance of Austria as the 'natural ally of England in the east', had done little to strengthen the European position of the Austrian Empire; it is even arguable that he had done something to weaken it. His continual

criticism of Austrian rule was in curious contrast to his sturdy defence
of Turkey against allegations of corruption and decay. Though
public advocacy of British liberal principles for other countries was
always sure of uncritical applause from the British public, there was
sound sense in the view expressed by Prince Albert in 1847,[5] and
Peel in the Don Pacifico debate of 1850, that it was foolish to
encourage constitutional reforms for which a state or a society might
not be ready. The habit of lecturing foreign countries on the
desirability of copying British institutions was not always wise and
rarely tactful. Successive Austrian governments could well have
wished to be saved from the candid friend whose candour was so
much more in evidence than his friendship.

The rift with Austria was all the more damaging in view of the
continued British distrust of France. Although Napoleon, as his policy
over Syria, China and Mexico in 1858–61 demonstrated, was still
anxious to cooperate with Britian, the old enmities and suspicions
on the British side were as strong as ever. The popular Volunteer
Movement of 1859–60, the strengthening of the navy, and Palmerston's massive fortifications programme, testified in striking fashion
to the standing conviction of the British public that the national
enemy was still their great neighbour across the Channel. It was
Palmerston's opinion, as indeed it had been Peel's, that only 'sufficient
defensive Strength on our Part can render our Relations with France
satisfactory and secure'; and under his guidance the naval and
military defences of the country which had caused so much anxiety
to Wellington in the 1840s were by the 1860s placed on an effective
footing. But the policy which inspired this rearmament was fundamentally pacific. In the last five years of his life, beneath the old
aggressive and sometimes reckless language, Palmerston displayed
a defensive, almost a static quality. When the Polish revolt broke
out in 1863 the lack of any cooperation between the two western
powers destroyed whatever chance may have existed of successful
diplomatic intervention. Though Palmerston, under pressure from
press and parliament, spoke bluntly to the Russian government, he
refused to join France in protesting against the Russo–Prussian
convention of mutual aid in repressing the revolt, and he rejected
Napoleon's proposal for a European congress. The whole episode
was a revelation both of Anglo–French disunity and their individual
weakness in the face of a determined central power. Having indirectly encouraged the rebels to prolong their resistance, the govern-

---

[5] In a letter to Baron Stockmar 2 September 1847, printed in T. Martin, *Life of the Prince
Consort.* 'We are frequently inclined to plunge States into Constitutional reforms to which
they have no inclination. This I hold to be *quite wrong* (*vide* Spain, Portugal, Greece), although
it is Lord Palmerston's hobby.'

ment's policy of 'meddle and muddle', as Lord Derby described it, eventually abandoned the Poles to their fate.

Similarly over the American Civil War, which engaged warm British sympathies and put a savage strain on the British economy, strong words were accompanied by a remarkable passivity of action. A series of awkward incidents took place, such as the arrest of two southern envoys taken off the British ship *Trent* on the high seas in 1861, and the government's failure to detain the *Alabama*, built at Birkenhead for the Confederate navy, in 1862; but Palmerston even at his most quarrelsome never went beyond an attitude of defensive jingoism. At bottom he wished neither to intervene nor to provoke hostilities.

The final demonstration of British powerlessness and pacifism came over Schleswig–Holstein. Despite Palmerston's rather threadbare joke, the matter though complicated did not defy understanding. In the middle of the century the dynastic change of succession in Denmark to an heir through the female line, raised the question whether the two duchies, personally united with the Danish crown for centuries, but bound by the Salic law of male inheritance, should be legally incorporated with Denmark, or the German Confederation (of which Holstein was already member), or divided. The issue, small enough in itself, was given international importance by the forces of German nationalism and Prussian ambition. In 1848–9, the revolutions in Germany had been an embarrassment for British policy despite the general sympathy for constitutional reforms. There was no belief in London political circles in the possibility or even desirability of German unification but there was an underlying fear that the spread of democratic republicanism would put Germany on the side of France besides having disturbing repercussions in Poland and Denmark. War in fact did break out between the German Confederation and Denmark over the duchies. In 1850 energetic action by Britain, Russia and France relieved Denmark from the pressure of its more powerful neighbour and Prussia (the military agent of the Confederation) was forced to agree (1851–2) to the integrity of all the Danish territories. The Treaty of London, however, was essentially a settlement imposed by the great powers and its terms were almost as distasteful to the Danes as the German Confederation.

Despite the Danish issue of 1849–51, and occasional friction over the German *Zollverein*, relations between Britain and Prussia, the old Waterloo allies, remained generally good for some years longer. It was the Crimean War that created the first serious rift. At the outset of the crisis Prussia seemed primarily concerned with organizing resistance by the other four powers to French ambitions, while Britain was endeavouring to unite Austria and Prussia in a common front against Russia. The British attempt to enlist Prussian support on the Eastern Question failed; and though in March 1854 Frederick William IV assured the British ambassador to St Petersburg that he would never fight on Russia's side, this was small comfort in London. What became ominously clear after 1856 was that the wreckage of the old alliances left by the Crimean War provided an unprecedented opportunity for the two powers which wanted territorial changes in central Europe. By 1857 British diplomats were beginning to fear a secret understanding between Bismarck and Napoleon aimed at Austria and involving compensation for France in the Rhineland. The accession to power of the prince of Prussia as regent and the despatch of Bismarck to St Petersburg temporarily improved Anglo–Prussian relations; and when the Austro–French war broke out in 1859, Prussia like Britain worked to localize the conflict and restore peace. After Bismarck came to power in 1862, however, it was apparent that even in Berlin the territorial settlement of 1815 no longer had any sanctity. In March 1863 the grant by the Danish king of a new constitution, annexing Schleswig but giving independent rights to Holstein, started a new crisis. Circumstances now were more favourable to German and Prussian ambitions than in 1849–51. The former partnership of Britain, Russia and France over the Danish duchies had long since broken up. Russia had been conciliated by Bismarck's assistance in repressing the Polish revolt of 1863; and Napoleon had been alienated by the brusque British rejection of his proposal for a great international congress to review generally the terms of the 1815 European settlement.

As the tension over the duchies increased, British diplomacy preached concession to Denmark and moderation to the German Confederation, a laudable activity which was frustrated as much by Danish obstinacy and unrealism as by German belligerence. Nevertheless, Palmerston himself was at least partly responsible for the intransigence of the Danes. In his public utterances (notably a speech in the House of Commons in July 1863) he had emphasized that the independence and integrity of the Danish monarchy was an important British interest and that if the German Confederation tried to impose its will by force, 'it would not be Denmark alone with which they would have to contend'. Bismarck himself was coolly indifferent to the British threat; the Prussian attitude was essentially that expressed by von Moltke in 1865 when he observed contemptuously that 'England is as powerless on the Continent as she is presuming'. The problem for Prussian diplomacy was one of method, not of end; and it was only with reluctance that Bismarck utilized the strength of German nationalism and the aid of Austria in pursuit of Prussian aggrandisement. Similarly it was Bismarck's ruthless methods rather than his general objective that aroused British distrust and fear.

By the beginning of 1864 the foreign policy of Palmerston and Russell was in pieces. Britain, the one real supporter of the *status quo*, was isolated and impotent. All chance of French cooperation had been destroyed by British suspicion of Napoleon's designs on the Rhineland; Russell's aggressive messages to Austria and the Federal Diet made German acceptance of British mediation impossible; British advice was ignored in Copenhagen. In the spring of 1864, while the Prussian and Austrian troops occupied by stages the whole Danish peninsula, proposals from Russell for a naval demonstration off Copenhagen were overruled by the rest of the cabinet with the vigorous backing of the Queen and only faint resistance from the prime minister. The inevitable parliamentary inquest in July was one of the most humiliating experiences Palmerston ever had to endure; and for a time it looked as if the Commons as well as the Lords would endorse a vote of censure on the government's handling of the Danish question. He was saved ironically by the votes of the pacifist radicals led by his old enemies Cobden and Bright and a few conservatives. Though public opinion, warmed by the recent marriage of the Prince of Wales to the Danish princess Alexandra, was sentimentally sympathetic to the Danish cause, there was no readiness in the country to go to war. Moreover, war against Prussia still seemed an unnatural event to leaders of both main political parties. Palmerston himself still at heart feared aggressive nationalism and French ambitions, and looked on the central powers as the guardians of order and stability in Europe. Even though he condemned the rapacity of the victors in the 1864 war, he could in September 1865 take comfort in the reflection (one which would have been familiar to Castlereagh and Wellington) that 'it is desirable that Germany, in the aggregate, should be strong, in order to control those two ambitious and aggressive powers, France and Russia, that press upon her west and east'.

By 1865 Palmerston and Britain were left as the last exponents of the principles of 1815. It was to be only a few more years before the revelation in 1870 of French weakness and Prussian military aggressiveness started a long, slow shift in British foreign policy. Already, however, the old confidence in the moral power of British influence on the continent had been shattered. It was clear that in future Britain would either have to do more or say less. The store of international credit accumulated by Pitt, Liverpool, Wellington and Castlereagh was exhausted and the principles they had followed no longer applicable. By 1866 the Vienna settlement was dead, the

Europe of Castlereagh, Metternich and Canning vanished, legitimacy and legality outmoded. The old antagonism between authority and liberalism was being resolved into a new and dangerous synthesis of the nationalism of 1848 and the militarism of the dynastic states. The 'concert of Europe', which with all its faults had contributed to the peaceful settlement of international problems, was no longer in existence; and Canning and Palmerston had been among its grave-diggers. For Britain 1864 marked the real beginning of 'isolation', not a splendid beginning but a realistic one. For too long British foreign policy, and indeed British public opinion, had been under the illusion that the rest of Europe was following, or could be encouraged to follow, the British path of constitutional development and social progress. Between 1864 and 1871 Europe was at last seen to be a different political world, moved by forces and ruled by methods incomprehensible to the peaceful, prosperous, domesticated society that had grown up in the shelter of the British Isles.

11 Peace and Prosperity: Taking Stock in 1865

I

When the Registrar-General and his staff prepared their report on the census of 1851, they pointed out that a significant stage had been reached in the evolution of British society. At this midway point in the century the urban population of Great Britain for the first time exceeded that of the country. Urban population they defined as residents in market towns, county towns and cities; so that many under this heading were still living in what was essentially a rural environment. Moreover the difference was not great: 10·5 million as against 10·4 million. Neverthless, the still unslackened growth of population made it certain that the process of urbanization would continue. Despite British emigration overseas and the tendency since the Famine of Irish migrants to go to America rather than to Britain, the 2·3 million by which the population had increased since 1841 exceeded, according to the census calculators, the increase during the whole of the second half of the eighteenth century. In the fifty years since 1801 ten millions had been added to the British population, almost the equivalent of the total increase in the island in all preceding ages.

In that same half century the proportion of land per person had fallen from 5·4 acres to 2·7, in England and Wales from four to two acres. In the towns the average density was over five persons to an acre, in the country over five acres to one person. People were living closer to each other, a majority in built-up areas. There was more social unity, less provincialism, more movement and mixture of people and families. Much of the urban growth had come from internal migration. A large proportion of the existing town population had been born in the countryside. 'In England,' concluded the *Census Report* with an unexpected touch of poetry, 'town and country are bound together not only by the intercourse of commerce and the interchange of intelligence, but by a thousand ties of blood and affection.'

They were also bound by 5,000 miles of iron railroad with 2,000 more under construction. In two great waves of railway promotion, the first in 1836–8 and the second in 1844–8, the capital had been raised to provide Britain with a new form of transport. On the trunk roads the horse-drawn coach had virtually disappeared and by 1865 the railway system that was to meet the country's needs for another century was substantially in existence. It had been a prodigious national effort. Between the opening of the Liverpool–Manchester line in 1830 and the Crimean War in 1854 some £250 millions had been invested in railway companies—the equivalent of almost five times the annual revenue of the state. At its peak in the late 1840s railway investment was absorbing half the private investment of the country and paying a £16 million wage bill for quarter of a million men. It was as though an entire major industry had been temporarily added to the nation's resources; and even when the boom passed away, the pervasive influence of the railways on almost every branch of the economy and every class of society was permanent and profound. Socially the trails of smoke and the distant whistle in every part of the kingdom marked the end of the old provincial isolation. Economically the productivity of British industry was now assisted by the best and most inexpensive transport system in the world. In a thousand different ways, from cheap Midlands coal for the London householder to the light reading literature provided by W. H. Smith's station bookstalls, the railways helped to remould Victorian society.

Despite railways, urbanization and industrialization, Britain still presented a largely rural appearance. Agriculture was still by far the largest single occupation; and by the 1860s agriculture was manifestly prospering. Lord Ernle, the historian of English farming, called the years from 1853 to 1863 a golden age. It was true that there had been considerable price fluctuation, especially for the arable farmer, round the middle of the century. Immediately after the repeal of the corn laws good harvests and large imports brought the price of grain down to panic levels. The Crimean War, which closed the Baltic to Russian corn, then saw a rapid return to high prices. After 1855 stability returned despite heavy foreign imports. A growing population and a rising standard of living kept up consumption; and foreign foodstuffs, especially wheat from North America, tended to even out fluctuations in price levels rather than depress them. Meat and dairy products rose in value, rents also, though part at least of the increase went back in estate improvements.

Urbanization and the railways in fact had come as a universal boon to the landed interest. The farmers benefited by cheaper and quicker access to larger and more compact markets, the landowner by the sale of land and higher property values. By 1860 the beneficial effects of free trade had completely allayed the old protectionist fears. The growth of industrial wealth had increased food consumption faster than either the domestic or foreign producer could easily match it. The enormous increase in the import of live cattle after 1842, for example, still more after 1846 when the duties were entirely removed, had more than borne out Peel's hope that Britain would develop a thriving fatstock rearing industry. So important and profitable was it by 1860 that it made corn growing, not as an isolated activity but as an adjunct to green crops and animal husbandry, a remunerative aspect of agriculture even at the reduced post-Crimean prices.

The inevitable decline of 'King Corn' in the face of this increasing diversification of agriculture was shown by the technical improvements in the middle of the century. These significantly were devoted almost entirely to arable farming. In the 1830s, as one farming expert unkindly said, the average British farmer 'despised science as much as he feared Free Trade'. Lack of capital, and recollection of the Swing riots of 1830, fortified this prejudice. When the Royal Agricultural Society, dedicated to scientific improvement, was founded by the gentry in 1838 it was denounced by some embattled farmers as a betrayal of their interests in that it disavowed by its non-political character the necessity of legislative protection. By the 1850s, however, scientific methods were spreading among both landowners and tenants. Peel's 1846 Improvement of Land Act, empowering state loans for drainage schemes (one of his most valuable 'compensations' for the repeal of the corn laws) resulted in an expenditure of £8 millions over the next twenty-five years, involving some two million acres as well as providing an example for privately financed drainage operations.

Even more important was the growing use of farm machinery. In the changed social and economic conditions of the mid-nineteenth century it was increasingly recognized that agricultural progress implied not a crude extension of arable acreage but the application of more intensive methods to the land already under the plough. The real mechanical revolution in British farming came in Victoria's reign. The process can be seen in the annual exhibitions of the Royal Agricultural Society. In the 1830s the main interest was in drills, in the 1840s in tile-making machines for drainage, in the 1850s in mechanical reapers and threshers, in the 1860s in steam tillage. At the Newcastle show in 1846 only one steamengine was on display; at Worcester in 1863 there were a hundred and thirty-five. For small farmers, unable to afford the capital outlay, there was already a well established practice of hiring them from middlemen. The growing demand was exemplified by the experience of one manufacturer of

agricultural steamengines who between 1852 and 1863 sold no less
than five thousand where in 1845 he had made only one steamengine
and not a single steam thrashing-machine. In agriculture the age
of steam had at last arrived. Not the least of its consequences was
that the British farmers with a smaller labour force were producing
more food than ever before. British agriculture was playing its full
part in feeding the island's mounting population and in the process
enjoyed a prosperity unknown in the years of high protection.

What sustained that prosperity, however, was the wealth
generated by the growth of British industry. Agriculture, which at
the start of the century had accounted for 33 per cent of the national
income, by 1851 has seen its share fall to 20 per cent. Its dominant
place in the economy had been taken by manufactures (including
building and mining) whose share had risen from 23 per cent in
1801 to 34 per cent in 1851. Coal output (the index of energy
consumption) had expanded between Waterloo and the death of
Palmerston more than fivefold. The UK registered shipping tonnage,
despite the competition of railways, had nearly doubled. The
leadership in this astonishing industrial expansion had been provided
by the textiles. Between the second and sixth decades of the century
imports of raw cotton and exports of cotton piece goods had increased
eightfold; imports of raw wool, despite a substantial increase in the
domestic supply, more than sixfold. Textiles in the 1850s constituted
60 per cent in value of the entire export trade; and though this high
proportion had been even higher in the 1830s, the extraordinary
dominance of textiles in the British economy remained. Coal and
iron, whose growth had largely depended on the textile industry,
were only just beginning to assume an independent role. Iron, steel
and machinery, a relatively negligible item before 1820, had
increased their share of British exports to 20 per cent; coal accounted
for 2 per cent. Substantially the wealth of Britain consisted in its
ability to make cheap cloth, iron, steel and machinery for the rest
of the world and transport them to the customer in British ships.
It was a unique position which could not last for ever; but while
it lasted Britain led the world economy.

Industrialization, sea power, and a world market not only fed,
clothed and housed the growing millions of British people, but had
raised their standard of living. It has been estimated that the national
income rose from about £190 millions in 1801 to £560 millions in
1851—in individual terms an increase from £12 to £20 per head
of population. Another index is provided by income tax returns. The
gross value of income from lands, houses, mines and other forms of
real estate assessed under Schedule A increased from £85.8 millions
in England and Wales in 1843 to £131·3 in 1865; in Scotland from

£9·4 millions to £16·2 millions. That under Schedule D (profits from trades and professions) from £52·7 millions in England and Wales in 1843 to £95·6 in 1865; in Scotland from £4·8 to £9·8 millions. Even allowing for the inclusion in 1853 of incomes between £100 and £150 (the effect of which was offset by lower rates) this was a substantial increase in the taxable wealth of the country.

After 1842 the trend was away from indirect taxation on consumption towards direct taxation on property and incomes. Despite sweeping reductions in customs and excise, however, the increased consumption of food and tobacco more than compensated for the revenue losses on manufactured goods and raw materials. The revenue from indirect taxation continued therefore to rise slowly from about £42 millions in 1840 to £45 millions in 1860. But the real transformation came in the proportion of national revenue raised directly from the wealthier section of the population—the property owners and income tax payers. In 1840 this had amounted to approximately £7·7 millions, in 1860 to £19·6 millions. Since in the same period the national revenue had increased from £51·5 to £70 millions, this meant that the proportion directly contributed by the wealthier classes (excluding their share of indirect taxation) had risen from about 15 per cent to 28 per cent. To this should be added the amount of local taxation which fell mainly on property, in 1860 possibly as much as £15 millions.[1]

II

The great increase in national wealth in itself furnishes little evidence as to its distribution. The large and familiar inequalities remained, though it is unlikely that rising productivity failed to benefit to some extent all classes. From 1843 onward there had clearly been a general and dramatic improvement in the material state of the country. Except for one bad year in 1847, wheat prices were consistently low from 1842 to 1852. In four years from 1844 to 1847 sugar consumption rose by 40 per cent in the wake of Peel's budgets. The 'Hungry Forties' was not a contemporary or even a Victorian

[1] These calculations are based on the figures given in Stafford Northcote's *Twenty Years of Financial Policy* (1862), appendix B. The figure for local taxation in 1840 is from G. R. Porter, *Progress of the Nation* (1847 edn), p. 527. It should be noted that Northcote's distinction is not between direct and indirect taxation but between taxation falling directly on property and other kinds. Under the latter heading he includes income-tax returns from schedules B, D and E. In 1860 these amounted to £4·5 millions. I have therefore deducted this amount from his total of indirect and added it to the total of direct taxation.

expression. It seems to have been coined by those neo-Cobdenites Mr and Mrs Fisher Unwin sixty years later and popularized by the book Mrs Unwin (Richard Cobden's daughter) published under that title in 1904 to combat Joseph Chamberlain's tariff reform campaign. All the indications suggest in fact that from the mid-1840s conditions improved for the working classes as a whole and from 1850 it is indisputable that there was a rise in real wages.

A great export industry like cotton, with its satellites iron and coal, was peculiarly subject to alternate boom and depression; but industry in general paid good wages. Probably the most permanently depressed and exploited class of workers were in those non-industrial employments characterized by an excess of labour, absence of union organization, lack of social mobility and traditionally low wages; often they were women. Charles Dickens in his *Sketches by Boz* (1836) called the London milliners' and staymakers' apprentices the 'hardest worked, the worst paid, and too often, the worst used class of the community'. Five years later Douglas Jerrold, journalist and wit but serious for once, wrote in even more scarifying language of 'the working Sempstress—the lonely, faded spinster—the human animal vegetating on two shillings *per diem*'. Factory acts, mines acts, trade unions, ten hour days, could do nothing for these unfortunates; only the cheaper food available from the mid-1840s onward and for a few hundreds of them the scheme of female emigration to Australia which Sidney Herbert was promoting between 1849 and 1852 could help.

The largest class of non-industrial, unorganized and 'unprotected' workers remained, as ever, the agricultural labourers and their families. Though a parliamentary enquiry into the condition of women and children employed in agriculture took place in the 1840s, no legislation resulted until after 1865. The House of Commons gentry, as Peel rather sharply pointed out in 1844, showed more zeal for imposing regulations on factory owners than on their tenant farmers. Yet even among this large and depressed class signs of improvement were visible by the middle of the century. The immediate cause was clearly the general fall in the cost of living that had come in the 1840s. Caird estimated in 1850 that the rural worker's main articles of food were a third cheaper compared with 1840 and that this single circumstance had 'added greatly to the comfort of the labourer'; other rural reformers agreed with him. Even when wages had not increased, S. G. Osborne wrote in 1852, the labourers were better off because everything they ate or used had got cheaper. 'After more than twenty years' active interest in their condition, I never saw them so comfortable as I have known them to be the last five years.' Charles Kingsley, his brother-in-law and another anglican parson, added his testimony in 1859. In the preface to a new edition of his rural novel *Yeast* (first published in 1851), he admitted that 'the labourers, during the last ten years, are altogether better off. Free Trade has increased their food, without lessening their employment.'

Other influences, more unevenly, were working to the same end. After the middle of the century agricultural wages were rising slightly even in the worst-paid areas. Another beneficial development was the increasing provision of allotments, disliked by the farmers by favoured by the Poor Law Commissioners as a substitute for the dying cottage industries. From Kent to the North Riding of Yorkshire (where in 1848 they were reported as 'very prevalent') peers and gentry were taking the lead in making land available. Local horticultural societies were beginning to offer prizes for best kept allotments and vegetable produce. In addition most villages of any size possessed a variety of organizations to assist their poorer inhabitants—sick clubs, burial clubs, coal clubs, clothing clubs— with a weekly subscription of a few pennies and relying heavily on donations from wealthy parishioners. Anglican clergy took a leading part in these charitable activities, as also in the movement for village schools and adult evening classes. Farmers were largely indifferent, if not actually hostile, and the gentry too were often out of contact with the rural poor. The resident parish clergy—gentlemen by status but not always in income—were often the labourers' only social ally. It was not accident that the two best known champions of the agricultural labourer in this period were both clergymen: the Reverend Sidney Godolphin Osborne of Dorset in the 1840s and Canon Edward Girdlestone of Devonshire in the 1860s.

Significantly both men were promoters of organized emigration schemes as a means of helping both those who left the countryside and those who stayed. The more important migration, however, was the silent drift of the country dwellers to the towns, the men often to general labouring, the girls to domestic service. By 1861 nearly 150,000 people born in Norfolk were living outside the county and its population had actually declined. After the mid-century the effect of this internal movement was to stabilize wages and in favourable circumstances even to push them up. At the same time mechanization and more intensive farming were creating a demand for more labour. For rural reformers the real problem was housing. To bad living conditions they attributed the evils they could see—dirt, disease, coarseness, drunkenness, and immorality—and those they suspected —incest, abortion, and infanticide. The insanitary one- or two-room cottage was still in 1850 the commonest type; neither farmer nor speculative builder had any economic incentive to build better. In many rural habitations, in Osborne's savage phrase, human existence was 'simply pig-life glazed and staircased'. Yet even here things were changing. By the 1840s landlords in many parts of the country, with more conscience and longer purses than their tenant farmers, were taking the lead in building cottages with the reformer's indispensable minimum of three bedrooms (for parents, boys and girls), gardens, and proper privies. Supreme examples were the fourth duke of Northumberland (died 1865), who was said to have built nearly 1,400 new cottages and repaired many more, and the seventh duke of Bedford who by 1857 had put up about 600 new cottages on his Bedfordshire and Devonshire estates. Essays on cottage architecture appeared in agricultural journals and the duty of landed proprietors to provide adequate cottage accommodation was emphasized. The final seal of royal approval was given by Prince Albert, himself a notable builder of farm cottages at Windsor, Osborne and Balmoral, who arranged for model labourers' houses to be shown at the 1851 Exhibition. Rural housing could not be transformed in one generation; but at least the problem was recognized and the remedies, however piecemeal, were being applied.

Though the southern agricultural labourer remained one of the worst-paid and worst-housed of the larger occupational groups, he was at least emerging from the debased conditions which had produced riot, machine-breaking and incendiarism in the earlier part of the century. Between farmer and labourer there was truce rather than social reconciliation. When opportunity offered, as at harvest-time, men often bargained for better pay or went elsewhere. Free trade, capital and mechanization—the indirect results of the industrial revolutions—had brought them marginal but recognizable benefits. There was certainly no desire on the part of the mass of people living in the country to go back to the days of corn laws and high food tariffs. Even so, their state was still not as good as the organized, industrial worker. The extensive researches into the diet of the working classes carried out in the early 1860s by Edward Smith (one of John Simon's able young medical men at the Privy Council office) demonstrated that outside the cotton famine years the Lancashire textile workers enjoyed a diet sufficiently rich in protein and carbohydrates to ensure health. By comparison the English farm labourers, though spending a larger proportion of their wages on food, were not so well nourished. A fifth of them had not enough carbohydrates; more than a third insufficient protein. Lowest of all in the scale were the domestic workers and sweated industries where definite malnutrition still existed.

In the industrial areas the aristocrats of labour lived on a scale unknown to the southern rural labourer and beyond the dreams of the half-starved London sempstress. In the Black Country round Dudley and Wolverhampton, for example, the iron-workers by the middle of the century were earning in good times 50s. a week, in bad seldom less than 16s. for a five-day week. A collier earned 20s. to 30s. to which his family might add another 10s. to 30s. These high wages had given rise, in the disapproving words of one cleric, to 'a deep and almost universally pervading sensuality'. The men spent recklessly and extravagantly on food (meat of all kinds, geese, duck, early green peas, new potatoes, and asparagus); on drink (beer and spirits in profusion, sometimes port wine consumed by the tumbler or basinful); on pleasure excursions in cars and carts; and in gambling. The habit of saving was almost non-existent; the wages were good but the money went as fast as it came. Yet the critics and moralists who deplored this spectacle and pointed to the thrift and foresight of the French working classes, admitted that the conditions in which the men lived were hardly conducive to elevated feelings—bad housing and sanitation, inadequate supplies of clean water, dirt, smoke, employment of women at the pithead (and sometimes illicitly and by connivance of the men, underground), and consequent neglect of children and household.

What also disturbed philanthropists and administrators was the class enmity still widely present which no amount of prosperity or good management seemed able to eradicate. Indeed, good wages in the colliery industry appeared to encourage men to work less than a full week, stop work or strike on flimsy pretexts. In the language of clergy, government inspectors, and Blue Books, there was still in 1850 a 'spirit of insubordination' in many occupations, especially the heavy industries, a lack of respect or loyalty to employers, and a readiness to use coercion against them whenever there was an advantage to be gained. In the coalfields of Staffordshire and the northeast there was a considerable circulation of cheap Chartist, socialist and 'infidel' literature, the staple diet of which seemed to consist of violent criticism of religion, society and of all classes except the industrial workers themselves. There were over a dozen papers of this class, mainly printed in London and some showing strong similarities to the writings of such French socialists as Louis Blanc and Blanqui. One national paper which sold widely in the manufacturing areas was the radical-Chartist *Reynolds's Weekly*, which proclaimed itself as devoted to 'the cause of freedom and the interests of the enslaved masses'. In 1861 it had a circulation of 350,000, equal to that of *The Times*, the *Standard* and the *Telegraph* put together. Although from the mid-1840s more effort was being made by clergy and gentry to repair the years of neglect, and a new breed of employer was appearing, younger, better educated and more

socially responsible, occupational and union loyalties often seemed
stronger than any social gratitude or local tie.

It was true that the larger unions by 1850 were beginning to
abandon direct coercion of employers as a central strategy in favour
of more efficient national organization, better financial assistance
for its members, and more effective social legislation. The so-called
'Junta' which emerged between 1852 and 1865 (W. Allan, R.
Applegarth, D. Guile, E. Coulson, and G. Odger, representing
respectively the engineers, carpenters, ironfounders, bricklayers and
shoemakers unions) was the first important group of unionists to offer
a sensible, cautious leadership. They were content to aim at what
was practicable and prepared to work with their contemporary
society rather than against it. Aided by middle-class allies—Christian
Socialists like J. M. Ludlow, Tom Hughes, and Charles Kingsley
and reforming rationalists like Frederic Harrison and Professor E.
S. Beesly, many of them barristers and literary men—the 'new
unionism' did much to break down the engrained distrust of trade
unions still prevalent in the public mind. At the same time, though
the chimera of a universal, consolidated trade union organization
had been abandoned after the 1840s, the growth of provincial trades
councils as permanent rather than as emergency joint-delegacies of
local unions helped to prevent the movement from becoming merely
an aggregate of individual craft unions.

Nevertheless, while the Junta disliked strikes and preferred to work
for the welfare of their members by other methods, the industrial
scene was not a picture of unbroken peace. The creation of the
Amalgamated Society of Engineers in 1850, the largest union of its
time with 11,000 members paying the unusually high subscription
of 1s. a week, led to aggressive action by its members and forceful
counter-action by employers. The great strike of 1852, the first to
attract national interest, ended in a defeat for the men; but though
the employers were successful, the union survived as an example of
how a powerful, skilled craft should be organized. Not all strikes
were unsuccessful. In the coalfields of Northumberland and Durham,
where there was a history of poor industrial relations, the tactics
of the miners in the 1840s of concentrating on individual mines caused
many employers to give in. Even enlightened firms had little cause
to be reconciled to unionism. The Derwent Iron Company at Consett
in Co. Durham was a large concern employing 15,000 workmen.
It was also an excellent employer, providing cottages, gardens,
drainage, roads, schools, libraries and churches, as well as paying
good wages. It was the last place where a strike might have been
expected. Yet a strike took place in 1849 which was ascribed largely
to the infiltration of unionists determined to 'win' at Consett.

In this case energetic measures by the management, helped by support from some of their own employees, proved successful. Often, even when many of the workmen were peaceful, the active unionists tended to force the pace and the rank and file were reluctant to stand aloof for fear of consequences. This was hardly surprising, since the consequences could sometimes be unpleasant. In the course of similar troubles at the same time in south Wales, one blackleg at Aberdare was killed in an explosion when a bag of gunpowder with a lighted fuse was thrown into his house. English colliers brought in by one colliery owner to replace the strikers were violently attacked and as a result ten Welsh miners were committed to gaol.

Animosity was not all on one side. Faced with strike action even benevolent employers tended to take measures which in the men's minds constituted provocation; and not all employers were either benevolent or sensible. The attempt by the London builders unions in 1858 to get a nine-hour day led to a prolonged strike in 1859–60 and a demand by the master builders for a repudiation of union membership as a condition of future employment. Neither side won, though the generous sums contributed by other unions prevented the men from being defeated. It would be misleading, however, to depict the state of the working classes solely in terms of the trade union movement. Though the membership of enrolled trade unionists had increased perhaps from 150,000 in the 1840s to 200,000 or even 300,000 in the 1860s, the majority of the urban and industrial workers were not in unions. Those that were saw the benefits of membership more in terms of insurance, sick benefit and social clubs than in any active militancy against employers. In the skilled trades wages by 1865 were possibly as much as 20 per cent higher than twenty years earlier and since there had been a steady recruitment from the poorly paid ranks of the country labourer and domestic worker to the better-paid occupations, the national improvement was greater than a mere comparison of wage rates might suggest. One sign of prosperity was that building societies, provident societies, savings banks and cooperative societies were becoming familiar elements of working-class life in the industrial north, as was also the spread of the Saturday half-holiday.

III

A feature of the middle decades of the century was the growing number of enlightened employers trying to establish a new style of industrial relationships. For some the motive was a practical realization that men who attended chapel and sent their children to school were likely to prove reliable employees. For some it derived from a new sense of social duty instilled at public schools in the tradition of Thomas Arnold of Rugby. For others it was part of the philanthropy enjoined by nonconformist ethics. Whatever the cause, the result was often a kind of industrial paternalism that could compare with the best efforts of the country gentry and clergy. An example was Price's Candle Company in London which in the 1850s was providing for its employees day and night schools, cricket fields and allotments, paid holidays, excursions to the seaside, bath houses, dining rooms and a chapel. Titus Salt, the Bradford millionaire, built an entire industrial estate for his workpeople called Saltaire, comprising some 500 dwelling-houses, complete with public bath and wash-houses, reading room, library, and a Congregational chapel in the classical style. Similar company housing estates were built by the Tredegar Ironworks in Monmouthshire and by the great manufacturer Akroyd of Halifax at Copley and Ackroydon.

If these were exceptional, there were many other employers—Bagnall's Ironworks at West Bromwich, Ransomes at Ipswich, the Stansfeld and Briggs Collieries near Huddersfield, Joseph Pease at Durham, John Bright at Rochdale, Lord Ellesmere's colliery at Worsley, the Ashworths at Bolton, Adams the lace firm at Nottingham, John Guest's Dowlais Ironworks and the Ebbw Vale Company in south Wales, and the Glengarnock Ironworks in Scotland—who were putting some of their profits into schools, sports grounds, reading rooms, and canteens, and promoting cricket, football, brass bands, benefit clubs, seaside excursions and Christmas entertainments. Only wealthy firms could afford large-scale philanthropy, and there were many more small enterprises which could not. Nevertheless, a standard was being set by which these others could be judged; and if some of the activities were dictated by no more than enlightened self-interest, even self-interested philanthropy was better than no philanthropy at all.

These developments reflected an attitude in society as a whole. The publicity given in the 1840s to the 'Condition of England' question, in government enquiries, popular novels, journalism, and a multitude of serious books, pamphlets and articles, like Douglas Jerrold's *Heads of the People* and Mayhew's revelations of the state of the London poor in the *Morning Chronicle*, affected most of the educated classes. Though perhaps more public concern for the state of the working classes was evinced in the 1840s than in any previous decade, that concern had been growing for many years. Even before 1830 individual bishops and clergy of the Church of England, for example, had tried to alleviate the lot of the poor; and the interest of the church quickened in the next twenty years. By the middle of the century bishops like Blomfield and J. B. Sumner, who had started their careers as Benthamite utilitarians, had abandoned theory in favour of compulsory regulation in such matters as sanitary reform. Both the older and the younger bishops were exhorting their clergy to take an interest in the physical as well as the moral state of the working classes. All the whig and eight tory bishops (including Archbishop Howley, Blomfield and Sumner) voted for the repeal of the corn laws. The episcopate, led by Blomfield, Thirlwall and Wilberforce, were even more solidly behind the Ten Hours Act of 1847.

On both issues they were concerned to identify the church not with a class but with the people as a whole. The optimistic and somewhat unworldly alliance between the Christian Socialists and the Chartist trade unionists in 1848–52 represented not an eccentric but merely an extreme example of anglican social sympathies. The church could offer no opposition in principle to the efforts of Maurice and Kingsley to establish closer links with the working classes. Their short-lived periodical *Politics for the People* in 1848 carried contributions not only from S. G. Osborne but from Archbishop Whately and a number of prominent anglican laymen.

A different aspect of this concern was the enormous amount of voluntary charitable activity. No assessment of Victorian social responsibility is complete that does not take into account what was being done by private philanthropy outside the scope of the poor law. It was not a new feature of British society. Most towns of any size or antiquity had an array of charitable foundations dating back many generations. But post-Waterloo distress had increased the calls on private generosity and public conscience. Every period of trade depression was marked by efforts to alleviate distress. In 1816 a fund launched to assist the Spitalfields weavers raised £43,000 at the first meeting and was swelled in a couple of days by another £5,000 from the Prince Regent. In the depression of 1826, apart from contributions amounting to £3,000 from the royal purse to aid local relief funds in England and Wales, a general national fund was organized in the City of London which at one point was distributing £5,000 a week. This organization—the Manufacturers Relief Committee—was revived in 1842 when a royal message was read in churches and chapels throughout the kingdom inviting subscriptions for the relief of distress in Lancashire and the industrial areas of Scotland. At the start of the Lancashire cotton famine a single county meeting in Lancashire raised £130,000 for relief to which Lord Derby, the chairman of the executive committee,

subscribed £5,000—a sum which was neither the first nor the last
of his contributions. Legislation was later passed to enable wealthier
parishes in the area to assist the hard-pressed districts, and a loan
of £1,500,000 was sanctioned for public works to provide
employment. But it was the aggregate of nearly £2 millions from
the public that enabled Lancashire to pass peacefully through a
period of acute economic depression which fifty years earlier would
have brought riot and bloodshed.

Equally important though less publicized was the permanent
network of charitable organizations which carried on their work in
both bad times and good. In a real sense early Victorian society
was organized to meet poverty, destitution and other social evils in
a way that the state was not. The poor law was the refuge of last
resort. Once family responsibilities broke down, the first resource
of the poor were the unofficial agencies that society had evolved over
many generations for precisely this purpose. Clearly some of this vast
but miscellaneous effort was wasteful, maladministered and misdirected; some forms of poverty and many individual cases remained
untouched. Yet in aggregate it represented a much greater
application of social resources, both in effort and money, than
anything attempted by central or local government. Even large
institutions—hospitals, dispensaries, charity schools, orphanages,
lunatic asylums, societies to assist widows, mendicity societies,
emigration societies, homes for the blind, deaf and dumb—normally
drew their main income from the subscriptions and legacies of the
wealthy inhabitants of their locality. Such support as they might
derive from town corporations or poor law authorities was merely
supplementary.

Because of the multiplicity of agencies involved it is impossible
to assess with any accuracy the total amount of money expended
in this way. But the temptation is probably to under- rather than
over-estimate it. In the main Macaulay was probably correct when
he claimed that in the 1830s and 1840s more was being done by
voluntary effort to relieve the poor than ever before; and there was
no slackening of effort in the later decades. S. G. Osborne observed
in 1860 that there was scarcely a physical or spiritual want or evil
for which some society did not exist. It has been estimated that the
annual expenditure by private charitable organizations in London
alone in the early 1860's may have been between £5 and £7 millions,
or as much as the entire official poor relief expenditure for the whole
country.

This philanthropic activity, together with the uncounted efforts
of individuals, was perhaps more effective in knitting society together
than bureaucratic state relief would have been. Certainly after the

repeal of the corn laws not only did many influential people think that it was the business of the wealthy, the educated, and the religious to bridge the social gap between rich and poor but they believed that they were succeeding. The change was perhaps first generally noticed at the time of the Chartist demonstration in London in 1848 when the crowds that went to Kennington Common—working people in their Sunday best with rosettes in their button-holes and their womenfolk on their arms—looked as if they were on a holiday outing rather than bent on overthrowing the government.

This impression was strengthened by the experience of the Great Exhibition three years later. Planned as a conscious demonstration of national harmony, as well as of national wealth and industrial inventiveness, it more than fulfilled the hopes of its sponsors. Many nervous people in high life feared the effects of attracting masses of country labourers and town artisans to London by special cheap days and organized railway trips. Clergy and landowners in rural districts, manufacturers in towns, sent whole trainloads of working men and their families to see the wonders of the Crystal Palace. Never before in any one year had the British population moved about so much. But all went well; there was no riotousness and little disorder, only an understandable increase in pickpocketing. The pleased surprise of the authorities at this gratifying circumstance was a measure of their previous apprehensions. In fact the poorer classes who attended the Exhibition seemed to be less interested in the more meretricious entertainments on show than in the products of their own craft or occupation. They took pleasure in identifying themselves with the new world of industry and technology which their country was displaying to the world. By many commentators the Exhibition was felt to be a national jubilee, emphasizing and strengthening the ties that bound society together. The *Illustrated London News* spoke in colourful journalistic prose of the obliteration of class jealousies and the 'fusion of society into one homogeneous and contented mass of mutually related and mutually dependent people'.

If this was exaggeration, at least it was exaggeration that reflected a good deal of public opinion. In the 1850s and 1860s this optimistic attitude became even more widespread. Not all radicals and reformers were pleased at the apparent quiescence of the working classes. 'The English proletariat,' Engels wrote acidly to Marx in 1858, 'is becoming more and more bourgeois, so that this most bourgeois of all nations is apparently aiming ultimately at the possession of a bourgeois aristocracy and a bourgeois proletariat, as well as a bourgeoisie.' Cooper, the old agnostic agitator turned Baptist lay-missionary, revisiting the Midlands, Yorkshire and Lancashire in the 1860s, nostalgically contrasted the passionate political convictions of the ragged Chartists thirty years earlier with the prosperous, well dressed working men he found in Lancashire, talking of their shares in the 'Coops' and building societies, and interested more in their whippets and racing pigeons than in politics. Others were more grateful in their comments. To S. G. Osborne, one of the severest critics of the middle and upper classes to which he himself belonged, it seemed in 1864 that prosperity had come because Britain was 'a people at peace among ourselves'. For those who could remember the years between 1815 and 1842 it would not have seemed an unjust verdict.

IV

The middle classes themselves were clearly growing in strength and organization. There were more professional men and more professions. By 1850 the number of barristers, for example, had increased fourfold since Waterloo; and even if only about a third of them actually pursued a legal career, their ranks were still overcrowded and an increasing number were glad to turn to government and administration. Solicitors in London had almost doubled in the same period and most of them were in active employment. Of the three old professions, in fact, only medicine seemed in the third quarter of the century to be relatively static. This was largely because of the Medical Health Act of 1858 which, by establishing a legal definition of medical practitioners, a medical register, and a General Medical Council, had eliminated a large number of unqualified men who had previously been free to attend to the Victorian public. Other, faster-growing professions were attaining status alongside the old—dentists, engineers, architects, surveyors, accountants, company secretaries, authors and actors. Together with the established organs of finance, trade and industry —the Bank of England, the Stock Exchange, the shipping, insurance, and commodity exchanges, and the provincial chambers of commerce (provided in 1860 with a national chamber)—they constituted a skilled and intelligent leadership for the middle classes as a whole.

To satisfy the intellectual needs of these classes a daily and weekly newspaper press, four times as great as in the reign of George IV, supplied information and views on public affairs. Higher interests were examined in a mass of religious periodicals. By the 1840s Evangelicals, Broad Churchmen, Tractarians, Unitarians, Methodists, Congregationalists, Baptists, Quakers, Roman Catholics and Jews, all had their denominational press. A slightly later but equally significant development was the growing number of periodicals devoted to particular social or professional interests. By the 1850s there were journals for sporting squires, for farmers, gardeners, doctors and musicians; for the theatrical world, for teachers, and artists; for the mining and railway industries; for engineers, chemists and economists. A wide range of relatively cheap subscription clubs, both in London and the larger provincial towns, had come into existence to attend to the social and personal comfort of the males of these classes. *Punch* (founded 1840), the *Illustrated London News* (1842) and such domestic literature as the *Family Herald* (1842), and the *Englishwoman's Domestic Magazine* (1852) catered for their wives and families, as did in a different way the growing number of seaside resorts like Brighton, Ramsgate, Broadstairs, Ryde, Torquay, Bridlington, Scarborough, Southport and Blackpool, which the railways had helped to transform from quiet watering places for the wealthy and invalid into popular holiday towns with serried rows of hotels and boarding houses.

Increasing professionalization and organization was also evident in those characteristically middle-class institutions, the churches. Perhaps the most striking fact to emerge from the religious census of 1851 was that churchgoing was an activity mainly confined to the middle and upper classes and those, like domestic servants and rural labouring families, who were under the eye of their social superiors. The public at large, though possibly not the professional clergy, were shocked to discover that over 40 per cent of the population did not attend any form of religious service on the census Sunday. In the three largest English provincial towns of Manchester, Liverpool and Birmingham it has been estimated that perhaps as many as nine in ten of the total population were non-attenders. Some of the working-class London boroughs were no better, and this after a generation of intensive urban missionary work by both anglicans and nonconformists. The churches and chapels were there; but the people were not filling them. It was not that the churches had lost the allegiance of the mass of the urban and industrial working classes; they had never possessed it. As Peel had drily pointed out as early as 1835, 'between the Dissenters and the Established Church there is an enormous neutral ground of infidelity'. It was a consciousness of this among the wiser men on both sides that had helped to dampen down sectarian rivalry.

After 1850 the old church-dissent conflict had degenerated into a welter of secondary issues: Maynooth, voluntaryism, church rates, ritualism, admission of Jews to parliament, clerical courts,

ecclesiastical discipline, civil divorce, university entrance and burial
grounds. Though the activities of the Liberation Society provoked
a Church Defence movement, which attained a mild prominence
between 1859 and 1863, much of the heat had gone out of confessional
warfare. Church and chapel were themselves divided on many issues.
The diversity of anglican opinion, from members of the Evangelical
Alliance at one extreme to Tractarian ritualists at the other, was
matched by the divisions within as well as between the three main
nonconformist denominations. The chief demand of the Liberation
Society was the abolition of church rates. But this was a symbolic
question devoid of much practical content. In the great majority
of towns compulsory payment of church rates had long been
abandoned, and in rural parishes there was little opposition—though
the inevitable exceptions gained wide publicity. A survey conducted
by the Liberation Society in 1866 disclosed that of over 1,500 parishes
making returns, only 150 still had compulsory payment. The case
for abolition was more on grounds of its virtual disuse than its
hardships to non-anglicans. Compromise and commonsense had
robbed the question of all but residual significance.

The decline of the church rate issue was only one aspect of the
larger transformation of the Church of England. Since the shock
of the 1828–32 legislation it had been engaged, slowly and sometimes
painfully, in redefining its position in English society. In the process
it had become more like its nonconformist rivals, just as they were
coming to resemble more closely the established church in all but
historic status. Though the outward trappings of the establishment
remained, legislation since 1828 had lopped off many of its privileges
and monopolies. In effect the church had been thrown back on its
own spiritual and physical resources. What happened after 1830 was
not simply reform but a profound change in the actual character
of the church. It could not be regarded any more as co-existent with
the state. Even parliament was no longer an exclusively anglican
or even Protestant institution. Once regarded as a kind of proxy
legislature for the establishment, it now contained not only dissenters,
Unitarians and Roman Catholics but, after a long campaign
culminating in the act of 1858, practising Jews. One logical if belated
consequence of this theological separation of church and state was
the revival of Convocation in 1854–5. The Church of England now
had, what the nonconformist sects had long possessed, its own annual
conference of clergy.

By comparison with the other churches, however, its resources of
wealth, influence and manpower were still impressive. Since the
beginning of the century the establishment by 1850 had built over
2,500 churches at a cost of over £9 millions of which over £7 millions

had come from private donations; another 1,000 new churches were built and over 300 reconstructed between 1851 and 1865. Its schools provided the bulk of education for the children of the English poor. The number of beneficed clergy had risen from nearly 11,000 in 1831 to nearly 18,000 in 1851, and their efforts were being supplemented by an army of deacons, lay-readers and district visitors. Pluralism and non-residence had been virtually eradicated, and significantly fewer of them were magistrates. The clergy were better trained, more professional, more urbanized, more zealous, more earnest, more respectable, and perhaps less individualistic. Bishop Pepys of Worcester could say with pride in 1854 that 'the sporting clergyman, so common a character in former days, is now rarely to be met with'. To some bishops it seemed as though the church was in a better state physically and morally than at any time since the Reformation —better supported by the wealthy, more respected by the poor. If there was a tendency on their part to ascribe much of the growing social harmony to the work of the clergy, rather than the improved state of the church to changes in society, there was at least a sober optimism over what had been achieved and what the future would bring.

There was a similar hopefulness in the nonconformist churches. They had reason to be confident. The returns of 1851 showed that of the total attendances (many probably attended twice) at church on census Sunday, nearly 3.8 million were at anglican churches, only slightly fewer (nearly 3·5 million) at dissenting chapels. Despite the notable Church of England revival in the towns, in most of the large industrial cities dissenting attendances outnumbered anglican. This position of near-equality was accompanied by the same kind of activity and organization that characterized the revived and transformed anglican church. Out of the shell of the old eighteenth-century dissenting sects had emerged the Victorian nonconformist churches, concerned less to convert the nation or bear unflinching witness to a peculiar truth as to cater in an efficient and responsible way for the needs of their members. Their own worldly success had ensured that their task in the mid-nineteenth century was consolidation rather than expansion, organization rather than individual evangelism.

In the 1830s and 1840s all the main nonconformist denominations —Wesleyan, Congregationalists, and Baptists—were giving close attention to the training of their clergy; all were bent on raising their own academic standards. They were producing better educated, more professional ministers but also men who would have greater expectations of security and status from the career they had chosen. Even Primitive Methodism, one of the few genuine radical

evangelistic movements of the early nineteenth century, did not
escape this apparently inevitable process of institutionalization. The
new nonconformist chapels that were going up all over the country,
particularly in the large towns, were witness to the social change.
No longer were they the austere barn-like structures that had satisfied
older generations. They were built expensively, on good sites, in the
classical or the later more popular gothic style, with organs and
stained-glass windows, reflecting the wealth and growing aesthetic
tastes of the congregations which financed them. 'The Author of our
prosperity,' said a successful Methodist factory owner in explanation
of an ornate chapel he and his brothers had erected near their own
homes, 'ought not to be worshipped in a house inferior to that in
which we dwelt.'[2] The dissenting denominations had their own
training colleges, their secondary as well as their elementary schools,
their London headquarters, their central libraries, their annual
conferences, their magazines, their own hymn books. They were
becoming in effect churches. Nonconformity had achieved parity
with the establishment, and in the process had become respectable
and middle class.

A more secular aspiration of the middle classes was towards better
secondary and higher education for their children. By 1850, for
example, even Gladstone (typically while opposing whig proposals
for an enquiry into the old universities) admitted that if Oxford and
Cambridge had a fault, it was that they 'have too much the character
of seminaries of the higher classes. I want to see them embrace a
larger number of the middle classes of society.' Russell's commission
of enquiry and the acts of 1854 (Oxford) and 1856 (Cambridge)
freed the two universities from the restrictions of their ancient
regulations and set up commissions to promote internal reforms. The
government of the universities was put into the hands of the resident
fellows; religious tests were modified so that dissenters could take
first degrees; and the degree syllabuses were widened to include more
scientific subjects. Given the great social and political influence of
the two senior English universities and the resistance (especially of
Oxford) to reform, this was perhaps as much as was practicable at
the time. Ten or fifteen years earlier, in the heat of the anglican-
dissenting conflict, even this much would have been impossible.

A greater and more characteristic achievement, since it came from
private initiative and required no legislation, was the rise of schools
catering specifically for the sons of the professional, industrial and
mercantile middle classes. The thirty years from 1840 to 1870 were
the classic age of new public schools. Thirty-one were started in this

---

[2] Quoted by W. Cooke Taylor in *Notes of a Tour in the Manufacturing Districts of Lancashire*
(1842), p. 62.

period compared with a mere half-dozen in the first four decades of the century. It was not that the seven traditional foundations—Eton, Harrow, Westminster, Charterhouse, Winchester, Rugby and Shrewsbury—were physically unable to cope with an increasing pressure, but that they were still looking mainly to the gentry and aristocracy for their clientele and were unduly narrow in their selection of pupils. The new schools were intended to provide a cheaper, more accessible, more professional education which, while retaining the classical tradition, often prepared directly for entrance into the army and navy, the Indian civil service and government departments at home.

The anglican bias was still strong. Compared with the six belonging to other denominations and two non-denominational, no less than twenty-three of the new schools were specifically anglican. As that earnest Tractarian Nathaniel Woodard had hoped, the new middle classes were being captured for the church, though less by the early Woodard schools like Lancing and Hurspierpoint than by the more immediately successful foundations like Marlborough, Cheltenham, Wellington, Rossall and Radley. Outside the ranks of the public schools there was also a growing number of revived grammar schools and endowed schools offering a classical education and boarding-house training for the children of parents who could not afford the more expensive establishments. Staffed for the most part by Oxford and Cambridge graduates, many of them in holy orders, the public and the grammar schools together formed a powerful medium through which the Victorian middle classes absorbed the ideals of a gentlemanly, classical and anglican education. For a society which was increasingly dependent on trade, industry and technology, it was a curious feature which did much to explain the pattern of British social and political development in the Victorian period.

V

In the activities of mid-Victorian society, bustling, opulent, expanding and self-confident, the directing hand of the state is not readily observable. After the heroic but isolated efforts of the 1830s and 1840s at industrial regulation, education and poor law reform, the tide of 'centralization' seemed to be receding, leaving behind as stranded wrecks the Railway Board which made a brief appearance in the mid-1840s and the Board of Health set up in 1848, reorganized after five years when Chadwick, Southwood Smith and

Lord Ashley were all dropped, and finally abolished in 1858. But
just as it is easy to exaggerate the practical results of the social
legislation of the immediate post-1832 period, so it is easy to ignore
the significance of the work being carried on more quietly and less
controversially in the 1850s and 1860s. The growth of state activity
was not so much arrested as camouflaged.

By the middle of the century, for example, the Board of Trade
had acquired a mass of miscellaneous responsibilites which more than
made up for the effect of free trade on its tariff reform activities.
The act of 1850 which established the general mercantile authority
of the Board, and that of 1854 which codified merchant shipping
legislation, brought some sort of order to the haphazard accumulation of two decades of administrative growth and in the process
turned the Board into the nearest equivalent which early Victorian
government possessed to a department of trade and industry. Even
the reabsorbed railway section continued to increase in size and to
exercise, by persuasion and advice rather than through its power
of legal compulsion, a considerable influence over such matters as
company regulations, accident precautions and conditions of service.
Though parliament in the 1840s had preferred to spend hundreds
of hours debating railway bills rather than give general powers to
government, the principle was never surrendered that in return for
the privileges of monopoly and compulsory land purchase the
railway companies must submit to inspection and supervision.

An analogous history was that of the education committee which
grew up in that 'potting shed for new administrative plants', in
Professor Smellie's neat phrase, the Privy Council. When the whigs
in 1839 set up a special committee of the Council to superintend
the disbursement of the enlarged parliamentary grant for education,
the state inadvertently acquired a permanent office for educational
policy, with Kay Shuttleworth, a former assistant poor law
commissioner, as its initial driving force. The sectarian rivalries which
prevented an agreed national educational policy between 1839 and
1847 did little to restrict the administrative development of the new
office. Even the defeat of Russell's bill in 1853 to allow large towns
to levy an educational rate was circumvented by the decision of the
committee to make capitation grants at first for rural and later for
all schools. Power of the purse and administrative initiative enabled
the committee to support in fact any educational development of
which it approved. By the end of the Crimean War, through building
grants, capitation grants, teacher-training subsidies, and salary
supplementations, the state through the committee was spending half
a million pounds annually and the figure was steadily rising. The
reorganization of 1856, which turned the old committee of Council

into a department of state under a parliamentary minister, was a belated recognition of the political importance of education—or at least, of the amount of money being spent on it. By 1862 this had risen to £840,000 and the schools directly assisted taught nearly half the children of the poor who went to school. The grant was also subsidizing nearly three dozen teacher-training colleges with over 2,000 students.

The unpopular Revised Code of 1862 was an attempt to rationalize and control the expensive and expanding system of multiple grants that had grown up since 1840. But the financial saving was counterbalanced by the criticisms which the new 'payment by results' system incurred and the damage done to the efficiency and morale of the schools. What was also becoming clear was that the assisted voluntary system was nearing the limits of its capabilities. The effort of the churches, particularly of the Church of England, to provide schools for the poor—'the most gigantic effort ever made by private charity to perform a public duty', wrote the *Quarterly Review* in 1861— had with all its defects supplied an elementary education for a higher proportion of children than in Holland or France and only marginally lower than under the compulsory Prussian state system. A whole new profession, numbering some 10,000 certificated teachers and 60 state inspectors had come into existence by 1868 with improved salaries and growing professional competence. But if education was to be not just a social duty but a social right, only the state, that had done so much to assist the voluntary effort, could apply the final compulsion, organization and finance necessary for an effective national system. The general readiness on the part of the informed public, the press and the churches themselves to accept this next step was a tribute to the central role played by the education department in the previous twenty years.

Over the same period another of the mid-century experiments in government had been quietly consolidating its position after a shaky start. Chadwick's famous *Enquiry into the Sanitary Condition of the Labouring Population of Great Britain* in 1842 was a landmark in the development of social policy. Intellectually it marked the realization of the Poor Law Commissioners that poverty was a complex phenomenon affected by many factors such as housing, working conditions, disease, thriftlessness and drunkenness. It stressed the importance of the medical officer and civil engineer in local government and the basic necessity for an urban population of pure water and piped sewage. Yet, as so often with the pioneer legislation at this time, the administrative solution not only fell short of its author's intentions but was soon reduced to even more modest proportions. The Public Health Act which eventually appeared in

1848 authorized (but except in districts of high mortality did not compel) local authorities to set up boards of health with powers for paving, sewage and water supply. The central board also established could in practice do little more than exhort, admonish and publicize. Chadwick, however, made no secret of his conviction that a national sanitary policy could only be secured by a powerful central department with powers of inspection and initiative, and that municipal control was preferable to private agencies. As a result he achieved the paradoxical feat of uniting against the board both the defenders of local government and the champions of individual enterprise. Earnest, insensitive and dogmatic, he was incapable of realizing that British society, with its strong individualistic tradition, did not take kindly to authoritarian regulation—or even the appearance of it. Even so, the compulsory vaccination act of 1853 and the compulsory appointment of medical officers for all the London districts in 1855 demonstrated the readiness of parliament to act with surprising vigour when a convincing case was made for state intervention.

For the Board of Health the apparent catastrophe of 1858 was more apparent than real. Most of its functions other than its compulsory powers (which in any case had not been used) were transferred to the Home Office, which was obliged in consequence to set up a special local government office to administer them. Equally important the Board's chief medical officer John Simon, together with responsibility for epidemic diseases, was assigned to that useful depositary the Privy Council Office. Like Chadwick, though with more emphasis on medicine, less on engineering, Simon regarded statutory regulation of the physical conditions of the poor 'an obligation of society'. But he was shrewd enough to know that no national policy would succeed unless there was general public assent to what was being done. In setting out to secure that consent he became the most effective propagandist in the history of the Victorian public health movement. After 1858 his central position in the Privy Council Office assured him of political influence at the centre of power. Getting together under a system of 'temporary appointments' a team of able young medical men, he carried out and publicized a series of pioneer studies in epidemic and preventible disease. By 1865 he had earned for his office a national reputation which was enhanced by the work undertaken by his inspectors during the cotton famine in Lancashire and the cattle plague of the mid-1860s. The conviction was growing that only greater central direction of this kind could hope to solve the problem of public health.

The prudent Simon reaped where the doctrinaire Chadwick had aggressively sown. Nevertheless Chadwick left his mark on English local government. Once the 1848 Public Health Act was on the statute book, an increasing number of municipalities began to make use of its provisions. Before the Board ended its first independent phase in 1854, no less than 284 towns had petitioned to come under the act, of whom 182 had already qualified. By 1865 over 570 localities had taken powers either under the 1848 act or the wider Local Government Act of 1858. Few of them were prepared to incur the cost of maintaining all the permissible full-time officials ranging from medical officers and borough engineers to inspectors of nuisances. But the principle of municipal responsibility for health and sanitation was being recognized and much actually accomplished. Between 1848 and 1871 the government authorized loans for these purposes totalling over £10 millions.

Other amenities were being added to urban life, many under the adoptive clauses of parliamentary legislation. Though the new borough councils set up in 1835 did not at first show much enthusiasm for taking on fresh civic responsibilities, local agitation, pressure from their own officials, and an occasional salutary epidemic resulted in a gradual extension of municipal enterprise. Baths, wash-houses, parks and playing-fields were appearing in the 1840s, museums and public libraries in the 1850s. Some corporations acquired their own water-supply; some their own cemeteries; a few their own gas-works. While full 'municipal socialism' only came after the consolidating act of 1875, the achievements of the middle decades of the century were not inconsiderable. By 1865 the towns and cities of Britain were pleasanter, and certainly safer, places to live in than they had ever been. The last great cholera epidemic came in 1865–6, killing over 14,000 persons a large enough figure but not as many as in the three earlier epidemics of the century. Though medical ignorance of the sources of infection for many common diseases[3] kept the crude death rate constant, the effect of sanitary measures was seen in the steady fall in the death rate from smallpox, enteric fever and cholera. While the population continued to rise, the death rate did not. Compared with continental states like France, Italy and Germany, the mortality in England and Wales remained low. London was a healthier place than either Paris, Brussels, Berlin, Vienna or St Petersburg; and British public health was rapidly becoming the best in the world.

Local government had also acquired another institution, perhaps

---

[3] Orthodox medical opinion still held that the main causes of such diseases as typhus, typhoid and cholera were lack of cleanliness and atmospheric contagion. Even a medical reformer like Florence Nightingale disbelieved in the existence of germs and as late as the 1870s medical students were taught that it was the effluvia from organic filth which produced fever. The germ theory only became established after 1875.

the most underrated of all the early Victorian contributions to the
civilizing of society: the county and borough police forces. The
compulsory police clauses in the Municipal Corporations Act of 1835
had resulted in a flood of applications from the new watch committees
for assistance and advice from the Metropolitan Police. In over 200
boroughs Scotland Yard men were sent down to help the authorities
in setting up their own forces. Not surprisingly what followed was
a flight of petty criminals into the unpoliced rural districts. A royal
commission which considered the problem recommended the
establishment of a national force to be trained by Scotland Yard;
but, like many of the bold proposals of the 1830s, this was too strong
for contemporary stomachs. The 1839 rural police act merely
permitted the county magistrates to set up their own individual
forces, with the home secretary having the right of approving the
appointment of chief constables and the regulations for each force.
By 1853, when a fresh review was made, it was clear that the early
legislation was inadequate. More than a dozen recalcitrant boroughs
had still not obeyed the 1835 act. Rural police forces had been set
up in only twenty-two counties and parts of seven others. There was
little uniformity between the various forces and some reflected the
views of ex-army and -navy chief constables who had a more military
conception of police work than the civilian 'preventive' principle
enshrined in Peel's Metropolitan Police—in one case at least
extending to the practice of sword-drill for all recruits and the issue
of cutlasses for night patrols.[4]

The new act of 1856, therefore, with a similar one for Scotland
the following year, both imposed a national system and tried to instil
some homogeneity into the forces already in existence. Every county
was required to establish a police force; the Home Office was given
powers of inspection for all forces, and further authorized to make
grants-in-aid of one quarter the cost on proof of efficiency. For this
the criterion in the early years was little more than a prescribed
proportion of police to population; but, as happened in other areas
of government administration, the right of inspection inevitably led
on to further controls: standard tests of efficiency, the merging of
small inefficient borough forces, the provision of expert advice, and
the gradual elimination of the eccentricities which chief constables
like Captain Harris in Hampshire and Captain McHardy RN in
Essex, had introduced into their commands. With the 1856–7 acts
Britain had for the first time professional police forces covering the
whole country. In England and Wales by 1865 there were over 23,000
men (including some 7,500 in London) to enforce law and order—

---

[4] In Hampshire under Captain Harris.

a larger force than the regular home army the Liverpool government had at its disposal in the disordered year of 1817. The nationwide police system that had been an unrealized dream of Peel's in the 1820s had within a generation come into existence.

Partly because of the police, Britain was becoming a more orderly and disciplined society. It was also becoming less coarse and brutal. The newspaper press was one index of changing manners. It was more decorous, less vigorous, than the violent, reckless but high-spirited journals of the Regency period. The vulgarity and venom of the Gillray, Rowlandson and Cruickshank cartoons in the earlier part of the century had given way first to the lithographs, cooler in tone and temper, of John Doyle, the famous HB, and then to the goodhumoured raillery of the *Punch* cartoonists Leech and Tenniel. Another sign was the growth of a more humane attitude towards animals. 'Humanity Dick' Mártin's campaign in the 1820s had its first successes in the Ill-treatment of Cattle Act of 1822 and the foundation in 1824 of the Society for the Prevention of Cruelty to Animals. After 1832 the old blood sports that had amused the English crowds since the middle ages began to die out as a result of the efforts of the legislature, the clergy and other reformers, assisted by the new police. An anglican parson in the Black Country told a factory inspector in 1850 that whereas twenty years earlier he used to see bulls, bears, badgers, dogs and cocks being brought in for baiting and fighting, he had almost put an end to such exhibitions in his parish. Dogs were still bred for fighting; but, to avoid the police, the contests were held secretly at night.

The old prize ring had never regained the peak of fashionable approval it reached in 1821 when eighteen leading pugilists of the day, including such famous names as Cribb, Spring and Belcher, took part in the coronation of George IV as muscular 'pages' guarding the entrance to Westminster Hall. After the Reform Act the sport steadily degenerated. The great Sayers-Heenan fight in 1860 which was watched by peers, MPs, authors, poets, service officers and (it was alleged) parsons, as well as the 'swell mob' from London, came as a last sudden flicker of a tradition that was already almost dead. The *Annual Register* found it curious that 'in these days of humanity and refinement' it should be called upon to chronicle such an event.[5] The growing humanity that affected the *Annual Register* was also visible in the administration of criminal justice. After 1841 no one was executed in England except for murder. In 1849, for example, of sixty-six criminals sentenced to death, only fifteen of nineteen

---

[5] The fight took place near Farnborough and lasted for thirty rounds and two hours twenty minutes until it was stopped by the police. By that time Sayers had a broken arm and Heenan was half-blind.

found guilty of murder were actually hanged. Even this was an unusually large number; in 1846 there had been only six executions.

Executions were, however, still public. It was not until 1864 that a royal commission recommended that they should take place in private and not until 1868 that this became law. Until then the popularity of hanging as a public entertainment demonstrated how much of the old brutal feeling remained in mid-Victorian society in curious juxtaposition to its technical modernity. In the middle decades of the century the Great Western railway used to offer cheap excursion tickets to see the London executions and similar facilities were made available elsewhere. One of the fifteen executions in 1849 was that of John Wilson at Liverpool for multiple murder (a woman, two children and a servant). On this occasion 'upwards of 100,000 persons were present, the railway companies running cheap trains from all available parts'. An even more notorious execution that same year was that of the Mannings, a married couple who had murdered the woman's lover for gain and whose detection and arrest was one of the first great feats of the small detective branch of the Metropolitan Police set up during Graham's home secretaryship in 1842. A husband and wife sharing the same scaffold was a titillating novelty and their execution at Horsemonger Lane gaol in November was watched by 'an immense assembly', many of them 'persons of apparent respectability and amongst them ... many well-dressed females', who paid high prices for comfortable viewpoints in the houses opposite and watched through opera glasses. A force of 500 police was present and crush-barriers were erected in an attempt to prevent the usual crowd injuries that happened on these occasions. The attractions of such spectacles were not confined to the great towns. When in July 1852 two Irish labourers were executed in the little Fife county town of Cupar, where no such event had taken place for twenty years, such a large crowd assembled, many coming a distance, that troops and special constables had to be mustered to guard the scaffold.

Such occasions were outlets for the sensationalism and cruelty still obviously present in Victorian society. A people accustomed to bare-knuckle pugilism, bull-baiting and public hangings could not lose its appetite for such scenes in a single generation. But other more civilized spectacles were beginning to appear. Football (by 1863 already split into the rival codes of association and rugby), cricket, rowing, athletics and in Scotland golf, were becoming growing attractions. It was possibly not entirely coincidence that the decade that saw the end of public executions was also marked by the foundation of the Football Association in 1863 and was followed by the start of the FA Cup competition in 1871 and the first England

v Scotland international match in 1872. The early development of
association football was largely the work of former public-school men;
but within a few years the game was taken up by the working classes
in Lancashire and the Midlands. Like any other large, urbanized
community Victorian Britain had its dark side of crime, pornography
and prostitution. In the slums of the great cities and in some of the
remoter rural districts the civilizing agencies of society were still
confronted with massive tasks. A large part of the poor in central
London, for example, never went near a church, cohabited without
the blessing of a marriage service, and defied the efforts of vaccination
officers and schoolmasters to get hold of their children. Yet by 1865,
in their piecemeal, empirical fashion, the Victorians were halfway,
perhaps more than halfway, towards solving those problems of public
order, education and health that had seemed so insuperable in the
age of Peterloo.

VI

What seemed to have changed least was the position of the traditional
governing classes. The county families that sent MPs to Westminster
in 1865 would have been familiar to George III in 1765, though
their members wore top hats and trousers instead of cocked hats
and breeches and travelled by train instead of coach. Palmerston's
cabinet of 1859 was composed of seven peers, two sons of peers, three
baronets and only three untitled commoners. This was a slightly more
aristocratic body than Liverpool's cabinet of 1825 which had five
commoners in a membership of thirteen. The lord lieutenant was
still head of the county hierarchy. The JPs still governed the counties
in petty and quarter session. Though the proportion of clerical
magistrates had declined, there were over 1,000 clergymen who were
JPs in the 1860s, amounting possibly to half the rural magistracy.
Clergy and squires were still the paramount figures in the English
countryside until the reforms of the 1880s. Even the more antiquated
institutions of shire government were capable of being brought into
use. County meetings, summoned by the sheriffs and attended by
peers, gentry and MPs, were held all over England and Wales in
1850 to protest against 'Papal Aggression'. When the volunteer
movement was launched to meet the presumed threat from France
in 1859, the government ruled that units could only be set up on
the recommendation of the lords lieutenant of England, Wales and
Scotland and were to act under their command. The overwhelming

political influence of the landowners had ensured that no elective
assemblies armed with general powers could be established in the
counties similar to those in the boroughs nor professional stipendiary
magistrates sit alongside the amateur justices of the peace. The
benevolent rural paternalism of the landed aristocracy was to
continue for almost a generation after Palmerston's death.

Even in such industrialized areas as the West Riding of Yorkshire
the Earl Fitzwilliam, in the 1860s as in the 1790s, was the uncrowned
king of local society and politics. The only two men from the non-
gentry class who became MPs for the constituency between the first
and second Reform Acts were Cobden in 1847 and 1852 and Francis
Crossley, the Halifax carpet manufacturer, in 1859. This was not
because the landowners had direct electoral control. It resulted from
a sensible adjustment of urban and landed interests and the
willingness of town liberals to accept aristocratic whig leadership
when exercised with tact and responsibility. In the view of an old-
fashioned liberal manufacturer like J. G. Marshall of Leeds the
harmless, political divisions into whig and tory, liberal and conservative, prevented the emergence of sharper and more dangerous
social confrontations between town and country, anglicanism and
nonconformity. Among the squires themselves, as the sporting
novelist Robert Surtees noted in *Plain or Ringlets* (1860), political
partisanship had greatly diminished. Agricultural prosperity, the end
of the corn-law controversy, cheap and easy communications by
rail with all parts of the country, the growth of London club life,
all helped to break down the old provincial and party feelings. While
the local party organizations established in the 1830s continued,
though often in a slightly moribund condition, the slackness of party
control at the centre and the absence of important political issues
meant that the period from 1846 to 1867 was the last golden age
of the independent MP—as it was also, in a social sense, for the
landowning class from which most of them were drawn.

It was true that the growing technicalities of administration made
it impossible to heap more direct powers on the county magistrates
after the fashion of the eighteenth century. What administrative
innovations took place in rural government tended to assume the
anonymous form of boards—poor law or public health, for instance,
or the Highways Boards of 1862. Alongside the old-style magistrate
was appearing a new-style expert: the poor law medical officer, the
sanitary engineer, the chief constable. But while these officials
represented a partial encroachment on the omnicompetence of the
country gentry in the government of the countryside, their traditional
position of prestige and power was still substantially intact.

The most important administrative reform of the period that

affected them—the Poor Law Amendment Act of 1834—had not only failed to bring about a large measure of centralization but was administered with a remarkable sensitivity to local conditions. In mapping the boundaries of the new unions adjustments had been made to suit the convenience of influential landowners and estates; JPs were *ex officio* members of the board of guardians in their district; and the plural voting system for the elected guardians ensured that, except in towns and large open parishes, the landowners and their tenants decided the elections, often without a contest. The clergy and squires showed no reluctance to serve on the boards. Peers and other magnates were found acting as poor law guardinas; and the position was not dissimilar with other boards. As long as the gentry were ready to carry out their traditional unpaid public duties, their influence ensured that there would always be the opportunity. Moreover, despite the growing variety of local agencies, the general administration of the counties were clearly more efficient and less corrupt than that of the towns. The County Rates Act of 1852 imposed a measure of standardization and control on county finance; but the generally recognized integrity and economy of county administrations made no further legislation necessary.

Cobden might grumble, as he did in 1849, that 'we are a servile, aristocracy-loving, lord-ridden people, who regard the land with as much reverence as we still do the peerage and the baronetage'. But the efforts of Hume and Milner Gibson in the 1840s to introduce a wider measure of democratic representation into county government was little more than a radical hobbyhorse—an expression of class jealousy rather than a realistic possibility. The same was true of the campaign of the 1850s and 1860s to abolish primogeniture as the basis for land inheritance. The Cobdenite *Freeholder* could proclaim in 1852 that 'Free Trade will be in vain if we do not have free trade in land'; but, like every other attempt to prolong the Anti-Corn Law League agitation for other purposes, the movement failed to attract the support of the liberal middle classes. It was in any case a pointless cry. The power of the landed interest did not depend on entail and primogeniture; nor was it saved by them when the great economic decline of the landed estates came the following century.

The real strength of the gentry and aristocracy lay elsewhere: in the structure of the state, in government, in parliament and the electoral system, in the church, the armed forces, the civil service, in local government and society. They were not an extraneous but an integral element in national life. They had taken a full share in the economic as well as the political development of the country. They had shown themselves on most occasions intelligent and flexible; they had made political concessions and yielded privileges when public opinion clearly demanded such surrenders; they had shouldered since 1842 a large share of taxation. The repeal of the corn laws in 1846 had in spectacular manner removed from them the odium of a class monopoly at no cost to themselves in either money or status. They had played a useful and sometimes prominent role in the social, religious, educational and other philanthropic movements of the period and had been rewarded by the moral approval of the public in addition to their existing social and political advantages. What was remarkable was not that British society, growing more urbanized and industrialized with each decade, was slowly slipping beyond their control, but that by a process of astute adaptation they had maintained that control so long and with so little resentment on the part of the rest of the community.

Bibliography

Abbreviations

BIHR *Bulletin of the Institute of Historical Research*
EHR *English Historical Review*
HJ *Historical Journal*
JBS *Journal of British Studies*
JEH *Journal of Ecclesiastical History*
SHR *Scottish Historical Review*
TRHS *Transactions of the Royal Historical Society*
Place of publication is London unless otherwise stated.

Bibliographies

The fullest guides are *The Bibliography of British History 1789–1851*, edited by Lucy M. Brown and I. R. Christie (Oxford, 1977) and *The Bibliography of British History 1851–1914*, edited by H. J. Hanham (Oxford, 1976). These may be supplemented for later years by the *Annual Bulletin of Historical Literature* published by the Historical Association and, more promptly, by the *Annual Bibliography of British and Irish History*, edited by G. R. Elton for the Royal Historical Society, which begins with the year 1975 (Hassocks, Sussex 1976–). All these take note of the more important articles in periodicals as well as books. Short basic guides for students are published by the Historical Association in 'Helps for Students of History'. Those of value for this period include I. R. Christie, *British History since 1760: a Select Bibliography* (no. 81, 1970), Owen Chadwick, *The History of the Church: a Select Bibliography* (no. 66, 1966), S. B. Chrimes and I. A. Roots, *English Constitutional History: a Select Bibliography* (no. 58, 1958) and E. M. Johnston, *Irish History: a Select Bibliography* (no. 73, 1972).

Documentary Collections

The two best are in the series *English Historical Documents* (edited by D. C. Douglas): vol. XI, 1783–1832, edited by A. Aspinall and F. A. Smith (1959), and vol. XII(I), 1833–74, edited by G. M. Young and W. D. Handcock (1956), with excellent introductions and bibliographies. For political and constitutional history see W. C. Costin and J. S. Watson, *Law and Working of the Constitution* (1952) II, 1784–1914, an imaginative selection marred by absence of commentary, and H. J. Hanham, *The Nineteenth-Century Constitution* (Cambridge, 1969). Useful for specific topics are J. F. C. Harrison, *Society and Politics in England 1780–1960* (New York, 1965), G. D. H. Cole and A. W. Filson, *British Working-Class Movements*

1789–1875 (1951), R. P. Flindall, *The Church of England 1815–1914* (1972) and J. Briggs and I. Sellars, *Victorian Nonconformity* (1973).

General Histories

Though beginning to date slightly the best textbook is still E. L. Woodward's volume in the Oxford History of England, *The Age of Reform* (2nd edn, Oxford, 1962), which has a good critical bibliography. Asa Briggs, *The Age of Improvement* (1959) covers the period from the 1780s to 1867, giving particular attention to social and economic factors. R. K. Webb, *Modern England from the Eighteenth Century to the Present* (1969) is a modern standard text embodying the results of recent scholarship. Written for an American public it explains clearly many things which British histories tend (not always justifiably) to assume are already known to their readers. É. Halévy, *History of the English People in the Nineteenth Century*, translated by E. I. Watkin and D. A. Barker (6 vols, revised edn, 1949–52) is a classic work by a Frenchman who brought a fresh objective mind to the period. His premature death before finishing the 1841–52 period left gaps in vol. iv. Two older, large-scale works are still worth consulting: Spencer Walpole, *History of England from the Conclusion of the Great War in 1815* (6 vols, revised edn, 1890) and Herbert Paul, *History of Modern England* (5 vols, 1904–5) which covers the years 1846–70. For Scotland, where the nineteenth century is still inadequately treated, see G. S. Pryde, *Scotland from 1603 to the Present Day* (1962) and the final volume of the Edinburgh History of Scotland (edited by G. Donaldson), *Scotland 1689 to the Present* by W. Ferguson (1968).

The rest of this bibliography will be confined to the more important and generally accessible books and articles on the topics covered in the separate chapters.

1 Country and People

Two general economic histories are indispensable for the study of British society in this period: J. H. Clapham, *An Economic History of Modern Britain* (Cambridge, 1926–32, reprinted 1950–52), i *The Early Railway Age 1820–1850*, and ii *Free Trade and Steel 1850–1886*, and P. Mathias, *The First Industrial Nation: an Economic History of Britain 1700–1914* (1969). Two other useful books are S. G. Checkland, *The Rise of Industrial Society in England 1815–1885* (1964) and H. Perkin, *The Origins of Modern English Society* (1969).

G. R. Porter, *The Progress of the Nation from the Beginning of the Nineteenth Century* (various edns, 1836–51) is a standard compendium of statistics. The author was head of the statistical department of the Board of Trade. An indispensable modern reference work though more narrowly economic in scope is B. R. Mitchell and P. Deane, *Abstract of British Historical Statistics* (Cambridge, 1962). The controversy between the optimistic and pessimistic schools can be examined in *The Long Debate on Poverty* (Institute of Economic Affairs, 2nd edn, 1974) and *The Standard of Living in Britain in the Industrial Revolution*, edited by A. J. Taylor (1975), collections of essays by various authors with introductions.

Ivy Pinchbeck, *Women Workers and the Industrial Revolution 1750–1850* (reprinted 1969) brings sanity and proportion to an emotional subject. The old trilogy by J. L. Hammond, *The Town Labourer 1766–1832* (1917), *The*

Skilled Labourer 1760–1832 (1919) and *The Village Labourer 1760–1832* (1911) have still not been supplanted. Written with distinction and sympathy they are valuable studies though subsequent research has modified their generally pessimistic conclusions.

For rural society J. D. Chambers and G. F. Mingay, *The Agricultural Revolution 1750–1880* (1966) provides a good survey based on recent scholarship. F. M. L. Thompson, *English Landed Society in the Nineteenth Century* (1963) is the standard authority on the social history of the landowning aristocracy. It can be supplemented by D. Spring, *The English Landed Estate in the Nineteenth Century* (Baltimore, 1963). Lord Ernle's classic *English Farming*, edited by A. D. Hall (1936) is still a standard text though it needs to be amplified for the later period by C. S. Orwin and E. H. Whetham, *History of British Agriculture 1846–1914* (1964). A useful special study is *Land and Industry: the Landed Estate and the Industrial Revolution*, a symposium edited by J. T. Ward and R. G. Wilson (Newton Abbot, 1971).

The middle classes as a whole lack a historian but a good account of the professions in this century is given in W. R. Reader, *Professional Men* (1966) which should be read in conjunction with the standard work by A. M. Carr-Saunders and P. A. Wilson, *The Professions* (Oxford, 1937).

Most of the working-class lives mentioned below for chapters 3 and 7 throw light on social conditions but no list should omit the view of the English countryside and its inhabitants (*c.* 1820–32) in William Cobbett's *Rural Rides*, available in many editions. Of the many accounts left by foreign visitors two may be singled out: *A Regency Visitor: the English Tour of Prince Puckler-Muskau 1826–28*, edited by E. M. Butler (1957) and *Industrial Britain under the Regency 1814–18*, edited by W. O. Henderson (1968), extracts from the reports of two Swiss, one German and one French observer. For the sporting world see E. W. Bovill, *The England of Nimrod and Surtees 1815–1854* (1959). John Ford, *Prizefighting: the Age of Regency Boximania* (Newton Abbot, 1971) is a short readable introduction to the subject. K. Chesney, *The Anti-Society* (Boston, 1970) is a colourful account of the Victorian underworld. A more scholarly examination will be found in J. J. Tobias, *Crime and Industrial Society in the Nineteenth Century* (1967) and there is a useful little collection of documents by the same author in *Nineteenth Century Crime: Prevention and Punishment* (Newton Abbot, 1972).

2 Government and Religion

For the influence of economic theory see L. C. Robbins, *The Theory of Economic Policy in English Classical Political Economy* (1952) and *The Classical Economists*, edited by A. W. Coats (1971) a collection of articles by different authors. For the structure of the state, F. W. Maitland, *Constitutional History of England* (1906) is still the best starting-point though it should be supplemented by D. L. Keir, *Constitutional History of Modern Britain* (6th edn, 1960). More detailed but essential works or reference are W. R. Anson, *Law and Custom of the Constitution*, I *Parliament*, and II *The Crown*, edited by A. B. Keith (4th edn, 1935) and Josef Redlich, *The Procedure of the House of Commons*, translated by A. E. Steinthal (3 vols, 1908), an historical survey. For the relations between monarch, cabinet and parliament see J. P. Mackintosh, *The British Cabinet* (1962) and A. S. Foord, 'The Waning of the Influence of the Crown', *EHR* LXII (1947). On the unreformed electoral system E. and A. G. Porritt, *The Unreformed House of Commons*

(Cambridge, 1903–9) is still the authority. J. H. Philbin, *Parliamentary Representation 1832, England and Wales* (Newhaven, Conn., 1965) is a valuable analysis for the years 1826–32.

The best short introduction to local and central government is K. B. S. Smellie, *A Hundred Years of English Government* (2nd edn, 1950). Emmeline Cohen, *Growth of the British Civil Service 1780–1939* (1941) is a good general survey. H. Parris, *Constitutional Bureaucracy* (1969) is a scholarly and comprehensive study of the broader aspects, including a useful chapter on the controversial questions of Benthamite influence, collectivism and *laissez-faire*. Of the many monographs on individual departments the more important are H. Roseveare, *The Treasury: Evolution of a British Institution* (1969), which ranges more widely than the title suggests; D. M. Young, *The Colonial Office in the Early Nineteenth Century* (1961), a lucid account with much that is of general significance for the period; R. Prouty, *The Transformation of the Board of Trade 1830–1855* (1973); and Ray Joncs, *The Nineteenth-Century Foreign Office* (1971), an administrative history. For local government there is still nothing to replace S. and B. Webb, *English Local Government from the Revolution to the Municipal Corporations Act* (9 vols, 1906–29).

For the churches in general see J. Stoughton, *Religion in England 1800–1850* (2 vols, 1884) and the more recent study by L. E. Elliott-Binns, *Religion in the Victorian Era* (2nd edn, 1946), which despite the title goes back to the start of the century. W. R. Ward, *Religion and Society in England 1790–1850* (1972) is particularly good on attitudes towards the establishment; see also A. Armstrong, *The Church of England, the Methodists and Society 1700–1850* (1973). A valuable study of the social and demographic aspects is A. D. Gilbert, *Religion and Society in Industrial England: Church, Chapel and Social Change 1740–1914* (1976).

The standard histories of the Church of England are J. H. Overton, *The English Church in the Nineteenth Century 1800–1833* (1894) and F. W. Cornish, *History of the English Church in the Nineteenth Century* (2 vols, 1910). These should be supplemented by more recent works. W. L. Mathieson deals with *English Church Reform 1815–1840* (1923). R. A. Soloway has much new material on the attitude of the episcopacy in his *Prelates and People: Ecclesiastical Social Thought in England 1783–1852* (1969). S. C. Carpenter offers a more general survey in his *Church and People 1789–1889* (1933). C. K. Francis Brown, *History of the English Clergy 1800–1900* (1953) is particularly full on the reforms of the earlier part of the century. M. H. Port, *Six Hundred New Churches* (1961) examines the work of the Church Building Commission of 1818–56. G. M. Howse, *Saints in Politics* (Toronto, 1952) is a sympathetic study of the Clapham Sect.

For dissent H. W. Clark, *History of English Nonconformity* (2 vols, 1911–13) is a standard text. The second volume deals with the period from the Revolution to the end of the nineteenth century. Though awkwardly arranged, B. L. Manning, *The Protestant Dissenting Deputies*, edited by O. Greenwood (Cambridge, 1952) is an indispensable record of the activities of the central representative body of the Three Denominations. A brief but valuable modern study is Ian Sellars, *Nineteenth-Century Nonconformity* (1967). The older histories of the individual sects tend to be interior accounts of their development. The attitudes of the authors as well as the information conveyed make them, however, valuable sources. They include *A New History of Methodism* by W. J. Townsend and others (2 vols, 1909); *History of English Congregationalism* (1907) by R. W. Dale, one of the notable nonconformist figures of the period; and H. B. Kendall, *Origin and History of the Primitive Methodist Church* (2 vols, 1906). Recent studies of the two smaller denominations are *The English Presbyterians* by C. G. Bolam and others, (1968) which covers the transition from orthodox Calvinism to Unitarianism, and A. C. Underwood, *History of the English Baptists* (1947).

3 The Peterloo Years

For the problems of the executive see J. Cookson, *Lord Liverpool's Administration 1815–1822* (Edinburgh, 1975), the first realistic exploration of the working of government and parliament after Waterloo. This should be supplemented by A. Mitchell, *The Whigs in Opposition 1815–30* (Oxford, 1967). There is no satisfactory life of Lord Liverpool though there is a recent essay on him in *The Prime Ministers*, edited by H. van Thal, 1 (1974). G. D. Yonge, *Life and Administration of the Second Earl of Liverpool* (3 vols, 1868) has useful material though insipid as a biography. For the two other ministers concerned with law and order, H. Twiss, *Life of Lord Chancellor Eldon* (3 vols, 1844) and G. Pellew, *Life of the first Viscount Sidmouth* (3 vols, 1847), though equally dull and uncritical have a wealth of informative material. For a modern assessment of Sidmouth see P. Ziegler, *Addington* (1965).

A good introduction to the social difficulties of the post-Waterloo years is R. J. White, *Waterloo to Peterloo* (1957). Nothing comparable exists for Scotland though Henry Cockburn, *Memorials of His Time* (1856) and *Letters on the Affairs of Scotland* (1874) by the whig solicitor-general for Scotland have much of interest on radical agitation and state trials. See also L. J. Saunders, *Scottish Democracy 1815–1840: the Social and Intellectual background* (1950). E. P. Thompson, *The Making of the English Working Class* (1963) despite its bias and exaggeration is eminently readable and provides a quarry of information even for those who do not accept his interpretation. A useful corrective is M. I. Thomis, *The Luddites: Machine Breaking in Regency England* (Newton Abbot, 1970). The standard account of the industrial troubles is still F. O. Darvall's *Popular Disturbances and Public Order in Regency England* (1934). The 1969 edition has a critical introduction and additional bibliography by A. Macintyre. A. Aspinall, *The Early English Trade Unions* (1949) has an illuminating collection of documents on the period 1791–1825 with a useful introduction. For their general history see S. and B. Webb, *The History of Trade Unionism* (1958, reprinted 1973) and H. Pelling's shorter *History of British Trade Unionism* (1963).

For Peterloo see D. Read, *Peterloo: the 'Massacre' and its Background* (Manchester, 1958, reprinted 1973) which sets the event in its context; Joyce Marlow, *The Peterloo Massacre* (1970) which concentrates on the actual episode; and R. Walmsley, *Peterloo: the Case Reopened* (1969) which argues in detail the case for a more sympathetic understanding of the magistrates. J. Stanhope deals competently with another dramatic episode in *The Cato Street Conspiracy* (1962) which should be supplemented by T. M. Persinnen, 'The Revolutionary Party in London 1816–1820', *BIHR* (1972). Among the many radical and working-class autobiographies should be mentioned that of Samuel Bamford who was present at Peterloo and later arrested. His *Passages in the Life of a Radical* and *Early Days* were edited by H. Dunckley in 1893 (2 vols) and by W. H. Chaloner under the title of *Autobiography of Samuel Bamford* (2 vols, 1967). For the radical movement in general the best introduction is S. Maccoby, *English Radicalism 1786–1832: from Paine to Cobbett* (1955). J. W. Derry, *The Radical Tradition: Tom Paine to Lloyd George* (1967) discusses some of the radical figures of this period. For radicalism and popular religion see R. F. Wearmouth, *Some Working-Class Movements of the Nineteenth Century* (1948) and *Methodism and the Working-Class Movements of England 1800–1850* (1937).

4 The Government and the State of the Nation

In addition to the books listed in the first paragraph of section 1 above, the following are important: H. W. V. Temperley, *Life of Canning* (1905) and W. Hinde, *George Canning* (1973), the best of the modern studies; N. Gash, *Mr Secretary Peel* (1961), and C. J. Bartlett, *Castlereagh* (1966), the most satisfactory account of a statesman who lacks an adequate biography. So too does Huskisson but A. Brady, *William Huskisson and Liberal Reform* (1928) is essential for his work in this period. Government economic policy can be followed in W. R. Brock, *Lord Liverpool and Liberal Toryism 1820–24* (1941), a pioneer study but now somewhat dated, and Boyd Hilton, *Corn, Cash, Commerce: the Economic Policies of the Tory Governments 1815–1830* (1977), based on wide research though concentrating unduly on the role of Huskisson.

George IV by R. Fulford (1935) is a lively sketch of that wayward complicated monarch. The same author's *Trial of Queen Caroline* (1967) is useful but see also Cookson's *Liverpool Administration. Radical Squibs and Loyal Ripostes*, edited by E. Rickword (1971) gives an amusing sample of the satirical pamphleteering. For the controversies over the corn laws and the discontents of the agriculturalists see D. G. Barnes, *History of the English Corn Laws 1660–1846* (1930) supplemented by T. L. Crosby, *English Farmers and the Policies of Protection 1815–52* (Hassocks, Sussex, 1977) and 'George Webb Hall and the Agricultural Association' by D. Spring and T. L. Crosby, *JBS* I (1962). For the Catholic question see the next section. For legal and criminal reform the indispensable authorities are W. S. Holdsworth, *History of English Law* III, edited by A. L. Goodhart and H. G. Hanbury (1952) and L. Radzinowicz, *History of English Criminal Law* (3 vols, 1948).

5 The Constitutional Revolution

N. Gash, *Sir Robert Peel* (1972) deals with his career after 1830. H. Maxwell, *Life of the Duke of Wellington* (2 vols, 1899) is still useful and Elizabeth Longford, *Wellington* (2 vols, 1969–72) the best of the many modern lives. There is still nothing to replace G. M. Trevelyan's *Lord Grey of the Reform Bill* (1920, reprinted 1952), a readable but inadequate biography.

For the foundation of the Metropolitan Police see two somewhat overlapping books by C. Reith, *British Police and the Democratic Ideal* (1943) and *New Study of Police History* (Edinburgh, 1956), and for a wider background, J. M. Hart, *The British Police* (1951) and C. Dilnot, *Scotland Yard: its History and Organization* (new edn, 1929). In addition to the books listed in section 2, much light is thrown on the religious issues of 1826–8 by R. W. Davis, *Dissent in Politics 1780–1830: the Political Life of William Smith MP* (1971). R. G. Cowherd, *The Politics of English Dissent* (New York 1956) is also useful. For the Catholic question see G. T. Machin's authoritative study, *The Catholic Question in English Politics 1820–1830* (Oxford, 1964). The situation in Ireland is covered by J. A. Reynolds, *Catholic Emancipation Crisis In Ireland 1823–1829* (Yale, 1954) and more generally by R. B. McDowell in his indispensable *Public Opinion and Government Policy in Ireland 1801–1846* (1952).

For a full list of books and articles on the Reform Act of 1832 see N. Gash, *Politics in the Age of Peel* (1953, revised edn with new introduction and additional bibliography, 1977) which deals with the issues raised by the bill and the working of the reformed structure in the following twenty years. The most modern account of the parliamentary reform movement is J. Cannon, *Parliamentary Reform 1640–1832* (1973) which has a good bibliography. J. R. M. Butler, *Passing of the Great Reform Bill* (1914) is still valuable but the definitive work is M. Brock, *The Great Reform Act* (1973), based on a careful examination of a wide range of sources and covering every aspect of the crisis. A. Aspinall, *Three Nineteenth-Century Diaries* (1952), gives the comments of two whigs and one tory during the crisis with a long, informative introduction. The best guide to the technical changes made by the act is C. S. Seymour, *Electoral Reform in England and Wales* (1915, reprinted with introduction by M. Hurst 1970). An account of the Irish and Scottish acts is given in Gash, *Politics in the Age of Peel*. For Scotland see also W. Ferguson, 'The Reform Act (Scotland) of 1832: Intention and Effect', *SHR* xlv (1966). For a different interpretation of the Reform Bill see D. C. Moore, *The Politics of Deference* (Hassocks, Sussex, 1976). For a more recent discussion of whig motives see the judicious analysis in the introduction to *The Holland House Diaries*, edited by A. D. Kriegel (1977), which give an illuminating insight into cabinet deliberations in the years 1831–40.

6 Parties and Politics

A short scholarly survey of the period is given by G. B. A. M. Finlayson in *England in the Eighteen Thirties: Decade of Reform* (1969) which has a good critical bibliography. A more impressionistic study is A. Llewellyn, *The Decade of Reform: the 1830s* (New York, 1971). N. Gash, *Reaction and Reconstruction in English Politics 1832–52* (Oxford, 1965) deals with some of the major problems confronting the political parties. An invaluable addition to the literature on politico-religious questions is G. I. T. Machin, *Politics and the Churches in Great Britain 1832–1868* (Oxford, 1977) which has an exhaustive bibliography.

For corn laws and education most of the books listed under those headings in sections 2, 4 and 5 are still relevant but see also J. L. Alexander, 'Lord John Russell and the Origins of the Committee of Council on Education', *HJ* xx (1977) for a fresh appraisal of whig policies in 1839. For the Tractarians, R. W. Church, *The Oxford Movement 1833–1845* (1891) still has value as a contemporary witness and there is a useful chapter on the subject in J. Hunt, *Religious Thought in the Nineteenth Century* (1896). For church reform and the Ecclesiastical Commission see Olive J. Brose, *Church and Parliament: the Reshaping of the Church of England 1828–1860* (1959). For the House of Lords see A. S. Turberville. *The House of Lords in the Age of Reform 1784–1837* (1958), supplemented by D. Large, 'The Decline of "the Party of the Crown" and the Rise of Parties in the House of Lords 1783–1837', *EHR* lxxviii (1963).

D. Southgate, *The Passing of the Whigs 1832–1886* (1962) is the nearest to a history of the whig-liberal party in this period. Further information can be gleaned from A. Aspinall, *Lord Brougham and the Whig Party* (Manchester, 1927), P. Ziegler, *Melbourne* (1976) and J. Prest, *Lord John Russell* (1972). For the radicals see S. Maccoby, *English Radicalism 1832–1852* (1935), supplemented by such radical biographies as J. K. Buckley, *Joseph Parkes of Birmingham* (1926) and Mrs Grote, *Life of George Grote* (1873). Relations between whigs and Irish nationalists are covered in A. Macintyre, *The Liberator: Daniel O'Connell and the Irish Party 1830–1847* (1965).

Their opponents are better served. Robert Blake. *The Conservative Party from Peel to Churchill* (1970) is a stimulating introduction. *The Conservatives: a History from their Origins to 1965*, edited by Lord Butler (1977) is a symposium covering a longer period in more detail. *The Conservative Leadership 1832–1932*, edited by D. Southgate (1974) is another symposium concentrating on the policies and personalities of the leaders. There is finally R. Stewart's detailed study *The Foundations of the Conservative Party 1830–1867* (1978), full of information, though its judgements on wider issues are sometimes open to question.

For party organization, both central and local, see N. Gash, *Politics in the Age of Peel*; D. Read, *Press and People* (1961) which deals with politics and opinions in three leading provincial towns, (Manchester, Leeds and Sheffield); and three valuable regional studies—R. W. Davis, *Political Change and Continuity c. 1760–1885* (1972) for Buckinghamshire, T. J. Nossiter, *Influence, Opinion and Political Idiom in Reformed England* (1965) for the northeast, and R. J. Olney, *Lincolnshire Politics 1832–1885* (1973). The party implications of the municipal corporations act are examined by G. B. A. M. Finlayson in 'The Politics of Municipal Reform 1835', *EHR* LXXXI (1966).

7 The 'Condition of England Question'

The 1830 rural riots were first examined in the Hammonds' *Village Labourer* (section 1). A more detailed and sophisticated study is *Captain Swing* by W. J. Hobsbawm and G. Rudé (1969). The best account of the Dorchester labourers is Joyce Marlow, *The Tolpuddle Martyrs* (1971).

For the industrial radical movement Wearmouth's *Working Class Movements* (section 3) is still useful. *Popular Movements c. 1830–1850*, edited by J. T. Ward (1970) has chapters on the factory movement, anti-poor law agitation, trade unionism, Chartism and anti-corn law agitation. See also D. Read, *The English Provinces c. 1760–1960* (1964) in which part 3 (1830–60) covers the same ground. For metropolitan activities see *London Radicalism 1830–1843*, edited by D. J. Rowe (1970), a selection from the papers of that indefatigable organizer Francis Place. For background see G. Wallas, *Life of Francis Place* (1918). The history of trade unions in this period is best followed in the Webbs' *Trade Unionism* (section 3). The agitation against the new poor law is examined by N. C. Edsall, *The Anti-Poor Law Movement* (Manchester, 1971) and the ten hours movement in J. T. Ward's authoritative *Factory Movement 1830–1855* (1962). For the men involved see C. H. Driver, *Tory Radical: the Life of Richard Oastler* (Oxford, 1946), J. C. Gill, *The Ten Hours Parson* (1959) a study of the Reverend G. S. Bull, and Georgina Battiscombe, *Shaftesbury* (1974).

Though there is now a copious literature on Chartism, the best introduction is still M. Hovell, *The Chartist Movement* (1918, reprinted 1950). The older account incorporating much original material by R. G.

Gammage, *History of the Chartist Movement* (1894, reprinted 1969) recaptures some of the contemporary flavour. The most useful modern account is J. T. Ward, *Chartism* (1973). Regional aspects, essential for any understanding of the movement, are analysed in *Chartist Studies*, a symposium edited by Asa Briggs (1959). For the movement in Scotland see L. C. Wright, *Scottish Chartism* (Edinburgh, 1953) and for Wales, D. Williams, *John Frost: a Study in Chartism* (1939). G. D. H. Cole, *Chartist Portraits* (1941) is the best introduction to the gallery of Chartist leaders, most of whom have found a modern biographer. Of the older Chartist autobiographies two may be singled out: *The Life of Thomas Cooper by himself* (1879, reprinted with introduction by J. Saville, Leicester, 1971) and *The Life and Struggles of William Lovett* (1876, reprinted with preface by R. H. Tawney, 1967). For the reaction of authority see the invaluable study by F. C. Mather, *Public Order in the Age of the Chartists* (Manchester, 1959) which can be supplemented by the details in N. Gash, *Sir Robert Peel* (1972) and J. T. Ward, *Sir James Graham* (1967). An unforgettable picture of the views of the commander of the Northern District is given in the second volume of the *Life of Gen. Sir Charles Napier*, by Sir William Napier (4 vols, 1857). For the part played by the League, see N. McCord, *The Anti-Corn Law League* (1958), which has a comprehensive bibliography. This, the first attempt to chip away the plaster of Victorian legend, replaces all previous accounts.

8 Peel's Decade

Most of the books in sections 5 and 6 are still relevant. T. L. Crosby, *Sir Robert Peel's Administration 1841–46* (Newton Abbot, 1970) is a condensed but useful account of the ministry. R. Stewart, *The Politics of Protection* (Cambridge, 1971) deals with the position of Stanley and the protectionists in 1841–52. See also Robert Blakes's classic biography, *Disraeli* (1966).

For Maynooth Machin's *Politics and the Churches* (section 6) is indispensable but see also his article 'The Maynooth Grant, the Dissenters and the Establishment 1845–7', *EHR* LXXXII (1967). For the ten hours bill see the factory question in section 7; for public health, section 11 below; for farming opinion, section 4. The following articles are also of value: W. O. Aydelotte, 'The Country Gentlemen and the Repeal of the Corn Laws', *EHR* LXXXII (1967); G. Kitson Clark, 'The Electorate and the Repeal of the Corn Laws', *TRHS* 5th series I (1951); Mary Lawson-Tancred, 'The Anti-League and the Corn Law Crisis of 1846', *HJ* III (1960).

In addition to the books on Ireland in sections 4 and 6, the situation in Ireland is also dealt with by K. B. Nowlan, *The Politics of Repeal* (1965), which studies Anglo-Irish relations in the years 1841–50. For the famine see *The Great Famine*, edited by R. Dudley Edwards and T. D. Williams (Dublin, 1956), a collection of essays by different authors, and Cecil Woodham-Smith, *The Great Hunger: Ireland 1845–49* (1964).

The Peelites after 1846 are studied from slightly different angles by J. B. Conacher, *The Peelites and the Party System 1846–52* (Newton Abbot, 1972), emphasizing leaders and issues, and W. D. Jones and A. B. Erickson, *The Peelites 1846–57*, good on organization and membership. The subsequent careers of the League leaders are best studied in the two standard lives. J. Morley, *Life of Richard Cobden* (1879 and many subsequent edns) and G. M. Trevelyan, *John Bright* (1913), bearing in mind that they were not typical of the parliamentary radicals.

Of many modern books on the Queen the best is Cecil Woodham-
Smith, *Queen Victoria: Her Life and Times* I, 1819–61 (1972), based on
careful work in the Windsor archives. Nothing however can replace the
revealing *Letters of Queen Victoria*, the first series of which (1837–61) was
edited by A. C. Benson and Viscount Esher (3 vols, 1908). For her husband
the best modern life is still R. Fulford, *The Prince Consort* (1949) but the
official laudatory *Life* by Sir T. Martin (3 vols, 1876–80 and other edns)
contains invaluable material.

9 The Decline of Party Politics

Most of the books on politics and religion in sections 5–8 are relevant. See
also G. I. T. Machin, 'Lord John Russell and the Prelude to the
Ecclesiastical Titles Bill 1846–51', *JEH* xxv (1974) and C. H. Stuart, 'The
Prince Consort and Ministerial Politics 1856–9' in *Essays Presented to Keith
Feiling*, edited by H. Trevor Roper (1964), which reviews the role of the
prince more widely than the title suggests.

For Palmerston the older standard life by H. C. F. Bell, *Lord Palmerston*
(2 vols, 1936, reprinted 1966) is still the most comprehensive and scholarly
survey though a little dated. D. Southgate, *The Most English Minister* (1966)
is less a biography than a study from printed sources of his foreign policy
and position in politics. *Lord Palmerston* by Jasper Ridley (1970), which uses
the Broadlands archives, is sometimes inaccurate on background but is
probably the best portrait of his character and personality. There is no
satisfactory life of Aberdeen though Frances Balfour's *Life of the Fourth Earl
of Aberdeen* (2 vols, 1923) has useful material. For his ministry see J. B.
Conacher's massive and scholarly book *The Aberdeen Coalition 1852–1855*
(Cambridge, 1968) which covers every aspect in great detail. Olive
Anderson, *A Liberal State at War* (1967) discusses the less familiar topics of
political opinion, economic and financial policy, and public morale during
the war. For further exploration of the influence of public opinion on the
drift into war see Kingsley Martin, *The Triumph of Lord Palmerston* (1924,
revised edn 1963).

The rise of Gladstone can best be followed in the standard *Life* by John
Morley (3 vols, 1912). Two good modern studies are Philip Magnus,
Gladstone: a Biography (1954) and, based on more recent research, E. J.
Feuchtwanger, *Gladstone* (1975). S. Buxton's *Mr Gladstone as Chancellor of the
Exchequer* (1901) is useful for his financial policy. The relations between
Gladstone and his prime minister are vividly brought out in the 1851–65
correspondence edited and introduced by P. Guedalla in *Gladstone and
Palmerston* (1928). J. R. Vincent, *The Formation of the Liberal Party 1857–1868*
(1966) is an interesting pioneer study of pre-Gladstonian liberalism. *Pressure
from Without in Early Victorian England*, edited by Patricia Hollis (1974) has
chapters on various reform movements in this period, including the
Liberation Society and the Administrative Reform Association. See also
G. I. T. Machin, 'Gladstone and Nonconformity in the 1860s: the
Formation of an Alliance', *HJ* xvii (1974).

10 Safeguard and Security

The Cambridge History of British Foreign Policy (1783–1919), edited by A. Ward
and G. P. Gooch (3 vols, 1923) is mainly of value for reference. The best

general textbook is R. W. Seton-Watson, *Britain in Europe 1789–1914* (Cambridge, 1937, reprinted 1945), a lively and incisive survey though dated on domestic history. H. W. V. Temperley and L. Penson, *Foundations of British Foreign Policy from Pitt to Salisbury* (Cambridge, 1938) has a useful selection of documents with an historical introduction. *Britain and Europe: Pitt to Churchill 1793–1941*, edited by James Joll (1950, reprinted 1961) concentrates on the more enduring strands of British policy. A larger work, two thirds documentary, by K. Bourne, *The Foreign Policy of Victorian England 1830–1902* (Oxford, 1970), provides the best general commentary since Seton-Watson and has a good critical bibliography.

Of the many monographs may be mentioned D. C. M. Platt, *Finance, Trade and Politics in British Foreign Policy 1815–1914* (Oxford, 1968), which discusses the influence of economic interests; H. C. Allen, *Great Britain and the United States: a History of Anglo-American Relations 1783–1952* (1956); C. W. Crawley, *The Question of Greek Independence 1821–1833* (Cambridge, 1930), the standard authority; J. R. Hall, *England and the Orleans Monarchy* (1912); E. J. Parry, *The Spanish Marriages 1841–1846* (1936) a good analysis of their impact on European diplomacy; H. W. V. Temperley, *England and the Near East: the Crimea* (1936); W. C. Costin, *Great Britain and China 1833–1860* (Oxford, 1937); and D. Beales, *England and Italy 1859–60* (1961). Conacher's *Aberdeen Coalition* (section 8) has a full treatment of the diplomatic side.

For foreign secretaries see C. K. Webster, *The Foreign Policy of Castlereagh 1815–22* (1925, reprinted 1947); H. W. V. Temperley, *The Foreign Policy of Canning 1822–27* (1925); and C. K. Webster, *The Foreign Policy of Palmerston 1830–41* (2 vols, 1951). For Palmerston's later policy see the various *Lives* in section 9 and Prest's life of Russell (section 6). See also H. Maxwell, *Life and Letters of the Fourth Earl of Clarendon* (2 vols, 1913) and *A Vanished Victorian: Life of the Fourth Earl of Clarendon* by his grandson George Villiers (1938), a lively narrative which draws on a wide range of sources.

There are useful chapters on the army and navy in *Early Victorian England* I, edited by G. M. Young (1934). For the navy see C. J. Bartlett, *Great Britain and Sea Power 1815–1853* (Oxford, 1963), a scholarly study of the interplay of technical developments and policy, and M. A. Lewis, *The Navy in Transition 1814–1864: a Social History* (1965). *The Royal Navy* by W. L. Clowes (7 vols, 1897–1903) though awkwardly arranged is a storehouse of information. The post-1815 period is dealt with in vols VI and VII. J. H. Briggs, *Naval Administration 1827–1892* (1897) gives a unique account of the Admiralty and its successive chiefs by a long-serving official. Corelli Barnet, *Britain and Her Army 1509–1970* (1970) is a stimulating introduction to the social and political aspects as well as the purely military. J. W. Fortescue, *A History of the British Army* (13 vols, 1899–1930) is a vast sprawling work of uneven value which is nevertheless an invaluable source of information. The administrative history of the army in this period is covered in vols XI and XIII.

The best succinct account of the military operations in the Crimea is probably still E. Hamley, *The War in the Crimea* (1891) by a soldier who took part in the campaign. C. Hibbert, *The Destruction of Lord Raglan* (1961) is a sympathetic study of the commander in chief with a good bibliography. G. MacMunn, *The Crimea in Perspective* (1935) defends the conduct of the campaign against civilian criticisms. C. S. Parker, *Life and Letters of Sir James Graham* (2 vols, 1907), J. Martineau, *Henry Pelham, Fifth Duke of Newcastle* (1908), Lord Stanmore, *Sidney Herbert* (2 vols, 1906) and *The*

Panmure Papers, edited by Sir G. Douglas and Sir G. D. Ramsay (1908), all have valuable sections on the central administration of the war. The collected despatches of *The Times* correspondent W. H. Russell, published in 1855, have been edited by N. Bentley under the title of *Russell's Despatches from the Crimea 1854–1856* (1966).

11 Peace and Prosperity

Many of the books listed in sections 1–6 on social, economic, religious and administrative topics are relevant here. Mid-Victorian society is described in a number of books. *Early Victorian England*, edited by G. M. Young (2 vols, 1934) is a symposium by various authors on social life *c.* 1836–65. W. L. Burn, *The Age of Equipoise* (1964) is an original and stimulating survey of the mid-Victorian generation. G. Kitson Clark, *The Making of Victorian Britain* (1962) corrects many conventional views. W. Johnston, *England as It Is* (2 vols, 1851) presents the contemporary view of a conservative-minded barrister.

On rural society see also Pamela Horn, *Labouring Life in the Victorian Countryside* (Dublin, 1976) and J. P. D. Dunbabin, *Rural Discontent in Nineteenth-Century Britain* (1974). For the involvement of the gentry in the poor law see P. A. Brundage, 'The Landed Interest and the New Poor Law: a Reappraisement of the Revolution in Government', *EHR* LXXXVII (1972) and 'The Landed Interest and the New Poor Law, *EHR* XC (1975). Two articles by F. M. L. Thompson are also of value: 'Whigs and Liberals in the West Riding 1830–60', *EHR* LXXIV (1959) which discusses the position of the landowning class in a large and heavily industrialized English county, and 'Land and Politics in England in the Nineteenth Century', *TRHS* 5th series XV (1965) which deals among other matters with the radical attack on entail and primogeniture.

The best introduction to the growing literature on the role of the state is D. Roberts, *The Victorian Origins of the Welfare State* (New Haven, 1959) which has a useful bibliographical essay. An excellent book for students is O. MacDonagh, *Early Victorian Government 1830–70* (1977) which has separate chapters on the more important extensions of state activity in these years—industrial legislation, poor law, local government, public health and police. W. C. Lubenow, *The Politics of Government Growth* (Newton Abbot, 1971) examines attitudes towards state intervention in the period 1833–48. For public health there are two good studies of Chadwick: S. E. Finer, *The Life and Times of Sir Edwin Chadwick* (1952) and R. A. Lewis, *Edwin Chadwick and the Public Health Movement 1832–1854* (1962). For his equally important successor see Royston Lambert, *Sir John Simon 1816–1904 and English Social Administration* (1963). C. Fraser Brockington, *Public Health in the Nineteenth Century* (Edinburgh, 1965) breaks new ground with valuable documentation. For education the standard work is S. J. Curtis, *History of Education in Great Britain* (1948). For the spread of boys' public boarding schools see T. W. Bamford, *The Rise of the Public Schools* (1967) and for elementary schools Mary Sturt, *The Education of the People* (1961). The authoritative study of railway administration is H. Parris, *Government and the Railways in Nineteenth-Century Britain* (1965).

The interplay of local and national politics in local government is explored by Derek Fraser in *Urban Politics in Victorian England: the Structure of Politics in Victorian Cities* (Leicester, 1976). This can be followed up in detail in two important local studies: *The History of the Corporation of Liverpool 1835–1914* by B. D. White (Liverpool, 1951) and *Bristol and its Municipal Government 1820–1851*, Bristol Records Society Publications xxix (1976) by B. Bush. Victorian concern about social problems is discussed by G. Kitson Clark in *Churchmen and the Condition of England 1832–1885* (1973) which has a wider scope than the title suggests. The Christian Socialists can be studied in C. E. Raven, *Christian Socialism 1848–54* (1920). P. W. Slossen, *The Decline of the Chartist Movement* (1967) gives a useful discussion of the changing attitudes of the working classes after 1848.

Appendices

Appendix A: Increase in population, 1801–61 (in millions with approximate decennial increase in brackets)

Year of census	England and Wales	Scotland	Great Britain	Ireland
1801	9·1	1·6	10·9	5·3 estimate
1811	10·4 (14%)	1·8 (12½%)	12·4 (14%)	6·0 estimate
1821	12·1 (16%)	2·1 (16½%)	14·4 (16%)	6·8 first census
1831	14·0 (16%)	2·4 (14%)	16·5 14½%)	7·8
1841	16·0 (14%)	2·6 (8%)	18·8 (14%)	8·2
1851	18·0 (12½%)	2·9 (11½%)	21·1 (12%)	6·6
1861	20·2 (12%)	3·1 (7%)	23·4 (11%)	5·8

Note: Figures adjusted to include army, navy and merchant seamen at home and abroad. Totals for Great Britain include the population of the Isle of Man and the Channel Islands.

Source: *Census of Great Britain 1851 Population Tables* I (1852); *Census of Great Britain in 1851* (1854); and Thom's *Statistics of the United Kingdom* (1868).

Appendix B: Yearly average price of wheat per quarter, 1811–64

	s.	d.		s.	d.		s.	d.
1811	95	3	1829	66	3	1847	69	5
1812	126	6	1830	64	3	1848	50	6
1813	109	9	1831	66	4	1849	44	6
1814	74	4	1832	58	8	1850	40	4
1815	65	7	1833	52	11	1851	38	7
1816	78	6	1834	46	2	1852	41	0
1817	96	11	1835	39	4	1853	53	3
1818	86	3	1836	48	9	1854	72	7
1819	74	6	1837	55	10	1855	74	9
1820	67	10	1838	64	4	1856	69	2
1821	56	1	1839	70	6	1857	56	5
1822	44	7	1840	66	4	1858	44	3
1823	53	4	1841	64	5	1859	43	10
1824	63	11	1842	57	5	1860	53	4
1825	68	6	1843	50	2	1861	55	5
1826	58	8	1844	51	3	1862	55	6
1827	58	6	1845	50	9	1863	44	9
1828	60	5	1846	54	9	1864	40	5

Source: tables published in the *Journal of the Royal Agricultural Society* XVII (up to 1855) and XVIII–XXV and I (second series) for subsequent years.

Appendix C: Distribution of parliamentary seats before and after the Reform Act of 1832

By the three Reforms Acts which became law in 1832 the total membership of the House of Commons remained at 658 but the constituent parts were altered.

England: fifty-six small boroughs were completely disfranchised (111 seats); Weymouth reduced from four to two members; thirty others lost one member—a total loss of 143 seats.
Twenty-two new two-member boroughs were created and nineteen with one member—a total additional borough membership of sixty-three.
Seven counties received a third member; twenty-six were divided into two districts each with two members; the Isle of Wight was given a separate member; Yorkshire an additional two members—a total additional county membership of sixty-two.
England therefore lost 143 seats and gained 125—a net loss of eighteen.
Wales: county representation increased by three; a new borough district (Swansea) created; and separate representation for Merthyr Tydfil—a total gain of five seats.
Scotland: eight new burgh seats.
Ireland: four large towns and Dublin University each received an additional member—a total of five.

In sum therefore the English representation was diminished and that of Wales, Scotland and Ireland increased. In England there was a marked increase in the proportion of county to borough seats.

The House of Commons before and after 1832 (pre-Reform figures in brackets)

	County seats		Borough seats		University seats		Totals	
England	(82)	144	(403	323	(4)	4	(489)	471
Wales	(12)	15	(12)	14	(—)	—	(24)	29
Scotland	(30)	30	(15)	23	(—)	—	(45)	53
Ireland	(64)	64	(35)	39	(1)	2	(100)	105
Totals	(188)	253	(465)	399	(5)	6	(658)	658

Index